# 'Alexander'

*On Aristotle
Metaphysics 12*

*Ancient Commentators on Aristotle*

GENERAL EDITORS: Richard Sorabji, Honorary Fellow, Wolfson College, University of Oxford, and Emeritus Professor, King's College London, UK; and Michael Griffin, Assistant Professor, Departments of Philosophy and Classics, University of British Columbia, Canada.

This prestigious series translates the extant ancient Greek philosophical commentaries on Aristotle. Written mostly between 200 and 600 AD, the works represent the classroom teaching of the Aristotelian and Neoplatonic schools in a crucial period during which pagan and Christian thought were reacting to each other. The translation in each volume is accompanied by an introduction, comprehensive commentary notes, bibliography, glossary of translated terms and a subject index. Making these key philosophical works accessible to the modern scholar, this series fills an important gap in the history of European thought.

A webpage for the Ancient Commentators Project is maintained at ancientcommentators.org.uk and readers are encouraged to consult the site for details about the series as well as for addenda and corrigenda to published volumes.

# 'Alexander'

*On Aristotle
Metaphysics 12*

Translated by
Fred D. Miller, Jr.

BLOOMSBURY ACADEMIC
LONDON • NEW YORK • OXFORD • NEW DELHI • SYDNEY

BLOOMSBURY ACADEMIC
Bloomsbury Publishing Plc
50 Bedford Square, London, WC1B 3DP, UK
1385 Broadway, New York, NY 10018, USA
29 Earlsfort Terrace, Dublin 2, Ireland

BLOOMSBURY, BLOOMSBURY ACADEMIC and the Diana logo are trademarks
of Bloomsbury Publishing Plc

First published in Great Britain 2021
This paperback edition published 2023

Copyright © Fred D. Miller, Jr., 2021

Fred D. Miller, Jr. has right under the Copyright, Designs and Patents Act, 1988,
to be identified as Author of this work.

For legal purposes the Acknowledgements constitute an extension of this copyright page.

All rights reserved. No part of this publication may be reproduced or transmitted in any form or by any means, electronic or mechanical, including photocopying, recording, or any information storage or retrieval system, without prior permission in writing from the publishers.

Bloomsbury Publishing Plc does not have any control over, or responsibility for, any third-party websites referred to or in this book. All internet addresses given in this
book were correct at the time of going to press. The author and publisher regret
any inconvenience caused if addresses have changed or sites have ceased to exist,
but can accept no responsibility for any such changes.

A catalogue record for this book is available from the British Library.

A catalog record for this book is available from the Library of Congress.

ISBN: HB: 978-1-3501-7935-6
PB: 978-1-3501-8562-3
EPUB: 978-1-3501-7937-0
ePDF: 978-1-3501-7936-3

Series: Ancient Commentators on Aristotle

Typeset by RefineCatch Limited, Bungay, Suffolk

To find out more about our authors and books visit www.bloomsbury.com
and sign up for our newsletters.

# Acknowledgements

The present translations have been made possible by generous and imaginative funding from the following sources: the National Endowment for the Humanities, Divison of Research Programs, an independent federal agency of the USA; the Leverhulme Trust; the British Academy; the Jowett Copyright Trustees; the Royal Society (UK); Centro Internazionale A. Beltrame di Storia dello Spazio e del Tempo (Padua); Mario Mignucci; Liverpool University; the Leventis Foundation; the Arts and Humanities Research Council; Gresham College; the Esmée Fairbairn Charitable Trust; the Henry Brown Trust; Mr and Mrs N. Egon; the Netherlands Organisation for Scientific Research (NOW/GW); the Ashdown Trust; the Lorne Thyssen Research Fund for Ancient World Topics at Wolfson College, Oxford; Dr Victoria Solomonides, the Cultural Attaché of the Greek Embassy in London; and the Social Sciences and Humanities Research Council of Canada. The editors wish to thank Errol Katayama, David Keyt, Anthony Preus, and Christopher Shields for their comments; Dawn Sellars for preparing the volume for press; and Alice Wright, Publisher, along with Georgina Leighton at Bloomsbury Academic, for their diligence in seeing each volume of the series to press.

# Contents

| | |
|---|---|
| Preface | vi |
| Conventions | viii |
| Abbreviations | ix |
| Introduction | 1 |
|    1. The challenge of *Metaphysics* 12 | 1 |
|    2. Who wrote the commentary on *Metaphysics* 12? | 3 |
|    3. Critical assessments of Ps.-Alexander | 8 |
|    4. Ps.-Alexander's interpretation of *Metaphysics* 12 | 10 |
|    5. Sources of Ps.-Alexander's commentary on *Metaphysics* 12 | 25 |
| Textual Emendations | 33 |
| Translation | 35 |
| Notes | 133 |
| Appendix I: Freudenthal's Comparison of the Two Alexanders | 199 |
| Appendix II: Comparison of Ps.-Alexander's Readings with the Aristotle Manuscripts | 203 |
| Bibliography | 209 |
| English–Greek Index | 223 |
| Greek–English Index | 231 |
| Index of Passages from Other Works | 243 |
| Subject Index | 249 |

# Preface

Book 12 (*Lambda*) of Aristotle's *Metaphysics* is the culmination of a treatise regarded as one of the greatest works of philosophy by an author known as 'the Philosopher'. It was covered in the commentary on the *Metaphysics* by Alexander of Aphrodisias, the premier ancient commentator. But, alas, Alexander's treatment of Book 12 is lost, except for fragments preserved in Arabic by Averroes. The author of the extant commentary on Book 12, is called 'Ps.-Alexander' in this volume, as explained in the Introduction.

Since this is the first selection from Ps.-Alexander's portion of the commentary on the *Metaphysics* to appear in the Ancient Commentators on Aristotle Series, the introduction to this volume includes a discussion of Ps.-Alexander's identity and a critical assessment of his work in addition to an overview of his interpretation of Book 12 and a brief account of his sources. I started work on this translation a number of years ago out of curiosity while studying the *Metaphysics* as a member of the Ohio Greek Philosophy Group. As I carried out this project, I became increasingly impressed with Ps.-Alexander's contribution. Although he is not of the same calibre as Alexander of Aphrodisias and is cavalier in his treatment of sources, his commentary is most definitely worthy of study. In addition to plausible textual readings and reconstructions, which are still treated seriously by modern editors, he offers informative insights into difficult passages and a comprehensive and illuminating exegesis of Book 12 as a whole, albeit drawing at times on Neoplatonic materials to fill out his interpretation.

In preparing the translation and notes I had the benefit of a wealth of past scholarship as indicated in the bibliography. Renewed interest in *Metaphysics* 12 over the past two decades has yielded a fresh windfall, including a Symposium Aristotelicum volume and two other edited collections, new critical editions of Book 12 by Stefan Alexandru and Sylvia Fazzo, several commentaries, and a plethora of journal articles. By serendipity Lindsay Judson's Clarendon volume on *Metaphysics* 12 was published several months before my deadline. After completing the first draft of my translation, I was able to make many improvements by consulting two previous translations, the sixteenth-century Latin version by Sepúlveda and a very fine recent Italian rendering by Rita Salis. Two earlier volumes in the present series included helpful translations of material which reappears in Ps.-Alexander's commentary: Robert Sharples' Alexander of Aphrodisias *Questions* and Ian Mueller's Simplicius *On Aristotle On the Heavens*. I should add that Mueller's work was especially valuable for the translation and notes in Chapter 8.

I am pleased to thank Errol Katayama, David Keyt, Anthony Preus, and Christopher Shields for commenting on a draft of the translation and notes, suggesting many improvements, and sparing me from embarrassing errors. The penultimate draft served as a text for a seminar on Aristotle's philosophical theology which I conducted in collaboration with Professor Christopher Shields at the University of Notre Dame and which was the source of helpful feedback and valuable new insights. Erika Gray, my daughter, skilfully assisted with the diagrams for Chapter 8. Mary Dilsaver and Tamara Sharp at the Social Philosophy and Policy Foundation provided indispensable clerical support. The library of Bowling Green State University and the affiliated Ohio Link system were a constant source of essential research materials. I am especially grateful to Richard Sorabji for commenting on early drafts of the translation and introduction and for offering valuable assistance and advice throughout the project.

Fate decreed that my deadline would fall during a global pandemic in 2020, so that I was obliged to finish my work confined to my home, where Aristotle's sublime speculations afforded a welcome respite from sublunary tribulations.

Finally, for the constant support and encouragement of my beloved wife Kathryn and family I am deeply grateful.

F.D.M.

# Conventions

[...]    Square brackets enclose words or phrases that have been added to the translation for purposes of clarity. (An exception is made for certain frequently recurring expressions which are obviously implied by the context.)

(...)    Round brackets, besides being used for ordinary parentheses, contain transliterated Greek or references to the text of the *Metaphysics* or that of Ps.-Alexander's commentary.

<...>    Angle brackets enclose additions to Hayduck's text.

†...†    Daggers enclose text that is evidently corrupt.

'...'    Quotation marks enclose direct citations from the *Metaphysics* and other works.

# Abbreviations

| | |
|---|---|
| Alexandru | S. Alexandru (ed.), *Aristotle's Metaphysics Lambda: Annotated critical edition based upon a systematic investigation of Greek, Latin, Arabic, and Hebrew Sources*, Leiden: Brill, 2014. |
| Barnes | J. Barnes (ed.), *The Complete Works of Aristotle: The Revised Oxford Translation*, 2 vols, Princeton: Princeton University Press, 1984. |
| Bonitz | H. Bonitz (ed.), *Alexandri Aphrodisensis commentarius in libros Metaphysica Aristotelis*, Berlin: Georg Reimer, 1847. |
| CAG | *Commentaria in Aristotelem Graeca*, 23 vols, Berlin: Reimer, 1882–1909. |
| DK | H. Diels, *Die Fragmente der Vorsokratiker, Griechisch und Deutsch*, 6th edn, ed. W. Kranz, 3 vols, Berlin: Weidmann, 1951–2. |
| Fazzo | S. Fazzo (ed., tr.), *Il Libro Lambda della Metafisica di Aristotele*, Naples: Bibliopolis, 2012. |
| Genequand | C. Genequand (tr.), *Ibn Rushd's Metaphysics: A translation with introduction of Ibn Rushd's commentary on Aristotle's Metaphysics, Book Lâm*, Leiden: Brill, 1986; based on M. Bouyges, M. (ed.), *Averroes, Tafsīr Mā Baʿd aṭ-Ṭabīʿa*, Beirut: Dār al-Mashriq, 1938. |
| Hayduck | M. Hayduck (ed.), *Alexandri Aphrodisiensis in Aristotelis metaphysica commentaria, consilio et auctoritate Academiae Literarum Regiae Borussicae*, Berlin: Georg Reimer, 1888. |
| *Index* | H. Bonitz (ed.), *Index Aristotelicus*, vol. 5, *Aristotelis Opera*, ed. I. Bekker, Berlin: W. DeGruyter, 1961/1870. |
| Jaeger | W. Jaeger (ed.), *Aristotelis Metaphysica*, Oxford Classical Texts, Oxford: Clarendon Press, 1957. |
| Judson | L. Judson, *Aristotle Metaphysics Lambda: Translated with an Introduction and Commentary*, Oxford: Clarendon Press, 2019. |

| | |
|---|---|
| Ross | W. D. Ross (ed.), *Aristotle Metaphysics: A Revised text with Introduction and Commentary*, 2 vols, Oxford: Clarendon Press, 1924. |
| Salis | R. Salis (tr.), Italian translation of *Metaphysics* 12 in G. Movia (ed.), *Alessandro di Afrodisia e Pseudo Alessandro Commentario alla 'Metafisica' di Aristotele*, Milan: Bompiani, 2007, 1870–2042. |
| Sepúlveda | J. G. Sepúlveda (tr.), *Alexandri Aphrodisiei commentaria in duodecim Aristotelos libros de prima philosophia*, Rome: Silber, 1527. |

# Introduction

## 1. The challenge of *Metaphysics* 12

Book 12 (*Lambda*) is, in the view of many, Aristotle's crowning achievement, the 'coping-stone' of his *Metaphysics*.[1] Here he brings together the main themes of his system in order to provide a fundamental explanation of the nature of reality. In the course of the argument he offers a synoptic glimpse of the universe, inviting us, in our mind's eye, to gaze inward from the outermost rim of the cosmos and behold at its centre a stationary earth surrounded by heavenly bodies embedded within rotating concentric spheres in a co-ordinated system whose imperceptible causes he will unveil. It is further revealed that the prime mover of this system is the ruler of the universe, the supreme god, who is continuously and eternally in the best possible state of conscious self-awareness, far surpassing what we mortals can only briefly experience. Aristotle thus fulfils the earlier promise that first philosophy is, for him, theology (6.1, 1026a19; 11.7, 1164b3). In its ancient audience this intellectual vision doubtless instilled a sense of wonder comparable in our own day to the first awe-inspiring photographs of the earth from outer space.

In detail, however, *Metaphysics* 12 places heavy demands on the reader. Beyond skeletal scaffolding, it lacks clear organization, so that it is hard to see how the first five chapters outlining the principles and causes of perishable substances are connected with the latter five chapters demonstrating the existence and attributes of eternal substances. The book opens abruptly without much stage setting, by declaring that substance is the subject of theoretical knowledge and then arguing for the priority of substance. This is followed, rapid fire, by a succession of distinctions, stated briefly with little by way of explanation or illustration. At one point W. D. Ross complains 'that Aristotle is jotting down notes from a treatise (or lecture), not writing a treatise in its finished form'.[2] Chapter 6 begins, anew, without much context, by asserting that 'there is necessarily an everlasting immovable substance' (1071b3–20) which must be actuality (*energeia*) and not potentiality (*dunamis*). What exactly is meant by this is disputed, and Aristotle himself points out that it is puzzling to claim that something is an actuality when there is no prior potentiality of which it is the actuality (as with the acorn that is potentially an oak tree). In Chapter 7 the pivotal argument for the existence of the prime mover is obscured by textual corruption and appears to beg the question (1072a23–5). There follows Aristotle's oft-quoted claim that 'it imparts movement by being loved, while other things impart movement by being moved' (1072b3–4). This implies that the prime mover is both a final cause and a moving cause, but Aristotle does not explain very clearly how these two modes of causality are related, even though he takes his predecessors to task for failing to answer this very question. Having argued that the prime mover is itself unmoved Aristotle adds daunting arguments that this mover is an intellect which is suddenly identified with the god, who enjoys a life continuous, everlasting, and vastly superior to our own. The last three chapters pose further difficulties of their own. Chapter 8, which deals with the question of how many immovable movers there are, seems so incongruous that Werner Jaeger argued that it must have been written at a later time and inserted in its present place by a later editor.[3] Chapter 9 explores further puzzles concerning the intellect, though commentators disagree over whether these puzzles continue the discussion of the divine intellect from Chapter 7 or start a new enquiry about intellect in general.[4] Finally, in Chapter 10, Aristotle takes up the question of how goodness is present in the universe, and he answers with two analogies which might be taken to point in different directions: the order in an army which depends on its general (top down) and the order of a household which involves the co-operation of its members (bottom up). He then launches into criticisms of his predecessors for failing to explain how their first principle is the source of universal goodness rather than elaborating his own answer to this question. The concluding evocation of Homer's 'let there be one sovereign' (*Iliad* 2.204) leaves unexplained how this is consistent with the multitude of immovable movers in Chapter 8.

Moreover, it is not always obvious how the arguments of *Metaphysics* 12 are related to the cosmological theories expounded in Aristotle's *Physics* and *On the Heavens*. In addition, there are problems common to Aristotle's writings, such as terms and doctrines only explained in other works, vague references to his predecessors, and numerous textual difficulties. Hence, there was a pressing need for a commentary on the scale of that attributed to Alexander of Aphrodisias. Unfortunately, however, the authenticity of the relevant part of his commentary has long been in question.

## 2. Who wrote the commentary on *Metaphysics* 12?

Alexander of Aphrodisias, the greatest of the ancient Peripatetics, was appointed by the Roman emperors Septimus Severus and Antoninus Caracalla to a chair of Aristotelian philosophy around 200 CE.[5] His voluminous writings included commentaries on Aristotelian treatises and original works on philosophical topics, such as *On Fate* and *On the Soul*, although many of these were subsequently lost.[6] Among his commentaries, that on the *Metaphysics* was the most influential, but the latter portion, concerning Books 6 (Epsilon) to 14 (Mu), has long been regarded as spurious. To allay early suspicions, Juan Sepúlveda[7] (1494–1573) offered several arguments for the authenticity of the doubtful books: that the Greek manuscripts which he had consulted, including 'the four earliest copies', all ascribed authorship to Alexander of Aphrodisias without qualification; that the disputed books seemed more similar in style to that of the rest of the commentary than to commentaries by others (for example, Michael of Ephesus); that the opinions expressed in the disputed books resembled those which Averroes ascribed to Alexander of Aphrodisias; and that the later commentaries mentioned no author later than Aspasius and Sosigenes, both of whom predated Alexander. Against this, the anti-Aristotelian Humanist Francesco Patrizi of Cherso (1529–1597) alleged that there were significant differences between the two parts of the commentary in style and content, and he conjectured that the real author was Alexander of Aegae, a first-century Peripatetic commentator.[8]

Some of the most important evidence, which bears directly on *Metaphysics* Book 12 and which is alluded to by Sepúlveda, comes from the commentator Averroes (Ibn Rushd, 1126–1198), whose *Long Commentary on the Metaphysics* (*Tafsīr Mā Ba'd aṭ-Ṭabī'a*) contains numerous excerpts from Alexander's commentary on Book 12, which were translated into Arabic along with Aristotle's text.⁹ In the nineteenth century, Valentin Rose argued that Averroes' excerpts differ in important ways from corresponding passages in the extant commentary. Rose based this conclusion on Hebrew translations of Averroes' commentary, since the Arabic original was still lost; but his contention was confirmed by Jacob Freudenthal upon the publication of a rediscovered Arabic manuscript of Averroes' commentary.¹⁰ Freudenthal distinguished thirty-two 'fragments' (translated into German) from Alexander's commentary, and pointed out numerous inconsistencies with the extant Greek commentary.¹¹ Freudenthal concluded that the author of the extant commentary of Book 12 was not Alexander of Aphrodisias (whom he assumed to be the commentator referred to by Averroes) and, moreover, displayed no familiarity with the real Alexander's work.¹² Since Freudenthal's thesis has met with almost universal acceptance,¹³ the author of the extant commentary on *Metaphysics* 12 will henceforth be referred to as 'Ps.-Alexander'. There are contending theories as to his true identity.

One clue is Ps.-Alexander's use of Neoplatonic language. 'Neoplatonism' is a modern label for a widespread movement in later antiquity which may be compared to a big tent supported by four poles: Platonism, Pythagoreanism, Aristotelianism, and popular religion (paganism eventually replaced by Christianity). The seminal work for this tradition was the *Enneads* of Plotinus (204–270), who advised his students to study Alexander of Aphrodisias and other commentators, according to Porphyry (234-*c.* 305) in his *Life of Plotinus* 14. In later antiquity, the commentators were mainly Neoplatonists who tried to show that the philosophy of Aristotle was in fundamental agreement with the philosophy of Plato and Pythagoras.¹⁴ It is, therefore, noteworthy that the extant commentary on *Metaphysics* 12 contains Neoplatonic terms in evidence only after Alexander of Aphrodisias: for example, *ontotês* ('being', 669,29), *stoikheiôtos* ('composed of elements', 679,2), and *ho polutimêtos nous* ('the highly honourable intellect', 710,36; 719,13 ff.).¹⁵ Hermann Bonitz called attention to such linguistic evidence and also noted parallels with the commentary on the *Metaphysics* of Syrianus (*c.* 375–437). Of the latter we have only the commentaries on Books 3–4 and 13–14,¹⁶ but in the case of Books 13 and 14 there are many passages which are virtually the same as the ones in Ps.-Alexander's commentary on those books. Bonitz remarked that in some cases Syrianus includes phrases missing from Ps.-Alexander's commentary, such as 'as Alexander the commentator also says' (e.g. 745,29–32). On this basis Bonitz inferred that Syrianus was referring back to the commentary of Ps.-Alexander, which was written after the real Alexander's but which Syrianus believed was genuine.[17] This thesis was defended more recently by Leonardo Tarán, who maintained that Ps.-Alexander was the source for Syrianus and that neither of them was acquainted with the real Alexander's commentary.[18]

Freudenthal also took note of Ps.-Alexander's Neoplatonic language, but he supposed that the commentator belonged to late antiquity between the mid-fifth century and the end of the sixth century.[19] For instance, in response to 'the thrice-most-blessed experience' (*to trismakariston pathos*) in which the human intellect grasps the divine intellect 'in a partless and indivisible present' (714,15–24), Freudenthal remarks: 'Here we find the belief in the ecstasy of the Neoplatonists, and the unification with God in the same expressions which we encounter in late Neoplatonists'.[20] He also disparages Ps.-Alexander's treatment of Hellenic anthropomorphism and Egyptian zoomorphism (709,28–710,35) as typical 'silly' Neoplatonic allegorical interpretation of pagan practices (1884, 56). Regarding the aforementioned parallels with Syrianus, he maintained that it was Ps.-Alexander who came later and copied Syrianus and that Ps.-Alexander deliberately omitted the references to the real Alexander.[21] Recently Concetta Luna has offered persuasive arguments in support of Freudenthal's claim that Ps.-Alexander copied Syrianus rather than vice versa. She offers a number of exhibit passages in which Ps.-Alexander repeats what Syrianus says without fully understanding it, in some cases because he lacked the original context.[22] Further evidence for a later date for Ps.-Alexander is the fact that he reproduces a number of passages, often almost verbatim, from the commentary on Aristotle's *On the Heavens* by Simplicius (c. 490–560), who attributes them to a lost commentary by Alexander of Aphrodisias. Inspection of these passages indicates that Ps.-Alexander copied them from Simplicius rather than the reverse.[23]

By the nineteenth century the scholarly consensus was shifting towards the Byzantine commentator Michael of Ephesus, who includes in a list of his works a commentary on *Metaphysics* Books 7–14 (*in PN* 149,8–16). The commentator is referred to as 'the Ephesian' by an anonymous scholiast (Paris gr. 1853) and by Ps.-Philoponus in his own commentary (*in Metaph.* 6,4).[24]

'Michael of Ephesus' is mentioned by a second hand in the title of the commentary on Book 6 (Epsilon) in Paris gr. 1876 (commentary manuscript A).[25] As for Ps.-Alexander's frequent polytheistic locutions, Rose argued that the commentator understood them as figurative references to 'the secondary intellects' (*hoi deuteroi noï*, 794,13).[26] Building on the research of earlier scholars (including Christian August Brandis and Felix Ravaisson), Karl Praechter compiled a large mass of evidence of similarities between the commentary on the *Metaphysics* and already identified writings of Michael of Ephesus. The data include word choice, syntax, and telltale mannerisms such as epanalepsis (i.e. redundant repetition of the initial conjunction of a protasis before the apodosis in a long sentence, as in English 'if ... if then ...'; e.g. 688,35–40).[27]

Who, then, was Michael of Ephesus? Although Michael himself indicates that he was from Ephesus (*in EN* 570,21) and there is some suggestion that he was a physician,[28] other biographical details, including his dates and an unnamed teacher (716,26), are a matter of inference and speculation. Formerly, scholars placed him in the eleventh century and conjectured that he was a pupil of Michael Psellus and taught in the school of philosophy founded by the Byzantine emperor Constantine IX Monomachus in 1045.[29] However, Robert Browning has more recently offered evidence that Michael was active somewhat later, in the early-twelfth century, based on a funeral oration delivered about 1150 CE for the Byzantine princess Anna Comnena (1083–1153/5?). In this speech, George Tornikes, Metropolitan Bishop of Ephesus, remarked that, after the death of the emperor Alexius Comnenus in 1118, his daughter Anna 'gathered together all the most eminent representatives of the logical sciences – and they were numerous and remarkable.... The works which philosophers of our time addressed to her bear witness to her love of learning, works concerning those writings of Aristotle on which commentaries had not been written until her time ... I have myself heard the wise man from Ephesus attribute the cause of his blindness to her, because he spent sleepless nights over commentaries on Aristotle at her command, whence came the damage done to his eyes by candles through desiccation.'[30] Browning conjectures that 'the wise man from Ephesus' was none other than Michael, who most likely wrote his commentaries between 1118 and 1138 (the latter being the date that Anna turned her full attention to writing her *Alexiad*). He further speculates that, in addition to Michael, Anna Comnena's 'philosophical circle' included Eustratius, Metropolitan Bishop of Nicaea (1050/1060-c. 1120), who addressed his patroness as a *basilis*, which can mean 'princess' (in the proem of *in EN* 6), and whom Anna in turn praised as 'skilled in the sacred and profane sciences, more confident in dialectics than those who frequent the Stoa and Academy'.[31] Browning more boldly declares that 'it is clear that Anna and her colleagues were bent on constructing a philosophical system, and not merely on glossing texts'.[32] Such a 'system' might be found in Eustratius, who sought to harmonize doctrines drawn from Plato as well as Aristotle in order to provide a philosophical bulwark for Greek Orthodox Christianity. Although Browning's thesis about the identity of Michael has been generally accepted, there is less agreement as to how extensive Anna's circle of scholars was and to what extent they shared Eustratius' mission of forging a new synthesis of Neoplatonic philosophy with Greek Orthodoxy.[33]

In any event, it is known that Michael composed a series of commentaries or collections of scholia, making use of whatever pre-existing materials (most often anonymous ancient sources) he could lay his hands on. These included a commentary on *Sophistical Refutations* which was mistakenly attributed to Alexander of Aphrodisias[34] and a commentary on *Generation of Animals* which was erroneously ascribed to Philoponus.[35] Michael also wrote on treatises of Aristotle which were outside the mainstream of the ancient commentary tradition including the minor psychological works[36] and other biological works,[37] as well as the *Politics* and *Rhetoric*.[38] Michael also collaborated with others in a project to prepare a comprehensive commentary on the *Nicomachean Ethics*. He contributed commentaries on Books 5, 9, and 10, while Eustatius wrote on Books 1 and 6. The anonymous Book 7 may have been written later, and the remainder consisted largely of scholia compiled from ancient sources.[39]

Most scholars now concur that the completion of Alexander of Aphrodisias' commentary on the *Metaphysics* was yet another contribution by Michael of Ephesus to the Comnenite project of reconstructing lost commentaries and filling gaps left by the ancient commentators. Nonetheless, he will continue to be called 'Ps.-Alexander' in this work, in view of the lack of universal agreement regarding his identity and in recognition of his own obvious intention to remain anonymous.

## 3. Critical assessments of Ps.-Alexander

Ps.-Alexander, the author of the extant Greek commentary on *Metaphysics* Book 12, is without a doubt the most controversial of the Aristotelian commentators. Those who place him in late antiquity often cast him as an unscrupulous poseur – a forger if he precedes Syrianus or a plagiarist if he comes after – who demonstrates his philosophical incompetence whenever he endeavours to offer an original interpretation. They supply plenty of evidence to support their verdict. In the spurious later books of the commentary, Ps.-Alexander speaks as if he were the author of the genuine books of the commentary: on Book 1 at 741,36–7; on Book 3 at 641,11–12; and on Book 5 at 567,24 and 630,31–2. His commentary on Book 12 contains extensive materials recycled from the real Alexander's *Questions* as well as shorter passages taken from the real Alexander's *On the Soul* and *Mantissa* and also materials lifted from Simplicius' commentary on *On the Heavens* – all without attribution or even misrepresented as his own (687,25). In addition, Ps.-Alexander seems at 703,4–7 to allege authorship of *On the Heavens* and also, perhaps, at 672,11–12 of *Generation and Corruption* (though the latter may be speaking for Aristotle himself). Freudenthal is particularly caustic, asserting that Ps.-Alexander 'is not one of those compilers who in naive impulsiveness introduce excerpts from earlier writings as their own, but a fraudster who commits fraud with conscious intent'. He has perpetrated 'literary theft' and 'shamelessly plundered' the works of Alexander, Syrianus, and Simplicius in order to embellish his forgery. Though Tarán assigns Ps.-Alexander an earlier date than Syrianus and Simplicius, he, like Freudenthal, regards Ps.-Alexander as an ancient Neoplatonist masquerading as the genuine Alexander.[40]

Scholars who identify Ps.-Alexander as Michael of Ephesus tend to be more respectful. For example, Karl Praechter, who in his review of the *Commentaria in Aristotelem Graeca* (published in 1909), remarked:

> [T]he Academy edition has brought to life a truly respectable interpreter of Aristotle in Michael of Ephesus … Michael's on the whole sober and intelligent exegesis may have furthered Aristotelian studies considerably in his time and can also provide essential services to the inexperienced reader of Aristotle today. Above all, he seeks to make Aristotle's concise expression more intelligible through paraphrase and to elucidate the context by

demonstrating the connection of thought; he also frequently eases one's concentration through examples. Yet he also has value for the experienced reader owing to his preservation of many sorts of valuable materials, however trivial they were to the author's overall historical-philological interests and owing to the perspective he permits on the philosophical tendencies of his time.[41]

H. Paul F. Mercken has similar praise for Michael's work on the ethics, observing that 'his painstaking compilation and editing of earlier scholia [is] motivated by nothing so much as the desire to elucidate Aristotle'. He continues, 'His Aristotelianism manifests itself in many ways. He chooses the physical and other treatises of Aristotle to comment upon; he stays close to the text of Aristotle, which he explains with reference to its general import (*dianoia*) as well as to its detailed form (*lexis*); he makes a wide use of other works of the Stagirite; and he does not attempt to make Aristotle fit into a Neoplatonist strait jacket'.[42]

A defender of Michael of Ephesus must nevertheless account for evidence of misappropriation and subterfuge. Freudenthal contends that it would be unreasonable to identify Ps.-Alexander with 'this man, unclear but learned for his time, trying assiduously to interpret the Aristotelian writings'. Robert Sharples also remarks, 'it is hard to think of a parallel in antiquity for the deliberate passing off of a spurious *commentary* as the genuine article'.[43] The charges of forgery and plagiarism seem less plausible if Browning is correct that Michael was engaged in a collaborative project to restore and complete the ancient commentaries. If Ps.-Alexander was Michael, *whom* after all did he expect to deceive? Rejecting the claim that Michael was a fraudster, Concetta Luna remarks that Michael was under great pressure to produce a large quantity of work in a short time and 'forced to use without too many scruples all the available materials'. In his commentary on *Nicomachean Ethics* 5, he acknowledges using scholia by earlier commentators (*in EN* 50,6–9). She argues: 'It is evident that the practice of incorporating into his own commentaries extracts more or less extensively taken from earlier commentators, notably Alexander of Aphrodisias, is a particular trait of Michael of Ephesus... There is no intention of producing a forgery. The commentaries of Michael are works made of bits and pieces.'[44] On this view Michael should be compared not so much to Konrad Kujau, who claimed to have discovered Hitler's diaries, but rather more to an anonymous ghost writer commissioned to complete an unfinished work of a deceased author such as Dicken's *Mystery of Edwin Drood*.

A more important question concerns Michael's competence. Although no one would seriously claim that Ps.-Alexander is a match for Alexander of Aphrodisias in terms of philosophical ability, it would be a mistake to underestimate his contribution. Mercken offers the following description of his methods:

> Michael's commentaries on the *Ethics* are according to his own work *skholai*, lectures or commentaries, written either with a view to or as a product of his teaching. In them he explains both the letter and the spirit of Aristotle's text, concerns himself with textual exegesis, points out the connection between various passages, spells out arguments that are too succinct for direct comprehension, advances parallel texts, makes cross-references throughout the Aristotelian corpus, and refers to other philosophers, especially to Plato.[45]

According to Mercken, Michael self-consciously continued in the tradition of the ancient commentators. He was not a militant Aristotelian, a doctrinaire Neoplatonist, or a Christian apologist. On the other side, Robert Sharples, an eminent scholar on Alexander of Aphrodisias, has offered an acerbic critique of Ps.-Alexander's commentary on *Metaphysics* 12, by pointing out many alleged mistakes and confusions. Often Sharples is on the mark, although in number of instances a case can be made in Ps.-Alexander's defence (as indicated in the notes to the translation in this volume). He concludes with the verdict that Ps.-Alexander's scattered scholia simply do not add up to a systematic interpretation of *Metaphysics* 12: 'pseudo-Alexander follows the Aristotelian text so closely that it is difficult to attribute to him any definite position'.[46] In order to assess this negative evaluation, it will be useful to consider the following selective overview.

## 4. Ps.-Alexander's interpretation of *Metaphysics* 12

Ps.-Alexander views *Metaphysics* 12 as a unitary whole, unlike many interpreters who treat the first five chapters and the last five as involving separate enquiries and view Chapter 8 as a later addition.[47] He begins by remarking that 'this entire treatise' is devoted to the first immovable principle of the universe (668,2–4). He clearly views the first five chapters as preparing the way for the final five. In discussing Chapter 1 he adds a distinction between first and second substance, which is not in Aristotle's text but which seems to foreshadow the prime mover, the first substance on which everything depends (668,16–17). In Chapter 4 again he notes that the separate entity 'which as the first of all moves all things'(1070b34–5) is 'the principle under investigation' (681,34–5 on 1070b34–5). Later, at the beginning of Chapter 6, he highlights the way in which the distinction between three kinds of substance made at the outset (1069a30-b1) provides the framework for the entire book, and he remarks that the ontological priority of substance to the other categories, argued for at Chapter 1, 1069a19–24, forms the basis for the argument in Chapter 6 (687,25–36). He sees Chapter 7 as anticipating Chapter 8, interpreting Aristotle's statement that 'these substances must be without matter; for they must be everlasting if, in fact, anything else is also everlasting' as referring forward to the many immovable movers of the heavenly spheres (689,7–14 on 1071b20–2). In addition, he takes Aristotle's distinction between 'simple' and 'one' (at 1072a32) to clear the way for a plurality of simple celestial movers (695,10–17). Further, he takes Chapter 9 to continue the discussion of the divine intellect in Chapter 7 (710,36), in contrast to some commentators who see it as taking up puzzles about the human intellect or thinking more generally. Finally, he interprets the Homeric adage at the end of Chapter 10 so as to be consistent with polytheism implied by Chapter 8 (721,23–33).

Aristotle's ultimate objective in Book 12, according to Ps.-Alexander, is to identify the cause in virtue of which the perceptible universe is a cosmos, or orderly whole, and hence good (714,35–715,5). On this account Aristotle views the cosmos as a comprehensive system involving perpetual coming-to-be and ceasing-to-be on earth and everlasting motions of celestial bodies in the heavens. To explain all this motion it is necessary to posit a first moving cause (*kinêtikon aition*). But what sort of cause is this? Where does it belong in Aristotle's fourfold distinction of causes: material, formal, efficient, or final? Although Aristotle takes his predecessors to task for failing to answer this question, he is not as forthcoming himself as might be expected. Ancient commentators debated this question, and modern scholars are still not in complete agreement. But before considering what

Ps.-Alexander's contribution to this fundamental issue is, it is necessary to consider in detail his interpretation of Book 12.

Ps.-Alexander takes Aristotle's point of departure to be that since time and therefore movement always exist without beginning or end, there must be an everlasting substance which undergoes this everlasting movement. The source for this movement must be an actuality (*energeia*) (688,12–22 on 1071b12–20). The argument has three steps: the first cause must be capable of bringing about movement (*kinêtikon*) and producing an effect (*poiêtikon*); it must be acting (*energein*); and its substance cannot be a potentiality (*dunamis*), 'for there will not be everlasting movement, since it is possible for that which is in potentiality not to be'. Ps.-Alexander understands the argument as follows: 'But, then, if it is capable of bringing about movement or producing an effect but is not acting in any way' (where "is not acting" means: if it is not an actuality in every way having no share at all of potentiality), there will be some time when there will not be movement; for what has the potential to be not acting will sometime be not acting.' Ps.-Alexander evidently takes Aristotle to presuppose the so-called principle of plenitude, according to which all potentiality is actualized. In a temporal context this implies that whatever is possible will be actualized at some moment in time, whatever is necessary will always be actualized, and whatever is merely possible (i.e. possible but not necessary) will fail to be actualized at some time.[48] Further, Ps.-Alexander understands the verb *energein* ('to act') in an occurrent sense, because the alleged cause fails to act at a particular time.[49] Thus the claim that the *energeia* of the prime mover is without *dunamis* implies that the prime mover is active at every moment in time in a way that Plato's Form of the Good is not.[50]

Ps.-Alexander finds a connection between Aristotle's astronomical speculations and his proof of the existence of the prime mover in his treatment of the passage at 1072a9–26 (see 691,30–692,35).[51] Pursuant to his earlier claims that the prime mover is an actuality and that actuality is prior to all potentiality, Aristotle explains why there is a perpetual cycle of generation (i.e. alternating coming-to-be and ceasing-to-be). He remarks that 'something must always remain, acting in the same way' and that 'another thing must always act now in one way and now in another', and then proceeds at the same dizzying level of abstraction. Ps.-Alexander understands Aristotle in a more concrete way as explaining the perpetual cycle of the seasons, which the commentator explains in terms of a simplified version of the theory presented in Chapter 8. This assumes that celestial bodies appear to orbit the earth because they are carried around by homocentric spheres that rotate around the earth. The cycle of the seasons is due to the sun, which is observed to have two different apparent motions – daily (across the sky from sunrise to sunset) and annual (altering its maximum elevation in the sky over the course of a year) – which have two different causes. The former motion takes place at the same rate as the daily motion of the fixed stars around the earth, while the latter motion is peculiar to the sun and is caused by a special sphere that carries the sun around the earth. The axis of this solar sphere is inclined at a slight angle to the earth's equator so that over the course of the year the sun appears higher in the sky, the days grow longer and temperatures rise, and then it appears progressively lower in the sky, the days are shorter, and temperatures fall (the northern and southern hemisphere experiencing opposite effects at the same time). The alternation of seasons is thus due to the solar sphere's motion, but what guarantees that this process will be everlasting? It must be due to the fact that the solar sphere is moved forever by something else. The source of this motion cannot be anything like the sphere of Saturn (presumably selected by Ps.-Alexander because it is the outermost planetary sphere) because Saturn's sphere is itself moved by the sphere of the fixed stars. Thus Saturn's sphere is a mere cog in the cosmic machinery passing on the motion of the fixed stars to the sun (which is presumably implied by the fact that Saturn rises and falls daily at the same rate as the sun and fixed stars). The real cause must therefore be the everlasting motion of the sphere of the fixed stars. This explains Aristotle's conclusion that the eternal cycle of coming-to-be and ceasing-to-be is caused by two motions: that of the solar sphere and that of the outermost sphere of the fixed stars. Nearly all subsequent commentators accept an interpretation of this difficult passage along these lines.

Ps.-Alexander, however, views this explanation of the cycle of generation as only a preamble to the proof of the unmoved mover (cf. 692,36–693,12). For this proof, he remarks, Aristotle employs a 'method of analysis', in this case analysing the factors involved in movement: namely mover, moved, and moved mover. He reads Aristotle's argument as follows: 'There is something which is moved with an unceasing movement ... There is, therefore, also that which it moves. And since what is moved and what imparts movement [is] also an intermediary, therefore there is something which imparts movement without being moved, which is everlasting and a substance that is also an actuality' (1072a23-6). Ps.-Alexander understands the argument to rest on a general principle: if Y is intermediary (*meson*) between X and Z, and both X and Y exist, then Z must also exist. As applied to moving bodies, X=that which is moved only, Y=that which both is moved and imparts movement, and Z=that which imparts movement only. On this construal the proof resembles a passage in *Physics* 8.5 where Aristotle also distinguishes three factors involved in movement: that which is moved, that which imparts movement, and that by which something imparts movement. The latter is a moved mover: it imparts movement while being moved itself. In contrast an unmoved mover is not that by which something else imparts movement (cf. *Phys.* 8.5, 256b14–20). It is noteworthy that the interpretation of the latter passage by Simplicius in his commentary on the *Physics* (1226,10–1227,33) is very similar to that in Ps.-Alexander's exegesis of 1072a23-6. Simplicius points out an analogous application of Aristotle's principle in which mead is the intermediary between the two extremes of wine and honey. It is interesting that Simplicius also describes the moved mover as an 'intermediary' (*meson*) between what is only moved and what is only a mover, although the *Physics* passage does not contain the word *meson*.

It must be noted, however, that Ps.-Alexander's interpretation depends on a peculiar Greek clause, which he construes as translated above: 'There is, therefore, also something which it moves' (1072a23-4). But the Greek phrase – *ti ho kinei* – translated as 'something which it moves' is ambiguous, since it could also be translated as 'something which moves it'. Against Ps.-Alexander's interpretation, W. D. Ross objects that the clause should in fact be translated the latter way, contending that 'from the existence of a *kinoumenon* [thing moved] there cannot be inferred the existence of something which it moves, but only the existence of something that moves it'.[52] In support of Ps.-Alexander, however, it could be replied that the fact that the planetary system is moved by the sphere of the fixed stars is precisely what has been established by the preceding astronomical explanation of perpetual generation. Ross' interpretation seems open to the objection that no basis has been given yet for the inference to the existence of an immovable mover from the existence of a moved thing.

Aristotle subsequently argues that there is a multitude of such movers, a doctrine which, as has been seen, Ps.-Alexander finds to be reflected throughout Book 12. In Chapter 8 Aristotle undertakes to determine their precise number based on the astronomical theory developed by Eudoxus of Cnidus (c. 408–c. 355 BCE), modified by Callippus of Cyzicus (c. 370–c. 310 BCE), and subsequently revised by Aristotle himself: to explain the observed motion of all the stars observed to move overhead, it must be supposed there is a series of nested homocentric spheres revolving around the earth. Outermost is the sphere containing the myriad fixed stars, and within are many other spheres which are responsible for the movement of the seven planets (or 'wandering stars'). The complex movement of each planet requires the co-ordination of several dedicated spheres, and Aristotle concludes that the movement of all seven planets requires fifty-five spheres in all as detailed in Chapter 8. His central argument in this chapter is that just as the motion of the outermost sphere of the fixed stars is due to the prime mover, as argued in Chapter 7, so also each of the fifty-five planetary spheres has its own immovable movers. Hence, there are fifty-five separate substances in addition to the prime mover.

In order to explain the argument of Chapter 8, Ps.-Alexander offers a systematic exegesis of the Aristotelian theory of homocentric spheres, drawing liberally on Simplicius' commentary on Aristotle's *On the Heavens*, which in turn cites Alexander of Aphrodisias and the latter's teacher Sosigenes. This includes the following ten theses: (1) All stellar motions are due to the motions of a nested series of geocentric spheres, each of which transmits its motion to the next sphere within it (700,12–14; 710,1–13). (2) Each sphere conveys its motion to the next sphere within, which adds a motion of its own (704,32–3). (3) The fixed stars have a simple rotational motion because they are embedded in the outermost sphere which has a simple rotational motion (703,10–12). (4) Each of the seven planets has a complex motion because it is associated with a series of spheres (each sphere having its own simple rotational motion) which jointly carry the planet and keep it moving forward (703,12–704,9). (Ps.-Alexander illustrates this for the moon and the sun but only gestures towards the other planets.) (5) Since the planets apparently move independently of each other, there is also associated with each outer planet a series of counteracting spheres (offsetting the spherical motions that contribute directly to the planet's motion) so that the motion of inner planets will not be affected (704,9–705,13). (6) The everlasting motion of each sphere is caused by a mover which is immovable *per se* and *per accidens*. This is true of the planetary spheres as well as the sphere of the fixed stars (700,12–14; 701,1–13). A corollary is that the immovable movers must be separate substances rather than the souls of the spheres. (707,1–11). (7) There are *at least* as many separate substances as there are spherical motions (706,24–31). This requires the assumption (discussed below) that each single motion has a unique cause. (8) These separate movers constitute a 'divine multitude' in which a number of subordinate movers are filled with the goodness of the prime mover (of the sphere of the fixed stars) which is 'overfull with its own noble attributes' (707,4–6.12–25). (9) There are *no more* separate substances than there are spherical motions, because there must be something for each such substance to move (707,28–708,3). (10) Every spherical motion must contribute in some way to the motion of a planet (either by carrying the planet directly or by counteracting one of the carrying spheres) (708,39). Based on these theses and on astronomical observation it is reasonable (*eulogon*) to suppose that there are exactly fifty-five immovable movers in addition to the prime mover (702,4–11; 705,36; 706,24–6; 708,21–2).

In his explication of Aristotle's theory of stellar motion, Ps.-Alexander calls attention to two general principles which warrant closer consideration. The first of these is Aristotle's premiss that 'a single movement is due to a single thing' (1073a28).[53] This assumption is needed for thesis (7) above, which requires that each celestial motion has its own dedicated mover. More precisely, as will be seen, Aristotle is assuming that every movement has a *unique* moving cause, unique in the sense that it does not cause any other movement. Now it is obvious that this principle would have to be carefully qualified in order to be remotely plausible. For it is frequently the case that when a mover brings about a movement, the object that is moved in turn brings about another movement in something else, and it by another, and so forth, where the latter movements are brought about indirectly by the initial mover. So the principle can hold only when a mover directly brings about another movement. Furthermore, the same thing can move different things with different parts of itself or at different times, and likewise a thing can be moved by many things with different parts and at different times. Let us suppose that all such qualifications can be made (although Aristotle does not attempt to do so), so that the principle is that each and every movement (suitably qualified) is directly caused by a unique mover (suitably qualified).

Ps.-Alexander remarks that Aristotle's argument that the everlasting movement of the sphere of the fixed stars has a single mover is based on the premiss that 'a single and continuous movement comes to be by one moving cause' (701,20; cf. 1073a28).[54] Moreover, Ps.-Alexander points out that the same principle is at work in the argument that there are at least as many unmoved movers as there are celestial motions: 'after finding how many spheres there are, he will declare that the number of the moving causes is as great as that of the spheres; for a single thing has a single moving cause' (700,37–8). After commenting on Aristotle's conclusion that there are fifty-five unmoved movers in all for the seven planetary bodies, Ps.-Alexander reiterates: 'after he has proven that the movement that is one, simple, and everlasting comes about from a moving cause that is one, simple, and partless, he confidently declares that, however great the number of the spheres and perceptible substances turns out to be, "the immovable substances and principles are reasonably supposed to be so many"' (706,21–4). Now it is obvious that Aristotle must be claiming that each spherical movement is directly caused by a single dedicated mover, or else his conclusion would manifestly not follow. Hence, the principle in play is that each and every single movement is directly caused by a unique mover.

This principle also seems to be at work in Aristotle's argument that there is one heaven: 'For if there are many heavens, just as there are many humans, the principle for each will be one in form but nevertheless many in number' (1074a31–3). The principle here is the immovable mover, which cannot be many in number because it is immaterial. Since the mover is one, the heaven in motion must be too. As Ps.-Alexander points out, the basis of the argument is the previous conclusion 'that the moving cause of the object that is one and is moved everlastingly and continuously is [itself] one' (709,6–7), which as was seen is based on the principle that a single movement is due to a unique mover.

It is noteworthy that this same principle is implied earlier at 1071a27–9, a passage which has received considerable scrutiny as possible evidence for a doctrine of individual forms. Aristotle says that the causes and element 'of things in the same species are different, not in form but because individuals have a different [cause]: your matter and form and mover, and mine, but they are the same in universal account.' Commentators disagree over whether

Aristotle means to confine the distinction between 'your' and 'my' to matter alone (as the principle of individuation) or he means to extend it to form and mover as well. Ps.-Alexander makes clear that he takes the distinction to apply to all three causes: 'Not only do different genera have different causes, but also things that belong to the same species are different, albeit in number. For your matter is different from mine in number, and similarly the form and efficient cause, "though [they are] the same in universal account". That is, for in so far as all things depend on matter, form, privation, and efficient cause, the causes of all things are the same, but in a way my causes are different from your causes, not the same' (684,20-7). In this comment Ps.-Alexander underscores the point by saying that these causes are different 'in number'. (For example, the matter, form, and efficient cause of Ps.-Alexander are all numerically different from those of Alexander of Aphrodisias.) This implies that each substance has a unique set of causes. The principle that each motion has a unique moving cause, which Aristotle needs for his theory of immovable movers, is an analogous application of this idea to movement.

The second general principle to which Ps.-Alexander calls attention involves Aristotle's concept of final causality. The principle is that when a thing acts for the sake of some aim for some beneficiary, the beneficiary undergoes a change but the aim itself does not. For example, when a healer treats a patient, the patient (the beneficiary) may become healthy but health itself (the benefit aimed at) undergoes no change. This distinction is mentioned at 1072b1-2 following Aristotle's argument that because the first cause is an immovable mover it must be the first intelligible object and the first object of desire (1072a27-b1). This sets the stage for the prime mover to make its appearance as final cause of everlasting celestial motion.

At this juncture, however, there intervenes a difficult sentence in the manuscripts: 'That the final cause is found among the things that are immovable is made clear by this distinction, since the final cause is for someone, of which the former is but the latter is not' (1072b1-2). Ps.-Alexander reads the sentence this way, but he notices and tries to explain an obvious difficulty: the clause 'since the final cause is for someone' does not make any distinction. He points out, however, that Aristotle does make such a distinction elsewhere:[55] 'the things that come about and that are done come to be and are done *for the sake of something* also come to be and are done *for someone*; for example, the things that come to be and are done are done for the sake of happiness are done for someone, for instance, for Socrates' (695,28-30; emphasis added). The solution favoured by most editors is to emend the text so that the clause reads 'since the final cause is for someone *and for the sake of something*'. Ps.-Alexander offers a slightly different solution. When a thing aims at a certain benefit (e.g. happiness) for a beneficiary (e.g. Socrates), the final cause is strictly speaking the benefit and it does not change. (This does not exclude the beneficiary from being a final cause in a secondary sense, as will soon be seen.) This permits Aristotle to say straightaway, 'it imparts movement in so far as it is loved' (1072b3), implying that the immovable mover is a final cause in the strict sense, that is, as aim or end.

This principle that the final cause involves aiming at an immutable end for the sake of a beneficiary which undergoes change comes into play again when Aristotle argues that there are no more immaterial substances than there are celestial motions (1074a17-31). Ps.-Alexander (707,28-708,39) understands Aristotle's argument as follows: each motion is unitary and continuous and hence has as its cause an individual substance (cf. 684,14-15). Further, each separate substance is intrinsically good and hence an end (*telos*) in the sense of a benefit, an object of yearning, and a final cause. But then there must be something of which each of them is the final cause, namely a particular celestial motion. Hence, there will be *no more* separate substances than there are celestial motions (1073a30-b1). This was thesis (9) above. Furthermore, there can be no motion that does not contribute to the motion of a star, which was thesis (10) above. Aristotle argues that a celestial motion exists for the sake of a star as its end (1074a28-31). On Ps.-Alexander's interpretation a star carried by a sphere is a final cause in a secondary sense of beneficiary, while the final cause in the strict sense is its mover in the sense of aim or goal.[56] Aristotle maintains that each and every motion must be for the benefit of a star, because, as Ps.-Alexander observes, nature does nothing in vain (cf. 708,6). For example, in the case of Saturn, the seven motions of its seven associated spheres are required to bring about the distinctive complex activity of this planet. Fifty-five spherical motions in all are required to account for all the activities of all the seven planetary stars. Therefore, there are precisely fifty-five immaterial substances in addition to the prime mover which is required to explain the motion of the outer heavenly sphere. Thus the explanation of how many immaterial substances exist depends on the principle that a final cause involves aiming at an immutable end for the sake of a mutable beneficiary.

Further, Ps.-Alexander offers some insights concerning the divine intellect, which he takes to be the subject of both Chapter 7, 1072b14–30 and Chapter 9. Modern scholars generally disagree over the meaning of Aristotle's climactic utterance: 'the act of thinking is an act of thinking of an act of thinking' (*he noêsis noêseôs noêsis*, 1074b34–5). There are, roughly speaking, three lines of interpretation on offer: the divine intellect thinks of itself alone; it thinks of what is essential to a divine intellect; or it thinks of the eternal verities of which it is somehow constituted.[57] The first interpretation was favoured by traditional commentators, but it is rejected by modern scholars such as Richard Norman, who caricatures it as the view that 'the Prime Mover is a sort of heavenly Narcissus, who looks around for the perfection which he wishes to contemplate, finds nothing to rival his own self, and settles into a posture of permanent self-admiration'.[58] Ps.-Alexander provides some support for each of these interpretations. Regarding the second, at least, he implies that each subordinate intellect directs its awareness towards the first intellect (707,18–19), which would be at least consistent with the idea that they share something in common with it. In support of the third interpretation, Norman appeals to a passage in Ps.-Alexander's commentary on Chapter 7 (696,32–697,6) which allegedly implies that 'the Prime Mover's self-thinking, albeit differing in duration, is of the same kind as our own normal abstract thought'.[59] Ps.-Alexander could be understood this way when he remarks that 'we do not always spend our lives this way, but [only] when our intellect actually becomes the intelligible objects' and that 'it is impossible for us to live this sort of life always rather than sometimes; but for the first cause …, it is possible'. Further, in this passage Ps.-Alexander goes on to say that 'its activity is nothing other than thinking of itself', and he might be thought to suppose that the divine intellect thinks of itself in the same way in which we humans do. In a later passage, however, Ps.-Alexander presents Aristotle's reason for holding that the first intellect does not think of anything other than itself: 'for a simple intellect thinks of a simple object, and no other intelligible object is simple except for it. For it is unmixed and immaterial and possessing no potentiality in itself. So it will think of itself alone. For in so far as it is intellect, it will think of itself as an intelligible object; and in so far as it is both intellect and actually intelligible, it will always think of itself. Further, in so far as it alone is simple, it will think of itself alone. For since it alone is simple, it is capable of thinking of something simple, and it alone is a simple intelligible object' (699,5–11). This seems to favour the interpretation that the first intellect thinks exclusively of itself or its own essence, which might be consistent with the view that a subordinate intellect in thinking of its own essence thinks of something it has in common with the first intellect.

The first interpretation is also supported by Ps.-Alexander's way of taking Aristotle's remarks about the absurd consequences of supposing the divine intellect thinks of anything other than itself (711,24–40 on 1074b21–7). It is absurd to suppose that the divine intellect, which is the best possible object leading the best possible life, thinks of random and evil objects. 'Nobody who lives well will put up with "cognizing about certain things", for example, in the case of fornication how to fornicate well, so it will be most impious to say that the most divine and best substance cognizes about random and evil objects' (711,28–31). A further absurdity results if it is supposed that the divine intellect could start thinking of something besides itself. 'For if it changes from the beholding of itself, it will think of something altogether better or worse; but there is not anything better than it; so it remains that it is worse. And this is a movement and a withdrawal from it own best way of carrying on. This is confirmed by what happens with human beings; for when good human beings think of evil objects, they become worse than they were as a result of thinking of such things. This is also confirmed by the fact that they feel remorse, which one feels when one has become bad' (711,34–40). It is noteworthy that Ps.-Alexander does not comment on the gulf between Aristotle's divine intellect and the omniscient Christian God by whom 'the very hairs of your head are numbered'. He evidently takes his remit to be exegetical fidelity rather than Christian apologetics.

Chapter 10, finally, raises the question of how goodness resides in the universe, which Aristotle answers by means of two similes: the universe is like an army in which order is instilled by a general, and it is like a household in which 'the free persons are least at liberty to do act haphazardly, but all or most [of their actions] are ordered' unlike 'the slaves and beasts' who 'are able to do little for the common [end] and for the most part do act haphazardly' (1075a11–23). Ps.-Alexander (715,31–716,9) adds a third simile which combines features of the two: the universe is like a polis where free persons have a liberty which is circumscribed: they are not at liberty to do anything whatever, but they are at liberty to be doctors or soldiers and to do without exception all the things that contribute chiefly to the maintenance of the polis. In contrast the slaves perform trivial acts such as cooking or chopping wood and random acts which contribute little to the maintenance of the commonwealth, since they are not at liberty to pursue more important vocations. This political simile helps to explain how the things making up the universe are 'co-ordinated' in relation to some one thing, namely, one nature and fulfilment of the whole, but not all of them in a similar way (1075a16).

Following his household simile Aristotle states: 'that sort of principle is the nature of each of them' (1075a22–3). Commentators disagree over what Aristotle means by 'nature' (*phusis*) here. Does he mean that nature is an overarching principle which applies to each and every individual, or does he mean that each individual's own nature is its guiding principle? In other words, does he view nature as a 'top-down' or as a 'bottom up' principle?[60] Ps.-Alexander avoids this dilemma by understanding Aristotle to intend both senses: 'the nature and principle of the things that contribute together to the nature of the whole' (716,10–12). Just as in the polis the individual citizens promote the common good by performing their own roles in a co-ordinated fashion, so in the universe the individual substances contribute to the nature of the whole in acting according to their own natures in a co-ordinated manner.

Ps.-Alexander's political simile foreshadows the evocation of Homer with which Aristotle concludes Book 12: 'The sovereignty of many is not good, there is one sovereign'. The commentator (721,23–33) reconstructs the argument as follows: 'since, in the affairs that are under our control, we fare badly whenever people do not co-operate with each other, this will also happen in the universe [at large]'. The term *arkhê* which is central to this discussion signifies a principle or cause in the metaphysical context and a ruler in a political context. 'Wherever there is a multitude of rulers there is disorder, since the rule of many is the very same thing as disorder. And yet existing things are ruled not badly but in a manner that is orderly and best. If, then, the rule of many is disorder and the reason that existing things are badly governed, whereas the affairs under our control that involve mutual co-operation are governed not badly but in the best way, there must not be many principles. For the sovereignty of many is not good, but there is one sovereign, one principle, one god.' Rather than stop here with Aristotle, however, Ps.-Alexander carries the reasoning a further step: 'For the causes of the planetary objects are gods, but they depend on participation in and on the will of the first and most blessed intellect'. The cosmos is thus a community of gods like Aristotle's ideal monarchy, in which there is one individual so pre-eminent in virtue that all the others should obey him not in turn but always, so that he may rule justly and make it possible for all the citizens to achieve moral excellence (cf. *Pol.* 3.13, 1284b25–34; 3.16, 1288a15–29). Ps.-Alexander thus interprets the Homeric adage in terms of the polytheism of Chapter 8 rather than the more obvious monotheism on which a Christian apologist might have fixed his attention.

The latter part of Book 12 is mainly concerned with criticizing earlier thinkers for failing to make clear the causal role of their proposed first principle: is it a material, formal, efficient, or final cause? As Ps.-Alexander recounts (718,8–23 on 1075b1–9), Empedocles treats Love as the good, he treats it as an efficient cause when he says it combines things to produce the Sphere (the merging of everything in the universe) but as a material cause in so far as it is part of the mixture and of the Sphere. 'After establishing this, Aristotle states: even if we agree that Love belongs to the substratum as matter and as mover, nonetheless it will be entirely different in account. And if this is the case, will it be because Love imparts movement or because it is matter? Empedocles ought then to have said in which of the two respects the being of Love belongs to it'. Again, Aristotle faults Anaxagoras for failing to explain how his principle, called 'the Intellect', can be both an efficient and final cause. And further, even if one concedes that the Platonic Forms or Pythagorean numbers are in some sense causes, they cannot be efficient causes, or even formal causes in the way that Aristotle understands them (720,13–24 on 1075b28–30). After all this criticism, it is surprising that Aristotle is not more explicit in stating his own final solution to the problem of causal modality.

Ps.-Alexander, as has been seen, emphasizes that the first principle is 'the good which is essentially the final cause', alluding to Aristotle's statement that it imparts movement 'in so far as it is loved' (695,35–9 on 1072b3). But is the prime mover strictly speaking anything more than a final cause?[61] Simplicius in his commentary on Aristotle's *Physics* reports that Alexander of Aphrodisias and other Peripatetics viewed the prime mover as merely a final cause, whereas Simplicius himself agreed with his teacher Ammonius that the prime mover was also an efficient cause in a robust sense (*in Phys.* 1360,24–1363,24). This latter interpretation seems to be supported by Aristotle's own description of the cause of everlasting motion as both *kinêtikon* and *poiêtikon* (1071b12; cf. 688,17–18), that is, both a moving cause and an efficient cause. Aristotle sometimes uses it to designate the starting point of movement as the 'efficient cause' (*poiêtikon aition*, e.g. GC 1.7, 324b13; DA 3.5, 430a12; GA 1.21, 729b13). This becomes a term of art with the commentators including Ps.-Alexander, who offers homely examples: the father is the efficient cause of the son, and the sculptor is the efficient cause of the statue (677,29–33; 678,31; 681,17–23). Accordingly, he refers to immaterial substances as the 'efficient causes' (*poiêtika aitia*) of celestial motions (706,32). Thus he implies that efficient causality converges with final causality in the case of the prime mover when he says that 'the mover and that for the sake of which it imparts movement are the same, and for this reason everything which moves that which is moved is [itself] moved for the sake of it' (718,27–8). As he states in a concise aphorism: 'everything is turning about from it (*ex autou*) and towards it (*eis auton*)' (719,14).

Ps.-Alexander leaves a clue as to how he understands this fused mode of causation in a passage mentioned above (in connection with thesis (8) of the homocentric theory): the prime mover 'is not needful, it is overfull (*huperplêres*) with its own noble attributes, whereas [the subordinate immovable movers] strive towards it and are filled with its benefaction' (707,18–19). This image of noetic superabundance is reminiscent of Plotinus (205–270 CE) when he describes the generation of the cosmic intellect: the One, 'is perfect because it seeks nothing, possesses nothing, and needs nothing, overflowing as it were, and its overfull condition (*to huperplêres*) makes something other than itself. This, which has come to be, turns back to it and becomes intellect upon looking at it' (*Enneads* 5.2.1). Although such imagery suggests how the immovable mover might be an efficient as well as final cause, it is alien to Aristotle. Such Neoplatonic terminology which percolates through Ps.-Alexander's commentary was derided by Freudenthal as redolent of Neoplatonic 'supranaturalism'.[62] Freudenthal also calls attention to a passage suggestive of mystical intuition: the human intellect apprehends the divine intellect by means of an instantaneous 'thrice-most-blessed experience' (*trismakariston pathos*) rather than through a process of discursive thought occupying a span of temporal parts (714,18–23; cf. 696,35–6). Ps.-Alexander describes our contemplation of the divine intellect as 'contact' or 'touching' (*haphê*), echoing Aristotle himself (714,26.34; cf. *Metaph.* 12.7,

1072b20–1; 9.10, 1051b22–6; *DA* 3.7, 430b27–31). Presumably the incorporeal substances, which Ps.-Alexander calls 'secondary intellects' (794,13), whose intellection does not depend on perception, will be in even more immediate noetic contact with the first intellect and subject to its direct influence. There is no need, then, to suppose that Ps.-Alexander's description of the prime mover as 'efficient cause' is motivated by the unstated Christian belief in God as creator.[63]

In conclusion, it should be clear from this selective overview that, far from offering a mere paraphrase and pastiche of purloined passages, Ps.-Alexander constructs a comprehensive interpretation of Book 12 understanding it to contain an integrated and coherent argument. Although he makes use of Neoplatonic ideas to fill crucial gaps and round out his interpretation, he seems on the whole to be more concerned with explicating Aristotle's actual views than with carrying out a Neoplatonic agenda.

## 5. Sources of Ps.-Alexander's commentary on *Metaphysics* 12

Building on a previous edition by Herman Bonitz (1847), Michael Hayduck (1888) based his critical edition on four principal manuscripts and a Latin translation, which are represented by the following *sigla*:

A:  a late-thirteenth-century manuscript in the Parisian Bibliotheque nationale de France, gr. 1876

M:  a sixteenth-century manuscript in the Munich Bayerischee Staaatsbibliothek, 81

L:  a twelfth-century manuscript in the Florentine Biblioteca Medicea Laurenziana, plut. 87,12 (also containing manuscript A$^b$ of Aristotle)

F:  a fifteenth-century manuscript in the Milanese Biblioteca Ambrosiana, 363, F113 sup. (also containing manuscript M of Aristotle)

S:  an early sixteenth-century Latin translation by Juan Ginés de Sepúlveda based on four unidentified Greek manuscripts

There is one manuscript, however, which Hayduck did not consult:

O:  a late-thirteenth-century manuscript in the Florentine Biblioteca Medicea Laurenziana, plut. 85,1

The latter (called 'the Ocean') is a capacious codex containing a number of commentaries on Aristotle's works, including *Metaphysics* 10 to 14. This manuscript was used by other editors for later volumes in the *Commentaria in Aristotelem Graeca*. Hayduck's neglect of O seems in retrospect to be unfortunate, because it is regarded as an important text and possibly even a source for manuscript A.[64]

The manuscripts relied on by Hayduck present certain difficulties. One, recognized by Hayduck himself, is that there are serious discrepancies between the four main manuscripts attributed to Alexander's commentary, so that Hayduck was compelled to divide these into two groups: A and M along with S represent the commonly accepted version (*recensio vulgata*), while L and F represent a variant version (*recensio altera*). The major disagreements occur in the commentary on Books 1 and 2 and the beginning of Book 3. Hayduck took note of some serious discrepancies between the two versions, though he failed to mention that the second group does not name Alexander of Aphrodisias as the author. In any case he often corrected the reading of the first group on the basis of the second. This would have been a mistake, however, if the so-called *recensio altera* was in fact a derivative work by a later author.[65]

Another problem was more recently uncovered through some meticulous detective work by Alexandru 1999, namely, that F differs in important ways from L. In the earlier books the copyist of F frequently omits passages which are found in L. More importantly, beginning from Book 11 (Kappa) F no longer contains Ps.-Alexander's commentary, but instead a commentary by George Pachymeres (1242-*c.* 1315), still unpublished, which draws on Ps.-Alexander's.[66] As a result of these difficulties, Hayduck's edition suffers from serious deficiencies. He sometimes prefers the readings of L and F in places where A and M are acceptable, although he also flags longer passages in the critical apparatus as instances of 'the more serious discrepancy of the alternative recension'. Fortunately, these problems are most serious in the early books. However, the interruption of Ps.-Alexander's commentary in manuscript F at the beginning of Book 11 obviously nullifies its usefulness as a source for Book 12.

As mentioned above, the commentary on Book 12 contains material recycled from the genuine Alexander. Anomalously in the commentary on Chapter 6 the lemma for 1071b3 occurs twice over. While the second occurrence (687,23) is succeeded by the usual commentary, the first (685,26) precedes a lengthy prolegomenon (685,30–687,29) which repeats with many minor alterations the first chapter of the genuine Alexander's *Questions*.[67] Subsequently in the commentary on Chapter 7, there are sections reproduced from Alexander's *de Anima* (697,19–39 from 85,11–86,6 and 86,14–87,1) and *Mantissa* (699,1–11 from 109,25–110,3). Still later, in the commentary on Chapter 8, following the lemma on 1073b17 (at 702,36) several short passages are taken almost verbatim from Simplicius' commentary on *On the Heavens*. In none of these cases does Ps.-Alexander acknowledge his source. There are also indications that Ps.-Alexander drew on various Neoplatonic scholia to which he had access but are now lost. Possible motivations for these questionable practices have been discussed in Section 3 above.

Finally, there is need for a word about the manuscripts of the *Metaphysics* which Ps.-Alexander himself may have consulted. Although he seldom mentions alternative manuscripts, he does frequently cite the text and call attention to difficulties which it presents. This has made his work quite useful for modern editors (although it should be noted that it is sometimes debatable whether he is actually quoting or merely paraphrasing). As for the *Metaphysics* itself, it is generally agreed that the text underwent many changes as it was copied and recopied over the centuries as scribes tried to correct errors of their predecessors and added new mistakes themselves. More recently, scholars have distinguished two groups of manuscripts, which often diverge from each other.[68] Each group is descended from a peculiar lost archetype, which are denoted by lower-case Greek letters, here transcribed as *alpha* and *beta*. Of the three manuscripts most widely used, E (Paris Gr. 1853) and J (Vienna Ph. Gr. 100) are likely copies of *alpha*, while $A^b$ (Laur. 87,12) is a copy of *beta*, of which C (Taur. 3 VII 23), M (Ambr. 363 F113 sup.),[69] and $V^k$ (Vat. 115) are also descendants. There remains considerable speculation as to when *alpha* and *beta* were created and as to how exactly they are related to each other as well as to Aristotle's original draft. A widely shared view currently is that *beta* was produced in an attempt to make Aristotle's text more reader-friendly, for example by smoothing out difficulties and adding glosses. In addition, according to some scholars, many of the revisions of *beta* were influenced by the genuine Alexander's commentary. It should also be noted that many manuscripts show the influence of both the *alpha* and *beta* traditions, which is not surprising since a new copy of a Greek manuscript was often prepared by consulting other copies in order to correct for errors and find clearer readings. Another complication (obviously relevant to the present volume) is that after 1073a1 (in Book 12 Chapter 7) Aristotle manuscript A$^b$ was written by a later copyist who relied on the *alpha* tradition instead of the *beta* tradition, presumably because it was necessary for some reason to copy a different manuscript.[70] For the remainder of the *Metaphysics*, the more recent manuscripts C, M, and V$^k$ serve as representatives of the *beta* tradition, although they also show evidence of contamination from *alpha* sources (this is especially the case for C).[71]

This leads finally to the question of whether the unidentified manuscripts consulted by Ps.-Alexander belonged to either the *alpha* family or the *beta* family or to some other tradition altogether. It is evident on inspection that in the commentary on Book 12 his lemmata and citations agree with *alpha* as often as with *beta* when the two families disagree with each other (about thirty times in each case). Moreover, Ps.-Alexander disagrees with both *alpha* and *beta* over fifty times, which may indicate access to manuscripts independent of those now extant. It is noteworthy that a number of these alternative readings have been taken seriously into account by modern editors and commentators.[72] The relationship of Ps.-Alexander's commentary to the transmission of Aristotle's text clearly warrants further investigation.

## Notes

1  Ross, vol. 1, cxxx.
2  Ross, vol. 2, 354.
3  Jaeger 1923, 219–27; cf. Arnim 1931; Ross, vol. 2, 384.
4  Brunschwig 2000, 275 even considers ch. 9 as 'a short-lived thought experiment'.
5  Alexander, *De Fato* ch. 1, 164,3–5, 13 ff. (Sharples 1983a); cf. Sharples 1987, 1177. All subsequent dates are CE unless otherwise indicated.
6  For a full inventory and description see Sharples 1987, 1182–99.
7  In the second edition of his Latin translation of the commentary (Sepúlveda 1536). His discussion is quoted in Bonitz, xv-xvii.
8  Patrizi 1581, 32–3.
9  See Bertolacci 2005 and Di Giovanni and Primavesi 2016 (and earlier Walzer 1958 and Peters 1968) on the Arabic translators used by Averroes, summarized as follows: Abū Bišr Mattā (d. 940) for 1069a18–1072b16; Usṭāṯ (ninth century) for

1072b16–1073a13; Mattā again for 1073a13–1076a4. Mattā was also the source for translations of Alexander and Themistius. Outside of Book 12 Averroes relied mainly on Usṭāt̲, although he also occasionally turned to other translators such as Abū Zakarīyāʾ Yaḥyā ibn ʿAdī (d. 974).

10 Rose 1854, 146–52; Freudenthal 1884.
11 Averroes had at his disposal only Mattā's translation of the first two-thirds of Alexander's commentary on Book 12, the last fragment from which is mentioned at *Tafsīr* 1623. There is a critical edition by Bouyges 1938, an English translation of the commentary on Book 12 by Genequand 1986, and a French translation by Martin 1984.
12 Freudenthal's monograph begins with a brief overview of the differences between the two Alexanders. This overview is updated and translated into English in the present volume as Appendix I.
13 Aside from an early challenge by Zahlfleisch 1900 (on which see Tarán 1987, 220 n. 19). Freudenthal's conjecture about Ps.-Alexander's actual identity is rejected by many scholars, as will be seen, and his supposition that the real Alexander was the direct source of the passages referred to by Averroes has been questioned by DiGiovanni and Primavesi 2016, who argue that the source is rather an ancient reviser of the real Alexander whose work was translated from Greek via Syriac into Arabic.
14 This Neoplatonic influence is amply demonstrated in two anthologies edited by Richard Sorabji: *Aristotle Transformed: The Ancient Commentators and their Influence* (1990; rev. 2016) and *Aristotle Re-interpreted: New Findings on Seven Hundred Years of the Ancient Commentators* (2016).
15 See Luna 2001. This informative monograph is the source of much of the information in this section.
16 Syrianus, *On Aristotle's Metaphysics 13–14*, tr. Dillon and O'Meara 2008 (*CAG* 6.1, ed. Kroll 1902).
17 Bonitz, xviii-xix, xxvi; followed by Kroll 1902, vi.
18 Tarán 1987.
19 Freudenthal 1884, 52–6.
20 Ibid. 22. Translations from Freudenthal are mine.
21 Ibid. 28–34.
22 e.g. Luna (2001, 47–50) on Ps.-Alexander 797,12–17 = Syrianus, *in Metaph.* 166,26–8.
23 See, for example, notes on translation 361, 362, and 393.
24 This Ps.-Philoponus has been identified as George Pachymeres (1242–c. 1310) by Alexandru (1999; 2003).
25 Hayduck 1888, note to 405,1.

26 Rose 1854, 149. Against this Freudenthal protested, 'The author of the last books of the commentary is not a Christian like Michael but an adherent of Greek paganism' (1884, 53–4).
27 Brandis 1836, note on 724a; Ravaisson 1837, 64–5; Rose 1854, 147; Praechter 1906, 1990. Much of this material is presented and augmented in Luna 2001, Appendix III.
28 Reported by Praechter 1909, 864 n. 2. A reference to the four humours (675,4) also suggests a familiarity with Hippocratic medicine.
29 Praechter 1990, 53.
30 Tr. Browning 1990, 406.
31 Anna Comnena, *Alexiad* xiv, 8, tr. Mercken. On Anna Comnena as the *basilis* see Browning 1990, 400 and Mercken 1990, 414. See also Lloyd 1987.
32 Browning 1990, 402.
33 Anthony Preus (1981, 8 ff.) concurs with this account, whereas Mercken (1990, 436–7) is somewhat guarded and de Vries is more skeptical (1987, 111 n. 10). Wilberding and Trompeter 2018, 3–6 provide a recent overview.
34 *On Aristotle's Sophistical Refutations* (*CAG* 2.3=Wallies 1898). An earlier version of this commentary is translated into Latin (Ebbesen 1981).
35 Ps.-Philoponus *On Aristotle's Generation of Animals* (*CAG* 14.3=Vitelli 1897).
36 *On Aristotle's Parva Naturalia* (*CAG* 22.1=Wendland 1903). This omitted *On Perception*, since Alexander of Aphrodisias' commentary on this was extant (*CAG* 3.1=Wendland 1901).
37 *On Aristotle's Parts of Animals*, *On Aristotle's Motion of Animals*, and *On Aristotle's Progression of Animals* (*CAG* 22.2=Hayduck 1904). The latter two are translated by Preus 1981. A commentary on the *History of Animals* is lost (Praechter 1990, 52 n. 71).
38 Gottschalk 1990, 68 n. 67. Immisch in his edition of the *Politics* included as an appendix scholia of *cod. Hamiltonianus* whose author refers (ad loc. 1282a3 ff.) to his exegesis of the *Parts of Animals*; cf. Praechter 1990, 52 n. 72. Barker (1957, 136–41) discusses translated selected scholia from Michael's commentary on the *Politics*.
39 Eustratius, Michael of Ephesus, and Anonymous *On Aristotle's Nicomachean Ethics* (*CAG* 20=Heylbut 1892). This includes the anonymous scholia on Book 5 rather than Michael's own commentary (found in *CAG* 22.2=Hayduck 1901). The entire commentary (including the scholia on Book 5 rather than Michael's commentary) was translated into Latin by Robert Grosseteste (*c.* 1168–1283); cf. Mercken 1990, 407–8. Recent English translations are tr. Konstan 2001, 2008, and Wilberding and Trompeter 2018.
40 Freudenthal 1884, 19–24, 33; Tarán 1987, 229.
41 Praechter 1990, 51 and 53.

42 Mercken 1990, 434. For a less favourable assessment see Ebbeson who complains that Michael 'vacuumed old books for useful passages that might serve as or in scholia on the *Elenchi*, then emptied the bag of the vacuum-cleaner and called the rubbish-heap a commentary' (1990, 448).
43 Freudenthal 1884, 53. Sharples 2003, 192 with n. 27.
44 Luna 2001, 69–71; translations of Luna are mine.
45 Mercken 1990, 434.
46 Sharples, 2003, 214.
47 This discussion observes the modern chapter divisions of *Metaphysics* 12, which are descended from Basilios Bessarion's Latin translation (1447–50). Ps.-Alexander sometimes divides Aristotle's discussions so as to cut across these chapter divisions, and in some cases he seems justified in doing so.
48 These are temporal applications of the so-called 'principle of plenitude'. See Hintikka 1973, 95–9 for an interpretation along these lines.
49 Although Ps.-Alexander explicates Aristotle's verb *energein* ('to act') in terms of the real Alexander's formula *amoirein dunameôs* ('to have no share of potentiality'), Ps.-Alexander understands it in his own way as a temporal occurrence (cf. note on translation 200 [688,17]).
50 The Neoplatonists countered this objection to Plato with a theory of 'beginningless creation' (cf. Sorabji, 1990b), but Ps.-Alexander does not pursue this line of thought.
51 Ps.-Alexander views 1072a9–26 as forming a continuous argument, which is obscured by Bessarion's chapter break at 1072a19.
52 Ross 1924, 2 and 374. Cf. Judson, 222 who objects that if 'which' is the object of 'moves' then 'therefore' is out of order.
53 See Beere 2003, 17 n. 29: 'I do not find in the literature a satisfying discussion of the premiss, "one eternal motion is moved by one mover"'. See also Bodnár 2016, 261. Ps.-Alexander is one of the few to recognize the importance of this assumption.
54 Ps.-Alexander remarks also that this is defended in the *Physics*, presumably at 8.6, 259b16–20: 'a motion is one only if the thing bringing about movement and the thing being moved are each of them one, since in the event of a thing's being moved now by one thing and now by another the whole motion will not be continuous but successive'.
55 Ps.-Alexander reports that Aristotle makes the distinction in the work *On the Good* (now lost). Aristotle makes the distinction at *DA* 2.4, 415b2–3, 21–2, and he also mentions at *Phys.* 2.2, 194a36 that he distinguishes two senses of 'that for the sake of which' (*to hou heneka*) in *On Philosophy* (also now lost).
56 For recent interpretations along these lines see Bodnár 2016 and Judson, 270–80.

57 Liatsi (2016, 229) compares Aristotle here to the Sphinx, though the oracle of Delphi seems equally apt. The first interpretation, which is the traditional understanding, is endorsed by Ross, vol. 1, cxli–xcliii and many others; the second by Menn 2012, Judson, 329–32 and others; the third by Norman 1969, Kahn 1985, Bordt 2006, and others. Of course, the various commentators disagree on details. Judson offers a more elaborate taxonomy of interpretations (323–4, 326–32).

58 Norman 1969, 63–4.

59 Ibid. 72–3.

60 Most commentators, traditional and modern, favour the latter interpretation. Sedley (1990, 2000) and Horn (2016b) argue for the former interpretation, but see Judson, 348–9 for a renewed defence of the latter view.

61 Present-day scholars continue to debate this question: the view that Aristotle's first principle is solely a final cause is supported by Ross, Vlastos 1963, Elders 1972, and recently Ross 2016; the view that it is also an efficient cause in a nontrivial sense is supported by Broadie 1993, Judson 1994 and 2019, Kosman 1994, Berti 2000a, Bradshaw 2001, Salis 2009.

62 Freudenthal 1884, 23 n. 1; cf. Merlan 1963, 35–7.

63 For a different interpretation see Golitsis 2016, 256–7.

64 See Harlfinger 1975, 18; Golitsis 2014; Moraux 1976, 275–6; Kotwick 2016, 25–6.

65 Golitsis 2014, 2016b (the basis for this paragraph) argues that the *recensio altera* was composed by an 'anonymous professor', most likely Stephanus (late-sixth to early-seventh century), who was also the probable author of the commentary on *Metaphysics* 6 attributed to Alexander of Aphrodisias.

66 Discussed by Burnyeat 2008, 231–6.

67 Alexander of Aphrodisias, *Quaestiones* (SEG 2.2=Bruns 1887), tr. Sharples 1992 and 1994.

68 Including Harlfinger 1979, Primavesi 2012, Kotwick 2016, and Golitsis 2016a. Oliver Primavesi is preparing a new edition of the *Metaphysics* which takes into account the *alpha* and *beta* traditions. See Primavesi 2012 for background and for his edition of *Metaphysics* 1. Fazzo and Alexandru provide valuable information on Book 12.

69 Aristotle manuscript M should not be confused with commentary manuscript M mentioned above.

70 Harlfinger 1979.

71 These manuscripts have recently been studied by Alexandru, Fazzo, Golitsis, Primavesi and other scholars. Undoubtedly we have not heard the final word on the textual history of the *Metaphysics*.

72 These results are tabulated in Appendix II.

# Textual Emendations

The following list notes departures from the Greek text in M. Hayduck's 1888 *CAG* edition *Alexandri Aphrodisiensis in Aristotelis metaphysica commentaria*.

676,3     Changing *hupo* to *apo* based on A with Bonitz.
680,39    Changing *katasuntetagmena* to *kata ta suntetagmena* (cf. 680,17).
684,18    Changing *holôs* to *holês*.
684,21    Omitting *ta* before *eidê* based on A.
685,3     Omitting *ê* based on A with Bonitz (missing from Sepúlveda's translation).
694,27    Adopting Salis' suggestion of *dê* after *hosa* ('igitur' in Sepúlveda's translation).
697,25    Omitting *touto gar en autêi ginetai* with Salis (missing from Sepúlveda's translation).
698,15    Changing *auto* to *autos* (cf. Alexander *DA* 86,29).
699,4     Accepting *aei* based on M (cf. Sharples 2004, 31 n. 70).
703,34    Changing *aêbmgd* to *aêbgmd* (with Sepúlveda's translation; cf. Mueller 2005, 127 n. 11).
706,14    Omitting *phêsi legein*.
709,14    Omitting *touto ekhei* (cf. Sharples 2003, 197 n. 46).
718,30    Changing *legonta* (Hayduck's emendation) to *legôn* based on the manuscripts (with Bonitz).

# 'Alexander'

*On Aristotle
Metaphysics 12*

Translation

# Scholia on Book 12 of the *Metaphysics* of Aristotle[1]

## [Chapter 1][2]

In the present book of the *Metaphysics*, to which it is customary for the Peripatetics to assign the title '*Lambda*'[3] Aristotle[4] composes an account concerning the first (*prôtos*) and immovable (*akinêtos*) principle (*arkhê*),[5] to which, indeed, this entire treatise (*pragmateia*) is devoted. But since the word 'principle' is spoken in many ways (for matter (*hulê*), form (*eidos*), and privation (*sterêsis*)[6] are each called a principle), he first articulates what they involve summarily and concisely, in order that we may have the account of them fresh in our minds and thus know easily how the principle about which we are enquiring (*zêtein*) differs from other principles. Furthermore, since he had enquired in the [book concerning] puzzles (*aporia*)[7] in addition to other issues as to whether all things have the same principles or different things have different ones, but it has not yet received a solution (*lusis*), he for this reason again takes up the account of causes (*aitia*) in order to prove (*deiknunai*) that in one way all things have the same principles but in another way they do not.

> **1069a18** The investigation is about substance; [for it is to substances that the principles and causes enquired about belong. For both, if the universe exists as a whole of some sort, substance is its first part; and, even if it exists through succession, substance is in this way also what is first, then quality, and then quantity. At the same time the latter are not even things that are (so to speak) without qualification, for example, qualities and movements – or else even the not-white and the not-straight [would be things that are without qualification]; at least we say that they are, for instance, 'there is not white'. Further, none of the other things is separable. The early [thinkers] also bear witness in effect to this; for they were enquiring into the principles, elements, and causes of substance.][8]

Since it has been proven that the science (*epistêmê*) set forth here is prior to all the other sciences, and the subject (*hupokeimenon*) of the first science is also first, and substance (*ousia*) is prior to all the other categories (*katêgoria*), substance will be the subject of wisdom (*sophia*);[9] and since, in turn, among substances one is first and another second,[10] that which is first of all will be the subject of wisdom. And after saying that the investigation (*theôria*)[11] is about substance, Aristotle concisely adds the reason for this, stating, 'for it is to substances that the principles and causes enquired about belong' (1069a18–19).[12] For by enquiring about the principles and causes of substance he enquires about substance itself, just as, also, one who enquires about the cause of the eclipse (*ekleipsis*) enquires about the eclipse itself. For the cause of the eclipse, as was stated in the second book of *Posterior Analytics*,[13] is the definition (*horos*) of the eclipse, and this is the eclipse itself. Having proven, then, that the science set forth here is the first and that the first science is about the first things, he proves that substance is prior to the other categories; hence, if wisdom is first, and the first science is concerned with the first things, if it is proven that substance is first, the present wisdom will be such as to investigate substance.

First, then, Aristotle distinguishes the ways in which it is possible to think of substance among the ten categories,[14] saying, [on the one hand] 'for both if the universe (*to pan*) exists as a whole (*holon*) of some sort,[15] substance is its first part (*meros*)' (1069a19–20), that is, substance will be the first part whether we understand all perceptible (*aisthêtos*) substance together with the accidents (*sumbebêkos*) as a sort of unity, or we think of the ten categories as broken up and separated (*khôrizein*) from each other and lying in succession, such that, say, quantity (*poson*) is first, then quality (*poion*), then substance, and then the rest.[16] And in the latter case substance will be prior to the others, then quantity, then quality,[17] and the rest similarly; for the latter alternative is indicated by 'even if[18] [the universe exists] in succession' (1069a19–20), that is, if we think of the categories as existing (*einai*) not as a unity (*heis*) but in succession and not existing within substance.

But since what he means is still in a way rather unclear, let it be made clearer with an example (*hupodeigma*). Socrates is indeed a substance, but he is also white as well as philosophical and musical. Therefore, of the whole (*holotês*) that is composed of the substance of Socrates and the white and philosophical and musical, the musical is a part; similarly, Socrates is also a part of the compound whole (*sunolon*) that is made up of the white and musical and philosophical and Socrates. And just as in the case of these things, so it is also with the entire perceptible substance and the nine [other] categories. For in the case of these things, too, the substance will be a part of the whole made up of perceptible substance and quantity and quality and the remaining categories; and similarly quantity will also be a part of what is generated from (*apogennêma*) substance and quantity and the other categories.

Having said, then, that whether we envisage (*phantazesthai*) it as becoming a unity and a single nature (*phusis*) distinct from these ten categories, or as coming to be through succession, in both ways substance is prior to the others, Aristotle offers an additional proof, saying, 'at the same time these are not even things that are (*to on*) so to speak without qualification (*haplôs*)' (1069a21–2).[19] He means by 'these' [the items in] categories apart from substance. And since Aristotle also wanted to make clear what the things are that are apart from substance, he added, 'for example, qualities [and] movements'[20] (1069a22). And what he means is in effect this: for how in general could those other categories be considered prior to substance, those very ones that are not things that are in their own right (*kath' hauto*) but are said to be and partake (*metekhein*) of being (*ontotês*) because they are affections (*pathê*) of substance? If, then, they are things that are on account of substance and it gives being (*to einai*) to them, it is evident (*phaneros*) that substance is prior to all of them.[21]

And 'or else even the not-white and the not-straight' (1069a22–3) is equivalent to saying: but even the not-white and the not-straight are called beings on account of the white and the straight. For we say that what is not white *is* and what is not straight *is*. Since, then, the white, though not a being in its own right, possesses its being from substance, and the not-white, being a privation of the white, both is and is spoken of on account of the state (*hexis*) – that is, being white – this is a clear-cut indication that substance is prior to the other categories.[22] For it is due to substance that the states (for example, of whiteness and heat) are, and are called, beings, and it is due to the states that the instances of not-whiteness [and] not-heat are, and are also called, beings.

'Further', Aristotle says, 'none of the other things is separable (*khôristos*)' (1069a24) from substance, but they possess being in it and need it for their being. Therefore, that from which other things are not separate (*khôris*), while it is separate from them, is prior to those other things.[23] And that substance is prior to the other things is also established (*sunhistanai*) from the testimony of the early [thinkers]. For they also, he says, were enquiring into the principles of substance and of nothing else, on the grounds that it is prior to the other [categories]; for nobody enquires into the principles of posterior beings while neglecting the principles of things that are prior and exist in the chief sense (*kuriôs*) (cf. 1069a25–6).

> **1069a26** Now, the present-day [thinkers] posit the universal<s>[24] instead as substances. [For the genera are universals, which they say are principles and substances instead because they enquire logically. The early [thinkers], on the other hand, posited individuals, for example, fire and earth, as substances, but not the common body.
>
> 1069a30 Now, there are three substances: one is perceptible (upon which all are agreed), of which it is also necessary to grasp the elements, [enquiring whether they are] one or many, and of this [i.e. the perceptible] the one is perishable and the other everlasting; and another is immovable.[25] And some say that the latter is separate (some of these divide it into two, some posit the Forms and mathematical objects as a single nature, and some posit the mathematical objects alone of these). The former sorts, then, belong to natural science, for they involve movement; but the latter sort belongs to another science, if there is no principle common to them.]

After proving that substance is prior to the other [categories] and, in addition to this, that wisdom, as prior to all the other [sciences], enquires into the principles and causes of substances, Aristotle subsequently (*akolouthôs*) discusses who considered which beings to be substances. He says, 'The present-day [thinkers]'[26] say that 'the universals (*ta katholou*) instead are substances' (1069a26–7), and he adds what the universals are: 'for the genera' (*genê*), he says, 'are universals', which they declare to be principles and substances, because they 'enquire logically' (*logikôs*) or emptily (1069a27–8).[27] For since they had neglected the things (*pragma*), that is, beings in the chief sense, they carried out their enquiry (*zêtêsis*) about not-beings (*to mê on*); for universals are not-beings since they possess being [merely] by means of thought (*epinoia*).[28] In this way the present-day [thinkers] say that universals are substances. And by these remarks Aristotle could not be alluding (*ainittesthai*) to Plato (for this is not the opinion (*doxa*) of Plato), but he might be talking about others who were Plato's contemporaries.[29] 'But the early [thinkers]' used to speak on the contrary of 'individuals' (*ta kath' hekasta*) as substances (1069a28-9). Heraclitus posited fire (*pur*) as a substance and principle, Parmenides fire and earth (*ge*) in his writings concerning opinion, Thales water (*hudôr*), and others other things.[30] But none of them said that the common (*koinos*), [that is,] universal body (*sôma*), which is predicated of every body, is a principle[31] (1069a29-30).

After saying these things, Aristotle states that there are three substances, and since different people formed different opinions (*dokein*) about them, he also mentions what they are. One substance, he says, is the perceptible, which everyone agrees exists; for many declare unintelligently (*anoêtôs*) that there is no intelligible (*noêtos*) and divine (*theios*) substance. One of these was Hippo,[32] who is called 'the godless (*atheos*)' since he denied that there was anything apart from perceptible nature. One substance, therefore, is the perceptible, on which everyone agrees; and of the perceptible, the one is perishable (*phthartos*), for example, plants (*phuton*) and animals (*zôion*), while the other is everlasting (*aïdios*), for example, the spheres (*sphaira*) and the stars (*astêr*) in them.[33] And Aristotle says 'of which it is necessary (*anankê*) to grasp the elements (*stoikheion*), [enquiring whether they are] one or many' (1069a32-3) - [and he means the elements] not of everlasting substance, but of perceptible substance, and the latter is predicated (*katêgorein*) both of the perishable and of the imperishable (*aphthartos*) bodies. We must enquire, then, into the elements of this [i.e. perceptible substance]. For just as in the case of animals and plants, their substrate matter is the elements, so also in the case of the spheres and the stars in them, their substratum is an element; it is, then, the fifth body (*pempton sôma*).[34]

There are, then, these two substances, and the third is the intelligible substance which is everlasting and immovable,[35] which some say is separate and different from the other substances down here. However, some also, such as Plato, divide the latter into two, namely, into mathematical objects (for Plato said that the mathematical objects (*mathêmatika*) are separate and exist in their own right)[36] and the Forms (*Eidos*) or Ideas (*Idea*).[37] Among the Pythagoreans,[38] however, some placed the mathematical objects and Forms in one nature, saying that the mathematical objects are not at all different from the Ideas; but others among the Pythagoreans (for not all the Pythagoreans were of the same persuasion (*hairesis*)) said that only the mathematical objects exist, since they did not recognize the Ideas too (cf. 1069a34-b1).

After stating, then, that there are three sorts of substance, Aristotle adds that 'the former sorts' (1069a36) (meaning by 'the former sorts' (*ekeinai*) both perceptible and perishable (*phthartikos*) substance and also perceptible and imperishable substance) fall under natural science (*phusikê*), and he has concisely advanced the reason: 'for', he says, 'they involve movement' (1069b1). For it belongs to natural science to investigate things which contain a principle of movement (*kinêsis*) or rest (*êremia*).[39] But intelligible and divine substance belongs not to natural science but to the philosophy set forth here.[40] And he has set down the reason why it does not belong to natural science to investigate (*theôrein*) it, with the words, 'if there is no principle common to them' (1069b1-2), which is equivalent to saying that, since (*epeidê*) perceptible substance has nothing whatsoever in common (*koinônein*) with intelligible substance, and there is no principle common to them,[41] it could not belong to natural science to investigate the latter [i.e. intelligible substance].[42] The meaning of the passage, I believe, is something of this sort. But the continuation of the text (*lexis*) at the beginning is of the following sort: 'Now, there are three substances: one is perceptible (upon which all are agreed), of which it is also necessary (*anankaion*) to grasp the elements, [enquiring whether they are] one or many'; and then 'of which' (it is clear that ['which' refers to] perceptible [substance]) 'the one is perishable and the other everlasting'[43] (1069a30-3).

> **1069b3** Perceptible substance is changeable. [But if change is from opposites or from intermediates but not from all opposites (for voice too is not white) but from the contrary, there must be something underlying that changes to the contrary; for contraries do not change. [Chapter 2] 1069b7 Further, something remains, but the contrary does not remain; so there is a third thing apart from the contraries, namely, matter.]

The text would be clearer if, instead of 'perceptible substance is changeable (*metablêtê*)', the words '*since* (*epeidê*) perceptible substance is changeable' had been written.[44] For, after Aristotle has said above (1069a30-31; cf. 671,7-21) that there are three substances, of which some are perceptible and of which it is necessary to grasp the elements, he next enquires into what the elements are of the perceptible perishable substances and of the perceptible imperishable substances.

Now (cf. 1069b3-5) Aristotle states the assumptions[45] that perceptible substance is changeable, that all change is from opposites (*antikeisthai*) and

intermediates (*metaxu*), and that change is not from random (*tukhos*) opposites but from the appropriate negation (*oikeia apophasis*),⁴⁶ as he has declared in    30
Book 1 of the *Physics*.⁴⁷ (For a white colour (*khrôma*) comes to be from not-white but not from any random [not-white]. For voice, too, is said to be not-white, but a white colour does not come to be from a voice but from the not-white colour that is the negation of white. And the musical comes to be from not-musical, though not from a house (since a house is not-musical too)    35
but from its appropriate negation. And human being comes to be from not-human, but not from any [not-human] but from the appropriate privation. And all the other things that come to be also come to be in a similar way.) Since, then, all change comes about either from opposites or from intermediates (for    672,1
instance, white comes to be from grey too) and an opposite does not persist in the presence of its opposite or come to be what underlies it (for in no way does heat (*thermotês*) underlie coldness (*psukhrotês*), but in the presence of the cold (*to psukhron*), the hot (*to thermon*) in fact perishes (*phtheiresthai*) and does not    5
exist);⁴⁸ since, then, these things are so, there must be a third thing, and this is matter,⁴⁹ which changes from hot to cold and from cold to hot.

## [Chapter 2]

> [**1069b9** If, then, there are four types of change (either in respect of 'what' or in respect of quality, quantity, or place), and simple change in respect of 'this' is coming-to-be or perishing, change in respect of quantity is growth or diminution, change in respect of quality is alteration, and change in respect of place is locomotion, then changes will be into the particular contrariety. It must, then, be matter which has the potential to change in both ways.]

Granted,⁵⁰ it has been proven in Book 5 of the *Physics*⁵¹ that movement occurs in three categories – quality, quantity, and place – and there is change both in these categories and in that of substance (for 'in respect of "what"' refers to the natural and substantial (*ousiôdês*) form): 'and simple (*haplous*) change in    10
respect of "this"'⁵² is coming-to-be (*genesis*) or perishing (*phthora*), – that is, change in respect of substance (for we spoke of the simple coming-to-be of substances in *On Generation and Corruption*)⁵³ – change in respect of quantity is growth and diminution, change in respect of place (*topos*) is locomotion

(*phora*), and change in respect of affection (*pathos*) is alteration (*alloiôsis*) (cf. 1069b9–13), for example, heat [and] whiteness. Since, then, these things are so, all change is therefore into particular types of contrariety (*enantiôsis*): change in respect of quantity is into a contrariety in respect of quantity (for instance, large and small, or complete (*teleios*) and incomplete (*atelês*)), change in respect of substance is into contrariety in respect of substance (that is, form and privation), and similarly for the rest of the changes. But if this is the case, matter must be a third thing, since it has the potential (*dunasthai*) to change (*metaballein*) from form to privation and from privation to form; and similarly [for changes] from great or complete into small or incomplete.

> **1069b15** Since what is is twofold, everything changes from that which is in potentiality [to that which is in actuality (for instance, from what is white in potentiality to what is white in actuality, and similarly also in the case of growth and diminution). Hence, not only is it possible to come to be accidentally from what is not, but also all things come to be from what is not, though from what is in potentiality and not what is not in actuality. And this is the One of Anaxagoras (for it is better than 'all things together') and the mixture of Empedocles and Anaximander; and, as Democritus says, 'all things were together in potentiality but not in actuality'. Hence, they have had a grasp of matter.]

All these things which were said before and the things which will be discussed have been stated with exactness (*akribôs*) in the *Physics*,[54] but Aristotle makes mention of these things here for reasons which we stated when we were at the beginning the book (cf. 668,4–12). Since that which is (*to on*) is twofold,[55] namely in potentiality (*dunamei*) and in actuality (*energeiai*) (for water which is water in actuality is air in potentiality), 'everything changes from that which is in potentiality to that which is in actuality' (1069b15–16). And it is neither the case that the things that come to be come to be (*gignesthai*) from what is not in any way nor, again, that what is [comes to be from what is not in any way], but rather [these come to be] from that which is in one respect but is not in another respect. For matter is a being in its own right, and but it is a not-being due to the privation in it, and Socrates is a being, but he is also a not-being, due to the otherness (*heterotês*) in him. For since he is other (*heteros*) than a horse, he is what is not, since he *is not* a horse. Hence, all the things that come to be come to be in their own right from what is, but they come to be accidentally (*kata sumbebêkos*) from what is not.[56] For that which is white (*leukon*) comes to be from not-white, and what is not white is a being in its own right, but it is a not-being accidentally, since it is accidental to it that it is not white.[57] And it is likewise for the other cases. For instance, it is accidental to water that it is not air (*aêr*) and to Callias that he is not a horse (*hippos*).

And not only, Aristotle says, do things that come to be come to be from what is, though accidentally from what is not, but it is also possible to say conversely that they come to be from what is in potentiality and from what is not in actuality (cf. 1069b18–20). For instance, the water from which the air comes to be is what is not in actuality, since it is not yet air. Hence, in actuality it is not air (that is, what is not), but in potentiality it is air (that is, what is). In this way, then, after explaining to us what it is that comes to be and changes from form to privation and from privation to form – namely, that it is matter – he adds, 'this is the One (*to hen*) of Anaxagoras' (1069b20–1). Aristotle is saying in effect that when Anaxagoras declares that all things were together (*homou*) and the universe was one, and the Intellect (*nous*) began to separate these things from some source, he is showing that he had envisioned[58] (*oneirôttein*) matter without comprehending it, and for this reason he did not teach it clearly to us. It is better, therefore, Aristotle states, to say that everything comes to be from one thing, since the one is capable of changing into all things, and then to make clear that this one thing is matter, than to say that all things were together. For who in hearing that all things were together can understand that this locution refers to the matter which is potentially all things?

Now, just as Anaxagoras, when he said that all things were together, had envisaged matter but failed to recognize it,[59] so also did Empedocles when he said that things here came to be from the mixture (*migma*) (and by 'mixture' he would mean the Sphere (*sphairos*))[60] (1069b21–2). Because he was unable to grasp it, instead of saying that they were from matter, he said that things here are from the mixture. Democritus, however, also indicates (*emphainein*) with 'all things were together in potentiality' that he had got hold of a notion of matter obscurely; for 'all things were together in potentiality' is equivalent to saying that there is in us that which is capable of being all things (cf. 1069b22–3).[61]

> **1069b24** Now, all things that change possess matter, but the matter is different. [And such everlasting things that are not generable but are movable by way of locomotion [possess matter that] is not generable but is 'from there to here'.]

Upon enquiring in [the book concerning] the puzzles[62] whether all things have one principle and one element or more than one, Aristotle proves through the arguments stated and transmitted in that book that they do not have one, and he will prove again that they also have one, so that all things will both have one principle and not have one. But how he does so, we shall show when we go over the text (cf. Chapters 4–5 below). Thus, all perceptible and perishable things and all perceptible and imperishable things possess matter, but different matter. For the matter of perishable things is capable of changing from one form into another, which is why some might call [the matter] perishable;[63] but the matter of ingenerable things (*agenêtos*) is not of this sort, but is movable only with respect to locomotion[64] (cf. 1069b24–6). For example, the sun (*hêlios*) which is now in Aquarius (*hudrokhoos*) will in a little while be in Pisces (*ikhthues*).[65]

> **1069b26** One might however raise the puzzle: from what sort of not-being is there coming-to-be? [For that which is not is threefold. If, then, the [thing] is in potentiality, nevertheless it is not <from> any random thing but different things [come to be] from different things. Nor is [the statement] that 'all things [were] together' sufficient; for things differ in their matter, since why else did things without limit, and not one, come to be? For the Intellect is one, so that if matter were also one, that of which the matter was in potentiality would have come to be in actuality. The causes and principles, then, are three: two are contraries – of which one is the account or form, the other privation – and the third is matter.]

In a manner that is altogether confusing and baffling and neither put in order nor in proper sequence, Aristotle brings forth the statements in this book with the same lack of clarity with which he carried on at the beginning.[66] For, after saying above (1069b18–20) that the things that come to be not only come to be from what is but also from what is not, and after inserting many remarks in between,[67] he places here the reason why he mentioned those things earlier, saying in effect: 'I did not mention there those things [merely] in passing (*parergos*) but also out of necessity.' For one might raise the puzzle: since that which is not is spoken in three ways – in one way it is the false (*pseudês*) (just as what is is the true (*alêthês*)), in another as that which is in no respect and in no way, and in another as that which is in potentiality – from which of these will there be coming-to-be?[68] And having asked (*erôtan*) this by way of a puzzle, he answers by stating, 'if then the [thing]⁶⁹ is in potentiality ...' (1069b28) – that is, if there is something that is what is not in potentiality, there will be coming-to-be from it. This is stated elliptically (*ellipôs*), and I believe it is because he spoke clearly about this a little while before. We ought, then, as I think, to infer: what is not in actuality but what is in potentiality. Hence, the whole sentence is as follows: if, then, a thing is what is not in actuality but is what is in potentiality, there will be coming-to-be from it. Let us make what he is saying clear with an example: the water which is not air in actuality is air in potentiality. Nevertheless, it is not from any random thing that is what is not in actuality but is what is in potentiality, that anything comes to be, but a human comes from human seed (*anthrôpeion sperma*) and menstrual fluid (*katamênion*),⁷⁰ and an olive tree (*elaia*) from something else and a vine plant (*ampelos*) from yet something else (cf. 1069b28-9).

And since, as we say, different (*allos*) things come to be from different things, Anaxagoras did not speak adequately when he said, 'all things were together', that is, there was matter from which all things came to be. Rather, he should have stated what sorts of things (*pragmata*) come to be from what sorts of matter. For things differ not only in respect of form but also in respect of matter (cf. 1069b29-32). For example, bits of flesh and bones are matter for human beings, bronze for a statue, water for bronze,⁷¹ and another matter for another thing. For if there were not proximate matters [for each] virtually without limit (*apeiron*) (for nothing comes to be from formless (*aneideos*) matter except for only the simple things (*ta hapla*)),⁷² everything would be one. For if indeed the efficient [cause] (namely, the Intellect) is one, if the proximate (*prosekhês*) matter for each thing had also been one, what has come to be would have been one (1069b31-2).⁷³

For 'that of which (*hou*)⁷⁴ the matter was in potentiality came to be in actuality' (1069b32) means that that which (*ho*) the matter had the potential to come to be would have come to be one and not many. For instance, just as what is the seed which is an ear of corn (*astakhus*) in potentiality comes to be only an ear of corn from it, and not a vine plant or olive tree as well, so also, if the matter were one, what has come to be would have been one, and not any random thing but what it was in potentiality. After saying these things, by way of a conclusion to these remarks, Aristotle then indicates the three causes or principles: matter, form, and privation (cf. 1069b32-4).

## [Chapter 3]

**1069b35** After these things [it must be demonstrated] that neither the matter nor the form comes to be, [I mean, the ultimate ones. For everything [that changes] is something, and it changes by something and into something. And that by which it changes is the first mover, and that which changes is the matter, and that into which it changes is the form. Therefore, it will go on without limit, if it is not only the round bronze that comes to be but also the roundness and the bronze; so it must come to a stop.]

The phrase 'it must be demonstrated' is omitted from the text, so that the whole would be written as: after these things, it must be demonstrated 'that neither the matter nor the form comes to be'. And that the first and formless matter has not come to be Aristotle has proven at the end of Book 1 of the *Physics*.[75] And that the form has not come to be either he showed in Book 7 of the present treatise.[76]

And straightaway, since he said that there are three principles – matter, form, and privation – he enquires as a consequence whether they come to be or not. And he proves this very briefly because he has already proven it at length in Book 7.[77] Therefore, he says, one must prove that the matter and the form – that is, the ultimate [ones] – do not come to be; but 'ultimate' (*eskhatos*) (1069b36) is added because the four humours (*khumos*)[78] which are matter for Socrates have come to be, but they are not the ultimate, that is, formless matter.[79] Again, flesh is a certain form but not the ultimate [form?], but Socrates is the ultimate [form?].[80] In this way, then, after distinguishing in addition what sort of matter and what sort of form he says do not come to be, he proves what he is claiming, saying that, if not only the bronze (*khalkos*) comes to be round but also the roundness (*strongulotês*) – that is, the form – [comes to be], the progression (*anodos*) will go on without limit (cf. 1070a2–4). For there will be some substratum of roundness, since everything comes to be from some substratum. And, again, there is the same argument concerning the substratum of roundness, whether it comes to be or not. For if it comes to be, there will also be a substratum of it and this will proceed without limit. If, again, the bronze comes to be from a moist exhalation (*hugra anathumiasis*), and this from water, and this from formless matter, and this from something else, the process will go on without limit, which is impossible. For this has been demonstrated in Book 2 of the present treatise.[81]

**1070a4** After these things, [it must be stated] that each substance comes to be from a synonymous thing; [for natural things are substances, and the other things [are too]. For things come to be either by art or by nature or by chance or spontaneously. Now art is a principle in something else, while nature is a principle in a thing itself (for a human being begets a human being), and the remaining causes are privations of these.

1070a9 Now, there are three substances: the matter which is a this-something by appearing (for whatever things are by contact and not by natural coherence are matter and substratum), while the nature is a this-something and a state-towards-which; further the third which is the individual [substance] composed of these, such as Socrates and Callias. Now in some cases the this-something does not exist apart from the compound substance (for instance, the form of house, unless it is the art; nor is there coming-to-be and perishing of these things, but it is in another way that there is or is not a house without matter as well as health and anything that depends on art), but if it does, it is in the case of things that are by nature. That is why, then, Plato was not incorrect when he said that there are as many Forms as things that are by nature, if indeed there are Forms †but of these things, for example, fire, flesh, and head†; for all these things are matter, and the last [matter] belongs to what is substance most of all.]

Here, too, we ought to understand in addition 'it must be stated'. After the things already said, Aristotle says, it is necessary to say as well that each substance comes to be from a thing synonymous (*sunônumos*) with itself.[82] For it is either by art (*tekhnê*), he says, that there come to be the things that come to be, or it is by nature (cf. 1070a6), and both [sorts] come to be from things synonymous with themselves. And it is clear that the things that come to be from art come to be from something synonymous with themselves. For instance, a house (*oikia*) comes to be from the form of a house which is in the soul (*psukhê*) of the housebuilder (*oikodomos*), and health (*hugieia*) in the body comes to be from the form (that is, the account (*logos*)) of health in the soul of the healer (*iatros*). And it is most evident that natural things also [come to be] from a synonymous thing. For a human being comes to be from a human being, and a horse from a horse. However, the things that come to be spontaneously (*automatos*) or by chance (*tukhê*) are failures (*apotuchia*) of nature and art.[83]

After saying that it is either by art or by nature that there come to be the things that come to be, Aristotle tells how art differs from nature: namely, art is a principle in the producer (*poioun*) but not in the product, whereas nature is a principle which is in the same thing that comes to be. 'For a human being begets a human being' (1070a8); and this statement is connected with the statement that 'after these things' it must be said that 'each substance comes to be from a synonymous thing'; for a human being begets a human being.[84] And the clause inserted before this, 'for natural things are substances, and the other things' (1070a5–6), is equivalent to saying that not only are things that come to be by nature substances but the other things are too, that is,[85] those that are subjects of the arts. Or else 'for natural things are substances, and the other things' is equivalent to saying: for the things that come to be by nature come to be from substances, that is, from things synonymous with themselves, and likewise, too, the other things, that is, the things that come to be by art. And the whole passage will be as follows: after these things it must be stated that each substance comes to be from a synonymous thing; for natural things and the other things are substances. And an indication (*sêmeion*) of this is that a human being generates a human being. 'And the remaining causes' (1070a8–9), – that is, either chance or spontaneity – are privations and failures and mistakes (*harmartêma*) of things that come to be <from>[86] nature and art.

After stating previously (1069a30–6; cf. 670,24–671,21) that substance is said in three ways – two of which are perceptible, namely the perishable and the ungenerated (*agennêtos*), and the third is the intelligible – Aristotle introduces another triad of substance: namely, the matter, the form, and the compound of matter and form.[87] For substances, he says, are three, 'the matter being a this-something (*tode ti*) by appearing (*tôi phainesthai*)'[88] (1070a9–10). What he means would be as follows: since the matter of Socrates consists of bits of flesh, sinews, bones (*ostoun*), hands, feet, head (*kephalê*), and so forth, whenever we think of them as lying in a heap haphazardly and without having grown together (*sumphuein*)[89] or become unified (*henoun*) with each other, but as being merely in contact (*haptesthai*) with each other like heaped up grains of sand, so that there are, let us say, hands and spleen and heart lying at the bottom (*edaphos*), and above these the head and belly, and above these the feet and entrails – whenever, then, we think of these things which are the matter of Socrates as being in this state and being situated in this way, then they are 'a this-something' by appearing. For Aristotle means by 'a this-something' Socrates or the animal in general, which [these parts] would have brought to completion if they had acquired order (*taxis*), unification (*henôsis*), and growth together (*sumphusis*) by nature's agency. Therefore, the hands, the feet, the head, and the other parts lying about in a disorderly (*ataktôs*) and haphazard manner are Socrates 'by appearing', that is, in appearance (*kata phantasian*). For we imagine (*phantazesthai*) that if nature were to acquire the power to order and unify (*henoun*) the matter before us, it would become Socrates. And when [these parts] are unified and conjoined and acquire order, then it is not in appearance that this sort of matter is Socrates, but in reality Socrates exists, and it is true to say that these things are Socrates. Therefore, material things which are one by contact (*haphê*) but not by growing together and being unified are a this-something in appearance (1070a9-11). Similarly, too, in the case of fire, air, water, and earth (*gê*). For whenever it is [merely] by contact that they are one, then they are Socrates in appearance; but whenever it is by the agency of nature that they are blended and altered and become Socrates, then they are Socrates in truth.

Therefore, one substance is matter, while yet another substance is the nature which is a this-something and a certain state towards which [there is coming-to-be].[90] And by 'nature', 'a this-something', and 'a state', Aristotle means the form;[91] for these terms are parallel. And [he says] 'towards which' (1070a12) instead of 'towards which nature and form there is the coming-to-be'; for every case of coming-to-be is directed towards some form. And yet another substance is the [compound] of matter and form, for instance, Socrates or Callias.

After saying that the third substance is the individual (*to kath' hekaston*), 'Socrates or Callias' (1070a12), Aristotle states that in some cases it is evident that there are not Forms or Ideas of particular things themselves, and those who posit the Ideas agree with this too. For they[92] said that there are Ideas of things that come to be by nature's agency but not of those that come to be by art. Therefore, in some cases there are not Ideas; for there is not a Form or Idea of a house, saw, or statue, unless, Aristotle says, even in these cases one[93] says that Ideas are the arts through which these things come to be (cf. 1070a14-15). Therefore, the forms of artefacts (*tekhnêtês*) exist not in reality (*hupostasis*) but only in thought (*epinoia*). In addition, their existence is not a result of coming-to-be and a temporal interval (*khronikê paratasis*) and in general a change of some substratum, nor is their non-existence a result of perishing. For this is indicated by the statement, 'nor is there coming-to-be and perishing of these things, but it is in another way that they exist or do not exist' (1070a15-16), that is, they exist without coming-to-be and they do not exist though without perishing, like contacts.[94] For whenever I envisage a form of a house, this sort of form is not a result of coming-to-be; for it is not the sort of form that has come about after undergoing any alteration, but [it exists] atemporally (*akhronôs*) and in the present (*to nun*), for the appearance (*phantasia*) of it occurs to me in the present moment. But whenever I do not imagine it, it does not exist; for not imagining also departs in the present moment.

Further, Aristotle called the same form of a house and of the health in our imagination (*phantasia*) 'a house and health without matter' (1070a16–17). This is why, he says, Plato was not incorrect when he said that there are Forms not of artefacts but of natural things.[95] For if there are Forms at all, they will belong to things that come to be by nature but not to things that come to be from art. For 'different from these things' (1070a19) suggests that there will be Forms of natural things which are different from these things, that is, from the perceptible objects here. But the words 'for example, fire, flesh, [and] head; for all these things are matter, and the last [matter] belongs to what is most of all substance' (1070a19–20) do not follow from the adjacent text, nor do they go with it; but they go with [the earlier clause] 'for whatever things are by contact and not by natural coherence are matter and substratum' (1070a10–11).[96] And the continuous text is as follows: 'For whatever things are by contact and not by natural conjunction are matter and substratum, for example, fire, flesh, [and] head; for all of these are matter, and the last matter (*teleutaia hulê*) belongs to what is substance most of all' (cf. 1070a10–11,19–20). Next is 'the nature, a this-something and a state-towards-which' and so forth (1070a11–12). And Aristotle says that the indivisible (*atomos*) substance, Socrates or Callias, is substance most of all. For fire is matter of this sort of substance; but, most of all, its matter is the last, that is, the proximate, matter[97] of it, for example, flesh, sinews, and bones.

> **1070a21** The things that impart movement, then, are [causes] in so far as they were things that have come to be beforehand, [whereas those that are causes in the sense of an account are simultaneous with their effects. For when the human being is healthy, then health exists too, and the shape of the bronze sphere exists simultaneously with the bronze sphere. But whether anything remains afterward also must be investigated. For nothing prevents it in the case of some things, for example, whether the soul is of this sort – not the entire soul but rather the intellect; for that all [the soul remains afterward] is probably impossible. It is evident, then, that there is no need (for these reasons

at any rate) for the Ideas to exist; for a human being begets a human being – the individual [human being begets] some [human being]. And similarly in the case of the arts; for the healing art is also the account of health.]

And this pertains to the discussion concerning causes.[98] What it means is that the things that impart movement – that is, the efficient causes (*poiêtikon aition*) – are prior in time (*khronos*) to their effects. For Sophroniscus is before Socrates, and the housebuilder is before the house. But the text contains some unclarity (*asapheia*). 'Therefore, the things that impart movement,' Aristotle says, 'are [causes] in so far as they are things that came to be beforehand' (1071a21), using 'are' (*onta*) instead of 'subsisting' (*huparkhonta*), so that what he means is that the efficient [causes] subsist and possess an account [i.e. form] prior in time to the products; but the formal causes (*eidikon aition*) are simultaneous [with their products]. For the roundness, which is essentially the form of the sphere, is simultaneous with there being the bronze sphere; and similarly health, which is a certain state and form, is simultaneous with there being the healthy person (cf. 1070a22–4). It is clear, therefore, that the formal causes are simultaneous with the things of which they are causes.

But whether forms remain once they are separated, that is, whether they [still] exist after their separation (*khorismos*) and do not pass into nothingness, is in need of extensive investigation (cf. 1070a24–6). Still, Aristotle says, in the case of some things nothing prevents it; for example, if the soul is a form of animate things, nothing prevents it – that is, since the soul is a form of animate things (*empsukhos*), nothing prevents a sort of soul, for example, the intellect or the rational soul (*logikê psukhê*) – from remaining, for non-rational souls (*alogos psukhê*) are mortal (*thnêtos*).[99] And for this reason he adds 'probably' (*isôs*) (1070a26).[100] And if the causes of all things are clear, there is no need for the Ideas to explain how these things come to be.[101] For Socrates came to be from Sophroniscus and Plato from Ariston; and similarly in the case of artefacts; for it is from the art of healing (*iatrikê*), which is an account and form of health,[102] that health comes to be (cf. 1070a26–30).

## [Chapter 4]

**1070a31** The causes and principles of different things are in a way different, [but in a way, if one is to speak universally and by analogy, they are the same for all. For one might pose the puzzle whether the principles and elements of substances and relatives are the same or different, and similarly for each of the categories. But it is absurd if they are the same for all. For relatives and substances will be from the same things. What then will this be? For apart from substance and the other categories there is nothing common, but an element is prior to the things of which it is an element. But, then, neither is substance an element of the relatives, nor is any of them an element of substance. Further, how it is possible for all things to have the same elements? For none of the elements can be the same as the compound of elements, for example, for B or A to be the same as BA.]

Next comes the solution of the puzzle about whether all things have the same (*autos*) causes and principles or not (cf. 668,9–10).[103] Now Aristotle says that in one way they are the same but in another way they are different. 'Universally', then, he says (and to make clear what he means by 'universally',[104] he adds 'and by analogy'[105] (*kata analogian*)), they are the same (1070a32). For since all things that come to be have matter, form, and privation, and all things that come to be exist because of matter, form, and privation, then all things have the same principles considered as universal. For matter, form, and privation are causes of all things. For instance, a statue's (*andrias*) matter is bronze, its form is a shape (*skhema*) of a certain sort, and its privation is the form which it was lacking, for example, that of a horse (*hippeion*); and a door's (*thura*) matter is wood (*xulon*), its form is a shape of a certain sort, and its privation is, say, [the absence of the form] of a box (*kibiôton*). Hence, considered as universal and by analogy (for as bronze is related to a statue, so is wood to a door) all things have the same principles: matter, form, privation. But considered as proximate and co-ordinated (*suntattein*),[106] they are different; for the matter of a statue, that of a door, and that of Socrates are different from one another. Similarly, too, in the case of form and privation: the form of a statue, of a door, and of Socrates are different, and their [respective] privations are also different.

The situation is similar in the case of the efficient cause as well: the cause as mover is the efficient cause of all things considered universally, whereas the proximate ones are different: for instance, Sophroniscus is the efficient cause of Socrates, and the sculptor (*andriantopoios*) is the efficient cause of the statue. Hence, if we ask whether the principles and causes of all things are the same or different, we must say that in one way they are the same and in another they are different: considered universally they are the same, but considered as proximate they are different.

After stating that the causes and principles of different things are different, in order to show that it is reasonable to mention this claim Aristotle adds that one might pose the puzzle whether the elements and the principles of substance, quantity, quality, relative (*pros ti*), and the remaining categories are different or the same.[107] And he proves that in the chief sense (that is, considered as proximate) they are not the same. For it is absurd, he says, to say that all things have the same element (cf. 1070a33–6). And he proves this by a dilemma (*diairesis*): if all things have one element, it is either different from all the categories, or else one of them will be an element of the rest. But it is also clear that it is not different from the ten categories. For since the elements are prior to the things of which they are elements (that is, to things composed of elements (*stoikheiotos*)), if indeed the ten most general (*genikos*) genera (namely, substance, quantity, quality, and the rest) have the same element, it will be prior to them. But there is nothing prior to substance and the remaining categories; nor is there anything in general apart from them. Therefore, there is not one element of all [the categories] (cf. 1070a36-b3). But, on the other hand, neither is substance an element of relatives and of the remaining categories. For how will a non-substance come to be from a substance? For a substance always (*aei*) comes to be from a substance. Nor will relatives be elements of substance. For how will a substance come to be from an accident?[108]

'Further, how is it possible for all things to have the same elements? For none of the elements can be the same as the compound of elements' (1070b4–6). This argument (*epikheirêma*) is the same as the one before it but is carried out differently.[109] For previously Aristotle said that the element is prior to those things of which it is an element, but here he says that the element is different from the things of which it is an element. For instance, Socrates who is composed of fire and earth and the intermediate [elements] is not the same as the fire and earth, but different. If, then, the elements are different from the things of which they are elements, if indeed there is one and the same element of the ten categories, it will be different from all the categories. But there is not anything besides these. Therefore, there is not one element of all things. And Aristotle proves by induction (*epagôgê*) that the elements are different from the things composed of them: B, he says, which is an element[110] of the syllable (*sullabê*) BA, is different from the syllable (cf. 1070b6).

**1070b7** Nor, then, [is it] any of the intelligible elements,[111] for example, being and one; [for these belong to each of the compounds as well. So none of them will be either a substance or a relative. But it is necessary [for them to be]. So not all things have the same elements.

1070b10 Or as *we* say, there is a way they do and a way they do not; for instance, perhaps [the elements] of perceptible bodies are, as form, the hot and in another way the cold, as the privation; and as matter the first thing which is potentially these in itself; and these things and the things composed of them are substances, of which these are principles (or anything that comes to be one from the hot and cold, for instance, flesh or bone). For what has come to be is necessarily different from these. These things, therefore, have the same elements and principles, though different things have different ones.

1070b16 But it cannot be said that all things [have the same principles] in this way but [different things have them] by analogy. Thus one might say that there are three principles – the form, the privation, and the matter – but each of these is different for each genus, for example, in colour there is white, black, and surface, or light, darkness, and air, from which [there is] day and night.

1070b22 Since not only the things present in a thing are causes but also what is external to them, for example, what imparts movement, it is clear that a principle is different from an element, although both are causes and the principle is divided into these; and that which imparts movement or rest is a sort of principle. Hence, there are by analogy three elements, and four causes and principles. But a different thing has a different [element], and the first cause, as moving, is different for a different thing. Health, sickness, body; [and] the moving [cause] is the art of healing. Form, disorderliness of a certain sort, bricks; [and] the moving [cause] is the art of housebuilding.]

Aristotle has made clear which intelligible elements he means, namely, one and being.[112] Now, he says, being and one cannot be elements of all things. He proves this on the basis of his previous claim that the elements are different from the things that have come to be from them (1070b4–6; cf. 679,9–11). If, then, one and being are elements of everything, everything will be different from one and being. But just as what is composed of fire and earth is neither fire nor earth, so also what is composed of one and being will be neither one nor being. Hence, substance, quantity, quality, and the remaining [categories]

will be not-beings and not-ones (*mê hen*), which is impossible. But if this is   30
impossible, the premiss from which it is inferred is false. But this was that one
and being are elements of all things (cf. 1070b7–10).

Further, with the clause 'for these are present in[113] each of the compounds
(*suntheton*) as well' (1070b8) we should understand in addition 'the simple
things', so that it would mean: for these, being and one, are present in
(*enhuparkhein*) each of the simple things and the compounds. And 'so none of
them[114] will be either a substance or a relative' (1070b8–9) would mean: none 'of   35
them' (that is, none of the things that have come to be from being and one as
from an element) will be; that is, none will be in any way, nor will they possess
any reality (*huparxis*). For just as, as was said (679,14–16), what is composed of
fire and earth is neither fire nor earth, so also neither will what is composed of   680,1
one and being be one and a being, but it will be not one and not a being. One can
understand 'neither a substance or a relative' (1070b9) as equivalent to saying: so
neither a substance nor a relative will be a being.[115] And it is also possible to
understand it in the following way: if, then, one were to say that being is an
element, then since the element is different from the things composed of it,   5
either it [i.e. being] itself or the things composed of it [i.e. being] will be a not-
being. For it is not possible that both being (that is, the element) is a being and
that the things composed of it are beings. But if one were to say that substance is
an element, then either it [i.e. substance] will not be a substance or else the
things composed of it (for instance, Socrates, Plato, and so forth) [will not be
substances]. Similarly if relative is an element, then relative will not be a relative
[or else the things composed of it will not be relatives].

Aristotle concludes by saying, 'so not all things have the same elements' and   10
causes, but in a way they are the same but in another way they are different
(1070b9–11). For, in so far as all things have, as elements, matter, form,
privation, and efficient cause, and all things depend on these things, then in
this respect all things have the same principles. But in so far as the matter of
a statue is different from that of an animal, and similarly the form and
efficient cause of a statue are different, one from the other, in this respect the   15
principles of all things are different and not the same. Therefore, all things
have the same principles (I mean form, matter, and so forth) considered as
universals, but considered as co-ordinated [their principles are] different and
not the same.

Aristotle then proves by induction that all things depend on matter, form, privation, and the efficient cause. For of the perceptible bodies, he says, 'perhaps' (1070b11) – that is, for the sake of argument – there is the hot as form, the cold as privation, and what can become hot or cold as matter. And 'in itself' is added (1070b13), since we say that the white has become cold, though not in itself. But in itself[116] the substratum of the white does become cold. Thus the hot is form, the cold is privation, and what is potentially these things is matter. Therefore, the hot (for the hot is the form and substance of fire) and the matter are substances.[117] And not only these are substances, but also what is composed of hot and cold, that is, of fire and water. For this is either flesh or bone or anything else of the sort (cf. 1071b13-15).

But the clause 'for what has come to be is necessarily different from those things' (1070b15-16) in no way fits in with the adjacent text,[118] though it would be continuous with the passage a little before: 'none of them [i.e. the elements], then, will be either a substance or a relative' (1070b8-9). And this would provide the basis for the substance not being a substance and the relative not being a relative; for what has come to be must be different from those things. For, as Aristotle has said (1070b4-6), what has come to be from an element is different from the elements. Therefore, of the things mentioned in the adjacent text (1070b11-21), the hot is form, the cold is privation, what can [become] these things is matter, and also the light is form, and the dark is privation. And out of air and light (*phôs*) (that is, of matter and form) there is day (*hêmera*), while out air and darkness (*skotos*) (that is, matter and privation) there is night (*nux*). Hence, all things have the same principles in this way (that is, by analogy), as we said (678,10-31), but not in the chief sense.

And since, Aristotle says, causes include not only these [i.e. form, privation, matter] considered as co-ordinated in us,[119] but also what is external (*ektos*) (namely, the mover (*to kinoun*) or the efficient cause), 'a principle is different from an element' (cf. 1070b22-4). For a principle is more universal (*katholikos*) than an element, since an element is also a principle but not every principle is an element.[120] For instance, a father is a principle but not an element. The principle, which is more universal, is divided into the following things, which are more particular (*merikos*): namely, into matter, form, privation, and the efficient cause. If, then, the principle is divided into these things,[121] it is clear that what imparts movement and rest (that is, the efficient cause) is a sort of principle.[122] Hence, the elements that are found to be everywhere by analogy are three: matter, form, and privation; but the principles and causes are four: matter, form, privation, and efficient cause (1070b24–6). And these four [principles] are different in different things, for example, in the case of animals the body of the animals as matter, health as form, sickness (*nosos*) as privation, and the healing art as efficient cause. And, again, the house is form, disorderliness (*ataxia*) of a certain sort is privation, the bricks (*plinthos*) are matter, and the housebuilder is the efficient cause. Hence, all things have matter, form, privation, and the efficient cause as causes, but different things have different causes (cf. 1070b26–30).

> **1070b30** Since what imparts movement in natural human beings is a human being, [and since in the case of things resulting from cognition it is form or its contrary, in a way there will be three causes, but in a way four. For the healing art is in a way health, and the art of housebuilding is in a way the form of a house, and a human being begets a human being. Further, apart from these things there is that which as the first of all things moves all things.]

Aristotle spoke of 'natural human beings'[123] owing to the human-being-itself (*autoanthrôpos*); for the latter is not natural. But what Aristotle now says, and said also in the *Physics*,[124] is that the efficient and formal (*eidikos*) [causes] are often the same. For Sophroniscus and Socrates are different in number (*arithmôi*) but the same in species, and the health in the body and the efficient cause of health (namely the art of healing) are the same in species (*eidei*) (for the healing art is [identical with] the account of health), and similarly the house and the art of housebuilding (*oikodomikê*) [are the same in species].[125] Hence, the efficient cause and the formal cause, not altogether but in a certain respect, are two in number (*arithmôi*) but one in species (*eidei*).[126] And on this basis in one way the causes are three, but in another way four.[127] Further, apart from these causes is 'the first of all things',[128] which is the principle here under investigation (cf. 1070b30–5).

## [Chapter 5]

> **1070b36** Since some things are separable and some are not separable, the former are substances. [And for this reason these things are causes of all

things, because without substances there will not be affections and movements. Further, these will be soul, perhaps, and body, or thought and desire and body.]

With these remarks Aristotle shows that the principles of substances are principles and causes of the existence of accidents. For since, he says, some things that are are separable and subsisting by themselves, such as substances, and other things (namely, the accidents) are inseparable (*akhôristos*) and incapable of existing by themselves but possess their existence in other things, for this reason 'the former' – that is, the things that are separable and subsisting by themselves – are 'substances', and for this reason 'these things'[129] – that is, the principles of substances – are also causes of the existence of all other things (cf. 1071a1). He has forcefully introduced the reason for this, saying that 'without substances[130] there will not be affections and movements' (1071a1–2). For since the principles of substances are causes of the substances existing, and substances, again, are the causes of the accidents existing, it is very clear that the principles of substances are causes of the accidents also existing. Next he says also what are the most proximate causes of the existence of animate things: these, he states, are 'soul, perhaps,[131] and body', as in the case of plants, or intellect and body and desire (*orexis*), as in the case of human beings, or body and desire,[132] as can be seen in the case of non-rational (*alogos*) beings (cf. 1071a2–3).

**1071a3** Further, in another way, by analogy, the principles are the same, [namely, actuality and potentiality. But these are also [different] at different times for different things and in different ways. For [in] some cases the same thing is sometimes in actuality and sometimes in potentiality, for instance, wine, flesh, or a human being. And these also fall under the aforementioned causes; for the form, if it is separable, is in actuality, and [also] the compound of both, as well as the privation, for example, darkness or diseased, while the matter is potentiality; for this is capable of being both.]

Aristotle has stated that the principles of all things are matter, form, privation, and efficient cause, and that by analogy they are the same but in the chief sense they are not the same but different, since both potentiality (*dunamis*) and actuality (*energeia*) are principles (for it is from one thing in actuality and another thing in potentiality that things that come to be do so. And, as he said in the *Physics*,[133] 'had this [fact of] nature been observed it would have resolved

all puzzlement'). Now he states that just as when we observed the matter, form, efficient cause, and privation in everything, we said that the principles of all things are the same, so also, since in everything there is seen potentiality and actuality, in the sense of the universal potentiality and universal actuality on which all things subject to generation (*en genesei*) depend, we might say all things have the same principles, but in the sense of the potentiality and actuality immanent in each individual (*hekastos*), we might say that they are different         15
and not the same. Consequently, we will say that the principles of all things are either the same or different both when focussing on matter, form, and so forth, and also when focussing on potentiality and actuality. Further, then, he says, in a different way and by another analogy (for it is not by the analogy concerning form, matter, and so forth, but by the analogy 'concerning potentiality and         20
actuality') the principles are the same (1071a3–5).

Nevertheless, both potentiality and actuality are 'at different times[134] in different things and in different ways. For [in] some cases the same thing is sometimes in actuality and sometimes in potentiality' (1071a5–7). For in the case of Socrates health is sometimes in actuality and sometimes in potentiality, because if Socrates is healthy (*hugiainein*) then health belongs to him in actuality and sickness in potentiality, but if he is sick it is the reverse. Hence,         25
health belongs sometimes to persons such as Socrates and Plato, but at other times to others such as Achilles and Alcibiades. But [it belongs] also 'in different ways'. For sometimes it exists potentially and sometimes actually. 'For instance, wine (*oinos*) or flesh or a human being' are examples (*paradeigma*) of 'sometimes in actuality and sometimes in potentiality' (1071a6–7). For the very liquid (*hugrotês*) which is now in actuality wine is in potentiality vinegar         30
(*oxos*); and what is now in actuality vinegar is in potentiality wine;[135] and similarly in the case of the remaining two. And as it is in these cases, so also in all cases. But also the potentiality, he says, and the actuality and the substratum of these 'falls' under, or is referred to, the aforementioned causes: that is, matter, form, and privation. For the actuality is like the form and the form like the actuality, while the potentiality is like the privation and the         35
privation is like the potentiality,[136] and the substratum of these is like the matter (cf. 1071a7–11).

Therefore, the meaning of what Aristotle says, I think, is as follows. In the text 'the form [is] in actuality' [is written] instead of 'the actuality is analogous

683,1 to the form and the form to the actuality', and 'if it is separable' instead of '[if it is] separable in thought' (1071a8–9). For the enmattered (*enülos*) forms are only separated in thought from matter.[137] And 'the compound of both' [is written] instead of 'not only is the form actuality, but also what is composed of
5 matter and form'. Alternatively, '*the form* [is] in actuality, if it is separable' [is written] instead of 'the light',[138] which would mean that the actuality (that is, the light) is what is separable; for it is separated from the transparency (*diaphanês*) in the air during each [day]. And he means by 'the compound of both' the day, which is composed of the light and the illuminated (*phôtizein*) transparency. And that he speaks of light, which he also says is separable, as actuality, I submit in evidence (*tekmairesthai*) his statement that darkness is privation.[139]

10 **1071a11** But in another way things which do not have the same matter differ[140] in actuality and potentiality, in which case they do not have the same form but a different one, [just as a cause of a human being is the elements – fire and earth as matter and the proper form – and furthermore some external thing, for instance, the father, and beyond these the sun and its oblique orbit, which are neither matter nor form, nor privation, nor the same in form but are movers.]

Since a human being makes a human being come to be and the sun [does too], and the sun and Sophroniscus are both efficient [causes] of Socrates, then, on the one hand, the matter of Sophroniscus (his flesh, bones, and sinews) and likewise
15 his form (that is, his actuality) do not differ at all in account from Socrates' matter and form. For the matters of both consist of flesh and sinews; and likewise, surely, their forms are the same and differ only as to [which of them is] prior or posterior; for Sophroniscus' matter and form are prior [in time] to Socrates' nature. On the
20 other hand, the matter and form of the sun are prior to the matter and form of Sophroniscus not merely in time, but also in account. For Sophroniscus' matter consists of flesh, whereas the sun's matter consists not of this sort but of some fifth body. And that the sun's form is also different from Sophroniscus' form I do not need to say.[141] Aristotle intimates these things by saying, 'in another way things which do not have the same matter differ in actuality and potentiality, in
25 which case they do not have the same form' (1071a11–13). This passage is elliptical (*ellipês*). It would be complete if it said that in another way things which do not have the same matter *or the same form* differ in actuality and potentiality, in which case they do not have the same form *or the same matter*.[142] And if this is

what he is saying, since Sophroniscus is the efficient cause of Socrates, while the sun and its oblique orbit (*loxos kuklos*) are too, the actuality (that is, form) of the sun and of its oblique orbit[143] differs from the actuality (that is, form) of Sophroniscus and Socrates; similarly, then, too, their potentialities (that is, their matters) [are different] (cf. 1071a15–16).

And he has added the reason for this when he said, [the external causes are] 'neither matter nor form nor privation' (1071a16), which is equivalent to saying that Sophroniscus' matter and form are the same as Socrates' matter and form, and similarly their privation; for both possess the privation that is opposed to the human form; but the form and matter of the sun and its oblique orbit are not the same as the matter and form of Sophroniscus and Socrates. Therefore, since the actuality and potentiality of these things (namely, of the sun its and oblique orbit) differ from the matter and actuality of Sophroniscus and Socrates, the former (namely, the sun and its oblique orbit) are different from Sophroniscus and Socrates, whose form and matter is not the same as the matter and form of the sun and oblique orbit. Further, if the sun and its oblique orbit differ from Sophroniscus and Socrates, then, inversely,[144] the actuality and potentiality of the sun and its oblique orbit differ from the actuality and potentiality of Sophroniscus and Socrates.

> **1071a17** Further, it must be seen that some [causes] can be stated universally while others cannot. [Indeed, the first principles of all things are this first [thing] in actuality and another which is in potentiality. Now, those things are not the universals. For the individual is a principle of individuals. For a human being is [a principle] of a human being universally, but there is none – rather, Peleus is [the principle] of Achilles, and your father is [the principle] of you, and this B is [the principle] of this BA, while in general B is the principle of the unqualified BA.
>
> 1071a24 In addition [there are] the forms of the substances, but different things have different ones, as has been said, of things which are not in the same genus (colours, sounds, substances, quality) except by analogy. And [the causes and elements] of things in the same species are different, not in form but because individuals have a different [cause]: your matter and form and mover, and mine, but they are the same in universal account.]

What Aristotle is saying is that we can speak of some causes universally and some not. For we will say that the cause of the universal statue is the universal sculptor, but that the cause of this statue is this sculptor. After asserting this he mentions 'the first' (that is, proximate) 'principles of all things' or 'this first [thing]'[145] (1071a18–19), that is, that which is particular. For the principle and cause of Socrates is *this* Sophroniscus. The principle of all things, then, is this actuality and this particular [thing] in potentiality (that is, this particular matter). For the cause of individuals is individual: for example, Peleus is [the cause] of Achilles, and this B is the cause of this syllable BA. For there are no universals,[146] and even if there were universals existing in reality and in their own right, their causes also would be universal; for example, if there were a universal human being, its cause would also be a universal, and of the <general>[147] syllable BA, [the cause would be] the universal B; but it does not exist (cf. 1071a19–24).

In addition to the aforementioned causes, there are also other causes and other principles. And these are 'forms of the substances,[148] but different things have different ones', as he has said (1071a24–5). For instance, horses and human beings have different [forms]. Not only do different genera have different causes, but also things that belong to the same species (*homoeidês*) have causes that are different, albeit in number.[149] For your matter is different from mine in number, and similarly the form and efficient cause, 'though [they are] the same in universal account' (1071a29). That is, for in so far as all things depend on matter, form, privation, and efficient cause, the causes of all things are the same, but in a way my causes are different from your causes, not the same (1071a28–9).[150]

> **1071a29** In the enquiry, then, about what are the principles or elements of substances and relatives and qualities, [as to whether they are same or different, it is clear that when they are at any rate spoken in many ways they belong to each thing, but when they have been distinguished they are not the same but different, except in the following way; and in this way they are the same by analogy, because they are matter, form, privation, and moving cause [are present], and in another way the causes of substances [are considered] as causes of all things, because they are destroyed when substances are destroyed. Further, [there is] the first [thing] in actualization. In another way, however, there are different first [causes], as many as are the contraries which are spoken of neither as genera nor in many ways. And, further, [there are] the matters. What are the principles of perceptible objects and how many they are, and how they are the same and how different – these things have been said.]

With these words Aristotle teaches us what we are obliged to answer 30
(*apokrinesthai*) if we are asked whether all things have the same or different
principles. And he says that 'when they are spoken of in many ways', that is,
universally (or matter considered as universal, and form and efficient cause
considered as universal), and in general by analogy and not as understood of
this thing or that, 'they belong to each thing', that is, the same principles belong
to all things (cf. 1071a31–2). But when the universal form, the universal matter, 35
and so forth have been divided into the causes of Socrates and Plato and so 685,1
forth, they are not the same but different, 'except in the following way' (1071a33)
– that is, by analogy – they are the same. And to make this more evident
Aristotle repeats the words again, and says that 'in this way they are the same[151]
by analogy, because [they are] matter, form, privation'[152] (1071a33), which is
equivalent to saying that since all things depend on matter, form, and privation, 5
they will have the same principles by analogy.

And 'in another way the causes of substances [are considered] as causes of
all things' is to say, in effect, that whenever we are asked whether the causes of
substances are also the causes of accidents, we must say 'yes' and add the
explanation (*aitia*) that if substances are destroyed (*anairein*) the rest are also
destroyed (1071a34–5). And that which destroys in addition (*sunanairein*) is 10
the cause of that which is destroyed in addition.[153] But these things were
discussed with exactness a little before (1071a1–2; 681,34–682,1).

'Moreover, [there is] the first [thing] in actualization (*entelekheia*)' (1071a35–
6). Moreover, he is saying, when we are asked whether the cause is the more
remote or the proximate, we should say that it is the first, that is, the proximate
[cause].[154] And, as Aristotle has often said,[155] Sophroniscus is the proximate
cause, that is, the cause in actualization, of Socrates. 'And in this way there are 15
different first [causes], as many as are the contraries (*enantios*)' (1071a36–7),
that is [to say]: but in another way one should call the contraries – that is,
the form or privation – first causes. Hence, what he means is that one should
sometimes call the cause in actualization (or the efficient cause) the first cause,
but at other times the contraries (that is, the form and privation); and these
contraries, he says, 'are spoken of neither as genera' (that is, as matter[156]) nor 'in
many ways' (that is, as universals), but as co-ordinated [proximate causes] 20
(1071a37). But in the passage 'in another way, however, there are [different][157]
first [causes], as many as are the contraries', the expression 'as many as are'

(*hosa*) is redundant. Moreover, he says, in another way 'the matters' will be called causes (1071b1).

And he concludes by saying what the principles are of perceptible objects[158] (namely, matter, form, and so forth) and how many they are (namely, in one way three and in another four); and how these are the same (namely, by analogy) and how different (namely, as proximate) has been discussed (cf. 1071b1–2).

## [Chapter 6]

**1071b3** Since there were three substances, two of which were natural …

From here on Aristotle discusses the primary cause and first substance, which in this work he also calls a god (*theos*).[159] First of all he establishes that such an everlasting substance exists in the following way. After first assuming that substance is prior to the other things (for this has been proven),[160] he states that[161] if there is not an everlasting substance but all substances are perishable, all things will be perishable;[162] for the other things are inseparable from substance and cannot exist separately from it. But it is not the case that all things are perishable, nor that all substances are perishable. And it is clear that not all things apart from substance are perishable; for it has been proven that movement is everlasting and imperishable.[163] For if [movement] had come to be, since everything that has come to be comes to be by something and from something, there would also be things from which movement comes to be. But if these things were in such a state that neither that which affects (*poiein*)[164] nor that which is affected (*paskhein*) was in need of any change in order for the latter to be able to be affected and the former to affect, then movement would already exist and would not have come to be. But if there was something as an impediment (*empodôn*) to them, some movement would have had to come to be, so that the one would affect and the other would be affected and the movement would have come to be from them. Thus there will necessarily be, before the movement came to be, a movement that has not come to be.

Since, therefore, movement is everlasting, and movement possesses its existence in that which is moved (*to kinoumenon*), then that which undergoes everlasting movement is also everlasting;[165] for it is not possible for a thing to undergo everlasting movement unless it is [itself] everlasting. For if one were to say that a movement is everlasting because one body receives it in succession (*diadekhesthai*) from another, in the first place he will not make the movement continuous (*sunechês*) and one. For [a movement] is continuous when the thing undergoing it is one. Hence, it will be possible for the movement to cease, unless there is some other everlasting cause of the orderly (*eutaktos*) and determinate (*hôrismenos*) succession (*diadochê*) of things that are moved. So the body which undergoes the everlasting movement is one and everlasting.[166]

But, then, the only movement that is everlasting and continuous is circular motion (*kuklophoria*). Hence, the body that undergoes this movement is everlasting. And this is consequently the best (*aristos*) of bodies, since what is everlasting is better (*ameinos*) than what is not everlasting. And what undergoes the first of all movements and is animate is then this[167] [i.e. the best of bodies]; for the best of bodies is animate, since an animate body is better than an inanimate (*apsuchos*) one; but the body capable of circular motion (*kuklophorêtikos*) is best, so that it is also animate; for the best of all bodies is animate, and the body capable of circular motion is of this sort.

But, then, everything that is moved is moved by something. And for this reason,[168] therefore, everything that is moved in virtue of the soul [is moved] by something, if at any rate that which is moved in virtue of the soul is moved in virtue of an impulse (*hormê*), and an impulse is in virtue of a yearning (*ephesis*)[169] for something; so the everlasting body would be moved in virtue of impulse and yearning for something. And if it is moved in virtue of an impulse and yearning, there must be something for which it yearns (*ephiesthai*)[170] and is moved, which is itself also everlasting and actual. For everything that is capable of moving something does impart movement, if it is something in actuality; and thus that which imparts movement always and continuously will be always the same in actuality, without any share (*amoiros*) at all of potentiality.[171] For if it is going to exist in potentiality (but no potentiality, as is proven in *On the Heavens*, is without limit), then, if it possesses the potential to not exist, it will sometime in actuality be non-existent. Hence,[172] it will be possible also for the movement to perish, if the thing that is going to impart movement does not exist in actuality. So it is without any share of potentiality.[173]

But it will also be immovable. For if this is also going to impart movement while being moved, it too will again need another mover and this [will go on] without limit.[174] But if it is immovable, it is also incorporeal (*asômatos*); for every body, in so far as it is body, is movable (*kinêtos*). So there will be some everlasting substance, simple and immovable in actuality, which is the cause[175] of the everlasting and continuous movement of the body capable of circular motion.

Further, the body capable of circular motion[176] will be moved by this [immovable substance] by means of thinking (*noein*) of it and possessing the yearning and desire for affinity (*oikeiôsis*)[177] with it [i.e. the mover]; for every body that is moved by some immovable thing [from which it is] separate is moved in this manner. The proof (*deixis*) is through analysis (*analusis*).[178] For there cannot be a demonstration (*apodeixis*) of the first principle, but we must establish the nature of that thing[179] by starting from things that are posterior and evident and by using the method of analysis in accordance with these things.

That the form which is capable of bringing about circular (*kuklôs*) movement is intelligible first and foremost and also an object of desire (*orekton*) first and foremost, may be proven from the foregoing. It is form that is chiefly intelligible. For matter, since it is none of the things that are in actuality, is intelligible by analogy and, as Plato says, 'by bastard reasoning (*nothos logismos*)'.[180] But form is intelligible, since it is a certain actuality,[181] and among the forms the form that is found in [the category of] substance and by itself[182] is more intelligible than that which is found in any other [category], because it also exists[183] to a greater extent, and among the forms in substance the most intelligible is simplest and always in actuality. For this is most intelligible because it exists most of all, by always being in actuality, and because it is simple and intelligible in its own nature. For the [parts] in composite objects are intelligible whenever the intellect has separated them from the things in which they are present and contemplates (*theorein*)[184] them as if they were simple. And the substance capable of moving all things is of this sort, I mean separable and simple and in actuality. It is this, therefore, that is intelligible most of all.[185]

But, then, it is also desirable most of all, since what is most noble (*kalos*) by its own nature is most desirable by its own nature, and this [object] is of this sort. For what is noble is present more in form than in matter, since [what is noble] is present more in what affects [something] than in what is †well†[186] affected (and what is affected is something potential whereas what affects [it] is actual), and more in what is determinate than in what is indeterminate (*aoristos*). So[187] what is noble is present in form rather than in matter, and in the form that is found in [the category of] substance rather than in any of the other genera. For it is due to this [i.e. substance] that the other things exist; and among those in [the category of] substance that which is most simple and without a share in potentiality is most noble; and it has been proven that the nature mentioned before is of this sort. So[188] it is chiefly and first of all both desirable and intelligible.

> **1071b3** Since, then, there were three substances, two of which were natural, and one was immovable, [and concerning the latter it must be said that there is necessarily an everlasting immovable substance. For substances are the first among things that exist, and if all substances are perishable, then all things are perishable. But it is impossible that movement should come to be or perish (for it always existed), nor that time should (for there cannot be a before and after if there is no time). Hence, movement is also continuous in the same way as time; for time is either the same as movement or an attribute belonging to it. But movement is not continuous except for movement in place, and movement in place is not continuous except for movement in a circle.
>
> **1071b12** But, then, if it is capable of bringing about movement or of producing an effect but is not acting, there will not be movement; for it is possible for what possesses a potentiality not to be acting. Nothing, therefore, is gained even if we were to posit substances which are everlasting – as do those who [posit] the Forms – unless there is a principle in them with the potential to bring about change. Even this, furthermore, is not sufficient, nor is another substance apart from the Forms; for if it is not acting, there will be no movement. Further, not even if it is acting, but its substance is potentiality, [is it sufficient]; for there will not be everlasting movement, since it is possible for that which is in potentiality not to be. There must, then, be such a principle whose substance is actuality. Further, then, these substances must be without matter; for they must be everlasting, if, in fact, anything else is also everlasting. So [they are] in actuality.[189]]

Concerning the first principle, as we said before (685,27-8), from here on Aristotle discusses what is its nature and its way of carrying on (*diagôgê*). In the first place he establishes that there is this sort of principle and he says what [it is] as follows. Since, he states, we said (1069a30-b2; cf. 670,24–671,7) there were three substances, two of which were natural, which also all agree exist, and of which one was ingenerable and imperishable, while the other [substance] considered as a whole was itself also ingenerable and imperishable (if indeed the cosmos (*kosmos*) is), though considered in terms of its parts it was generable (*genêtos*) and perishable, and the other [i.e. the third] was immovable, we must discuss the immovable substance, he says, and prove that there necessarily exists some substance, immovable and everlasting (cf. 1071b4–5).

Having already proven that substances are prior to the other things, namely, quantity, quality, and so forth, Aristotle uses this to prove the claim under consideration, giving in effect[190] the following deduction. If all substance is perishable, none of the beings that are other than substance will be everlasting,[191] since they all possess their existence in substance (cf. 1071b6). And yet there is something apart from substance that is everlasting and imperishable, namely movement and time. So there is also some everlasting substance, which undergoes the everlasting movement.[192] For every movement belongs to something. And that movement is everlasting has been proven in Book 8 of the *Physics*;[193] and [Aristotle thinks] the claim that time is also everlasting is worthy of elaboration (*paramuthia*),[194] saying that, if time is generable and perishable then neither did it exist before nor will it exist afterward (cf. 1071b7–8). And yet the [relation of] before and after is something belonging to time.[195] So there was time before time came into existence, if indeed there is a before preceding time; and there will again be time succeeding the existence of time, if indeed an afterward succeeds the perishing of time.

After proving that there is some substance that is moved everlastingly (*aidiôs*), Aristotle in the first place goes on to demonstrate what this is in the following way (cf. 1071b9–11). The everlasting movement is one, and the one [movement] is continuous, just as time is too.[196] For time is either the same as movement or something belonging to movement.[197] But continuous movement is no different from movement in place, and this is circular movement. So the everlasting movement is circular. Hence, the everlasting substance is that which undergoes this movement.

After proving in this way, then, that there is an everlasting substance, which undergoes circular and everlasting movement, and having proven in the *Physics*[198] also that everything that is moved is moved by something, Aristotle concludes that the thing that brings about the everlasting movement is thus something capable of bringing about movement (*kinêtikos*) and producing an effect (*poiêtikos*),[199] a thing that is immovable and everlasting and that is a form and actuality in every way and has no share (*amoirein*) at all of potentiality.[200] 'But, then, if it is capable of bringing about movement or producing an effect but is not acting (*energein*) in any way' (where 'not acting' [is written] instead of 'it is not an actuality that in every way has no share at all of potentiality'), there will be some time when there will not be movement; for what has the potential to be not acting will sometimes be not acting (1071b12–14).[201] But it has been proven that it is impossible for there not to be movement. Thus it is impossible also for any potentiality to be present in that which brings about everlasting movement. But even if the bodies in circular motion were devoid (*apallasthai*) of potentiality, because they were everlasting, how would they differ from the first principle? Rather, they are not altogether devoid of potentiality. For they are devoid of the potentiality by which things that come to be and perish come to be and perish, but they are not in the least devoid of the potentiality of being moved. For the hemisphere (*hêmisphairion*) that is over the earth (*gê*) in actuality is under the earth in potentiality.[202]

After saying, then, that the primary and everlasting principle is actuality having no share at all of potentiality, Aristotle adds, 'nothing is gained even if we were to make substances everlasting' (1071b14–15) and so forth, which is equivalent to saying: whether we assume that the first principles are Ideas or that they are numbers (*arithmoi*),[203] nothing will be gained with a view to how it is that the things that exist always possess existence, unless this thing itself is a certain form and a certain nature which is an actuality that has the potential to [bring about] change and everlasting movement.[204] Nor should any other nature and other substance be assumed apart from the Forms if it is not an actuality, nor will it[205] be sufficient to bring about everlasting movement. But the statement 'for if it is not going to act, there will not be movement' (1071b17) is the same as saying: for if the substance apart from the Forms [not only] does not act but remains not acting, as those who posit the Forms[206] declared (for while saying that the Ideas are immovable and in no way acting whatsoever, they said that certain emanations (*aporrhoia*) descended from them and coalesced with the matter here so that all the individual things came to be) – if, then, one were to assume a substance that is in the same state as the Ideas, movement will not exist. For movement does not exist without that which acts and imparts movement. And 'further not even if it is going to act' (which is equivalent to saying: and yet not even if the substance distinct from the Forms is acting and bringing about movement), but its substance[207] and nature is a certain potentiality (that is, if some potentiality has been joined with it, and it is not entirely without a share of potentiality), not even in this case will the movement be everlasting[208] (cf. 1071b17–18). For necessarily what is in potentiality (that is, what possesses the potentiality not to act) sometimes does not act. 'So there must be such a principle whose substance is an actuality' that has no share at all of potentiality (cf. 1071b19–20).

And in the words 'further, then, these substances must be without matter'(1071b20–1), the term 'these', I think, means 'the remaining', and it would mean that not only the thing capable of moving the fixed (*aplanês*) sphere[209] must be such as we have said, but also the remaining principles which move Saturn's (*Kroniakê*) sphere, Jupiter's (*Zeus*) sphere, and the remaining spheres, which are principles subordinate to the first [principle], and these therefore must be immaterial (*aülos*) and everlasting, if at any rate anything else is everlasting too (cf. 1071b21–2). For since, also, something else, namely, that which is capable of moving the sphere of the fixed stars, is everlasting, these too must be everlasting. Or else, 'if at least anything else is everlasting' (1071b22) would mean that since the unity (*henas*) of the seven spheres[210] is everlasting, the things capable of moving them must also be everlasting.

**1071b22** And yet there is a puzzle. For it seems that everything that acts has a potential [but not everything with a potential acts, so that potentiality is prior. But then, if this is so, none of the things that are will be; for it is possible for things to have the potential to be but yet not to be. And yet, if it is as the theologians say who make [things] come to be from Night or as the natural theorists who speak of 'all things together', the same impossibility results. For how will a thing] be moved, if there is not some actual cause? For lumber at any rate will not move itself, but the art of building [will move it]; nor will the menstrual fluid or earth, but the seeds and the semen will.

1071b31 This is why some, such as Leucippus and Plato, suppose there is always actuality, for they say that there is always movement. But why there is and what it is they do not say, nor the cause [why things are moved] this way [or that]. Now nothing is moved at random, but something must always be present, just as, in fact, a thing is moved by nature in one way, but by force, either by intellect or by something else, in another way. Further, what sort [of movement] is primary? For this makes an incalculable difference. But now not even Plato can state what he sometimes thinks is the principle, namely, that itself which moves itself; for, as he says, the soul is both later and coeval with the heaven. To think, then, that potentiality is prior to actuality is in one way correct and in another not (and it has been said how).]

After Aristotle has shown that the principle into which he is enquiring is an actuality[211] that has no share at all of potentiality, a puzzle, he says, arises concerning the things that have been proven. For one might be puzzled about the following: if potentiality is prior to actuality (and this is confirmed (*pistis*) by induction), and the first principle is actuality, potentiality would be prior to it; thus the first principle has another principle,[212] namely, potentiality, from which actuality has come to be. And Aristotle himself, too, attempts to prove that potentiality is prior to actuality: 'for it seems (*dokein*)', he says, 'that everything that acts has the potential' (1071b23); for just as we say that, because every human being is an animal but not every animal is human, animal is prior to human, in the same way also,[213] since everything that acts has the potential but not everything with the potential acts, potentiality will be prior to actuality.

But then, if potentiality is prior to actuality, 'there will be no beings in existence' (1071b25), which is equivalent to saying: so at some time there were no beings in existence. For it is possible for what has the potential to exist not yet to exist.[214] And I think that in the words 'for it seems that [everything] that acts [has the potential to act]' (1071b23), the term, 'seems' indicates that he does not himself agree with the proposition that everything that acts has the potential, so that the meaning is that it seems so to others. The statement 'But then, if this is so, there will be no things in existence; for it is possible to have the potential to exist but not yet to exist' (1071b25-6) is, I think, adduced as a solution to the [puzzling] claim that potentiality is prior to actuality; for if from the statement that all potentiality is prior to all actuality, it is inferred that 'there was some time when there were no beings in existence' (which, however, was proven to be impossible in *On the Heavens*),[215] then it is [demonstrably] false to say that all actuality is preceded by potentiality. But if, as we have said, this is a solution to the puzzle, why does he go back and solve it again? Rather, this is not foreign (*allotrioun*) to that keen intelligence (*ankhinoia*) typical of Aristotle.[216] For as substantiation (*parastasis*) of the truth (*alêtheia*) everywhere, and especially in this treatise, he has made mention of the same matters twice and as many times he clearly articulates the issues concerning them.

After proving, then, that actuality is prior to potentiality, or form to matter (for all potentiality is in a way matter; for instance, Socrates is the potentiality and matter of the [act of] writing), he criticizes (*aitiasthai*) the theologians (*theologos*)[217] for making potentiality and matter prior to actuality (cf. 1071b26–7). For example, when Hesiod says, 'Verily, first of all Chaos (*Khaos*) came to be, and then broad-breasted Earth (*Gaia*)' and 'but to the other [i.e. Hate] gloomy Night gave birth first',[218] by 'Chaos' and 'Night' he is alluding to matter. For darkness or Night is matter due to its intangibility (*alêptos*), and Chaos because it is capacious (*khorêtikos*) and receptive (*dektikos*) of forms. Anaxagoras, too, when he said, 'all things' were 'together', was alluding to matter (cf. 1071b27–8).[219] But [Aristotle] is not criticizing the natural theorists (*phusikos*), namely, Empedocles and Anaxagoras; for these said that actuality was prior to potentiality, as Aristotle says, since Empedocles postulated Love (*philia*) and Hate (*neikos*) as actuality, and Anaxagoras postulated the Intellect (cf. 1072a4–7 and 691,31–6). Rather, he is criticizing the theologians. For 'the same cause'[220] (1071b28) would not signify (*sêmainein*) this, namely, that the same absurdities follow for the theologians and natural theorists, but 'the cause' is equivalent to [saying that] the same absurdity follows for all the theologians, who make potentiality prior to actuality. Or it might mean that the same absurdity will follow for both the theologians and the natural theorists – not for all of them but as many of the natural theorists and theologians as assume that potentiality is prior to actuality. For if, he says, potentiality is prior to actuality according to these persons, how will matter be moved from itself if there is not the actuality that imparts movement? (cf. 1071b28–9). For the pieces of wood do not themselves move themselves to generate a box, but it is the art of building (*tektonikê*), which is an actuality [that moves them]; nor does the menstrual fluid move itself to generate an animal but the semen (*gonê*) does so, nor does earth [move itself] to generate a plant but it is the seed [that moves them].[221]

That is why in order to avoid these absurdities some theorists, for example, Leucippus and Plato, assume that actuality is prior to potentiality, and that this actuality is movement. For both Leucippus and Plato said there was always movement. For [the Demiurge] took over, Plato says, the matter which was in discordant (*plêmmelôs*) and disorderly motion.[222] And Leucippus stated that the atoms undergo movement in the void (*kenon*) through time without limit.[223] And they declared that movement is actuality (cf. 1071b31–3); but as to why movement is actuality and what this movement is, whether it is circular or some other sort, and why some things are moved this way and other things that way, of these things they do not state the cause.²²⁴ For since something must be everlasting, as has been proved, one would have had to state the cause due to which the sphere of the fixed stars is moved from east (*anatolê*) to west (*dusmê*), and why the planetary (*planômenos*) [spheres] are moved in reverse.²²⁵ For it is not at random that everything which is moved effects its movement, but by nature a stone (*lithos*) [is moved] in one way, namely, downwards, and the fire upwards, but by force (*bia*) [they are moved] in a different way, [for instance] a stone upwards and the fire downwards. Therefore, a stone is moved downwards 'by nature', but human beings are moved 'by intellect', since they are moved because they yearn²²⁶ for something, [for example] forcing (*biazesthai*) their body to go upstairs or up a tree in a way in which it is not naturally in motion (*pheresthai*) (for the natural motion of our body is downwards); and 'by something else' they are moved 'by force', for example, the non-rational animals by imagination²²⁷ (1071b34–6).

One would, then, have had to state the cause of these things and in addition to these things what sort of movement is primary. For there is a great difference between natural and unnatural movement, and between the first movement and the other sorts (cf. 1071b36–7). And he makes another criticism of Plato: Plato says that there was movement even before the cosmos came to be, if indeed the matter was undergoing disorderly movement, and again he says that the soul which had come to be at the same time as the heaven and which moved itself is the fount and cause of the existence of movement. Hence, Plato says that there was movement before the heaven came to be as well as the soul that had come to be along with it. If, then, there was movement before the heaven came to be as well as the soul that had come to be along with it, it is false that the soul which is moving itself is the fount of movement (cf. 1071b37–1072a2).²²⁸

After saying these things, again, as a particular solution of the puzzle posed before (690,1–3) which states that if indeed potentiality is prior to actuality the principle will not be actuality, Aristotle adds, 'to think that potentiality is prior to actuality' is in one way to speak 'correctly' but in another way 'incorrectly' (1072a3–4). For in the case of one and the same thing it is true that potentiality is prior to actuality.²²⁹ For instance, Socrates was musical in potentiality before, and he has become such also in actuality. Nevertheless,²³⁰ there was some other prior thing which was musical in actuality and which brought Socrates into actuality. Thus, in relation to one and the same [person], in the case of things generable and perishable, potentiality is prior to actuality, but in relation to the mass (*khuma*) of all humans actuality is not at all posterior to potentiality. And if in the case of these things potentiality has not come to be beforehand, it will be posterior to a far greater extent in the case of actuality understood in the chief sense. But there has been discussion of these matters in *On the Soul*.[231]

> **1072a4** Anaxagoras bears witness that actuality is prior [(for the Intellect is an actuality) as well as Empedocles (Love and Hate), and those who say that there is always movement, such as Leucippus. Hence, Chaos and Night did not exist for time without limit, but the same things always [existed] either in a cycle or in some other way, if indeed actuality is prior to potentiality. Now if, then, [there is] always the same thing [either] in a cycle [or in another way], something must always remain, acting in the same way.
> 
> 1072a10 And if there is going to be coming-to-be and perishing, something else must be always acting in one way and in another. It is necessary, therefore, that it act in one way in virtue of itself and in another way in virtue of something else; so [it must act] either in virtue of [yet] another thing or else in virtue of the first thing. It must then be in virtue of this [i.e. the first]. For [otherwise] that is again the cause of both it and that [i.e. the second and the third]. Therefore, it is better [to say that it is] the first. For that was the cause of its always occurring in the same way, and another thing was the cause of its occurring in different ways; but it is clear that of its always occurring in different ways both [are the causes]. This, therefore, is the way the movements are. Why, then, should one enquire after other principles?]

Following his demonstrations Aristotle was in the habit of offering the judgements (*hupolêpsis*) of others as added confirmation of his own statements. Thus after proving that actuality is prior to potentiality he also calls on Anaxagoras and Empedocles as witnesses (*marturesthai*). For the former made actuality,[232] that is, the Intellect, prior to the mixture, whereas Empedocles made Love and Hate prior (cf. 1070a5–6). However, those who said that movement always exists also made actuality (that is, movement) prior to potentiality. Hence, if actuality is prior to potentiality, 'Chaos or Night did not exist for a time without limit' – that is, potentiality did not exist prior to actuality – 'but the same things' which exist now – for example, there was 'always' the cosmos, 'either in a cycle (*periodos*)', as Empedocles claimed,[233] 'or in some other way', as

Aristotle intends (1072a7–9). Following the clause 'now if [there is] always the same thing in a cycle…' he omits (*elleipein*) the phrase 'or in some other way', so that the whole passage is: now if indeed this cosmos always exists, either 'in a cycle', as Empedocles says, or in another way, as *we* say,[234] 'something must always remain acting in the same way' and its nature is actuality' (1072a9–10).

But if it is necessary that there is also always coming-to-be, there must be something acting in a different way (that is, being moved obliquely (*loxôs*)), so that it brings what is capable of making things come to be (*genêtikos*) (namely, the sun) closer or takes it further away.[235] So, necessarily, the thing that is moved obliquely 'acts in virtue of itself in one way' (or it is moved obliquely and it brings the sun or takes it further away), and 'in another way in virtue of something else' (that is, the sun comes to be over the earth and under the earth every day in virtue of something else). '[E]ither in virtue of another thing' the sun is acted on in the latter way, for instance, say, by Saturn's sphere, or 'in virtue of the first', for instance, in virtue of the sphere of the fixed stars (1072a10–14).

And completing the argument, Aristotle says: so, necessarily, it is in virtue of the movement of the sphere of the fixed stars that the sun comes to be over the earth and under the earth, rather than[236] in virtue of Saturn's sphere. And the reason why it is in virtue of the sphere of the fixed stars that the sun's motion necessarily occurs over the earth and under the earth every day, he has added with the statement: 'for that is again the cause of both it and that'[237] (1072a14–15), that is to say: for the body of the sphere of the fixed stars will again be the cause of the star in Saturn's sphere coming to be over the earth and under the earth each day, and also of 'that', namely, the sun.[238] For the sphere of the fixed stars is the cause of both Saturn (*Kronos*) and the sun setting (*dunein*) and rising (*anatellein*) again. Hence, it is more correct to state that the sphere of the fixed stars is the cause of the sun rising and setting than that it is Saturn's sphere. For 'that' (or the sphere of the fixed stars), is (as we said) the cause of the sun always being carried in the same way (that is, being carried under the earth and over the earth), whereas the cause 'of [its occurring] in different ways' (1072a15–16) (for example, occurring sometimes in Scorpio (*skorpion*) and sometimes in Capricorn (*aigokerôs*)) is the oblique alignment (*loxôsis*) of the constellations of the zodiac (*zôdiakos*) through which it is carried.[239] Further, the words 'but it is clear that of what [occurs] always in another way, both' (1072a17) (and a comma is needed after 'in another way') can be put more clearly: but of what occurs always – that is, the regular and alternating occurrence of night and day as well as coming-to-be and perishing – the causes are 'both' – namely, both the sphere of the fixed stars and the solar (*hêliakos*) sphere which undergoes oblique motion. Therefore, the sphere of the fixed stars is the cause of nights and days coming to be, and the solar sphere and the sun are the cause of coming-to-be and perishing.[240]

After saying these things, Aristotle adds, 'This, therefore, is the way the movements are' (1072a17–18), which is equivalent to saying: not only do we say these things about the movements of the sphere of the fixed stars and the solar sphere but also this is the way they are. If, then, these movements are causes of things coming to be the way they come to be,[241] why is there a need to enquire into other principles such as those spoken of by those who posit the Ideas?

## [Chapter 7][242]

[**1072a19** Since it is possible [that things are] this way (and if they are not this way, they will be from Night and 'all things together' and from not-being), these [difficulties] may be resolved. And there is something that is always moved with an unceasing movement, namely, circular movement, and this is clear not only by reason but by fact, so that the first heaven must be everlasting. There is, therefore, also that which it moves. And since what is moved and what imparts movement [is] also an intermediary, therefore there is something which imparts movement without being moved, which is everlasting and a substance that is also an actuality.]

After saying these things, Aristotle states, 'since it is possible that [things are] this way', these problems would be solved (*luein*); 'and if they are not this way' (and a comma must be inserted after 'in this way'), 'they will be from Night and "all things together" and from not-being'[243] (1072a19–21). For in this way there is continuity of the text. But what it means is: since, as has been proven, actuality is prior to potentiality, and because the movement of the sphere of the fixed stars and of the solar sphere (and these spheres are also themselves actualities, even if not [actualities] in the chief sense), are causes of days and nights and of coming-to-be and perishing, every puzzle would be solved: namely, the one puzzling over whether potentiality is prior to actuality, the one asking why the sphere of the fixed stars is moved in one way and the sun's sphere in another, and the one enquiring what sort of movement is primary. For concerning all these things it has been stated that the movement that moves the others together with (*sunkinein*) itself, which is the movement of the sphere of the fixed stars, is the first of the movements, and is moved the way it is moved because nights and days come to be, but the solar sphere in the reverse direction, because there must be coming-to-be and perishing; and there is always coming-to-be and perishing always because there must always be something. If, then, it is possible that [things] are this way, as we say, all these issues would be resolved; 'and if they are not this way' (that is, if one were to say that they are not this way), 'they will be from Night and "all things together" and from not-being' (1072a19–20), that is, potentiality will be prior to actuality, and everything will be from potentiality, which has been proven to be impossible.

After saying these things, he again uses the method of analysis[244] to discuss the first principle. For, 'there is,' he says, 'something that is always moved with an unceasing (*apaustos*) movement', and this is circular movement (1072a21–2). And the fact that circular movement is everlasting is clear not only by reason and demonstration but also by fact (*ergon*)[245] and by tradition from our forebears (*progonos*). There is, then, 'the first heaven', [that is], the sphere of the fixed stars, which is moved everlastingly, and there is 'that which it moves'[246] (1072a23–4), [namely,] the entire planetary body.[247] For the planetary body is moved by the first and fixed body. There must, therefore, be that which only imparts movement. For since there is that which is moved only (namely, the planetary body), and there is also as intermediary (*mesos*) that which at the same time both is moved and imparts movement, such as the sphere of the fixed stars, there must be also a third thing, that which[248] imparts movement only. And it is that everlasting thing which imparts movement without being moved, being a substance and actuality[249] (cf. 1072a24–6). The thought, then, expressed in all his statements has been stated.

In the passage, however, 'since what is moved and what imparts movement [is] also an intermediary, therefore there is [something][250] which imparts movement without being moved' (1072a24–5), first of all a comma must be inserted after 'intermediary';[251] then one must understand 'and there exists also that which is moved only';[252] and then one must attach 'therefore there exists something which imparts movement without being moved', and so on, so that the whole passage will read as follows: since that which both imparts movement and is moved at the same time is an intermediary between that which is moved only and that which imparts movement only, and two of these exist – that which is moved only and that which both imparts movement and is moved at the same time – there must also exist that which is immovable.[253]

> **1072a26** The object of desire and the intelligible object impart movement in the following way: [they impart movement without being moved. And the first of these objects are the same. For the object of appetite is that which appears noble, but the first object of wish is that which *is* noble. And we desire things because they seem [noble] rather than believing they are [noble] because we desire them; for the act of thinking is a principle. And the intellect is moved by the intelligible object, and one of the columns is intelligible in itself; and in this column substance is the first, and of substance that which is simple and actual [is first].]

Having said that the object of desire and the intelligible object[254] impart movement in this way, Aristotle concisely adds how they impart movement by saying that it is without being moved [themselves] (cf. 1072a26-7). In this way, he says, every object of desire and every intelligible object impart movement in such a way that they are not moved but while remaining immovable they move other things, as the hay moves the ass and the picture (*eikôn*) moves the lover.[255] But since every object of desire and every intelligible object is so called from that which is an intelligible object and an object of desire in the first place and in its own right, and some things are objects of desire but not intelligible, such as bread, and conversely some are intelligible but not objects of desire, such as bad things (*kakos*),[256] he proves that that which is intelligible in the first and chief sense and that which is an object of desire in the chief sense are the same (cf. 1072a27).

First of all, however, he teaches us the difference between the object of appetite (*epithumêton*) and the object of wish (*boulêtos*), stating that 'the object of appetite is that which appears noble' (1072a27–8). For that which is noble[257] in the chief sense is an object not of appetite but of yearning (*ephetos*) and desire; for appetite (*epithumia*) is different from yearning, since appetite resides in the appetitive (*epithumêtikos*) and non-rational part of the soul, whereas yearning is in the rational (*logistikos*) part;[258] and the first and chief object of wish is not that which is apparently noble but that which is noble in its own nature.²⁵⁹ And we desire (*oregesthai*) [something] because it seems so, rather than, conversely, it seems so because we desire it²⁶⁰ (cf. 1072a28).

After speaking, then, in this way about these things, Aristotle concludes that the first intelligible object and the first object of desire are the same, stating, 'for the act of thinking (*noêsis*) is a principle' (1072a30), that is, the object of desire is a principle²⁶¹ of movement (for the object of desire must be understood for the principle of thinking); for this moves the intellect, and the movement is the intellect's act of thinking;²⁶² for the object of desire moves the intellect into actively thinking, whether the object of desire exists or not. And yet the intellect is moved by the intelligible object. If, then, the intelligible object moves the intellect and makes it actual, and the object of desire moves it too, the intelligible object and the object of desire turn out to be the same. But the first cause is intelligible in the chief sense and is intellect in its own nature. So it [i.e. the first cause] is intelligible in the chief sense and intellect in the chief sense and an object of desire in the chief sense.

And after saying, 'the intellect is moved by the intelligible object', Aristotle adds 'and one of the columns (*sustoikhia*) is intelligible' – intelligible 'in itself' (1072a30–1). But some things are intelligible in themselves and some are not in themselves, as we shall see in a little while. By 'one of the columns'²⁶³ Aristotle means that of the noble,²⁶⁴ under which are, according to the Pythagoreans, substance, light, triangle (*trigônos*), odd (*perittos*), and such things that they reckoned there. Therefore, the things under the column of the good (*agathos*) are all intelligible, but substance is the most intelligible of these things, and of substance, again, the most intelligible is 'that which is simple and actual' (1072a32), which is both intelligible in the chief sense and an object of desire in the chief sense.

Since Aristotle has said that substance is intelligible in itself and actual in total distinction from certain intelligible objects which are intelligible neither in themselves nor in actuality, it is worthwhile – or, even more, necessary – to say which things are intelligible in themselves and in actuality and which are not of this sort. All forms, <then>,²⁶⁵ that are enmattered and possess their being in matter come to be intelligible by the intellect's agency, though they are intelligible [only] in potentiality and neither in themselves nor in actuality. For by separating them from the matter together with which they have their being, the intellect itself makes them actually intelligible; and at that time each of them, when it is thought of, is actually intelligible and becomes intellect, not beforehand when they were not like this in their own nature.[266] For the actual intellect[267] is nothing other than the form which is thought of, so that also each of the objects, though not intelligible without qualification, becomes intellect whenever it is thought of. For just as actual perception (*aisthêsis*) is the same as the actual perceptible object and the actual perceptible object is the same as actual perception, so also the actual intellect is the same as the actual intelligible object and the actual intelligible object is the same as the actual intellect. For by grasping the form of the object of thinking and having separated it from the matter, the intellect both makes it actually intelligible and it becomes itself an actual intellect.

And if any of the things that exist, as has been proven,[268] is in itself incorporeal and immaterial, it is intelligible actually and in virtue of its own nature, and it possesses actual intelligibility from itself,[269] and not from the intellect that separates it from its matter (for it is an intellect [that is] is both immaterial and intelligible), but it is actually an intellect and actually[270] an intelligible object, as Aristotle will say shortly after. Hence, whichever forms that the intellect separates from their matter and makes intelligible are not intelligible in the chief sense and in themselves (an indication of this is that if they have been separated from the intellect that has thought of them and separated them from their matter and has made universal from particular objects, they perish and do not exist). But whichever [things] possess being in themselves from themselves are intellects in the chief sense and intelligible objects in the chief sense.

> **1072a32** But the one and [the] simple are not the same; [for 'one' signifies a measure, while 'simple' signifies that the object is in a certain state.
> **1072a34** But, then, both that which is noble and that which is an object of choice in itself are in the same column, and what is first is always best or analogous to it. That the final cause is found among the things that are immovable is made clear by this distinction, since the final cause is for someone †and of something†, of which the former is [movable] but the latter is not.
>
> **1072b3** And it imparts movement in so far as it is loved, whereas it is what is moved that moves the other things. Now if something is moved, it is also possible for it to be otherwise; hence, if the first locomotion is also an actuality in the way that it is moved, in this respect, however[271], it is possible for it to be otherwise, [i.e.] in respect of place, even if it is not in respect to substance.

But since there is something which imparts movement although it is itself immovable, and which exists in actuality, it is in no way possible for it to be otherwise. For locomotion is the first sort of change, and the first sort of locomotion is circular; and it [i.e. the immovable mover] brings about this sort of movement. So of necessity it exists; and in so far as it is necessary, [it exists] nobly, and thus it is a principle. For that which is necessary exists in so many ways: as what is by force because it is contrary to impulse, as that without which the good does not exist, and as what cannot [be] otherwise but [exists] without qualification. So it is on such a principle that the heaven and nature depend.]

Aristotle foils the following potential objection (*enstasis*) against his claim that things undergo this sort of motion: if the first and immovable substance is simple, and what is simple is one, then the immovable substance is one. But he will prove that there are also other immovable substances in this book.[272] He foils this, then, by asserting that the simple and one are not the same thing. For 'one' signifies a measure (*metron*); for example, we speak of one human being and one horse whereby we measure[273] human beings and horses. 'Simple', however, does not signify a measure but rather the state the simple is in, namely, not compound.

'And yet both that which is noble and that which is an object of choice (*hairetos*)[274] are in the same column' (1072a34–5), namely, [in the column] containing that which is intelligible in its own right, so that the first cause which is intelligible and noble in its own right is an object of choice and best both in its own right and because of itself. And by analogy, too, that which is first will be called best (cf. 1072a35–b1). Thus we could say that in so far as it is prior in worth (*axiôma*) and nobility the actual intellect is best in comparison with the dispositional [intellect],[275] and we would say, in turn, that circular movement is best in comparison with straight (*euthus*) movement.

After saying these things, Aristotle states, in addition to the things we mentioned, 'that' among the things that are immovable 'there is also the final cause (*to hou heneka*),[276] is made clear by this distinction' (1072b1–2), meaning a distinction in which he has often said that he has made the reduction of the contraries (*anagôgê tôn enantiôn*); and he has made this distinction in his book entitled *On the Good*.[277] In the clause 'since (*gar*) the final cause is for someone'[278] (1072b2), the word 'since' (*gar*) must be understood as taking the place of the conjunction 'but' (*de*), so that it means: but the final cause is for someone. For the things that come about and that are done (*prattein*) come to be and are done for the sake of (*heneka*) something and for someone; for example, the things that come to be and are done are done for the sake of happiness (*eudaimonia*) are done for someone, for instance, for Socrates. And in the words 'of which the former is and the latter is not' (1072b3), the term 'of which' would refer to the things for the sake of which the action occurs, while 'the latter is not' refers to the thing acting.[279] The meaning would be: the final cause, in the strict sense, is the latter; but the final cause is not, in the strict sense the former. For what undergoes movement for the sake of the good is not good, but the good, which is in the strict sense a final cause, *is* good.

Now, [a thing] is moved until it gets a grasp of (*katalambanei*) its good; and once it gets a grasp of it, it makes a stands (*histasthai*). But if the first cause, which is strictly speaking also first good, is unlimited, never will what is yearning for it grasp the whole of its goodness (*agathotês*), as it has possession of the partial goods. For this reason it will impart movement always in so far as it is loved (*eran*) while being ungraspable (*akatalêptos*).[280]

After saying these things Aristotle tells also how the first cause moves everything: that it moves the body capable of circular motion 'in so far as it is loved' (1072b3) and an object of yearning.[281] And by being moved proximately by it the heaven itself moves the other things.[282] And since every movement seems to disestablish (*existanai*)[283] the thing from which it originates and he said before that the heaven is moved, lest one might suppose that the heaven is disestablished in its own nature, he states, 'if now something is moved, it is possible for it to be otherwise' (1072b4-5), that is, since the heaven is moved, it is possible for it to be otherwise. And as to how it is possible for a thing that is moved[284] to be otherwise, he adds, 'hence if (*ei*) the first locomotion is also an actuality (*energeia*)[285] in the way that it is moved, in this respect, however (*de*), it is possible ...'[286] (1072b5-6). And a comma needs to be inserted after 'it is moved'. What he means is the following: if the actuality of the heaven is the first locomotion, because it is moved and possesses movement in general, in this way it will be said that it can be otherwise, undergoing motion in place or circular movement. And 'even if it is not in respect of substance' (1072b6-7) – or, in other words, even if it is not changed[287] in respect to its own nature or disestablished from it (because it is everlasting) – nothing prevents it from being moved[288] in respect of circular motion, even if it is not necessary.

After saying these things Aristotle states, 'since there is something that imparts movement, which exists in actuality,'[289] as was said, 'and is immovable, it is not possible for it to be otherwise' (1072b7–8) or to be moved in any way. And he proves this by saying in effect that if indeed it were possible for it [i.e. the prime mover] to be moved in any way, then it would be moved with the first of movements. But the first movement is circular movement;[290] and he has proved that it brings about this movement (cf. 1072b8–10). But if it brings about circular movement, it could not itself undergo this movement because one movement belongs to [only] one thing. And if circular movement exists of necessity, then that which brings about this movement also exists of necessity.

'And in so far as it is necessary,[291] [it exists] nobly, and thus it is a principle'[292] (1072b10–11). A comma is needed after 'necessary'. What this means is that, since the necessary is said in one sense to be that which is [brought about] by force, and in another sense that without which excellence (*to eu*) does not exist (for instance, without learning (*mathêsis*) knowledge (*epistême*) does not come to be present), and in another sense that which cannot be otherwise is necessary, such as are the demonstrative (*apodeiktikos*) principles, then he says that, since the first cause exists of necessity, in so far as it exists of necessity, it exists nobly, and 'thus' – that is, in the sense of 'that without which not' – it is 'a principle'. Hence, if we are asked in what way it is necessary that the first cause is necessary, we must say that it is necessary because excellence does not exist without it.[293] And he concludes by saying 'so it is on such a principle that the heaven and all[294] nature depend' (1072b13–14).

> **1072b14** It is the way of carrying on such as is the best for us for a short time [ – for it is always in this state, for this is impossible for us – since its activity is also pleasure; and for this reason waking, perceiving, and the act of thinking are most pleasant, while our hopes and memories [are so] because of these things.
>
> 1072b18 And the act of thinking in itself belongs to that which is best in itself, and that which is [the act of thinking] most of all is of that which is [best] most of all. And the intellect thinks of itself by participation in the intelligible object; for it becomes an intelligible object by touching and thinking of it, so that the intellect and intelligible object are the same. For that which is receptive of the intelligible object, that is, the substance, is the intellect, and it is acting when it possesses it.]

Whenever our intellect (*ho hêmeteros nous*), which is potentially the intelligible objects, has, as a result of the highest knowledge (*akra epistêmê*) and an exceedingly good life (*euzôïa*), actually become the intelligible objects, then we live the life that is best, most blessed (*makarios*), and surpassing every pleasure (*hêdonê*) – a life (*zôê*) which is indescribable (*anërmêneutos*) in words, but is known by those who have had this blessed experience.[295] Aristotle says, therefore, that the way of carrying on[296] such as is best for us for a short time (for we do not always spend our lives this way, but when our intellect actually becomes the intelligible objects), this life is always possessed by the first cause. For it is impossible for us to live (*zên*) this sort of life always rather than sometimes (cf. 1072b16), while for the first cause, as we shall see a little later, it is possible. For since its activity[297] is nothing other than thinking of itself, and its activity is its pleasure, in addition, then, it always lives this life, by which I mean, in fact, thinking of itself.[298] This life and way of carrying on, therefore, which we sometimes attain, is <the way>[299] the first cause always is, that is, it [i.e. the first intellect] is always the best life (*aristê zôê*).

And for this reason, Aristotle says, we say that perception and waking (*egrêgorsis*) and the act of thinking are most pleasant (*hêdus*), because while they are certain activities they are sorts of effigies (*indalma*) and shadows (*skia*) of the activity whereby we act and the life which we lead, whenever our intellect comes to be in a way the intelligible objects (cf. 1072b17–18). Again, we love (*philein*) hopes (*elpis*) and memories (*mnêmê*) because of activities: since we remember (*mimnêskein*) some activity or we hope to be acting, we love hope and memory (cf. 1072b18–19). If, then, we value (*agapein*) hopes and memories because of the activities, and we welcome (*aspazesthai*) these things in this way because we sometimes become active, this [sc. activity] must be an object of wonder (*thaumastos*).

And, Aristotle says, 'the act of thinking in itself is of that which is best in itself' (1072b18–19). And by 'the act of thinking in itself' he means the actual intellect,[300] which is different from the dispositional intellect, which again as dispositional is different from the potential intellect. For the dispositional intellect is a form and a potentiality[301] and a completion (*teleiotês*) of the potential intellect, a disposition which occurs in it as a result of its comprehension (*perilêpsis*) of the universal and its capacity to separate forms from matter, which [i.e. the forms] are in a way the same as each other. For that which has grasped a form of something separately from the matter possesses that which is both common and universal (for instance, when it has grasped the form of human being separately from the material (*hulikos*) circumstances, it possesses the common human being; for the difference (*diaphora*) of the individuals [i.e. human beings] from each other is received from the matter (†for this occurs in it†),[302] since their forms, at least in respect to which they are human beings, are not distinct). And, again, that which has comprehended what is common to individuals grasps the form separately from the matter; for it is this that is common and the same in them. And this dispositional state occurs in the intellect at the beginning in the transition (*metabasis*) from the continuous activity concerning perceptible objects, just as [the intellect] obtains from them a theoretical vision (*theôrêtikê opsis*) of the universal, which at first is called a thought (*noêma*) or a notion (*ennoia*), and when it becomes abundant, variegated, and many-faceted so as to have the potential to produce this even separately from its perceptual basis (*aisthêtikê hupobathra*), it is already an intellect. For whenever it comes into a dispositional state as a result of continuous activities in such a way that it has the potential to do the rest by means of itself, then there comes about the intellect called 'dispositional', since it is analogous (*analogos*) to the knower (*epistêmôn*) which is intermediate between being called a potential knower and being actively engaged in knowledge. This intellect, to the extent that it seems to fall short of the intellect that is actively engaged in knowledge, surpasses the intellect that is potentially knowing. And when this disposition is acting, the actual intellect comes to be. For the dispositional intellect is in a way the aggregate of thoughts that are laid aside and at rest (*êremein*).

And[303] since the actual intellect is none other than the form that is being thought of, just as actual perception is the actual perceptible object,[304] it is the dispositional intellect[305] (that is, the intellect that is able to think by itself and receive the forms of objects that are intelligible in themselves) which is already able to think of itself; for since it is itself the form that is being thought of, if indeed by thinking of it, it becomes what it thinks of (cf. 1072b19–21). So the intellect that possesses the disposition to think of forms possesses the disposition and potential to think of itself. For what has the potential to think comes itself to be thinking, and it is, whenever it thinks, thinking of the intelligible form beforehand and in virtue of itself,[306] and accidentally [thinking of] itself, because whenever it thinks it accidentally becomes the object of which it thinks. Now, before the intellect is actually thinking, that which is thinking and that which is being thought of are related to each other and are opposed to each other as correlatives; and whenever they are acting, they become one and there ceases to be the opposition (*antithesis*). For they can no longer fit under[307] the rubric of relatives. That is why the actual intellect becomes the same as the intelligible object, and it is reasonable (*eulogôs*) to say that it thinks of itself.[308] Thus the actual intellect thinks of itself, since it[309] becomes what it thinks of. For it thinks of the forms separately from matter, since it is not this but the being [i.e. essence] of this that it thinks of, as was said before (697,21–8).

Now, since the actual intellect is best in itself, its act of thinking, by which it thinks of itself, is the act of thinking in itself[310] also of the object that is best in itself. The actual intellect is best, not because it becomes the forms separately from matter by thinking of them, but because it becomes in a way the first intellect,[311] to the extent that it is able, by thinking of it. If, therefore, the act of thinking in itself is of what is best in itself, then also the act of thinking that is most of all in itself[312] will be thinking of what is best in itself most of all (cf. 1072b19). And in virtue of the act of thinking by which the first intellect thinks of itself, it is both that which thinks and that which is thought of. Therefore, the actual intellect thinks of itself 'by participation (*metalêpsis*) in the intelligible object' (1072b20). For [it does this] by possessing a disposition, as was said, to think of the forms by 'touching' (*thinganein*)[313] (1072b21). Moreover, the actual intellect is like the form of the potential intellect, so that it possesses as well the disposition to think of itself. Hence, whenever it thinks of itself, the same thing becomes the intellect and the intelligible object.

'For that which is receptive of the intelligible object, that is, the substance', or rather of the intellect, is itself 'the intellect'. And this is the sort of intellect that 'is acting when it possesses' in itself the intelligible objects when it has separated them; for it has separated [them] from the matter and [actively] keeps them in its possession and thinks of them (cf. 1072b22-3).

**1072b23** Hence, it is the former rather than the latter[314] which is the divine [state] that the intellect seems to possess, [and contemplation is the pleasantest and best thing. If, then, the god is always in the good state that we are in sometimes, it is wonderful; and if it is more so, it is still more wonderful. But [the god] is in this state. Furthermore, life belongs to it. For the activity of the intellect is life, and it is that actuality. And its activity in itself is a life that is best and everlasting. We say, then, that the god is a living being that is everlasting and best, so that a life and duration that is continuous and everlasting belongs to the god; for this is the god.]

Of all the things belonging to the intellect the most divine is contemplation (*theôria*).³¹⁵ Therefore, the divine [state] which the actual intellect possesses (and thinking of oneself is a divine [state]), 'this [belongs] more to that' (1072b23), that is, to the first intellect.³¹⁶ Therefore, [understanding] 'that' as that which essentially seems to be a most divine and honourable (*timios*) [state] of the actual intellect, and 'this' as thinking of itself, Aristotle states that this belongs rather to that [state of] the first intellect. For the first intellect thinks of itself with the most exactness, more so than even the actual intellect [thinks] of itself.

Now, the actual intellect does not think of itself in the way that the first intellect [thinks] of itself, nor [does it do so] always, but [only] at times and infrequently. But the first intellect thinks of itself always (cf. 1072b24–5). For the first intellect does not think of anything other than itself. For that it is thought of by itself by being intelligible, and that it will always be an object of thinking by being intelligible in actuality and by its own nature – are clear from that which is thinking <always> in actuality.³¹⁷ And [the first] intellect is itself alone always actually thinking. So it will always be thinking of itself.

This is still more the case in so far as it is simple; for a simple intellect thinks of a simple object, and no other intelligible object is simple except for it. For it is unmixed (*amigês*) and immaterial and possessing no potentiality in itself. So it will think of itself alone.³¹⁸ For in so far as it is intellect, it will think of itself as an intelligible object; and in so far as it is both intellect and actually intelligible, it will always think of itself. Further, in so far as it alone is simple, it will think of itself alone.³¹⁹ For since it alone is simple, it is capable of thinking (*noêtikos*) of something simple, and it alone is a simple intelligible object.³²⁰

And 'contemplation', in which it thinks of itself, is 'pleasantest and best' (1072b24). If, therefore, the god is always in a good state just as we are in a good state some of the time, the divine would be an object of wonder. And if it is in an indescribably better and greater state than the actual [human] intellect, then to the extent that it surpasses it, it will be so much the more wonderful (*thaumasios*). But it is in fact in this state. So the divine is most wonderful and highly honourable (*polutimêtos*) (cf. 1072b24–6).

But then, too, life belongs to the first intellect. 'For the activity of the intellect is life, and it[321] is the activity' (1072b26–7); so it is this life. Therefore, its activity, which is also an activity in virtue of itself,[322] 'is a life that is best and everlasting' (1072b28). Next, from the things that have been proven to belong to the first intellect, Aristotle defines it, saying that the first intellect is 'a living being everlasting [and] best' (1072b29); for there are also other everlasting living beings, but the best is the first intellect itself alone. Hence, if the god is an everlasting living being, and everything everlasting is contemplated continuously (for if it is intermittent (*dialimpanein*), it is not everlasting), 'a life and duration (*aiôn*) that is continuous' (for the life that is coextensive with each individual is a duration)[323] 'belongs to the god; for this is the god' (1072b30), namely, the everlasting and best life.

> **1072b30** Those, however, who suppose, as do the Pythagoreans and Speusippus, [that the noblest and best thing does not exist in the principle, because while the principles of plants and animals are causes, that which is noble and complete is present in what results from them, are not right in their opinion. For the seed comes from other things that are prior and complete, and the first thing is not seed but that which is complete; for instance, one would say that the human being is prior to the seed, not the human being that came from the seed but a different one from whom the seed came.
>
> 1073a3 That, therefore, there is some substance that is everlasting, immovable, and separate from perceptible objects is evident from the things that have been said. And it has been proven also that this substance cannot possess magnitude but is partless and indivisible. For it imparts movement for an unlimited time, and nothing limited possesses unlimited potentiality; and given that every magnitude is either unlimited or limited, it cannot be limited because it possesses no magnitude, and it cannot be unlimited because there is no unlimited magnitude at all. But then [it has been proven also] that it is unaffectable and unalterable. For all the other movements are posterior to movement in place. With respect to these things it is clear that this is how they are.]

Having proven that the god, the first principle, is a living being which is everlasting and best, Aristotle criticizes the Pythagoreans and Speusippus for claiming that the noblest and best thing does not reside in the principle and that the principle cannot be called best, because the seed and menstrual fluid are principles[324] of animals and are not best, but rather what has come to be from the seed and menstrual fluid is best. Now they are not right, Aristotle says, in holding that the incomplete seed and menstrual fluid are principles, but it is the father and mother (*mêtêr*), who in addition to being complete are also prior to the seed and menstrual fluid. Hence, the human being is prior to the seed, not the human who has come from the seed, but the father from whom came the seed (cf. 1072b30–1073a3).[325]

And Aristotle concludes by saying that it is clear, therefore, that there is a substance that is everlasting, separate, and different from perceptible objects (cf. 1073a3–5).[326] It has been proven also in *Physics* Book 8[327] that this sort of substance is incorporeal and partless (*amerês*). And he recalls what he said there, that this sort of principle brings about everlasting movement, and that what brings about everlasting movement necessarily has unlimited potentiality (*apeirodunamos*). For this has also been proven in that work.[328] But unlimited potentiality cannot exist in a limited (*perainein*) body. For this has also been proven in that work.[329] But that an unlimited body cannot exist in general has been proven in Book 3 of the *Physics*, and it has also been proven in the first book of *On the Heavens*.[330] So what has unlimited potentiality is incorporeal. 'But then' the first cause 'is also unaffectable (*apathês*) and unalterable (*analloiôtos*)'.[331] For if it were moved in general, it would undergo the first sort of movement which is movement in place; but it has been proven[332] that it does not undergo this movement, but if not this one, then, for sure, scarcely does it undergo the other kinds (cf. 1073a5–11).

## [Chapter 8]

**1073a14** But whether we should posit one substance of this sort or more than one [and how many, must not be overlooked; but we must also recall the assertions made by others, that they have said nothing concerning the number [of substances] that can even be clearly stated. For the theory of Ideas contains no special investigation of this (for those who say there are Ideas say that the Ideas are numbers, but concerning the numbers they sometimes speak of them as unlimited and at other times as limited to ten; but as for the reason why there are so many numbers nothing is said with demonstrative rigour).

1073a22 We must, however, conduct our discussion on the basis of things that have been laid down and determined. For the principle and the first of the things that exist is immovable both in itself and accidentally; and it brings about the first everlasting and single movement. But since it is necessary that what is moved is moved by something, that the first mover is immovable in itself and that everlasting movement is imparted by something everlasting and a single [movement] by a single thing, and since we see, apart from the simple locomotion of the universe, which is moved by the first immovable substance, other motions, which are the everlasting motions of the planets (for the body in circular [motion] is everlasting and never still; and these things have been proven in the works on natural science), then it is necessary that each of the motions is also moved by a substance that is immovable in itself and everlasting. For the nature of the stars is everlasting, being a sort of substance, and it is necessary that the mover is everlasting and prior to what is moved, and that what is prior to substance is necessarily substance. It is evident, therefore, that there are necessarily just as many substances which are everlasting in their nature, immovable in themselves, and without magnitude for the aforementioned reasons.

1073b1 That they are substances, therefore, and that one of these is first and another second according to the same order as the motions of the stars, is evident. But at this juncture the number of the motions must be investigated on the basis of the mathematical science that is most akin to philosophy, that is, astronomy; for this yields theoretical knowledge concerning substance that is perceptible, albeit everlasting, whereas the other [mathematical sciences] are not concerned with any substance, for instance, the science concerned with numbers and geometry. Now, that the motions are more numerous than the objects in motion is evident to those with an even moderate grasp, for each of the planets has more than one motion. But as to how many they are in fact, we now report what some of the mathematicians say (in order to provide some notion of it), so that that there may be some definite amount for our thought to grasp. But, as for the rest, we must partly enquire for ourselves and partly learn from [other] enquirers, and if anything opposed to what is said here appears to be the case to those who treat of these issues, we must to be friendly to both sides but be persuaded by those who are more exact.]

After proving that the first principle is one, being incorporeal and moved neither in itself nor accidentally,[333] but is immovable in every way, Aristotle
15  enquires: is there one substance of this sort or more than one, and if there is

not one but more than one, how many of them must we posit? 'But[334] it must not be overlooked, but we must recall' and ponder (*enthumeisthai*) 'also the assertions' and sayings (*gnômê*) 'of others' (1073a15–16). And he adds why we must recall them: [namely,] they have said nothing that is clear concerning the amount (*plêthos*) of such causes, whether the causes of this sort are three or twenty or some other number (*arithmos*) (cf. 1073a16–17).[335]

For those who posit the Ideas as causes of the things in this [perceptible realm] say nothing as to whether they also posited [them as] causes of movements. Nevertheless, since they assumed them to be in general causes, although they say nothing in detail (*eskeumennôs*) concerning their amount, they should have discussed the number of causes. Evidently, however, they only say that the Ideas are numbers,[336] sometimes defining number as far as ten and making it terminate (*apoperatoun*) in ten,[337] and sometimes saying that it is unlimited, because they sometimes say that they are unlimited and sometimes that they are limited [i.e. finite]. For if the Ideas are numbers, and number comes to a stop when it reaches ten, then there are ten Ideas. Again, if the Ideas are number, and number is without limit, then there are Ideas without limit (cf 1073a18–21). Hence, they did not make any peculiar affirmation concerning them, either that we must say only that they are unlimited or only that they are limited, but it is without 'demonstrative rigour' (*apodeiktikê spoudê*) (1073a22) that they discuss the issues involving the Ideas.

After criticizing them for failing to give a demonstrative account concerning the number of Ideas, even though they say that the Ideas are causes of the things in this [perceptible realm], Aristotle himself proposes to discuss how great the number of the moving causes is. In the first place he establishes that there are also different moving causes of Saturn and Jupiter (*Zeus*) and the remaining planetary stars (*planêtês astêr*).[338] For, as he will say (1074a24–31), the spheres too have come to be[339] on account of the stars; then, after finding how many spheres there are, he will declare that that the number of the moving causes is as great as that of the spheres; for a single thing has a single moving cause (cf. 1073a27–8 with 701,20).

And, again, he will refer to all these under the first cause, by which I mean the living creature that is everlasting and best, which he has proven to be immovable both in itself and accidentally (cf. 1073a23–5), and similarly also the moving [causes] of the other spheres; for these too are immovable in themselves and accidentally.[340] But why will the sphere that is first and belonging to the fixed stars not be moved by its own proper soul? Or else the sphere of the fixed stars and the remaining spheres are moved by their own proper souls but not in the way animals are (for the souls of animals propel or force the bodies in which they are present),[341] but rather in the way discussed in Book 2 of *On the Heavens*:[342] they are moved by the first [cause] as an object of yearning and desire. Let these things, however, have been already determined.[343] 'We must, however', says Aristotle, 'conduct our discourse on the basis of things that have been laid down and proven'[344] (1073a22–3): that the first principle, the first of all the things that exist, is immovable both in its own right and accidentally, and that, clearly, as the object of yearning it brings about the first, everlasting, single movement (cf. 1073a24–5).

'But since it is necessary that what is moved is moved by something, and that the first mover is immovable in itself' and accidentally (1073a26–7) (for even if souls are the first moving [causes] of living creatures, nonetheless they also are moved accidentally),[345] and since it is necessary that 'everlasting movement' comes to be 'by an everlasting' moving [cause] 'and a single' and continuous [movement comes to be] 'by a single thing' (1073a27–8) – for this has also been proven in the *Physics*[346] – if there was a single movement, since, in fact, as has been proven (cf. 700,38), a single [movement] comes to be by a single moving [cause], it would also be necessary to say that the mover is a single thing.

And since, beyond the simple movement of the universe (Aristotle means by 'universe' the sphere of the fixed stars,[347] which we say is moved by the first and immovable substance as an object of yearning), we see (*horan*) the other motions of the planets which are also everlasting themselves (for that a body capable of circular motion[348] is everlasting, not standing still (*astatos*), and never at rest, has been proven in *On the Heavens*),[349] since, then, we see this, it is necessary that each motion of the planetary [objects] is 'moved by' a substance 'that is immovable, that is, immovable in virtue of itself'[350] (1073a32–4). And if it would have been written 'by [a substance] immovable and in itself',[351] it would signify the same thing by this phrase. And it is necessarily not only by a substance which is immovable in itself that it is moved but also by one that is everlasting. And Aristotle adds the reason why the moving [causes] of the spheres of the planets are everlasting and substances when he says, 'for the nature of the stars is everlasting' (1073a34), which is equivalent to saying: since the stars which are moved by them always exist, necessarily also the mover, since it is prior to what is moved, is everlasting; but if it is prior, it is necessarily a substance; for the priority of a substance to the substances is due to the fact that other things cannot exist separately from substance (cf. 1073a35–7).

If, then, a simple cause is capable of bringing about a single and simple movement, as has been proven, and a single and simple movement comes to be by a single and simple cause,[352] it is evident that however many movements or moved things there are, there will be that many movers which are by nature both everlasting and immovable in themselves. And of these one is the first, another is the second, and another is the third; for the movers will be related in the same way as the things moved by them (cf. 1073a36-b3). But the meaning of his statements has already been stated, and the clause 'because they have said nothing concerning the amount that can even be clearly stated' (1073a16–17) is expressed in a roundabout manner (*periphrazesthai*); for the statement is equivalent to saying: concerning the amount they have said nothing clear.

After Aristotle has said these things and as he is going to discuss how great is the number of spheres – since he will state in this way, simply and without demonstration, that there are fifty-five (for he has stated elsewhere (cf. 1073b17–1074a12) the reason why there are so many among them) – he says, 'but at this juncture the number of spheres[353] must be investigated on the basis of the mathematical science that is most akin to philosophy'[354] (1073b3–5), which is equivalent to saying: we now, separately from demonstration, say that there are fifty-five, in order that we may discover from these the number of movers as well; for we do not now propose to prove how many spheres there in fact are; but if anyone seeks the demonstration of this too, let him turn to astronomy (*astronomia*).

After saying that it is from astronomy (*astrologia*), the [science] most akin to philosophy, that we must study theoretically how great is the number of spheres, Aristotle adds the reason why astronomy is most akin to philosophy, in comparison with the other mathematical sciences (*mathêmatikê epistêmê*), [namely,] geometry and arithmetic, stating, 'this yields theoretical knowledge concerning substance that is perceptible,[355] albeit everlasting', whereas geometry (*geômetria*) and arithmetic (*arithmêtikê*) are concerned with the attributes of magnitudes (*megethos*) and arithmetic with those of numbers (cf. 1073b5–8).

20   Since he said above that the motions are more numerous [than the planets], he adds 'that the motions are more numerous is evident' to one who has an even moderate grasp of mathematical subjects (1073b8–9). And that they are more numerous is clear. But as to how many motions (that is, of spheres)[356] there in fact are, we say what 'some of the mathematicians' (*mathêmatikos*) (1073b11–12) state (he is speaking of Eudoxus and Callippus)[357] for some
25   notion of how to determine how great the number of them is, so that we might be guided by them towards the discovery of the moving causes. But we must, he says, not abide by the statements made before us concerning the number of spheres, but we must enquire for ourselves as well and find it out, and learn from however many of the rest also who enquire about these things, and from whatever claim is evident to those who treat of these subjects beyond the
30   statements made by us here. We must 'be friendly' to those coming later and those coming before us for having discovered anything, but 'be persuaded by those who are more exact (*akribês*)' (1073b16–17).

After saying this Aristotle straightaway recounts what Eudoxus has said concerning the spheres and the number of them, and also what Callippus has said. And after showing the addition to the spheres which Callippus made (for Eudoxus posited that the total was twenty-six, whereas Callippus made it thirty-
35   three), Aristotle himself added twenty-two spheres to the thirty-three as follows.[358]

> **1073b17** Now, Eudoxus posited that the motion of the sun and the moon [in each case][359] involves three [spheres, of which the first is that of the fixed stars; that the second [rotates] along the [circle] through the middle of the constellations of the zodiac; that the third [rotates] along the [circle] aligned obliquely to the breadth of the constellations of the zodiac (while [the circle] along which the moon is carried is aligned more obliquely to the breadth [of the constellations of the zodiac] than is the sun's); and that [the motion] of the [remaining] planetary stars involves four spheres in each case. And of these [four spheres] the first and second are the same as those for the aforementioned [i.e. the sun and moon] (for the [sphere] of the fixed [stars] carries all the [other spheres], and the [sphere] that is placed in order under this and is in motion along the [circle] through the middle of the constellations of the zodiac is common to all [the spheres]). But the poles of the third [spheres]

of every [planet] are on the [circle] through the middle of the constellations of the zodiac, while the motion of the fourth [sphere] is along the [circle] which is aligned obliquely to the equator of the former (and the poles of the third sphere are different for the other planets but are the same for Venus and Mercury).

1073b32 Callippus, however, posited the same position (that is, the [same] order of distances) as Eudoxus, and he also assigned the same number [of spheres] to Jupiter and Saturn as Eudoxus, but he held that two spheres should be assigned in addition to the sun and moon, if one were going to account for all the appearances, and one [in addition] to each of the remaining planets.

1073b38 But if all [the spheres] when put together are going to account for the appearances, then it is necessary that in the case of each planetary [star] there are other spheres, though one fewer, which are counteracting and which always put back in the same position the first sphere of the star which is placed in order beneath it; for only in this way is it possible for all of them to produce the motion of the planets. Hence,[360] the spheres in which some of them are carried are eight [altogether] and those in which the others are carried are twenty-five, and of these [spheres] only those in which the one [planet] placed lowest is carried do not need to be counteracted, the counteracting spheres of the first two will be six, and the spheres of the later four will be sixteen. Therefore, the number of all the spheres, both those bringing about motion and those counteracting them, will be fifty-five. But if one were not to add to the moon and the sun the movements which we have mentioned, the spheres will be forty-seven in all.]

Now, the discussions of how many spheres there are, in what way they are moved, and due to what cause this occurs, by Eudoxus and Callippus and later by Aristotle, have been stated with great care in the second book of *On the Heavens* in the interpretation (*exêgêsis*) of the text[361] from 'and, further, for the following reason the other motions involve one body' up to 'but the potentiality of any limited body is related to a limited [body]',[362] and by and large we have also interpreted (*exêgeisthai*) there the present passage: 'Eudoxus posited that the motion of the sun and the moon (*selênê*) is in three [spheres]' up to 'Let the number of the spheres be so great' (1073b17–1074a15). So one who wishes may obtain clarification concerning the present text from the former. But since some of the passages have not been made clear there, it is worthwhile to examine them now.[363]

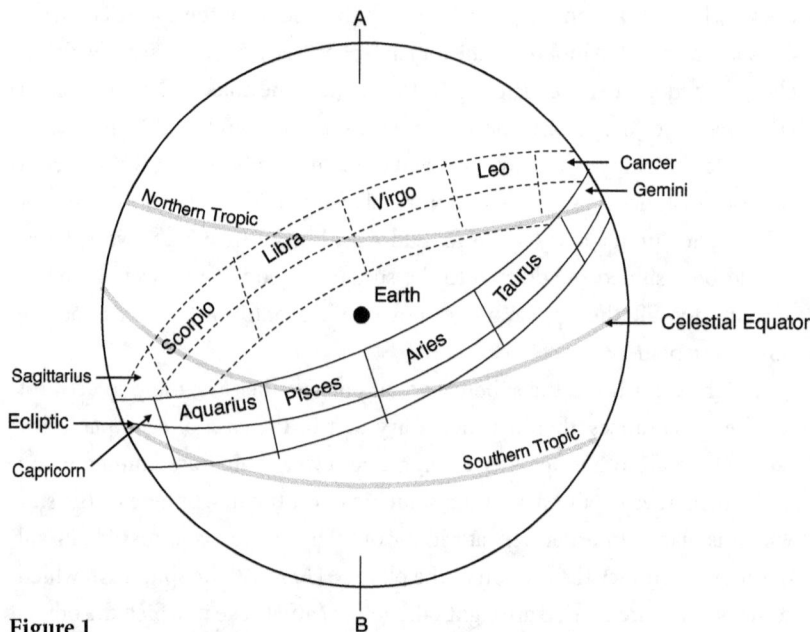

**Figure 1**

10   By the first of these passages, 'of which the first is that of the fixed stars' (1073b18–19), Aristotle does not mean (as one might think) that the sphere of the fixed stars[364] (see Figure 1) is first (although it *is* also first); but what he means is this: of the three spheres,[365] according to Eudoxus, that bring about the motion of the sun, the one that is first and surrounds the remaining two and undergoes the same movement as the sphere of the fixed stars (for he said that it is moved
15   from east to west (*dusis*), for the reason which we discussed in *On the Heavens*),[366] this first sphere was regarded by Eudoxus as fixed relative to the remaining two which are surrounded by it. And he said that not only the first sphere of the sun is fixed, but also that [the spheres] of Saturn, Jupiter, and each of the other stars
20   which are first and larger, are fixed, so that the first [i.e. outermost sphere] is a single sphere of the fixed stars, in which there is the mass of the stars filling up the constellations of the zodiac (*zôidia*), while there is one sphere of Saturn, another of Jupiter, and so on in succession, which Theophrastus described as 'starless (*anastros*)'.[367]

And by 'the third[368] is in the [object] aligned obliquely to the breadth (*platos*) of the constellations of the zodiac' (1073b20–1), he meant that it is in the circle (*kuklos*) aligned obliquely (*loxoun*) to the breadth of constellations of the

zodiac (as was stated in *On the Heavens*),³⁶⁹ the circle which the sun seems to   25
describe by its own centre (*kentron*) when it is carried (*pherein*)³⁷⁰ by the sphere
in which it is embedded (*endein*), which also seems to veer from the solstitial
constellations (*ta tropika sêmeia*),³⁷¹ because the sun is not always, when it
makes its turning (*tropê*), seen to rise from the same places.³⁷²

The phrase '[the circle] along which the moon is carried is aligned more
obliquely to the breadth [of the constellations of the zodiac] than is the
sun's' (1073b21–2) is equivalent to saying: the breadth of the oblique    30
alignment of the circle which the moon seems to describe by its centre is
greater than the breadth of the obliqueness of the circle which the sun
seems to describe by means of its own centre; for this was ascertained from
the fact that the sun and the moon do not rise from the same places in their
turnings (see Figure 2).³⁷³

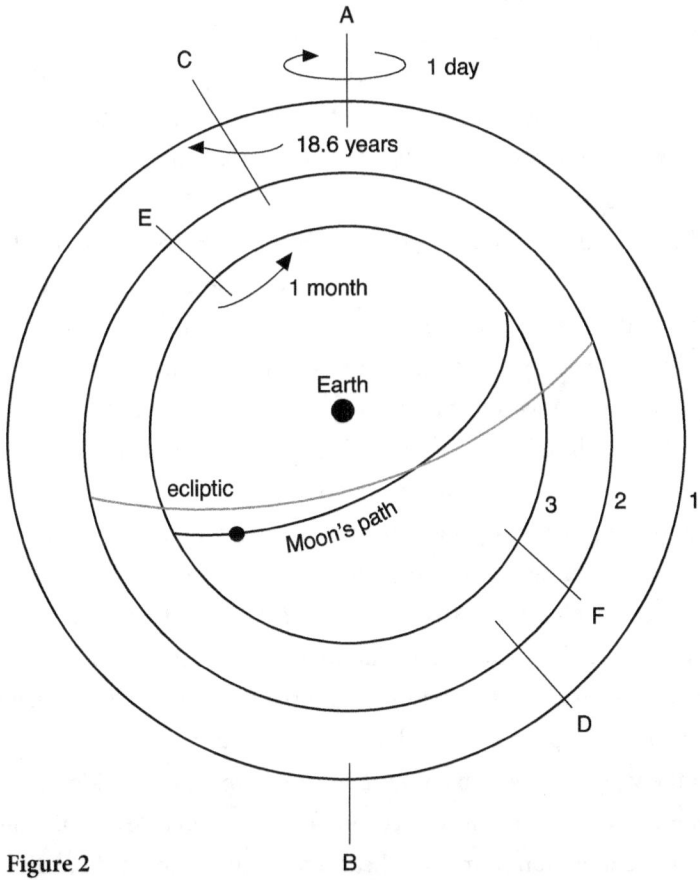

**Figure 2**

For let the horizonal (*horizôn*) circle be <AGBCMD>,[374] let the equinoctial (*isêmerinos*) circle be DEB, let the circle aligned obliquely to the breadth of the constellations of the zodiac which the sun seems to describe by its centre be AEC, and let the circle which, again, the moon seems to describe by its centre be GEM. And let the sun rise in the season when it makes its summer (*therinos*) turning from point (*sêmeion*) A and, when it is at the equinox (*isêmeria*), from point D. It is clear that the greatest breadth of the obliqueness is the arc (*periphereia*) DA. But let the moon, when it makes its turning to the north (*boreion*), rise from point G. Now, it is evident that the greatest breadth of the obliqueness of the moon is the arc DG, and it is greater than the arc DA, that is, greater than the greatest breadth of the obliqueness of the sun (see Figures 3A and 3B). This is indicated by the phrase '[the circle] in which the moon undergoes motion is aligned more obliquely to the breadth [of the constellations of the zodiac] than is the sun's' (1073b21–2).

Further, the phrase 'the poles (*polos*) of the third [sphere] of every [planet] are on the [circle] through the middle of the constellations of the zodiac' (1073b28–9) means: the third spheres all have their poles in the circles which are described through the middle of the constellations of the zodiac by the centres of the stars.

And the words '[Callippus] posited the same order (that is, of distances (*apostêma*))'[375] (1073b33–4) mean: the sorts of spheres that Eudoxus had said were first and second, these too Callippus said were first [and second];[376] and however far Eudoxus had said that Saturn's sphere was situated from Mercury's, Callippus also said it was that far.[377]

And the words 'that in the case of each planetary [star] there are other spheres, though one fewer, which are counteracting (*anelittein*)' (1074a1–3) mean: since the spheres carrying Saturn are four, let there be three counteracting spheres; for the three are one less than the four. Again, since [the spheres] moving Mars (*Arês*), according to Callippus, are five, let four counteracting spheres be added to them; for the four are one less than five; and similarly for the other [planets]. But the reason why Aristotle found it necessary to add the counteracting spheres is stated in *On the Heavens*.[378]

And the words 'and which always put back in the same position (*thesis*) the first sphere of the star which is placed in order (*tattein*) below' (1074a3–4) will be clear if we draw some circles.[379] Let there be three circles: AB, DE, and FG.

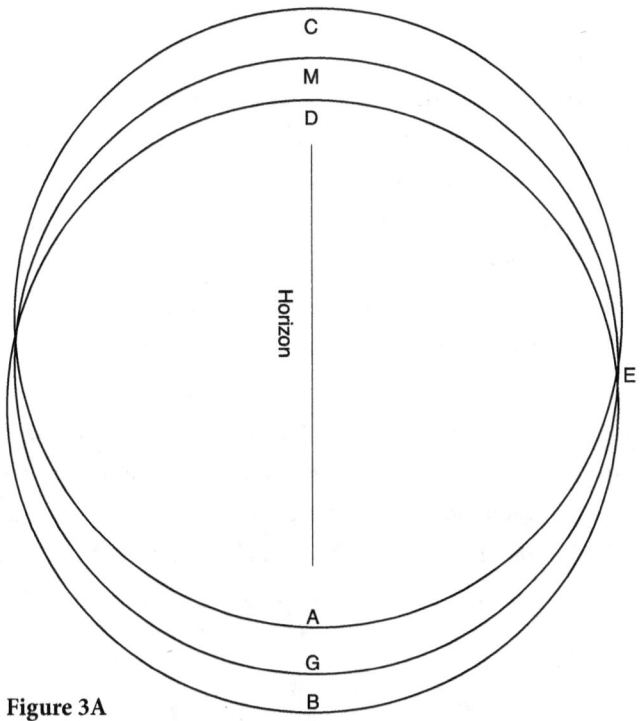

**Figure 3A**

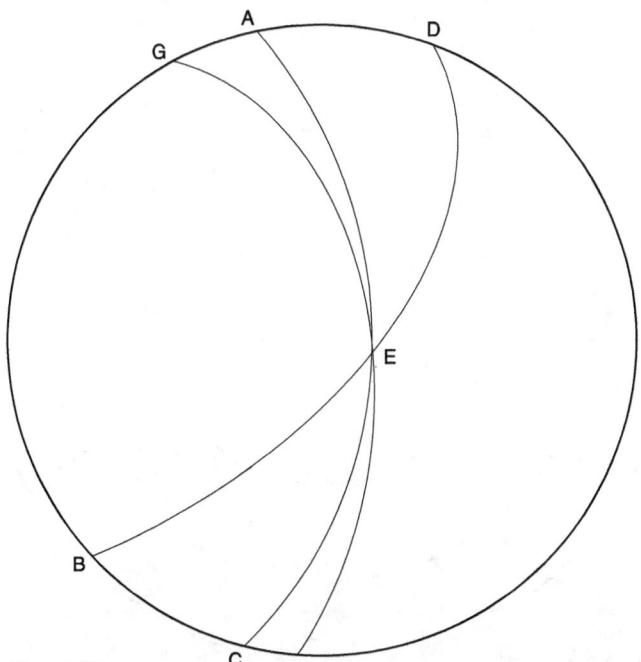

**Figure 3B**

25  And let there be a star, for instance, Jupiter, in FG, and let it be the point K. And let A be a point, and D and F, and B, E, and G. But let us not think of them as stars, but only as points [on the respective circles]; and let A, D, and F be on the same straight [line],[380] and similarly B, E, and G. And let the sphere AB be moved towards point B, so that A travels to where B [now] is. Further, let DE and FG be moved equally fast (*isotakhôs*) towards D and F [respectively], so that E and G
30  travel to D and F [respectively]. Since, then, the spheres ED and GF are moved in the same direction at equal speed, it is clear that the movement of sphere GF will be twice that of sphere ED (see Figure 4A).[381]

For, however great is the movement of the GF sphere, so much, too, will be imparted to it by the movement of sphere ED, since they undergo motion in the same direction. Hence, in the time in which E went to D, in the same time
35  G would travel through the whole circle GF and go again to G – unless sphere AB, which undergoes motion opposite (*antipheresthai*) to DE and pulls it towards B, does not allow it to impart to sphere FG another movement as great

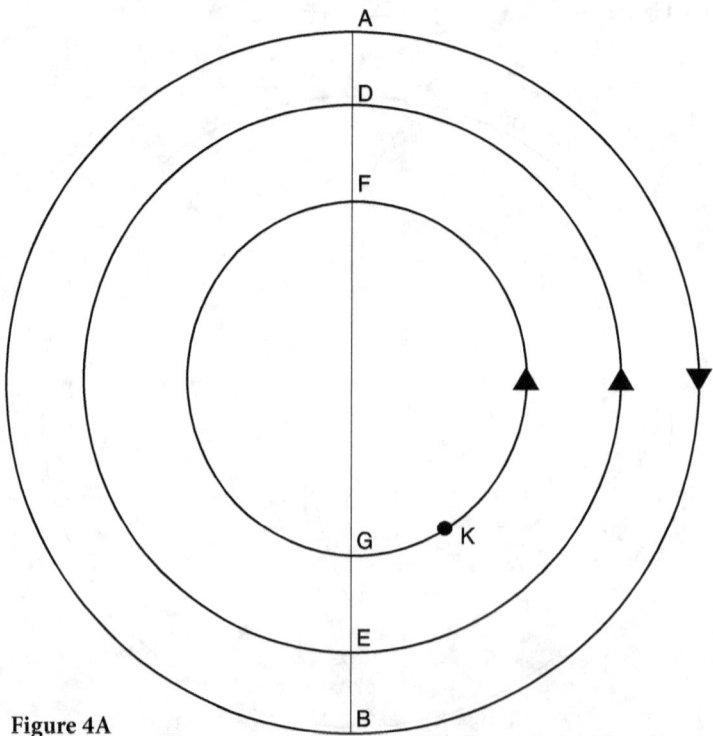

**Figure 4A**

as it is moved itself.[382] Hence, AB impedes (*empodizein*) DE and pulls it towards B,[383] and DE impedes FG,[384] and for this reason FG will always maintain the same position as the position of AB; hence, whenever G goes to F, and F is where G now is, then A will also go to where B now is, and B to where A is, and the points A and F and B and G are at all times in the same straight line, and when A rises, F rises too; and, again, when B sets G then too, and never do they rise before (*proanatellein*), or set before (*produnein*), A and F. And if AB and GF are in motion in the same direction, there will be the same result (see Figure 4B). And let sphere DE be thought of as counteracting.[385]

This, then, is what he means by the words: 'and which always put back in the same position the first sphere of the star which is placed in order beneath it' (1074a3–4). What he means by 'in this way' (1074a4) is: let the counteracting [spheres] be thought of in such a way that they make the first and outermost of the spheres moving Jupiter always keep the same position in relation to the sphere in which the star is embedded, and never make the points belonging

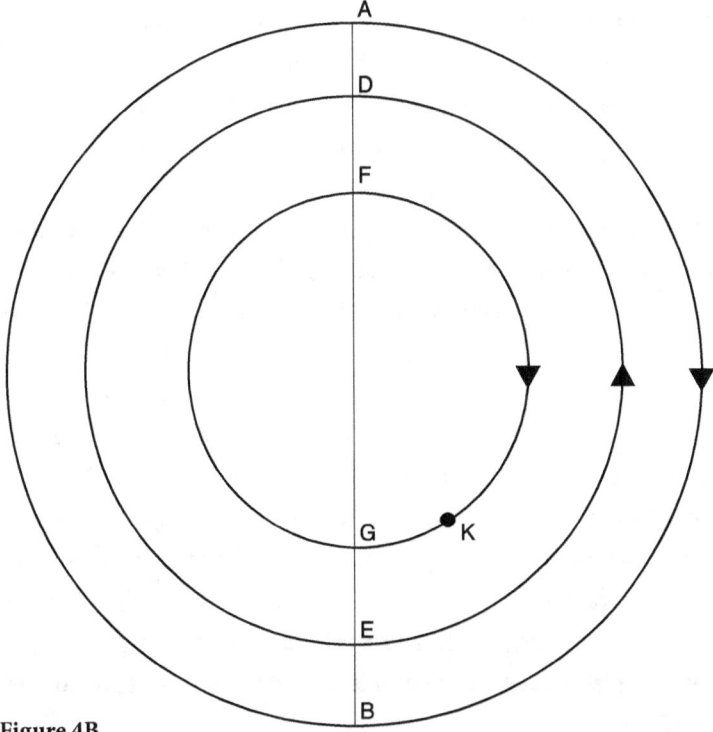

**Figure 4B**

to the first sphere precede the points belonging to the sphere in which the star[386] is embedded, but make them always rise together (*sunanatellein*) and set together (*sundunein*).

The words 'hence,[387] the spheres in which some of them undergo motion are eight and those in which the others do so are twenty-five' (1074a6–7) are equivalent to saying: hence, according to Callippus the spheres of the sun and the moon are eight [altogether], and those of the others – Saturn, Jupiter, and so forth – are twenty-five [altogether]. For the phrase a little before, 'but he [i.e. Callippus] held that two spheres should be assigned in addition to the sun and moon' (1073b35–6) is equivalent to saying: one to each. For since Eudoxus posited six spheres for the sun and moon, and Callippus says that the former are eight, it is clear that he posited in addition one to each of the former.[388] Similarly, he posited one in addition to each of the remaining spheres of the five stars. For since Eudoxus had said that four [spheres] belonged to each of the remaining five stars, Callippus made them five.

And the words 'of these only those in which the low one[389] is carried do not need to be counteracted' (1074a7–8) mean: only those spheres which carry the moon (which is the lowest of all the stars) do not need to possess counteracting spheres.

And the words 'the counteracting spheres of the first two will be six' (1074a8–9) mean: the spheres of Saturn and Jupiter will be six; for since the spheres carrying Saturn are four and those carrying Jupiter are four, and for each star there must be one less counteracting sphere, the counteracting spheres of Saturn and Jupiter will be six [altogether], and in the case of the remaining four – Mars, Venus (*Aphroditê*), Mercury (*Hermês*), and the sun – since there are five moving spheres in the case of each, there are four [counteracting spheres for each planet]. So the counteracting spheres of Saturn and Jupiter become two times three in all, and the spheres of Mars, Venus, Mercury, and the sun become four times four; hence, they are twenty-two in all. But the spheres carrying Saturn and Jupiter were eight, and those for the remaining five were twenty-five. Therefore, if these thirty-three are added to the twenty-two counteracting spheres, there will be fifty-five spheres in all.[390] For the spheres carrying the moon, as was said, have no need for counteracting spheres, because it is last; for thus Aristotle has said that only those spheres in which the star placed low[est] in order is carried do not need to be counteracted (cf. 1074a7–8).

The additional sentence, 'and if one were not to add to the moon and the sun the movements which we have mentioned, the spheres will be forty-seven in all' (1074a12–13) gives rise to confusion (*tarakhê*).³⁹¹ For if we were to take away the two spheres of the sun and the two spheres of the moon which Callippus has added, and also, clearly, the two other counteracting spheres from the sun (for since the former spheres have been taken away, the latter spheres that are going to counteract them must be taken away with them too), six spheres will be taken away: two which carry the sun and two which counteract these in addition to the two posited by Callippus in addition for the moon.³⁹² And if these are taken away from the fifty-five spheres, it no longer results that the remaining spheres will be forty-seven in all but instead that forty-nine are left. [Aristotle however says that forty-seven are left,]³⁹³ either because he has overlooked (*epilanthanesthai*) that he has taken away not four but only two spheres from the moon, unless we must say that he has taken four from the sun, which he himself posited in addition as counteracting, and the [two] spheres of both [the sun and moon] which Callippus [posited], then since there are eight taken away from the fifty-five, the remaining spheres are forty-seven, and thus results the number stated by Aristotle; or else, as Sosigenes says after considering the matter, it is better to hold³⁹⁴ that an oversight (*parorhama*) was committed by the copyists, than to make the seventh and eighth spheres the same.³⁹⁵

> **1074a14** Let, then, the number of spheres³⁹⁶ be this many, so that the immovable³⁹⁷ substances or principles [may be reasonably supposed to be just as many. For let it be left to more formidable [thinkers] to speak of what is necessary.]

After Aristotle has recounted the number of the spheres and stated that there are altogether twenty-six spheres according to Eudoxus and thirty-three according to Callippus, and fifty-five based on his own observation (*paratêrêsis*), and after he has proven that the movement that is one, simple, and everlasting comes about from a moving cause that is one, simple, and partless, he confidently declares that, however great the number of the spheres and perceptible substances turns out in fact to be, 'the immovable substances and principles are reasonably supposed to be so many' (1074a15–16). And since he has recounted only, but has not actually proven, that the spheres are fifty-five and has said that it is reasonable (*eulogos*) to suppose that the immovable substances are so many, he adds 'for let it be left to more formidable [thinkers] to speak of what is necessary' (1074a16–17) – as if he were saying: although we have recounted that there are fifty-five spheres, we do not say that there are necessarily this many; if any [thinkers] who are more formidable (*iskhus*) and superior[398] to us were to say it, these would proclaim that it is necessary and not [merely] reasonable, as we do – [he is] expressing these matters altogether philosophically (*philosophôs*).

But what are the efficient causes of the spheres which Aristotle now offers? Are they the souls or forms of the spheres? Or does he not speak of the souls of the spheres,[399] since they are not gods? For since they are forms of the spheres, they are in them, and they move them in a circle through the mediation of one and the same movement of their nature (for it is not the case that the movement of the soul is one thing and the movement of the nature another), and the spheres possess from their nature the suitability for movement which is congenital (*autophuês*), unforced (*abiastos*), and adapted to their form, and from their soul the locomotive (*metabatikos*) activity which is natural for them owing to their nature.[400] Therefore, he does not speak of their souls, but of different substances that are incorporeal and separate from body, and which are subordinate to the first intellect[401] to the same degree as the spheres (if one may say so) are to the sphere of the fixed stars, but higher than the souls of the spheres. Hence, the spheres are moved both by their own souls, as was said, and by gods of this sort, just as the sphere of the fixed stars is moved by the first intellect. And the sphere of the fixed stars is moved without limit because of the first moving cause; for the soul of the sphere of the fixed stars is not the cause of its being moved without limit, nor does it possess [unlimited motion] by its own agency but by that of the first moving cause.[402] For just as it possesses movement from soul, as was said,[403] so also being without limit and always in the same manner and in the same way and about the same things and in the same thing and all characteristics of this sort attach to the heaven from the immovable intellectual cause.

Therefore, just as the heaven is moved by the first moving [cause], so also the planetary spheres are moved by their own moving [causes], which are each completed (*teleioun*) and made good (*agathunein*) by the first moving [cause], in some cases more so and others less, in the case of Saturn's sphere more so and those of the sun's sphere less, and similarly for the others. And moving causes of this sort are called best (cf. 1074a19–20), not in the same way as the first [moving cause] on which they depend (*exertasthai*) (for it is not needful, [being] overfull (*huperplêrês*) with its own noble attributes, whereas they strive towards it and are filled with its benefaction (*agathodosia*)), but they are called best in comparison with the spheres that they move; for the latter yearn for the former on the grounds that they are best; for a thing yearns for that which it loves as what is best. Hence, the highly honourable intellect is called best without qualification, as also the first heaven is [called] great without qualification, whereas these [i.e. the lesser movers] are called best in relation to the spheres moved by them, just as also a particular magnitude is called great or greater, for instance, say, the ten-cubit length is not [great] without qualification but in relation to a particular two-cubit or five-cubit length (cf. 1073b1–3).

**1074a17** If, however, there can be no motion that does not contribute to the motion of a star, [and, furthermore, every nature and every substance that is unaffectable and has by itself attained the best must be held to be an end, then there could be no other nature beyond these, but rather this is necessarily the number of the substances. For if there were others, they would impart movement as being an end of motion; but it is impossible for there to be, in fact, other motions apart from the ones just mentioned.

1074a24 Further, it is reasonable to suppose this from the objects in motion. For if everything imparting motion is naturally for the sake of the object in motion and if every motion belongs to something in motion, no motion will be for the sake of itself or for the sake of another motion, but it will be for the sake of the stars. For if a motion is for the sake of [another] motion, the latter must also be for the sake of something else. Hence, since it is impossible for this to go on without limit, the end of any motion will be one of the divine bodies carried through the heaven.

1074a31 That there is one heaven, is evident. For if there are many heavens, as there are humans, the principle for each will be one in form but nevertheless many in number. But the things that are many in number possess matter; for there is one and the same account of many things, for instance, [the account] of human being, whereas Socrates is one; but the essence does not possess matter [namely, the first], since it is an actualization. The first immovable mover, therefore, is one both in account and in number; and so, also, that which is moved always and continuously one alone; so there is only one heaven.]

After stating that it is reasonable to suppose that there are as many movers as there are things that are moved, someone might be about to say: what prevents there from being some substances that are incorporeal and [existing] in virtue of themselves, but which do not impart movement? And if this is possible, it is not reasonable that there are as many incorporeal substances, neither more nor less, as there are objects moved. To forestall this objection which might be raised against his claim, Aristotle says: if, then, everything that has attained the best is an 'end' (*telos*)[404] (1074a20) and this itself is best and an object of yearning (for every god is best even if not as the first [god]), necessarily something yearns for it; for every object of yearning is the object of the yearning of something that is yearning. If indeed, then, certain other substances are best, and everything best is an object of yearning, these [others] are necessarily objects of yearning. But if this is so, the things yearning for them are necessarily moved by them. But if indeed there are things moved there will also be movements; for nothing is moved without movement. But, then, there are no movements beyond the fifty-five, so there are neither moved things beyond these nor movers.

Aristotle advances the argument hypothetically, saying, 'if, however, there can be no motion that does not contribute (*sunteinein*) to the motion of a star' (1074a17–18), and it must be understood in addition that there would be no other movement, for if there will be, it will be in vain. And he can be construed as saying that there is no other movement apart from those that have been mentioned; and if this is so, there will be no things moved apart from those already mentioned, and hence no movers either. If, then, there is no motion that does not contribute to the motion of a star (for both the motions of the spheres that carry the stars and those that counteract the motions of the stars make a contribution together (*suntelein*)), and all the movements contributing to the motions of the stars are so many[405] and none is left out, there is no other movement apart from these. For if there is, it will be in vain (*matên*), but neither the god nor nature makes anything in vain. But if there is no other movement, there is also neither moved thing nor mover. Hence, with this sort of argument, by proving that there is no other movement, Aristotle has at the same time demonstrated there is no other substance.

The words 'further, every nature and every substance that is unaffectable and by itself' (1074a19–20) are in a preliminary way indicative (*deiktikos*) that there are no other substances. What this means is as follows: further, if we must suppose that every nature and substance is unaffectable and in virtue of itself (that is, an incorporeal object of this sort) – that is, a cause that is best, yearned for, and a final cause[406] (*telikê aitia*) – then there will be no other nature apart from the aforementioned moving causes, but there are necessarily fifty-five not counting with them the first cause as well; for if[407] there were other substances apart from these, 'they would impart movement', since they are necessarily final causes and objects of yearning. This is indicated by the phrase: 'as being an end of motion' (1074a20–3). For the object of yearning is an end of motion, and of movement in general,[408] that comes about due to it. But it is impossible for there to be motions other than those that have been mentioned (cf. 1074a23–4).

And Aristotle adds the reason why it is impossible for there to be other motions: if there is also another motion, it will be either for the sake of a body in motion or for the sake of another motion (cf. 1074a25–9). But if indeed the motion is for the sake of a motion, it will be either for the sake of itself, such as walking (*badisis*) for the sake of walking, which is quite ridiculous (*katagelastos*), or for the sake of another motion such as whitening (*leukansis*) for the sake of sweetening (*glukansis*). But if this is so, there will also be sweetening for the sake of another motion, and so on without limit. It remains, then, that if there is another circular motion (*periphora*) apart from those we have mentioned, then it is for the sake of a body in motion.[409] But these are all the motions that contribute together to the motions of the bodies in motion. There is, then, no other motion apart from these; hence, neither is there another particular immovable and incorporeal substance apart from those we have mentioned. And I think that what he means is along these lines.

The phrase 'the end of every motion will be one of the divine bodies which are carried through the heaven'[410] (1074a30–1) is equivalent to saying: any circular (*enkuklios*) motion possesses some star as its end and it occurs for the sake of the star; for that for the sake of which something occurs is the end of what occurs because of it.[411]

After saying these things, Aristotle proves that 'the heaven'[412] or cosmos is one (cf. 1074a31–8). For it was necessary, since he has proven that the first cause is one, to enquire whether in addition the substance which is brought forth (*paragein*) and moved everlastingly by it is one or many. He says, then, that if the cosmos is not one but many in number, like Socrates, Plato, and Callias, but one in species,[413] there will be as many things that are best in themselves and best in the chief sense as there are cosmoses. For he has proven that the moving cause of the object that is one and is moved everlastingly and continuously is [itself] one.[414] Hence, the first principles and the things that are best in the chief sense will be more than one in number but the same in species. For, in so far as they are animals and in so far as they are everlasting and in so far as they are best, they will not differ at all, just as Socrates and Plato do not differ in so far as they are animals. So, there will be everlasting best animals which are many in number but the same in species. But things that are the same in species but different in number are this way owing to their matter; for individual human beings are different from one another owing to their matter,[415] since the forms at least in virtue of which they are human beings or horses, do not differ at all. And yet the first and best [cause] has been proven to be immaterial and actuality.[416] There are not, therefore, many everlasting best animals. Hence, neither can there be many cosmoses.[417]

In the phrase 'for there is one and the same account of many things, for instance, [the account] of human being', the word 'one' [is written] instead of ['different', i.e.]: for the account of the human being, in so far as it is a human being, is different; and 'Socrates is one', that is, that [i.e. the account] of Socrates[418] in so far as he is Socrates is different (1074a34–5). If this is so, then if indeed the first causes are many, the account of each one of them will be different in so far as they are individual (*atomos*) and particular. Hence, they will also be compound and enmattered, and the account of the form that is predicated of them in common will be different, which is quite impossible. And 'the essence (*to ti ên einai*) does not possess matter, [namely, the first]' (1074a35–6) [is written] instead of: the first essence – or rather, the first form, the account, and the actuality, which I call the first everlasting animal – does not possess matter.

> **1074a38** It has been handed down from those who were ancient and very old, in the shape of a myth [bequeathed to posterity – that these are gods and that the divine encompasses the whole of nature. And the rest has been added later mythically for the persuasion of the many and with a view to the usefulness of the laws and for the [common] advantage. For they say that these are human in form or are like certain other animals, and they say other things that follow from and are like those just mentioned. If, of these remarks, one were to take separately only the first – that they held that the first substances were gods – one would hold that it is divinely expressed and that, although in all likelihood each art and philosophy has oftentimes been

discovered as far as possible and once again perished, these beliefs of theirs have been preserved like remnants up to the present. The belief of our first forefathers and that from the first people are to this extent evident to us only.]

After proving that gods exist, which are as numerous as the spheres and depend on the divine and best substance and exist by its agency, and which consequently are able to be the best and to be called the best, Aristotle says that not only do we possess this notion about them, but that 'from those who were ancient (*arkhaios*) and very old (*pampalaios*)' we have inherited 'in the shape of a myth (*muthos*)' (1074a38-b2) [the belief] that gods exist, we ourselves do not intimate[419] through the myths any gods other than the ones about which we have been speaking. There are, therefore, gods and a divine multitude that encompasses the whole of nature and the entire cosmos (cf. 1074b3); but it does not encompass it corporeally in the way a bushel (*medimnos*)[420] encompasses the grains of wheat in it (for everything divine is partless), but in the way that one who steers (*kubernein*) something makes it good and always brings forth the order and the orderliness (*eukosmia*) that it possesses.

After saying that [these views] were bequeathed 'in the shape of a myth' (1074b1-2), Aristotle stated the reason why they spoke mythically (*muthikôs*) concerning the gods, [and] he adds, 'The rest has been advanced[421] later mythically with a view to persuading the many' (1074b3-4). He is saying, in effect, that since this was the only thing they declared clearly, namely, that gods exist, all the rest that they said concerning them, for instance, that Cronus and Rhea begot Zeus and so forth, they said 'mythically' in order to persuade the many and make them conform to the laws (*nomos*), and, in general, with a view to what is advantageous (*to sumpheron*) for the human way of life (*bios*) they declared these things mythically (cf. 1074b4-5).

For since they were wise (*sophos*) and cognizant of the fact that festivals (*panêguris*) and drinking parties (*sumposion*) have a calming effect on human beings and unify them and cause them to be friendly towards each other and to die for each other's sake – these things are the foundation of poleis, whereas solitary existence turns men into beasts (*apothêrioun*) and divides them and causes them to slay one another – and since for this reason they wished to establish festivals and drinking parties, they fabricated (*plattein*)[422] myths, [announcing,] for instance, that on this day Zeus was begotten from Rhea, and for this reason people had to gather together and celebrate the god's birthday (*genethlios hêmera*) and join in the communal feast. And also when they had made them in human form (cf. 1074b5–6), they had done this not in vain but with a view to the general welfare; for because they wished to turn humans away from striking each other, they had made the gods in human form (*anthrôpoeidês*), intimating by this that one who strikes a human being strikes and wantonly insults (*hubrizein*) a divine form.

And not only do they make them in human form, but for the even greater benefit of the human race they make the gods similar also to certain other animals (cf. 1074b6). For when the land of the Egyptians brought forth such a great multitude of snakes (*ophis*) that no other [greater] harm befell those dwelling there, whose nature and providential (*pronooumenos*) god let loose the so-called ibises (*ibis*) as killers (*phoneutria*) of the snakes, the wise men living there, wishing to deter the Egyptians from killing the ibises (for some people were killing them, even though they were the saviours (*sôteira*) of the Egyptian race), laid down a law proclaiming that no Egyptian was permitted to kill an ibis. The reason why, states the law, is that the gods appear to them in the form of ibises.[423]

Of these mythical utterances concerning the gods, Aristotle says, 'if one were to take separately the first one' – that what we call first substances and gods were also regarded by our forefathers as gods – 'one would hold that it is divinely expressed' (1074b8–10). And just as in all likelihood when arts and sciences have oftentimes perished in floods (*kataklusmos*) some remnants were left,[424] from which again the arts and sciences were rediscovered as far as possible, so also with regard to the belief that ancient peoples held concerning the gods (they held that gods exist), some remnants of this belief have survived up to the present. But from these sorts of remnants, he says, and from our forefathers' judgement this alone is clear to us, namely, that they too thought that gods exist (cf. 1074b10–14).

# [Chapter 9]

[**1074b15** The issues concerning the intellect involve certain puzzles.[425] For while it seems to be the most divine of things that are evident, the question of how it can be this sort of thing involves certain difficulties. For if it is thinks of nothing, in what does its dignity consist? It would rather be like someone asleep. And if it thinks but something else is dominant over it (for what is its substance is not this, the act of thinking, but potentiality), it would not be the best substance. For it is because it thinks that it is worthy of honour.

1074b21 Further, whether its substance is an intellect or an act of thinking, of what does it think? For either [it thinks] of itself or of something else; and if [it thinks] of something else, it is either always of the same thing or something different. Does it make any difference, then, whether it thinks of what is noble or of a random object? Or is it too absurd for it to be cognizing about certain objects? It is clear, therefore, that it thinks of what is most divine and honourable, and that it does not change; for change [would be] for the worse, and this would be already a sort of movement.

1074b28 First, then, if it is not an act of thinking but a potentiality, it is reasonable [to suppose] that the continuousness of the act of thinking is toilsome for it. Next, it is clear that there would be something else more honourable than the intellect, namely, the object of its thinking. For thinking and the act of thinking will belong even to one who is thinking of the worst object. Hence, if this ought to be avoided (since there are also some objects which it is better not to see than to see), the act of thinking would not be the best thing. So, it is of itself that it thinks, since it is the most excellent object, and the act of thinking is an act of thinking of an act of thinking.]

'The issues concerning the intellect' which is highly honourable[426] and first, Aristotle says, 'involve certain puzzles'. For it is evident[427] that this sort of intellect is the most divine thing of all and the best; and 'what state it is in' and how it carries on (*diagein*) in the best way 'involves certain difficulties' (1074b15–17).

He shows the problem by means of dilemma: Does it, he asks, think or not think? If it does not think but rather is in a condition like someone who is sleeping (*katheudein*),[428] what other greater dignity (*semnos*) could it possess? (cf. 1074b16–19). But if it thinks, does the whole intellect also think of itself as a whole, or does some part of it think while a part does not think? [If the latter,] it is just as in the case of the soul of a human being; for it is not the whole soul that thinks but only a part of it, namely, what is called the intellect. If, therefore, it thinks in this way, it is not the whole substance of it that is best but that [part] by which it thinks, just as it is not the entire soul of a human being that is honourable but the intellect or rational (*logikos*) part by which we think (cf. 1074b20–1). But [the statement that] its entire substance is not best is absurd.

'And if it thinks', Aristotle says, but 'something else is dominant (*kurios*) over it' (1074b18–19) – that is, if it thinks but its whole substance is not intellect, but something else is dominant over its thinking, just as is also the case with us (for it is not the soul but the intellect that is the cause and is dominant over our thinking) – if, then, something else is what is dominant[429] over the intellect's thinking ('for this, its substance, is not the act of thinking'[430] (1074b19–20), that is to say: for its substance cannot be an act of thinking and intellect, if indeed it is not its whole substance that thinks but only a part), it would not be its substance that is the best, but that in virtue of which it thinks will be the best. And the conclusion of the argument is as follows: if the intellect thinks of nothing, what other greater dignity could it possess? For nothing is more dignified than the act of thinking and contemplating. And if it thinks, while its whole substance is not the act of thinking and intellect, but something else is dominant over its thinking (for its entire substance cannot be intellect, if indeed it is not the whole[431] that thinks but it thinks only in some respect), if, then, these things are so, the first intellect would not be the best substance, which is quite impossible. So what this followed from is also impossible, namely, that it is not the whole that thinks and that its whole substance is not intellect.

Further, Aristotle says, if its whole substance, as has been proven, thinks and it is intellect or the act of thinking, of what does it think? 'For' it thinks 'either of itself or of something else'. And 'if' it thinks of 'something else', it is either 'always' the same thing, or now one thing and at another time 'something else'[432] (1074b21–3). And if it is at another time something else, are the objects of which it thinks at different times all good, or must we suppose that it also thinks of random and evil objects (*phaulos*), and does it make no difference whether it thinks of evil objects or even the contraries of these? We must therefore suppose these things, or else we have to say that just as in our case it is 'absurd' and nobody who lives well will bring himself to 'cognize (*dianoeisthai*) about certain things' (1074b23–5), for example, in the case of fornication how to fornicate (*porneuein*) well, so it will be most impious (*asebês*) to say that the most divine and best substance cognizes about random and evil objects. It is clear, therefore, that it thinks no evil; rather, it thinks of the most divine and most honourable object. But the intellect itself is most divine and most honourable; hence it thinks of itself, and it does not change from thinking of itself to start thinking of something else as well. For if it changes from the beholding (*periôpê*) of itself, it will think of anything altogether better (*kreitton*) or worse (*kheiros*); but there is not anything better than it; so it remains that is worse. And this is a movement and withdrawal (*ekstasis*) from its own⁴³³ best way of carrying on (cf. 1074b25–7). This is confirmed by what happens with human beings. For good human beings, when they think of evil objects, become worse than they were as a result of such an act of thinking. This is also confirmed by the fact that they feel regret (*metamelesthai*), and one feels regret when one has become bad.

After saying above (1074b19–20) that its substance is an intellect and act of thinking, Aristotle now confirms this by saying: 'first, if' its substance is 'not an act of thinking' and intellect and it is not substantial (*ousiousthai*) in so far as it is an intellect and act of thinking, 'but is a potentiality'⁴³⁴ of intellect by which the intellect can think (for the intellect is one thing and its potentiality is another, just as a colour is one thing and the potentiality by which the colour can be seen is another), if, then, it is a potentiality of intellect, and it has been proven that it is continuously and always thinking, 'the continuousness of the act of thinking (*to sunekhes tês noêseôs*)' will be 'toilsome (*epiponos*) for it'⁴³⁵ (1074b28–9). For if it is substantial in so far as it is intellect and an act of thinking, the continuousness of the act of thinking will not be toilsome for it, just as being human is not toilsome either for a human being, due to the fact that it is substantial in so far as it is human; but continuously walking (*badizein*) is toilsome for a human being because it does not have substance in so far as it is walking. Therefore, just as in the case of a human being, it will also hold in the case of the first intellect, and the continuousness of the act of thinking will not be toilsome for it, if it is an intellect and act of thinking.⁴³⁶ But how will the continuous act of thinking be toilsome for our intellect if it is substantial in so far as it is intellect? Rather, our intellect is not an actual intellect the way the first intellect is, but is [only] potential. First, then, Aristotle says, if [the first intellect] is not an intellect [in actuality] but a potentiality, the continuousness of the act of thinking will be toilsome. In addition, the first intellect will not be the object of value (*timios*), but rather [the thing of] which it thinks whereby it is brought from potentiality into actuality.⁴³⁷ For that which completes and brings what is potential into actuality is of greater value that that which is completed (cf. 1074b29–30).

The words 'for, also, thinking and the act of thinking will belong even to one who thinks of the worst object' (1074b31–2) are stated elliptically, I think, in that 'further' (*eti*) is omitted, so that there is the beginning of another argument that the first cause is not a potentiality. Hence, 'for, also' (*kai gar*) is in my view equivalent to 'further' (*eti*),[438] so that the entire phrase is as follows: further, 'thinking and the act of thinking will belong even to one who thinks of the worst object' (1074b32). And the proof proceeds on the claim (*axiôma*) that for contraries there is the same potentiality. Aristotle would then be saying: further, if its substance is not an act of thinking and an intellect but a potentiality, and contraries have one and the same potentiality, then to the same first cause which thinks of the noblest objects will belong the act of thinking, or rather the thinking of the worst objects, which is quite absurd. 'Hence' if thinking of the worst objects 'ought to be avoided'[439] (for it is better not to think of these things, just as not seeing the most shameful (*aiskhros*) objects is better than seeing them), then, since from the claim that the first cause is a potentiality it follows that it thinks of evil objects, which is impious, the first and most divine and best substance will not be a potentiality (cf. 1074b32-3). For in the phrase 'the act of thinking would not be the most divine and best thing' (1074b33), the term 'the act of thinking' [has been written] instead of 'potentiality'.[440] So, [the first] intellect is also not a potentiality, and it thinks of itself as the best object. If, then, being an act of thinking it thinks of itself, or rather of the act of thinking, it is[441] also the act of thinking of an act of thinking.[442] Or rather, it, that which thinks (*to nooun*), is it, the object of thinking (*to nooumenon*) (cf. 1074b33-5).[443]

> **1074b35** Evidently, however, knowledge and perception, and opinion, and cognition are always of something else, and are of themselves [only] in passing. [Further, if thinking and being thought of are different, in virtue of which of them does excellence belong to it? For being an act of thinking is not the same as being an object of thinking.
> 1074b38 Or is knowledge in some cases the thing: in cases of productive [knowledge], without matter, is it the substance or essence, while in cases of theoretical [knowledge] is the account, the thing, also the act of thinking? Since, then, the object of thinking and the intellect are not different in the case of things that do not possess matter, they will be the same, that is, the act of thinking will be one with the object of thinking.]

Having stated that the best and most divine object is an act of thinking, since the act of thinking is necessarily related to intelligible objects in the same way that perception and knowledge are related to perceptible objects and knowable (*epistêtos*) objects, Aristotle considers the following objection based on this which could be raised against what he has said: if indeed knowledge is of something else and not of itself (for instance, the art of healing is of health and not of itself; for it always studies what health is and how it could come to be, but accidentally it sometimes also studies itself, for example, that art of healing is an art concerning those who are healthy (*hugieinos*) or diseased (*nosôdês*) or neither of these), and similarly perception is of perceptible objects and opinion is of opinable objects (*doxastos*), then, in these cases, if the most divine and best cause is the act of thinking, it would be of something else and not of itself (cf. 1074b35-6). Aristotle conjoins another puzzle with this one and solves the second by means of the first.

The second puzzle is as follows: 'if thinking is one thing and being thought of is another'[444] (1074b36-7) (for thinking is infallibly grasping (*aptaistos katalêpsis*) the intelligible object, and being thought of consists in the object of thinking being grasped by that which thinks), and the first intellect is itself that which thinks and is itself the object of thinking, 'in virtue of which of them does excellence' and the best belong 'to it' (1074b37), in virtue of thinking or in virtue of being thought? 'For being an act of thinking is not the same as being an object of thinking' (1074b38), that is, thinking and being thought of are not the same; hence, it follows that enquiry is reasonable.

After saying these things, Aristotle solves the first puzzle by stating that 'in some cases knowledge' and the knowable object are the same (1074b38-1075a1). For instance, the art of housebuilding is nothing other than the form of a house, and the art of healing, similarly, is nothing other than the form of health.[445] And if this is so, and if the most divine and best thing is an act of thinking, the latter will be the same as the object of thinking. And he adds 'in some cases' on account of composite objects. For housebuilding is not the same as the entire house, namely, this particular house composed of bricks and timbers, but it is the same as its form which is thought of separately from the matter. Hence, on this basis, the second puzzle is solved, which he tacitly passed over since its solution was already obvious. For if the first intellect is itself the act of thinking and the object of thinking, excellence will belong to it in virtue of both: in virtue of thinking and in virtue of being thought of. 'In some cases', then, he says, 'knowledge' is 'the thing' (*pragma*) and 'the knowable'; and he adds what sort of knowable object is the same as knowledge: 'in cases of productive [knowledge], without matter, [it is] substance' (1075a1-2); that is, the substance or the form without matter[446] is the same as knowledge. (And using the word 'knowledge' (*epistêmê*) he refers to housebuilding and similar cases of productive knowledge[447] (*poiêtikê*).) But 'in cases of theoretical (*theôrêtikê*) knowledge', for example, geometry, arithmetic, and the like, it is 'the account' (and he adds what the account is), 'the object and the act of thinking' are the same[448] (1075a2–3). For the act of thinking that the moon is eclipsed (*ekleipein*) is the same as the cause in virtue of which the eclipse occurs, and the cause of the eclipse is the same as the eclipse; hence, the act of thinking of the eclipse is the same as the eclipse.[449]

After saying these things, by way of conclusion Aristotle adds: 'since, then, the object of thinking and the intellect are not different in the case of things that do not possess matter, they will be the same' (1075a3–4). This is equivalent to saying: in the case of objects that are intelligible in the chief sense, which are immaterial and existing by themselves, the intellect and the object of thinking are not different but are the same; for the objects that are intelligible in the chief sense, as was said in *On the Soul*,[450] are intellects and the intellects are intelligible objects. If this is so, then 'also the act of thinking will be one with the object of thinking'[451] (1075a4–5), that is, it will be the same. And he adds to these things in addition another puzzle, saying:

> **1075a5** Further, it remains to enquire[452] (*zêtêzein*) if the object of thinking is composite; for [if so, it] would undergo change in the parts of the whole. [Or is everything that does not possess matter indivisible? Just as, therefore,[453] the human intellect (or at least the intellect of composite things) is in a certain condition in a certain time (for it does not possess excellence in this or that, but it is in a certain whole that it possesses the best, which is something else), so the act of thinking is in this condition, being itself of itself, throughout the entire duration.]

And Aristotle means: if every object of thinking (for the statement concerning every object of thinking must be understood as universal) is composite, it is not in the present or in a very brief time that the intellect will think of the object of thinking, but it could change from thinking this to thinking that with a part of itself, and this will come about through a temporal interval; for in one time it will think this with a part and in another time that (cf. 1075a5–6). And he solves [the puzzle] by saying that 'everything that does not possess matter' (that is, the intelligible objects) is 'indivisible (*adiairetos*)' (1075a7) or partless and that there is no composition of them.

In addition to these things, Aristotle tells also how the first intellect thinks of itself, and he says that it does not do so through time, which would be to say that in one part of time a part of it thinks this, and in another [part of time, a part of it thinks] that (for it would then be divisible into parts), but being partless[454] it thinks of itself in the partless and – if it is permissible (*themis*) to say so – indivisible present. For 'just as', he says, 'the human intellect (*anthrôpinos nous*)' (or if we do not wish to refer to it as 'the human intellect', let us refer more universally to the intellect 'of composite things'),[455] 'just as, therefore,[456] the human intellect or[457] the intellect of composite things is in a certain time' (1075a7–8), for instance, when it acts and undergoes the thrice-most-blessed (*trismakaristos*) experience (for then the human intellect is 'not in this' part of time 'or in that' thinking of this or that [part] of the best and grasping (*ephaptesthai*) it as far as it is capable of having grasped it; for otherwise the first cause would also be divisible into parts; but it thinks of itself 'in a certain whole', that is, in a partless and indivisible present moment), so through its entire duration[458] the first intellect itself thinks of itself partlessly and atemporally.

Aristotle states sufficiently in the third book of the treatise *On the Soul*[459] how the actual intellect thinks of the object that is intelligible in the chief sense. The human intellect, he says, does not, then, possess excellence, the best way of carrying on or the act of thinking (that is, the contact with and contemplation) of the best and first intellect – since the first intellect is clearly another intellect subsisting apart from the human intellect.[460] So the human intellect does not possess this best way of carrying on in time and through time but it does so 'in a certain whole' (1075a8–9). And by 'a certain whole'[461] he means the indivisible present, which is a limit of time but is not time [itself]. For since the divine intellect is a sort of form of the human intellect, whenever [the human intellect] has the potential to grasp it, and every form supervenes (*epigignesthai*) in the indivisible present moment,[462] it is clear that the knowledge (*gnôsis*) of and contact with the first intellect supervenes in the human intellect in [one and] the same present moment.

## [Chapter 10]

**1075a11** We must investigate also in which way the nature of the whole possesses the good and the best, [whether it is as something separated and itself by itself, or as its order. Or is it in both ways, like an army? For its excellence is in its order and it is also the general, and more so he [is], since he is not due to the order but it is due to him. And all things are co-ordinated in a way, but not in a similar way, even swimming things, winged things, and plants; and they are not in such a way that one thing has no relation to any other, but [they are related] in some way. For all things are co-ordinated in relation to one thing – but as in a household the free persons are least at liberty to act haphazardly, but all or most [of their actions] are ordered, while the slaves and beasts are able to do a little for the common [end] and much of what they do is haphazard; for that is the sort of principle that is the nature of each of them (I mean, for example, that it is necessary for all things to have become dispersed), and there are thus other things which they all have in common with a view to the whole.]

715,1 What Aristotle is enquiring about is whether, since 'the nature of the whole' (1075a11) (he means by 'the whole' this perceptible cosmos)[463] is good and best, one must say that the cause in virtue of which this cosmos is good and best is something different (that is, a certain substance and nature which exists by itself) or that it is the order itself in virtue of which it is ordered, so that the
5 good and the best of this cosmos is its order.[464] And he answers by saying, 'or it is in both ways' (1075a13). For one ought to say that the good and best of the universe is twofold: both its order (for it is also due to this that it possesses the good and the best) and the first intellect; for it is due to the latter most of all that it possesses the noble and the best.

And Aristotle readily makes clear what is meant through an example. For
10 just as, he says, an army possesses excellence in its order and this sort of order is good and best for it, but 'the general (*stratêgos*) is also' what is the excellence and good of an army (*strateuma*)[248] and 'he is even more' its excellence since the order of the army is due to the general rather than the general being due to the order (1075a14–15), so, too, the excellent, the good, and the best belong
15 to the universe due to its order, but it is also due to the first intellect, through whom the order of the universe exists.

After saying these things, Aristotle says devoutly (*theophilôs*) and philosophically that nothing that exists is so in vain but 'all things are co-ordinated' (1075a16) and they contribute together, even if many of them are unknown (*agnoein*) to us, to the fulfilment (*sumplêrôsis*) and culmination (*apartismos*) of one single cosmos – that is, to its nobility, best condition, and excellence. And he recounts what things have been co-ordinated towards the fulfilment of the whole: winged things (*ptênos*), swimming things (*plôtês*), plants, and so forth. But even if all things in every way make a contribution together, still they do so 'not' all 'in a similar way' (1075a16–17) but some more so and others less. Presumably, however, even if some of them contribute a great deal[466] and others [only] a little to the fulfilment of the whole, still they do not do this in such a way 'that one thing' does not have any commonality (*koinônia*) 'in relation to another' (1075a17–18), but rather there is something common to them all: either both substratum and shape, or substratum alone, or neither substratum nor shape but [only] colour. For example, the imperishable and divine bodies have neither substratum nor shape or form in common with bodies subject to generation, though perhaps they have brightness (*lampron*) in common, even if their brightness is not altogether similar to the brightness found in objects subject to generation; but they do have both form and substratum in common with each other. Things subject to generation, on the other hand, have proximate matter in common [only] with certain others, whereas all of them have formless matter in common with all.

These things,[467] therefore, as Aristotle says, 'are co-ordinated' in relation to some one thing, namely, one nature and fulfilment of the whole, 'but not' all of them 'in a similar way'[468] (1075a16). But [it is] 'as in a household' or in a commonwealth (*politeia*)[469] [where] 'free persons (*eleutheros*)[470] are' in no way 'at liberty' (*exeinai*) (that is, allowed (*ephienai*) and granted) to do this or not to do it (1075a19–20), though they are at liberty to practise healing (*iatreuein*) or serve as soldiers (*strateuesthai*) and to do all the things that generally contribute principally to the maintenance of the polis, of if not all things (for there are some things, such as street cleaning and the like, which freemen would not do), still they are at liberty at any rate to do most things [of this sort]. As for 'slaves (*andrapodon*) and beasts' (rather, non-rational animals), the things done by them are small and contribute little to the maintenance of the polis, but most of the time they 'act haphazardly' (*tunchanein*)[471] (1079a21–2). That is, their actions that take up little of their time contribute also little to the maintenance of the polis, while most of their time they are acting but none of their actions are beneficial for the maintenance of the polis. For at that time[472] slaves (*doulos*) were not at liberty to serve as soldiers or administer the laws or practise philosophy (*philosophein*) or do anything else that contributed greatly to the maintenance of the commonwealth, but [only] to chop wood (*xulotomein*) or cook (*magireuein*) or perform similar tasks. Just as it is, then, with these persons, so it is also with things that contribute to the nature of the whole, some contribute a great deal to the nature and maintenance of the whole, others less.

After taking the commonwealth as an example, Aristotle shifts the discussion from this to the nature of the whole and states, 'this is the sort of principle that is the nature of each of them'[473] (1075a22–3), that is, the nature and principle of the things that contribute together to the nature of the whole. And now he is not speaking about all things without qualification but about things subject to generation and perishing (*en phthorai*). Such, then, is the nature and principle of these things; and as for the sort [of nature and principle], he says, 'I mean, for example, that it is necessary that all things come to having been dispersed (*diakrinein*)' (1075a23–4), that is, it is necessary for all things subject to generation (for it is concerning these things, as was said, that he is now speaking) to come to having been dispersed, or rather for one thing to come to be from another.[474] For the nature of things subject to generation came together into this, and this is common to them: all things come to be from all things, compounds from elements and, in a different way, elements from compounds. Hence, it is clear that all things subject to generation have in common their coming-to-be from one another.

After saying that all things subject to generation have a commonality in respect of their matter and their coming-to-be from one another, Aristotle adds, 'and there are other things which they all have in common with a view to the whole' (1075a24–5), that is, not only do they have a commonality with respect to their coming-to-be from one another for the fulfilment of the whole, but also with respect to other things such as colours, shapes, and magnitudes. For all these contribute together to the nature of the whole; for without magnitude and shape no perceptible object exists. In this way, then, our teacher[475] (*kathêgemôn*) has explained the present passage. But perhaps in the passage 'it is necessary that all things come to have been dispersed' (1075a23–4) the words 'all things' should be understood to refer not only to things subject to generation, but rather to all things, even, I affirm, the bodies that are divine and capable of circular motion themselves, so that the phrase would mean: it is necessary for all things, both those that are subject to generation and those that are capable of circular motion, to be dispersed, or rather to establish the whole cosmos, so that 'have been dispersed' is used in place of 'establish' (*sustênai*). For thus Anaxagoras said that Intellect, by dispersing [collections of] things with similar parts from one another, established the universe.[476]

And the words 'and there are thus other things which they all have in common with a view to the whole' (1075a24–5) would be a continuation of the example of the commonwealth,[477] as if he said: just as in the case of the establishment of the commonwealth all things have something in common with one another, so there are also certain other things which have something in common and assist one another in the fulfilment of the whole, as in the case of a house some people build it, others carry clay, still other finish timbers, but all of them do all these things with a view to producing the wholeness of the house.

> **1075a25** The impossible and absurd consequences for those who say otherwise – [as well as what sorts of things are said by those who speak in a more refined manner, and what sorts of statements involve the fewest puzzles] – ought not be overlooked.[478] [For all of them make everything from contraries; but they do not speak rightly of 'all things' or 'from contraries', nor do they say how there will be things out of the contraries in which the contraries are present. For contraries are unaffected by each other. For us, however, this is reasonably solved by means of a third thing. Others, however, make one of the contraries matter, like those who make the unequal matter for the equal or the many for the one. But this [puzzle] is solved in the same manner, since the matter which is one is not the contrary of anything.
>
> 1075a34 Further, all things outside of the one will participate in evil; for the bad itself is one of the [contrary] elements. Others say that the good and the bad are not principles; and yet the good is most of all a principle in all things. And others say rightly that this is a principle but not how the good is a principle, whether it is as an end or as a mover or as a form.
>
> 1075b1 Empedocles also speaks absurdly; for instance, he makes Love the good, and this is a principle also as mover, since it brings things together, and as matter, since it is a part of the mixture. Now, even if the same thing happens to be a principle both as matter and as mover, still the being, at least, of these is not the same. In virtue of which is Love [the principle]? It is absurd, also, for Hate to be imperishable, and this is itself the nature of the bad.
>
> 1075b8 Anaxagoras makes the good a principle that imparts movement, since the Intellect imparts movement. But it imparts movement for the sake of

something, so that [the latter] is different, except in the way *we* speak of it; for the art of healing is in a way health. But it is absurd not to posit also the contrary to the good, that is, to the Intellect. But all those who speak of the contraries do not make use of the contraries, unless one fine-tunes [their statements].

1075b13 And why some things are perishable and others imperishable, nobody says. For they derive all the things that are from the same principles. Further, some derive the things that are from that which is not, while others, so that they will not be compelled to do this, make all things one. Further, why there will always be coming-to-be and what the cause of coming-to-be is, nobody says. And for those who posit two principles there is necessarily another principle more dominant than these. And for those who posit the Forms there is yet another more dominant principle. For why did things participate or why do they participate [in the Forms]?

1075b20 And for other [thinkers] there is necessarily something contrary to wisdom, that is, the most honourable knowledge, but not for us. For that which is first has no contrary at all, since all the contraries possess matter, and they exist in potentiality. However, the contrary, ignorance, [is opposed] to the contrary, but that which is first has no contrary.]

After expressing his own opinions, which he has stated in all of his other treatises, Aristotle now sets out concisely what the others have said, stating, 'it ought not to be overlooked' what absurdities and impossibilities (*adunatos*) result for those who stated the matter differently from the way we do. And he sets out the things that are said by them. 'For all of them', he says, 'make everything from contraries', though they are not right to say either that 'all things' have come to be (for not all things have come to be) or that [they came to be] 'from contraries' (for not all things have contraries; for instance, the body capable of circular motion has no contrary)[479] (1075a28–9). Hence, in as much as some things have come to be and others have not come to be, these [thinkers] did not judge rightly when they said that all things have come to be. Likewise, since some things have contraries and some do not, they went wrong when they declared that contrariety (*enantiotês*) belongs to everything. But even with regard to those things that have a contrary, they do not say *how* contraries come to be from a contrary (cf. 1075a29–30). For instance, whiteness (*leukotês*) does not become blackness (*melania*), nor is whiteness at all affected by blackness.[480] 'For us,' Aristotle says, this question 'is solved' by positing a third thing, the matter [or] substratum (1075a31–2).

'But others', such as Plato, made 'one of the contraries' the substratum of the other. For he made the bad and the unequal (and by 'the bad' and 'the unequal (*to anison*)' he meant the matter) a substratum for the other contraries, respectively the good and the equal (*to ison*) (by 'the good' and 'the equal' alluding again to the Form). Since Plato at times called matter bad[481] and at other times unequal and at still other times many, and, similarly, he called the Form at times good and at other times equal and at still other times one,[482] having stated that they make the unequal the substratum for the equal, Aristotle adds 'or the many for the one' (1075a33). But not even these, he says, have stated the manner in which a contrary underlies a contrary. And he reproaches them for saying that matter is a contrary; for not the matter but the privation is contrary to the form with which it coexists. Hence, they are correct when they say that matter underlies form, but their statement that it is contrary to form is not correct; for contraries are never capable of coexisting.

And since Aristotle says that matter is both more[483] and most of all what underlies, speaking on his own behalf, he states: but 'for us is solved' this sort of absurdity (cf. 1075a31,35). For even if we say that matter is what underlies, still we state that it is not contrary to anything, but the things that contend over it are form and privation.[484] And another text is transmitted which is as follows: 'and since one matter[485] ...', which would be to say: and since the first matter is not contrary to anything (for it is without quality (*apoios*)), but earth and fire and the intermediates,[486] which are the most proximate matter, possess contrariety with one another.

Further, Aristotle says, if the bad underlies and everything derives from the bad, then everything will participate in the bad[487] and nothing will be good except the One, which he has said exists in virtue of itself (cf. 1075a34-5). But the followers of Plato made the good and the bad principles, while 'others', such as the Pythagoreans, object saying that the good is not a principle[488] (1075a36-7). And the sense in which the Pythagoreans did not want the good and best to be a principle, has been stated in the present book where we explicated the passage 'those, however, who suppose, as the Pythagoreans and Speusippus do, that the noble and best does not reside in the principle' (699,28-37 on 1072b30-2).[489] But others,[490] Aristotle says, when they say that the good is a principle, speak rightly; however, although when they say that the good is a principle, they do not define it and say whether it is final, efficient, or formal (cf. 1075a38-b1).

Aristotle, moreover, accuses Empedocles of 'absurdly' (*atopôs*) making Love a principle. For when Empedocles speaks of Love as bringing [things] together and capable of producing the Sphere, it appears that he wants it to be an efficient cause.[491] On the other hand, by making it a part of the mixture and of the Sphere, Empedocles indicates that he understands it to be a material cause (*hulikon aition*) (1075b1–4). After establishing this, Aristotle states: even if we were to agree that Love belongs to the substratum both as matter and as mover, nonetheless it would be entirely different in account.[492] And if this is so, will it be because Love imparts movement or because it is matter? Empedocles ought then to have said in what respect the being of Love belongs to it (cf. 1075b4–7). Besides if Love is, as Empedocles intends, the good, then Hate will be bad;[493] for if the former [i.e. good and bad] are contraries, the latter [i.e. Love and Hate] will be too;[494] but if this is so, how can he say that 'Hate is imperishable' (1075b6–7)? For after Love has come together along with all things and made the Sphere, then necessarily Hate perishes. For Hate and Love will not exist simultaneously. It is false, therefore, to say that Hate is imperishable as Empedocles maintains.[495]

Anaxagoras made the good, or rather the Intellect, the principle capable of bringing about movement.[496] But since the mover imparts movement for the sake of something, there will be something for the sake of which the Intellect imparts movement; but then let him say what this is (cf. 1075b8–9). Unless, Aristotle says, Anaxagoras speaks as we do[497] (1075b9). We say that the healing art is in a way the form of health,[498] [and] when it brings about a certain movement for the sake of health, it is for the sake of itself that it brings about this movement. If, therefore, Anaxagoras also speaks in this way concerning the Intellect, namely, that the mover and that for the sake of which it imparts movement are the same, and for this reason everything that moves that which is moved is [itself] moved[499] for the sake of it [i.e. the Intellect], in speaking this way he would be speaking like a reasonable person. But Aristotle accuses Anaxagoras of another 'absurd' claim when he says that Anaxagoras does not make the bad contrary to it, although he says[500] that the Intellect is good; for when one of the contraries is present it is necessary for the other to exist (cf. 1075b9–11).

To these [thinkers] in turn Aristotle also adds another complaint (*enklêma*) common to them all, saying: if one 'is not negligent (*rhathumein*)'[501] (1075b12) or hesitant to go over their statements but considers them accurately, he will find that they make all the principles of which they speak contraries, although they do not use them in [explaining] the coming-to-be of things but turn instead to something else (cf. 1075b12). And in many ways he rebuked them for this and he often attained the requisite clarity. Further, those who speak of principles and generate (*gennan*) all things from the principle that they posit, such as those who posit water as a principle and say that both heaven and earth and all things have come to be from it, have neglected to state the cause 'why some' of these things 'are perishable and others imperishable' (1075b13). For it was necessary to say why among things that are from the same principles some are perishable and others imperishable. Now, because Aristotle made the heavenly things from a distinct [principle] (namely, from the fifth body) but things subject to generation from other [principles], he was also able to say why some of them were perishable and others imperishable. But the other [thinkers] could not, because they posited the same substratum for everything.

Further, Aristotle says, other [thinkers] such as the followers of Hesiod[502] generate everything from not-being; but let them say why. And those such as the followers of Parmenides, in order not to concede this (for it is a common opinion of all natural theorists that nothing comes to be in any way from not-being), say that being is one and ungenerated. But, also, why there is coming-to-be and what is the cause of everlasting coming-to-be, nobody says[503] (cf. 1075b14–17).

After saying these things Aristotle states in reference both to 'those who posit two principles', such as the contraries, and to those who posit the Forms, that these [principles of theirs] do not suffice for [explaining why] things are in the state they are, but that 'it is necessary' to posit 'another principle more dominant than these'[504] (1075b17–18), which he has called the highly honourable intellect. For everything is turning about from it and to it.[505] And he lays down the reason why it is necessary to suppose that there is another more dominant principle, saying: for since the things here [in the perceptible realm] come to be by participation (*methexis*) in the Forms according to those who speak of them,[506] how, he asks, will matter participate in them, unless there is something else more dominant which moves both of them, namely, the matter and the emanation (as they call it) that comes to be from the Form in the matter (cf. 1075b19–20)? For if certain emanations which have emanated (*aporrhein*) from the Forms and combined with the matter become the things here, then it is altogether necessary that there is a mover, the matter to receive the emanation, and the emanation to be combined with the matter.

'And for other' theologians[507] who say that the contraries are principles, 'there is necessarily according to them something contrary to philosophy[508] and the most honourable' and firmest (*bebaios*) 'knowledge' (1075b20-1). For if knowledge is the same, as was said a little before (cf. 1074b38, 1075a1; 713,17-37), as the knowable object, if there is a contrary to the principle, that is, the object that is knowable in the chief sense, it will also be [contrary] to knowledge. But these [thinkers] faced the absurd consequence that there is something contrary to wisdom, whereas we, Aristotle says, do not face it in the least. For nothing is contrary to the first cause, the highly honoured intellect; hence, nor is it [contrary] to the knowledge of it.

And Aristotle has concisely given the reason why nothing is contrary to the first cause, when he said, 'all the contraries possess matter' and the contrary is in matter and potential (1075b22). For the white is potentially the black (*melas*). Hence, if indeed there is a contrary to the first principle,[509] but no contrary exists by itself rather than in a substratum or in matter, and the first principle, being most immaterial and an actuality, is also without any share of potentiality[510] (cf. 687,19-22), then there could be no contrary to the first principle. Hence, neither will ignorance (*agnoia*) be the contrary of knowledge concerning [the first principle]; for if ignorance is contrary to this sort of knowledge, the object of ignorance will also be the contrary of the first principle[511] (cf. 1075b23-4).

**1075b24** Further, unless[512] there are other things beyond perceptible objects, there will not be a principle or order [or coming-to-be or heavenly objects; but a principle will always have a principle, as alleged by all the theologians and natural scientists.

1075b27 But whether Forms or numbers are [principles], they will be the causes of nothing; or if not, at least not of movement. Further, how from things without magnitude will there be what has magnitude and is continuous? For number will not produce a continuous thing: neither as mover nor as form.

1075b30 Neither, however, will any of the contraries be what is [essentially] capable of producing [an effect] and of imparting movement; for it would be possible for it not to exist. But, then, producing [an effect] is posterior to potentiality. So the things that exist would not be everlasting. But they are. So one of these [alternatives] must be rejected. And how this is so has been stated.

1075b34 Further, as to what it is by which the numbers are one, or the soul and the body, or in general the form and the thing, nobody says anything. Nor is it possible to say unless it is, as we say, that the mover does it. And those who say that the mathematical number is first and that thus there is always another successive substance and that there are different principles for each [substance], make the substance of the universe episodic (for one substance contributes nothing to the other by existing or not existing) and they posit many principles. But the things that exist do not wish to be governed badly. 'The sovereignty of many is not good; [there is] one sovereign.']

It is not in passing that Aristotle now asserts this, but since he is about to contradict (*antilegein*) the Pythagoreans and Plato, he establishes first of all that there are intelligible substances, and thus subsequently enquires into what [these are] and whether they are the Ideas of Plato or the Pythagorean numbers. If, then, there is not, Aristotle says, a principle that is intelligible, incorporeal, and [existing] in its own right, 'there will not be order and coming-to-be' (cf. 1075b25). And why do I say [only] that there will not be *coming-to-be*? Nor will there be the heavenly (*ouranios*) objects themselves (cf. 1075b26), which in *On the Heavens* have been shown to be ingenerable and imperishable.[513] But if there is always going to be something, a principle will have a principle and the latter will have another and so on without limit, as the theologians[514] say (cf. 1075b26–7). For if Heracles[515] has as its principle [i.e. source] Zeus, which has Cronus, which has another [principle],[516] or again if the Forms are the principles of the things here [i.e. perceptible particulars], and the numbers are principles of the Forms, and the Dyad (*duas*) and the One are principles of the numbers, the progression will go on without limit.[517]

Besides, if the Ideas are principles, as Plato says, or numbers, as the Pythagoreans say, they will be the 'causes of nothing', as is proven Large *Alpha* [*Metaphysics* 1] and will be proven in the following two books [i.e. Books 13 and 14].[518] 'But if not . . .', that is, if one were to say that it is false to claim that Forms and numbers are not causes of anything because they are, one should concede this point to him for now, but [still maintain that] Forms and numbers will in no way be causes 'of movement'.[519] After conceding, then, that the numbers are causes, Aristotle asks: how 'from' numbers which are 'without magnitude' (*amegethos*)' and are mutually discrete[520] (*diorizein*) – 'will there be what has magnitude and is continuous? For number will not produce a continuous thing.' For it is impossible for a unit to be made continuous with a unit. And the phrase 'neither as mover nor as form' will be in place of: nevertheless number will be neither a moving cause nor a formal cause (1075b28–30).[521]

After saying that neither the Forms nor numbers are capable of imparting movement, Aristotle says that 'none of the contraries will be capable of producing [an effect] and of imparting movement' (1075b30–1), such as, say, the bad or the unequal. For a contrary is a potentiality and it has the potential to act, so that there was a time when it was not acting; for every actuality is posterior to a potentiality[522] (cf. 1075b31–3). When, therefore, it was not acting and or producing [anything], there were none of the things that exist, which [would be] impossible; for it has been proven that the things that exist are everlasting.[523] So the statement that the contrary is capable of producing contraries 'must be rejected' (1075b33). For since the contrary is a potentiality, as was said, it passes later into actuality. And it has been said, Aristotle states,[524] that potentiality is in a way prior to actuality (cf. 1075b34). For it was said that potentiality is prior to actuality in the case of one and the same thing, for instance, Socrates, but by no means for all cases (cf. 691, 27).

Further, Aristotle asks, in virtue of what are the numbers one, or what unifies three units and makes the number three or unifies the seven units to make the number seven, and similarly for the others[525] (cf. 1075b34). But,[526] also, what is it that unifies the soul with the body and makes them one? 'And in general', he says, what unifies the form and the thing? (I believe by 'thing' (*pragma*) he means the matter.) Further, then, how the form and the matter become one, 'nobody' says. 'Nor is it possible to say' (1075b35–6) if they make the Forms actual and [subsisting] by themselves, unless they were to say, as we say, that since the form does not subsist by itself but has the potential to supervene on the matter by means of a determinate movement of the matter, then whenever [the matter] is moved by that which moves it, it receives the form. For it is not necessary to enquire into how the roundness is one with the wax,[527] since it is not the roundness subsisting by itself that is united with the wax, but it supervenes by means of a determinate movement of the wax without existing by itself. But those who hold that the Forms also subsist by themselves cannot say how the matter (which was in another place) and the Form, having subsisted in separation from each other, came together, and one thing has come to be[528] out of them.

But the Pythagoreans too, Aristotle says, or also Plato,[529] who say that from the number three has come to be the plane (*epipedon*) and from it triangles and from them pyramids (*puramidês*) and from them fire, and again out of the [number] five[530] justice (*dikaiosunê*) and out of the unit the heaven and yet another thing out of something else, make the nature of things that exist 'episodic' (*epeisodiôdês*)[531] (1075b37–1076a1), that is, they say that nothing has anything in common with anything else but that [each thing] is foreign (*allotrioun*) [to every other]. Hence, if indeed fire, say, is foreign to earth in every respect and nothing is in common to them, whether fire exists or not, it makes no contribution (*sumballesthai*) to the existence of earth; and similarly also in the case of the other [elements] (1076a2). (For it is because *we* say that everything has something in common with everything in some respect that we say that one substance contributes to and co-operates in the existence of another substance.) But what does that which is from a principle differing in all respects from another, for instance, from the unit, contribute to that which is from another principle, for instance, from the triangle or cube (*kubos*)? [Nothing,] for[532] the unit and the cube have nothing in common.

Hence, since, in the affairs that are under our control, we fare badly whenever people do not co-operate with each other, this will also happen in the universe [at large]. Thus, because of this, the things that exist will be badly governed (*politeuein*), as well as because the Pythagoreans and their ilk posit many principles (cf. 1076a3). For wherever there is a multitude of rulers (*arkhos*) there is disorder, since the rule of many (*poluarkhia*) is the very same thing as disorder. And yet existing things are not ruled badly but in a manner that is ordered (*tetagmenôs*) and best. If, then, the rule of many is disorder and the cause of existing things being badly governed (cf. 1076a3–4), whereas the affairs under our control that involve mutual co-operation are not governed badly but in the best way, there must not be many principles.[533] For the sovereignty of many (*polukoiraniê*) is not good, but there is one sovereign (*koiranos*),[534] one principle, one god (cf. 1076a4). For the causes of the planetary [motions] are gods, but they depend on participation in, and on the will (*boulêma*) of, the first and most blessed intellect.

# Notes

## [Chapter 1]

1 [668,1] This is the title as it appears in commentary manuscript M. Although the author is not mentioned here, the discussion of Book 12 is part of the complete commentary on the *Metaphysics* attributed to Alexander of Aphrodisias. However, only the commentary on the first five books is regarded as his actual work. The heading for the first five books is 'commentary' (*hupomnêmata*), while for the last nine it is 'scholia' (*skholia*). Although the commentator on Book 12 is now thought by most scholars to be Michael of Ephesus, he is referred to in this work as 'Ps.-Alexander' for reasons discussed in Introduction §2.

2 Bracketed chapter headings mark divisions deriving from Bessarion's translation of the *Metaphysics* (1447–50) and commonly used by modern editors and translators. Ps.-Alexander's discussions sometimes overlap these divisions (e.g. see notes 44 and 242).

3 [668,4] Although the letter *lambda* would ordinarily represent the eleventh book of a treatise, in the special case of the *Metaphysics* it refers to Book 12, because Book 2, which was presumably added later, was called *Elatton* (Small) *Alpha*, to distinguish it from Book 1, which was called *Meizon* (Large) *Alpha*.

4 [668,4] In the commentary on Book 12 Aristotle is mentioned by name only occasionally (690,3; 691,30; 692,1; 701,9–10; 703,1; 704,20; 705,38; 706,12–13; 710,25; 717,29; 719,2), mainly to distinguish him from other thinkers. However, 'Aristotle' without brackets is added frequently throughout this translation for the sake of clarity.

5 [668,3] i.e the prime mover of the cosmos. As in this case more important terms are transliterated at their first occurrence, and thereafter only if the translation differs notably from that previously given. Noteworthy occurrences of these terms are listed in the Greek-English Index.

6 [668,6] These three principles are distinguished in *Phys.* 1.7, 191a8–12 and may be illustrated in connection with a statue: the bronze is its matter, its shape is its form, and the absence of this shape before it was moulded is the privation.

7 [668,9] Ps.-Alexander sees Book 12 as, in part, carrying out the programme of Book 3, which sets out a series of puzzles to be investigated in the following books.

The specific puzzle mentioned here is discussed at 3.4, 1000a5–1001a13 (subsequent line references are to the *Metaphysics* unless otherwise noted).

8 [668,15] The brief lemma preceding a section of the commentary is often, as in this case, a sentence fragment. This translation also adds in brackets additional material from the *Metaphysics* in order to provide the requisite context for Ps.-Alexander's commentary, which follows Aristotle's text almost line by line. For the sake of consistency and in order to minimize confusion, the translation of the lemma is generally made consistent with Ps.-Alexander's later citations and paraphrases. Passages where the lemmata diverge from the extant manuscripts of the *Metaphysics* (henceforth 'the Aristotle manuscripts' as distinguished from 'the commentary manuscripts') are discussed in the notes.

9 [668,16] 'Wisdom' (*sophia*) is the highest form of knowledge, as explained in *Nicomachean Ethics* 6.6–7. Knowledge is judgement concerning things that are universal and necessary. When knowledge of the things that are highest by nature is acquired by means of demonstration from the intellection (*nous*) of first principles, it is accounted wisdom (*sophia*, 1141b2–3). Ps.-Alexander assumes that wisdom is concerned with the first causes and principles of things, which Aristotle claims at *Metaph.* 1.1, 981b28–9. On the claim that substance is first of all the categories, see below at 669,1–21.

10 [668,17] By the 'first substance' Ps.-Alexander presumably refers to the prime mover (cf. 685,27). However, the distinction between first substance and second substance is absent from Aristotle's text here, which mentions only the contrast between substance and other categories (the distinction in *Cat.* 5 between primary and secondary substance does not seem relevant here). Nor is this distinction mentioned here by Alexander of Aphrodisias as paraphrased by Averroes (fr. 2F=*Tafsīr* 1406), though he does state earlier that Book 12 is concerned with 'the principles of the first substance which is absolutely real' (fr. 1F=*Tafsīr* 1394; tr. Genequand). The numbering of fragments with 'F' from Averroes follows Freudenthal 1884. In subsequent notes the latter commentator will be referred to as 'Alexander in Averroes' as distinguished from Ps.-Alexander (see Introduction, 3–4 for further discussion).

11 [668,20] The translation assumes that Ps.-Alexander understands *theôria* as simply 'investigation', although it is possible that he understands it as 'theoretical knowledge' (*theôretikê epistêmê*), equivalent to wisdom (cf. 1.1, 991b30–982a1).

12 [668,20] Clauses in quotation marks such as the foregoing are assumed to be citations of Aristotle's *Metaphysics* as indicated in Hayduck's edition (unless otherwise indicated). Important disagreements in the text as cited with the wording of the Aristotle manuscripts will be discussed in the notes.

13 [668,23] The reference is to *An. Post.* 2.2, 90a15. A lunar eclipse is defined as the privation of light from the moon as a result of the earth blocking light from the sun. Here the cause of the eclipse is mentioned in the definition. By recognizing the cause one is able to explain the other properties of the eclipse, including shape, colour, duration, periodicity, and so forth.

14 [669,2] The ten categories are listed in *Cat.* 4, 1b25–2a4 (cf. *Top.* 1.9, 103b22–3) and illustrated as follows: substance: man, horse; quantity: four-foot, five-foot; quality: white, grammatical; relative: double, half, larger; place: in the Lyceum, in the marketplace; time: yesterday, last year; position: lying, sitting; possession: being shod, being armoured; acting: cutting, burning; affection: being cut, being burnt. Manuscript L and Sepúlveda read 'nine' (*ennea*) instead of 'ten' (*deka*), perhaps understanding 'together with the nine (other) categories' (cf. 669,18 and see Salis n. 8).

15 [669,3] Ps.-Alexander understands *to pan* ('everything') to refer to the universe, that is, all of *perceptible* nature, or 'nature as a whole' (cf. 12.8, 1074b3). The term 'whole' (*holon*) implies that the universe possesses some sort of formal unity (cf. 10.1, 1052a22; 5.6, 1016b12; 12.10, 1075a11).

16 [669,7] Aristotle's argument takes the form of a constructive dilemma with a disjunctive premiss: either the universe exists as a sort of compound whole consisting of substance and the other categories, or it exists as a succession of categories, e.g. substance, quantity, quality, etc. (Quantity is 'first' only in the sense that it is the first among the non-substantial categories.) Ps.-Alexander fixes on the first horn of the dilemma (which he takes to reflect Aristotle's own view) and expounds it by means of the analogy of the whole consisting of Socrates and his accidental characteristics. In contrast, Alexander in Averroes remarks that in the second case, involving a succession of categories, one 'is even more inclined to believe that substance is the true existent' and he adds that Aristotle 'mentions the two views as a precaution, not because he believes in the first kind of priority' (fr. 3F=*Tafsīr* 1408; tr. Genequand). On the different interpretations of Aristotle's argument, see Berti 2016, 69–71.

17 [669,8] This reverses the order of quality before quantity found in the Aristotle manuscripts. On the priority of quantitative unity to qualitative see 611,27–612,7 on 10.1, 1053b4–6.

18 [669,9] The citation reads *ei kai*, commonly translated 'even if', meaning, perhaps, that even if the universe consists of successive parts, substance will be first. However, the Aristotle manuscripts read *kai gar ei ... kai ei* ('for both if ... and if').

19 [669,25] Regarding the placement of *haplôs* the commentary manuscripts disagree with the Aristotle manuscripts (which also disagree with each other). In terms of word order Ps.-Alexander's citation suggests that it modifies 'things that are' (*onta haplôs hôs eipein*) whereas that of EJ suggests that it modifies 'so to speak' (*onta hôs*

*eipein haplôs*). However, A[b] unequivocally implies that it modifies 'so to speak' (*onta hôs haplôs eipein*). The translation preserves the ambiguity.

20 [669,26] Following Ps.-Alexander, Jaeger and Bonitz read *hoion* ('for example') at 1069a22, since not all non-substances are qualities and movements. However, most editors read *allà* ('but') with the Aristotle manuscripts: 'but [they are] qualities and movements' (see Judson note on 1069a22).

21 [669,31] This argument that substance is prior 'in being' to items in the other categories is easier to follow in the Greek. The Greek verb *einai* (like the English 'to be') has two different uses: an *incomplete* use, when it needs to be completed by a predicate (as in English, 'Is she going?', 'Yes, she *is*.') and a *complete* use (as in 'To *be* or not to *be*, that is the question.'). Ancient Greek does not have a separate verb for existing, but forms of *einai* may be translated by forms of 'exist' when they have the complete use. Forms of 'be' are used when *einai* has the incomplete use or when it is uncertain which use is in play. Further, anything to which *einai* applies can be said to partake of being and hence be called 'being' (*to on*, from *on*, a participle of *einai*, is translated 'being', 'that which is', or 'thing that is' depending on context). Hence, 'Socrates is white' entails that the white (i.e. this instance of whiteness) partakes of being and, hence, that the white is a being. The gist of the present argument is that any item in a category other than substance (e.g. an instance of a quality such as whiteness) can truly called 'a being' only if it is present in some substance (e.g. Socrates) which is a being in its own right. For discussions of the verb *einai* and related forms see Kahn 1973 and Brown 1994.

22 [669,37] This argument for the priority of substance builds on the preceding argument, with an added wrinkle that is again clearer in the Greek. What makes 'Socrates is white' true is that Socrates possesses (*ekhei*) the quality of whiteness, which is thus a state (*hexis*, more literally 'possession', also translatable as 'property' or 'condition') of Socrates. What makes 'Socrates is not white' true is that Socrates lacks the quality, for example, if Socrates were to be sunburned. Therefore, 'the white is' is true provided there exists a substance possessing whiteness, and 'the not-white is' is true provided there is substance lacking whiteness. Thus, as something that is, a privation is posterior to substance to an even greater extent than is a quality.

23 [670,3] The present argument, on Ps.-Alexander's interpretation, is that substance is *ontologically* prior to items in other categories because it is ontologically separable from them: that is, it can exist without them but they cannot exist without it (cf. *Cat.* 5, 2b3–6; *Metaph.* 7.1, 1028a31-b2; 12.3, 1070a13–18; 12.7, 1073a3–5). For example, Socrates may be white, but he can exist without his whiteness, while his whiteness cannot exist without him. Hence, Socrates is ontologically prior to his own whiteness. This argument holds, however, only for

the accidental or non-essential characteristics of a substance, such as Socrates' being white or hot or musical. The translation assumes that *einai* is used here in the complete sense (see note 21). On Aristotle's concept of ontological separability see Fine 1984, Spellman 1995, Miller 2014, and Katz 2017.

24 [670,8] Translates *to katholou* (singular), evidently a copyist error. The plural 'the universals' (*ta katholou*) is cited at 670,12, in agreement with the Aristotle manuscripts.

25 [670,8] The translation of this sentence at 1069a30–2 follows Ps.-Alexander's reading; cf. note 43.

26 [670,13] Translates *hoi nun*. Ps.-Alexander understands a reference to Platonists and Pythagoreans in Aristotle's day (see also note 38). Aristotle's discussion is framed in terms of his distinction between universal (*katholou*) and particular (*kath' hekaston*), for example, at *Int.* 7, 17a39-b1: 'I call a universal that which is by its nature predicated of a number of things, a particular that which is not; human, for instance, is a universal, Callias a particular'. Aristotle also speaks of human as 'predicated universally' of Callias and all other particulars who happen to be human. Further, one universal can be predicated of another universal, for example, animal of human, and in this case human is called a species (*eidos*) and animal a genus (*genos*) (cf. *Cat.* 5, 2b17–21). In the *Categories* (generally regarded as one of his earliest works) Aristotle defends a view diametrically opposed to that of the Platonists, who regard the universal as more of a substance than the particular. He argues that an individual human such as Callias is a substance in the strictest sense and that 'the species is more a substance than the genus' (2b37–3a1, 2b22). However, it is unlikely that the Platonists would have said literally, 'a *genus* is a universal'. This is probably a restatement, in Aristotle's own terminology, of Platonic doctrine. Cf. *Metaph.* 7.14, 1309a24–34 and 8.1, 1042a14–16, where Aristotle says that the Forms are closely connected with the universal and the genus and that the genus is a substance more so than the different species and the universal more so than the particular (cf. 13. 5, 1079b8–9).

27 [670,14] 'Logically' (*logikôs*) is closely related to dialectic, which relies on reputable beliefs to seek definitions (cf. *Top.* 8.12, 162b27). Aristotle elsewhere suggests that Plato postulated the Forms because he was preoccupied with *logoi* (definitions or accounts) which cannot have as their objects perceptible things in flux (cf. *Metaph.* 1.6, 987b31–3). Ps.-Alexander understands 'logically' to have a negative connotation, suggestive of logic-chopping (*GC* 1.2, 316a11; *EE* 1.8, 1217b21; cf. *DA* 1.1, 403a2), although Aristotle uses the term elsewhere in the *Metaphysics* in a more favourable way in connection with his own investigation of essence (cf. *Metaph.* 4.3, 1005b32; 7.4, 1029b13; 7.17, 1041a28).

28 [670,16] Or 'for thought'. This apparently means that universals exist *only* in (or for) the intellect. It is unclear whether Ps.-Alexander intends to attribute this view

to Aristotle or he is only speaking for himself. Aristotle does say that universals 'exist in a way in the soul' (*DA* 2.5, 417b3–4) but the qualification 'in a way' seems important, since he does not deny that universals exist independently of the mind but rather that they are substances existing separately from the particular things of which they are predicated (see especially *Metaph.* 7.13). A similar view is found in Themistius: 'the universals stand as notions in thought' (*in Metaph.* 2,6). The genuine Alexander may go further in his own work *On the Soul*, in suggesting that universals as such come into existence only when they are thought: e.g 'the universal and common things have their existence (*huparxis*) in the individuals that are in matter; but when they are thought apart from matter they come to be common and universal, and they are intellect at the time when they are thought. But if they are not thought, they are not any more' (90,4–7; tr. Sharples in Sorabji 2004, v. 3, 152). The final words 'they are not any more' could be understood as 'they do not exist any more'. However, they could also be taken more weakly as 'they are not intellect any more'. Alexander is even more emphatic about the genus, saying that it 'is a mere name' or construct, possessing the property of being common 'in its being thought of, not in some reality (*hupostasis*)' (*Quaest.* 2.28, 78,18–20; 2.28, 79,16–18; tr. Sharples). His position, however, seems to be closer to conceptualism than to nominalism. For discussion see Tweedale 1984, Sharples 1987, 1199–1202, and Sorabji 2016b.

29 [670,19] In contrast most other commentators understand Plato as Aristotle's target here. Ps.-Alexander may be trying to downplay the disagreement between Plato and Aristotle. The 'contemporaries of Plato' probably include Speusippus and Xenocrates (see note 38).

30 [670,20] The Presocratic philosophers theorized that the cosmos was composed of a particular stuff (e.g. water in the case of Thales). On Aristotle's interpretation this stuff is a particular substance, and different objects in the cosmos consist of different portions of this stuff (e.g. the water in the Tigris River and the water in the Euphrates). Aristotle describes the views of these theorists more fully in *Metaphysics* 1.3.

31 [670,23] Fire, earth, air, and water have in common that they are all bodies. However, no Presocratic claimed that *body* as such is the first principle. That is, according to Ps.-Alexander, none of them treated body qua universal as a principle. For the expression 'common universal' see 7.13, 1038b11.

32 [670,27] Hippo (late-fifth century BCE) claimed that the soul is water. Cf. 462,29–31 for a similar report about Hippo, whom Aristotle dismisses as a philosophical lightweight (cf. *DA* 1.2, 405b2; *Metaph.* 1.3, 984a3).

33 [670,31] Aristotle endorsed a geocentric theory in which the earth has a stationary location in the centre of the universe and is surrounded by heavenly bodies embedded in rotating transparent spheres. (In ch. 8 Aristotle will speculate about how many spheres are required in order to explain the observed motions of celestial objects.) His terminology reflects his astronomical viewpoint and varies somewhat from ours: he uses *astêr* for both the fixed stars (which we call 'stars') and for the seven wandering stars or planets (*planêtês*), which include the moon and sun as well as Mercury, Venus, Mars, Jupiter, and Saturn. Aristotle describes the heavenly bodies as 'everlasting' (*aïdios*; the alternative 'eternal' suggests atemporality.) Ps.-Alexander uses these terms in a similar way, and the present translation will conform to their usage and the meaning will be almost always obvious from the context. Incidentally, although Ps.-Alexander describes the spheres as 'perceptible' (as implied by Aristotle's text), Aristotle elsewhere indicates that the material of the spheres is too attenuated to be visible to human beings (*Cael.* 2.4, 287b14–21). See also note 209.

34 [670,37] The fifth body is a celestial body in addition to the four sublunary elements (earth, water, air, and fire). The heavenly objects consist of what Aristotle himself calls the 'primary body' (*prôton sôma*), which he describes as 'primary, simple, ungenerated, indestructible, and wholly unchangeable' (*Cael.* 1.3, 270b1; 2.1, 283b26–9; 2.3, 286a10–11; 2.6, 288a34-b1). Aristotle's ancient commentators customarily called this body *aithêr*, though Aristotle himself attributes the latter term to early cosmologists (1.3, 270b19–24). See Bonitz *Index* 15b10–18.

35 [670,38] Aristotle will argue that this eternal and immovable substance is the prime mover or god in ch. 7. He will also argue that an additional fifty-five immovable movers are required to explain planetary motion in ch. 8.

36 [670,38] Cf.13.1, 1076a17–22: 'Some say that the mathematical objects – i.e. numbers, lines, and the like – are substances, and again that the Ideas are. And ... some posit them as two kinds – the Ideas and the mathematical numbers – and others posit them as having one nature, and others say that the mathematical substances are the only ones'. Aristotle also says that Plato treats the mathematical objects as 'intermediates' between the Forms and perceptible particulars (1.6, 987b14–18; 7.2, 1028b19–20). This distinction is suggested by 'the divided line' passage in Plato's *Republic* (510B-511D), which posits between belief (*pistis*) and understanding (*noêsis*) an intermediate state of awareness called cognition (*dianoia*) concerned with mathematical objects.

37 [671,3] The translations 'Form' (*eidos*) and 'Idea' (*idea*) are capitalized when they refer to Plato's theory of Forms to distinguish them from Aristotle's theory of forms.

38 [671,3] Ps.-Alexander here distinguishes two groups of Pythagoreans, those who identified Forms with mathematical objects and those who held that only

mathematical objects exist. (In contrast Alexander in Averroes says that only the latter was the view of the Pythagoreans, while the former was the view 'of somebody else than Plato or Plato according to the interpretation of some of his disciples'; fr. 5F=*Tafsīr* 1427; tr. Genequand.) It is hard to reconcile what Ps.-Alexander says here with remarks in the commentary on Book 13: that there are three groups of Pythagoreans, namely, those who distinguished mathematical objects from Forms, those who identified Forms with mathematical objects, and those who recognized only mathematical objects (723,37–724,7); that the Pythagoreans recognized only mathematical objects while Speusippus and Xenocrates identified Forms with mathematical objects (766,6–8); and, again, that the followers of Xenocrates and Speusippus recognized only mathematical numbers (782,31–2; cf. 745,31–2 regarding the followers of Xenocrates). Aristotle himself describes the views of the Pythagoreans elsewhere in the *Metaphysics*, for example, that 'number is the substance of all things' (1.5, 987a19; cf. 1.8, 13.8, and 14.3). He also implies that Speusippus followed the Pythagoreans in recognizing the mathematical objects rather than the Forms (see 7.2, 1028b21–4 with 12.7, 1072b30–4; 12.10, 1075b37–1076a1; 13.1, 1076a20–1; and 14.3, 1090b13–20). It was probably Xenocrates (not mentioned by name by Aristotle in the *Metaphysics*) who identified the Forms with numbers (see references in Guthrie 1978, 473–4).

39 [671,11] Cf. 11.1, 1059b16–18: 'natural science' (*phusikê*) is 'a discipline concerned with the things that have in themselves a principle or movement or rest' (cf. 6.1, 1026a12; 11.7, 1064a15). The term *phusikê* refers here not to physics in the narrow sense delineated in Aristotle's *Physics* but covers all the sciences concerned with perceptible substances, including those which we call astronomy, chemistry, meteorology, biology, and so forth.

40 [671,13] Cf. 668,24: 'first philosophy' ('primam philosophiam') in Sepúlveda's translation. The reference is in fact to what Aristotle calls 'first philosophy' (*Phys.* 1.8, 191a36; 2.2, 194b14; *Metaph.* 11.4, 1061b19) – and also 'wisdom' (6.1, 1026a23–32; 10.4, 1061b17–19) or 'theology' (6.1, 1026a19; 11.7, 1064b3) – and was eventually called 'metaphysics' (after the title *Meta ta phusika* assigned by later editors to Aristotle's work).

41 [671,16] Translates *autois* (neuter) as in manuscript A, echoing *autois* in the citation at 671,13. Manuscript L (followed by Hayduck) has *autais* (feminine) which makes the reference to substances explicit.

42 [671,17] On objects that do not belong to natural science cf. *Phys.* 2.7, 198a27–8; *DC* 3.1, 298b19–20; *GC* 1.3, 318a5–6. Alexander in Averroes by contrast remarks that 'natural philosophy is only concerned with moving substances and takes over their principles from first philosophy. This discussion of the immovable substance is reserved to first philosophy' (fr. 6F=*Tafsīr* 1428; tr.

Genequand). For different interpretations see Frede 2000, Donini 2002, Lefebvre 2012, and Berti 2016.

43 [671,21] Ps.-Alexander omits Aristotle's final clause: 'and another is immovable' although he alludes to it earlier at 670,37–8. Editors have long regarded as corrupt the text in the Aristotle manuscripts EJA$^b$ (see Judson note on 1069a30–3), and many have looked to Ps.-Alexander for clues to a more reliable reading. The manuscript version is translated as follows: 'There are, then, three substances: one is perceptible, of which <u>the one is everlasting and the other is perishable, upon which all are agreed</u>, ... <u>and the other is the everlasting, of which it is necessary to grasp the elements</u> ...' (1069a30–2) The most conspicuous problem with the received text (indicated by underlining) involves the repetition 'the one is everlasting ... and the other is everlasting' (*hê men aïdios ... hê de aïdios*). This repetition is absent from Ps.-Alexander's version and from Aristotle manuscripts C$^2$MV$^k$. (The final *hê de aïdios* was evidently absent also from the primary text used by Alexander in Averroes, though he notes its presence in a variant manuscript. He rejects it because it implies that in Book 12 Aristotle is only concerned with the elements of *everlasting* substances; cf. fr. 4bF=*Tafsīr* 1421.) Most modern editors concur in bracketing the final phrase, though they otherwise follow EJA$^b$ for the most part. Other disagreements concern the precise antecedents of the phrase 'upon which all are agreed' (*hên pantes homologousin*) and 'of which it is necessary to grasp the elements' (*hês kai anagkaion ta stoikheia labein*). In both cases the antecedent is the feminine noun *ousia* ('substance') but there are still three possibilities: 'perceptible' (*aisthêtê*), 'perishable' (*phartê*), or 'everlasting' (*aïdios*) substance. Whereas the manuscripts imply that 'upon which all are agreed' refers to *perishable* substance and 'of which it is necessary to grasp the elements' to *everlasting* substance, Ps.-Alexander takes both phrases to concern *perceptible* substance (cf. 670,28–34). Either version is possible, but Ps.-Alexander's is arguably more consistent with the context. For all thinkers would agree that there is perceptible substance, and Aristotle is concerned in Book 12 with the elements of both types of perceptible substance. After exploring the alternatives, Frede favours Ps.-Alexander's version (2000, 78–80). The translation of this sentence accompanying lemma 1069a26 follows Ps.-Alexander's construal.

44 [671,24] This implies that Ps.-Alexander regards 1069b3–9 as offering a continuous argument beginning '[Since] perceptible substance is changeable ...' and ending 'so there is a third thing besides the contraries, namely, matter'. This continuation is obscured by the absence of 'since' (*epeidê*) at 1069b3, which permits the customary but problematic chapter break with 'further' (*eti*) at line 1069b7.

45 [671,27] Literally, 'Aristotle says that since ...'. This is the beginning of a lengthy sentence (including a long digression) extending until 672,7 which spells out all of the assumptions required in order for Aristotle to posit matter as a third thing involved in change. The present translation breaks up such unwieldy sentences to make them more readable.

46 [671,30] Ps.-Alexander introduces several technical terms which recur throughout Book 12. These are explained elsewhere in Aristotle's works (notably in *Cat.* 10, *Top.* 2.8, *Metaph.* 10.3–4 and 7). Opposites (*antikeimena*) are pairs of items which cannot coexist. Three main types are of opposites are relevant here. (1) 'Contradictories' (*apophaseis*), i.e. affirmation and negation, e.g. sick and not-sick. (2) 'State' (*hexis*) and 'privation' (*sterêsis*), i.e. a characteristic or absence of that characteristic normally possessed by a specific sort of subject, e.g. sight and blindness. (3) 'Contraries' (*enantia*), opposites which normally belong to certain sorts of subjects. There are two kinds of contraries: (a) those with intermediate states (*metaxu*), e.g. white and black with grey as an intermediate colour, and (b) those without intermediates, e.g. odd and even in the case of numbers. Contradictories are such that one is present if and only if the other is not; hence, 'Socrates is sick' is true if and only if 'Socrates is not sick' is false, and vice versa. This is not the case with state/privation or with contraries, in which cases neither may be present if the subject is of the wrong sort. E.g. a stone is neither sighted nor blind, and a song is neither white nor black. Moreover, contrary characteristics and their intermediates must all be of the same kind, e.g. white, black, and grey are colours. Likewise, a thing is in a state of privation when, though it does not possess a certain characteristic, it does possess some other characteristic belonging to the same kind as the one it lacks, e.g. it is black or grey instead of white. This is the basis for Ps.-Alexander's distinction between an 'appropriate negation' (or 'appropriate privation') and a merely 'random opposite'.

47 [671,31] See *Phys.* 1.5, 188a31-b3: '... no random thing naturally acts on, or is affected by, another random thing, nor does it come to be from anything whatsoever, unless one might suppose it to happen accidentally; for how could white come to be from musical, unless musical was accidental to white or to black? Rather, white comes to be from not-white – though not from anything that is not white but from black or one of the intermediate colours, and musical comes to be from not-musical, though not from anything that is not musical but from unmusical or one of the intermediate states.'

48 [672,5] Modern editors of the *Metaphysics* begin a new chapter here; see note 44.

49 [672,6] Aristotle argues in *Physics* 1.7 that change involves three factors: form, privation, and substratum or matter.

## [Chapter 2]

50 [672,7] Here there begins a long tortuous Greek sentence extending for twelve lines. In such cases, where the meaning is not obscured, the first conjunction *epeidê* ('since') is translated 'granted' or the like and the sentence is broken up for the sake of readability.

51 [671,31] See *Phys.* 5.1-3 *et passim*. Ps.-Alexander mentions three types of 'movement' (*kinêsis*) while Aristotle's text mentions four types of 'change' (*metabolê*). Aristotle sometimes uses 'movement' also to cover all four types of change: see *Phys.* 4.10, 218b19; 8.7, 261a27.

52 [672,11] Ps.-Alexander reads *kata tode* (as do most Aristotle manuscripts) but understands *kata to tode*. Ross adds *to* as do some later Aristotle manuscripts (e.g. J, according to Alexandru, who also notes that *to* is written as a correction in E).

53 [672,12] *GC* 1.2, 315a26.

54 [672,26] The reference is to *Physics* 5.1. In the following discussion it is assumed that the verb 'to be' (*einai*) has an *incomplete* use: hence, 'that which is' (*to on*) is understood to refer to that which is *something*, e.g. white or human; cf. note 21.

55 [672,22] Or 'there are two modes of being' in scholastic jargon. The Aristotle manuscripts have *to on* ('that which is', participle with definite article) while the lemma has *on* ('what is' participle without article), although *to on* is present in the paraphrase at 672,26. This distinction will generally be reflected in the translation, although it is not always clear whether it makes a difference. Sometimes, however, it will be less awkward to translate these expressions as 'being'; cf. again note 21.

56 [672,33] Cf. *Phys.* 1.8, 191b13-15: 'nothing can be said to come to be without qualification from what is not, but a thing may come to be from what is not, that is, accidentally'. The relevant distinction between 'accidentally' (*kata sumbebêkos*) and 'in its own right' (*kath' hauto*) is explained in *Metaph.* 5.7: things are said to be 'accidentally' if they happen to possess certain non-essential characteristics which are not necessarily related to each other. For example, if a particular human being is both a musician and a builder, then the musician is said to be a builder accidentally, and the builder to be a musician accidentally. However, he is also said to be a human being in his own right. The distinction also applies to not-being as in the present case. In the case of Socrates, for instance, it is true both that he is (*sc.* a human) in his own right and that he is not (*sc.* a horse) accidentally.

57 [672,36] For example, if a grey object becomes white, then the white comes to be from what is not white, and what is not white, namely the grey, is not a not-being in its own right but is only a not-being accidentally because grey *is not* white. In such examples the term 'accidentally' can also be translated 'coincidentally'.

Sharples (1992, 81 n. 249) notes a similar discussion in Alexander *Quaest.* 1.24, 38,25 ff. and Simplicius, *in Phys.* 238,8–14.

58 [673,9] The verb *oneirôttein* is commonly associated with *oneira*, 'dream vision'. Here 'the One of Anaxagoras' refers to the primordial mixture from which the universe arose. Anaxagoras wrote a treatise beginning with the words, 'All things were together; then Intellect came and put them in order' (DK 59B1). In Anaxagoras' cosmology everything was originally mixed together but was separated due to the activity of cosmic Intellect (see 1.8, 989a33-b21). 'The Intellect' (*ho nous*) of Anaxagoras is capitalized to distinguish it from Aristotle's 'intellect'. On the identification of 'all things together' with matter see also 1071b28; cf. 690,13–14.

59 [673,16] The Aristotle manuscripts also include a reference to Anaximander (1069b22) who is not mentioned by Ps.-Alexander.

60 [673,17] In Empedocles' cosmology the universe undergoes a succession of great cycles during which its four eternal roots or material constituents – earth, water, fire, and aether – are alternately brought together by Love or separated by Hate (cf. DK 31B22,26,35). When Love is fully ascendant the universe is a perfectly blended 'sphere' (*sphaira*). Ps.-Alexander implies that 'things here' (i.e. in the present-day world around us) have resulted from the divisions within this sphere brought about by Hate (see 1.3, 984a8–11; 1.4, 985a21–9; 1.8, 989a20–6).

61 [673,22] Aristotle's text at 1069b23 is uncertain. Ps.-Alexander reads *homou* ('together'), whereas *hêmin* ('for us') is found in most Aristotle manuscripts (including E¹JA^bC, although some manuscripts including H^aM have *homou*, which is also noted as a variant reading by a later scribe in E). Ps.-Alexander, however, uses the term *hêmin* in his interpretation. Regarding Democritus, Aristotle may be alluding to the atomic *panspermia* ('all-engendering seedbed'); cf. *Phys.* 3.4, 203a20; *DC* 3.4, 303a16; *DA* 1.2, 404a3. However, Ps.-Alexander (followed by Bekker's edition of the *Metaphysics*) takes Aristotle to imply that Democritus has the concept of potentiality, an attribution for which there is no other evidence. Ross (while accepting *homou*) avoids this implication through a different punctuation of Aristotle's text: instead of saying that 'all things were together' (as these earlier thinkers claim) it would be better to say 'all things were together in potentiality but not in actuality'. (Note the phrase 'but not in actuality' is missing from Ps.-Alexander's citation.) Jaeger follows Ross' punctuation but with the emendation *men* for *hêmin*. It is noteworthy that Alexander in Averroes (unlike Ps.-Alexander) reads 'for us' and maintains that the words 'in potentiality' were a correction added by Aristotle rather than part of his quotation of Democritus (fr. 9F=*Tafsīr* 1445–6; cf. Freudenthal 1884, 45). For further discussion of this passage see Charles 2000, 106–10 and Judson note on 1069b21–4.

62 [673,24] cf. 3.4, 1000a5–1001a3.
63 [673,30] The point of this remark is that it is not strictly correct to say that when air, for example, comes to be from water, the *matter* underlying this process is 'generable' or 'perishable'. It is 'generable' only in the sense of being matter for coming-to-be and perishing. See 1069b35–1070a4.
64 [673,31] Celestial bodies are said to possess 'local matter' (or 'topical matter', *topikê hulê*) which changes location but does not come to be or undergo any other sort of change; cf. 8.1, 1042b5–6; 8.4, 1044b6–8; 9.8, 1050b21–2.
65 [673,32] As the year progresses the sun changes its position with respect to the stars (which are fixed in the outer celestial sphere according to Aristotle's astronomy), and it appears to move through the zodiac, a band of twelve constellations or stars. It takes the sun a little over a month to move from one constellation to the next. In antiquity it passed from Aquarius to Pisces in mid-February. Ps.-Alexander presumably regards these different locations of the sun as in a sense 'contraries'; cf. 672,14–19.
66 [673,36] Echoing this complaint, Ross remarks 'that Aristotle is jotting down notes from a treatise (or lecture), not writing a treatise in its finished form' (vol. 2, 354).
67 [673,36] The historical digression at 1069b20–6 interrupts Aristotle's argument.
68 [674,6] Ps.-Alexander lists the three senses of not-being as distinguished at 11.11, 1067b25–30 (cf. Charles 2000, 89 n. 2 and Judson, 98). There is a somewhat different threefold distinction at 9.10, 1051a34–b2 and 14.2, 1089a26–31, which seems less relevant to the present context.
69 [674,7] The commentary manuscripts have *to* while the Aristotle manuscripts have *ti*, 'something'.
70 [674,15] Cf. *Phys.* 1.5, 188a32–3: 'nothing by nature acts on any random thing or is affected by any random thing, nor does anything come to be from anything whatsoever, except accidentally.' In Aristotle's embryology the offspring receives its form from the father's seminal fluid and the matter from the mother's menstrual fluid; cf. *GA* 1.2 *et passim*. By adding this detail Ps.-Alexander obscures the point that a single thing comes to be from a single matter non-randomly and spoils the parallel the analogy with the olive tree and vine plant. Sepúlveda's more expansive translation, 'a human being is from a man by way of a woman, and is begotten by means of female menstrual fluid' ('homo ex humano femine, et mensibus muliebribus gignitur'), is doubtless due to his concern to preserve the analogy rather than to his reliance on a variant manuscript.
71 [674,21] Aristotle distinguishes between two classes of watery substances: liquid (e.g. oil) and fusible, including metals such as bronze which are normally solid but meltable when heated as described in *Meteor.* 4.6–10 (cf. 675,13–14)

72 [674,22] The 'simple things' (*hapla*) are the basic elements: earth, water, air, and fire. 'Formless matter' (*aneideos hulê*) is the ultimate matter which has no form of its own but persists throughout the most fundamental change, e.g. when one element is transformed into another. Although later commentators referred to this as 'the first (or prime) matter' (*hê prôtê hulê*), including Ps.-Alexander himself (e.g. at 674,34), modern scholars disagree over whether this concept can be found in Aristotle himself.

73 [674,24] 'For when there is one agent and one matter there must be one effect', as Aquinas (*Commentary on Metaphysics*, 2439) succinctly paraphrases.

74 [674,25] Ps.-Alexander reads *hou*, which is also in the Aristotle manuscripts and attested in the Latin and Arabic translations. Jaeger reads *ho* (what) following Ps.-Alexander's paraphrase.

## [Chapter 3]

75 [674,35] *Phys.* 1.9, 192a25–34.

76 [674,36] At 7.8, 1033b5–8; cf. 8.3, 1043b16–17.

77 [674,35] See 7.8, 1033a24-b19; cf. 494,26–496,6.

78 [675,4] Ps.-Alexander alludes to the theory which explained the healthy functioning of the body in terms of the harmony of four humours or bodily fluids – blood, phlegm, yellow bile, and black bile – and explained disease as due to the imbalance of these humours. The theory had its origins in Hippocratic writings (especially *On the Nature of Man* and *On Humours*), was expounded in a more systematic form by Galen of Pergamum (129–216? CE), and became widely accepted in later antiquity. However, although Aristotle occasionally refers to the various bodily fluids, there is actually no evidence of such a theory in his writings.

79 [675,5] The precise meaning of 'ultimate' depends on the point of view. In the case of matter, for example, a house is built out of boards which are made of wood which is made out of earth, but elemental stuffs like earth themselves contain prime matter which is intrinsically formless. The boards are the house's *proximate* matter while the prime matter is its *remote* matter, although either of these might be called 'ultimate' depending on the point of view. Analogously, we might think of the house's 'proximate form' as its fully developed form, i.e. the way the boards are assembled in the completed house, as distinguished from the 'remote form' its materials possessed at the outset, and again either form might be called 'ultimate'. Most commentators understand Aristotle in this passage to mean that neither the proximate matter nor the proximate form comes to be. However, Ps.-Alexander

understands him to mean here that neither prime matter nor the fully developed form comes to be, so that Aristotle is using 'ultimate' equivocally at 1069b36. This untoward implication may be avoided if instead Aristotle's point here is the same as at 7.8, 1033a24-b5: when we make a bronze sphere, for example, we do not make the bronze and the spherical shape as well, for in that case we would also have to make the latter two out of something, and so on to infinity. Note that 'ultimate matter' has the sense of proximate matter in at 7.10, 1035b30 and of prime matter at *Meteor.* 4.12, 390a15. See notes 72 and 97 on the concepts of prime matter and proximate matter respectively.

80 [675,6] The sentence is translated literally. It seems to imply oddly that Socrates is a form. Perhaps what Ps.-Alexander means to say is that the ultimate (i.e. fully developed) form of Socrates is distinct from the mere form of flesh.

81 [675,16] cf *Metaph.* 2.2, 994a3–5.

82 [675,19] Commentators disagree over the force of Aristotle's synonymy thesis (i.e. that every substance comes to be from something synonymous with itself), but it is generally agreed that synonymy for Aristotle is not a relation between things that merely share the same name. 'Synonyms' (*sunônuma*) are defined more strictly in the *Categories* as things that 'have a common name and the account of being corresponding to the name is the same'; e.g. a human being and an ox are called by the common name 'animal' and the account of being (i.e. definition of 'animal') is the same (*Cat.* 1, 1a6–8). In this sense 'synonymous' is evidently equivalent to 'having the same form' (*homoeidês*, as argued by Judson 2012; 2019, 114; cf. 2.1, 993b25). However, Ps.-Alexander (along with other commentators) holds that 'synonymous' has an extended sense in the case of artefacts: for instance, a material house is synonymous with a house in the mind, assuming that the concept or account (*logos*) of a house is the same as the form of a house (cf. 675,22–4).

83 [675,27] 'Chance' (*tukhê*) and 'spontaneity' (*automatos*) are defined in *Physics* 2.5-6. An outcome occurs by chance when it promotes (or frustrates) human purposeful choice but occurs accidentally and not for that reason. An outcome is spontaneous when it promotes or frustrates an end (which may or may not be a chosen end) but occurs accidentally and not for that reason. Spontaneity thus extends to outcomes affecting the natural ends of children, animals, and even inanimate objects. Although spontaneity encompasses chance, Aristotle often describes events as 'spontaneous' to distinguish them from 'chance'.

84 [675,32] This suggests that 'for a human being begets a human being' (1078a8; cf. 674,25–6) is misplaced in the manuscripts of Aristotle. For it illustrates not the claim immediately preceding it 'nature is a principle in a thing itself' (1070a7–8) but the earlier claim 'each substance comes to be from a synonymous thing'

(1070a4–5). Bonitz and Ross object that transposing 'for a human being begets a human being' to immediately after 'each substance comes to be from a synonymous thing' would break the connection of the latter with 'for natural things and other things are substances'. But that is clearly not Ps.-Aexander's intention (cf. 676,1–2).

85 [675,34] Translates *êtoi* (also rendered elsewhere as 'or' in the epexigetical sense), so that Ps.-Alexander understands 'the other things' (*ta alla*) to be restricted to the products of art, here and again in line 37. He also understands the scope of 'for' (*gar*) at 1070a8 to end with *ta alla* (as is punctuated by Ross and Jaeger). Hence, according to Ps.-Alexander the synonymy thesis is confined to natural substances and artefacts and does not include the products of spontaneity or chance, which are mere 'mistakes' of nature or art. In contrast, Alexander in Averroes understands 'the other things' more widely and takes it to be another subject of 'comes to be from a synonymous thing', which leads him to expatiate on how the synonymy thesis might apply to the products of chance and spontaneity (fr. 10a-cF=*Tafsīr* 1457–65). He may have consulted a text at variance with Ps.-Alexander's source (as well as our extant Aristotle manuscripts), which may also account for the striking disparity (noted by Freudenthal 1884, 47–9, 81–5) between the treatments by the two Alexanders.

86 [676,3] Reading *apo* ('from') with A (Bonitz) instead of *hupo* ('by the agency of') with L (Hayduck).

87 [676,7] E.g. the matter is the bronze, the form is the shape, and the compound of matter and form is the statue. See also *Metaph.* 7.3, 1029a2–7; 8.1, 1042a26–31; 8.2, 1043a26–8; *DA* 2.1, 412a6–9.

88 [676,8] Aristotle's unusual phrase *tôi phainesthai* (translated 'by appearing') has prompted much speculation. Ps.-Alexander interprets it as the more familiar expression *kata phantasian*, 'in appearance'. The latter expression, however, can be taken in either of two ways: as it appears in *imagination* or as it appears in *perception*. Ps.-Alexander (followed by Bonitz) understands it in the former way as 'in our imagination' (*en tôi hêmeterai phantasiai*, cf. 677,11–12): we can imagine a mere heap of Socratic bodily parts being assembled into an actual Socrates through the agency of nature, whereupon they would be a 'this-something'. Ps.-Alexander describes a haphazard heap of body parts presumably because this is how he construes Aristotle's remark that the materials 'exist by contact and not by natural coherence' (1070a10–11) and he supposes that such a heap can at best be imagined to be combined into a coherent substance. (Sharples 2003, 189 takes a less charitable view of Ps.-Alexander's interpretation.) In contrast, Alexander in Averroes (followed by Ross) understands *tôi phainesthai* as 'as it appears in perception' (as if Socrates' body parts are assembled so as to appear lifelike), and considers four different interpretations of Aristotle's claim so understood

(fr. 11F=*Tafsīr* 1467–72). See Freudenthal 1884, 45–6; Elders 1972, 103–5; Salis, n. 113; Judson, 118–19 for discussion of this difficult passage.

89 [676,11] Through the process of growing together (*sumphusis*) things in contact with each other form a coherent and continuous whole (see *Phys.* 5.3, 227a23–7; *Metaph.* 5.4, 1014b22–6).

90 [676,30] The word order is different in the Aristotle manuscripts: *tode ti eis hên kai hexis tis*, 'a this something towards which [there is coming to-be] and a certain state', which Ross finds 'intolerably harsh'. Most editors emend the text in agreement with Ps.-Alexander's paraphrase: *tode ti kai hexis tis eis hên*. Zingano (2016, 147–9) sides with the manuscripts.

91 [676,31] i.e. substantial form (cf. 672,10). Aristotle frequently uses 'nature' (*phusis*) in the sense of 'form' (*eidos*); cf. Bonitz *Index* 839a16–39. He calls form a 'this-something'(*tode ti*) at *Metaph.* 5.8, 1017b24–6 and 8.1, 1042a29, although he more often speaks of the hylomorphic compound (e.g. an individual animal) as a 'this-something' (cf. *Metaph.* 7.13, 1038b5) or says that the matter is called a 'this-something' in virtue of the form (cf. *DA* 2.1, 412a8–9). Aristotle remarks that forms are a kind of state (*hexis*) at *GC* 1.7, 324b17–18. Cf. *Metaph.* 8.5, 1044b31–4 and *DA* 2.5, 417b16 where *hexis* and *phusis* are juxtaposed.

92 [676,38] i.e. Plato and his followers; but Aristotle's text does not mention Plato until a few lines later at 1070a18 (cf. note 95). Aristotle's transition to Plato is rather abrupt but his point is to show a parallel between his own account of forms and Plato's theory of Forms. Ps.-Alexander shifts accordingly to his interpretation that for Aristotle the forms of artefacts, in contrast to those of natural entities, exist only in thought or imagination (cf. Themistius *in Metaph.* 6,32). For criticism of this interpretation of Aristotle on artefacts see Katayama 1999, 37. On the distinction between natural entities and artefacts see also 8.3, 1043b19–21; cf. 3.4, 999b18–20.

93 [676,40] This would not be Plato; cf. 677,12–13.

94 [677,6] According to Aristotle, there is no process by which the 'contact' (*haphê*) between bodies comes to be or ceases to be. Such contacts simply exist or they do not. See *Metaph.* 8.3, 1043b14–16 and *Cael.* 1.11, 280b22–9.

95 [677,13] Alexander in Averroes reads 'those who posited the Forms', understood to refer to Plato (fr.12F=*Tafsīr* 1481–2). See also 1.9, 991b5–7 and 13.5, 1080a5–6.

96 [677,20] Ps.-Alexander's contention that the words *hoion pur sarx kephalê*, 'for example, fire, flesh, [and] head', are misplaced from 1070a10 (where they originally preceded 'for such things as are by contact' and so forth) must be evaluated in the light of textual issues at 1070a19–20. The manuscripts and commentators differ over whether to read *álla* ('different') or *allà* ('but'), which are acute paroxytone or grave oxytone respectively, the Greek words differing only in accent. The word *álla* is found in Ps.-Alexander's paraphrase (as well as in a scribal correction in A[b]) and

is assumed by the Latin translations. On this reading Aristotle's text would be translated 'there are as many Forms as there are natural things, if there are Forms <u>different</u> from these things (*álla toutôn*), for example, fire, flesh, [and] head'. It is hard to see what Aristotle could have meant by this (though Judson takes it as a maladroit way of saying that Plato did not posit forms of fire, flesh, etc.; cf. Judson, 371–2.) Hence Ross accordingly follows Ps.-Alexander in reading *álla* ('different') transposing the *hoion* ('for example') clause in his Oxford translation to 1070a10, and understanding *toutôn* ('these') to refer to the (particular perceptible) things in our world. (Ps.-Alexander's transposition is indicated by a later scribe of J; see Jaeger's note at 1070a9.) The alternative is to read *allà* with EA$^b$CM (assumed by Alexander in Averroes fr. 13aF=*Tafsīr* 1483) so that Aristotle's text would be translated 'there are as many Forms as there are natural [kinds] (if there are Forms) <u>but</u> of these things (*allà toutôn*), for example, fire, flesh, [and] head'. However, this seems to commit Plato to questionable Forms of fire, flesh, etc. (which are called into question at *Parm.* 130C-D). Alexander in Averroes interprets along these lines but he was relying on a 'muddled' translation (cf. Genequand, 100–2 nn. 78, 79). A third alternative followed by Jaeger is to emend *álla* to *all' ou* on the alleged basis of *allou* in J (translated 'though not' in Barnes' Revised Oxford Translation). Unfortunately, however, *allou* has subsequently been found to be a mistaken reading of J, which has instead *alla* with no accent (cf. Alexandru and Fazzo). Consequently Ps.-Alexander's proposal remains an attractive alternative.

97 [677,26] The term *prosekhês* ('proximate') describes matter in its most developed state as found in a completely formed substance (cf. note 79). Aristotle refers to it here as the 'final' (*teleutaia*) matter and elsewhere as the 'ultimate' (*eskhatê*) matter (7.10, 1035b30; 8.6, 1045b18).

98 [677,28] The word *aitia*, 'causes', present in the Aristotle manuscripts, is missing from the lemma. This paragraph distinguishes 'efficient' (*poiêtika*) causes from 'formal' (*eidika*) causes in terms of whether or not they precede their effects. Although *poiêtikon aition* here means 'efficient cause', Ps.-Alexander also uses *poiêtikon* alone in the sense of 'efficient cause' (see the Greek-English Index in this volume). Aristotle's familiar distinction of material, formal, efficient, final cause (set forth in *Physics* 2.3 and *Metaphysics* 5.3) is only vaguely alluded to in *Metaphysics* 12; cf. note 127.

99 [678,4] On the distinction between rational and non-rational parts of the soul see *EN* 1.13, 1102a26–1103a3 and *EE* 2.1, 1219b26–1220a2. Ps.-Alexander associates the non-rational soul with imagination and appetite (cf. 691,6 and 694,3). For similar suggestions that some part of the soul might be able to exist in separation from the body see *Metaph.* 6.1, 1026a5–6; 8.3, 1043b18–21; *PA* 1.1, 641a32-b10; *GA* 2.3, 736b15–29; *DA* 1.4, 408b18–30; 2.1, 413a3–7. On the interpretative controversy over the separation of mind see Miller 2013.

100 [678,5] Contrast Alexander in Averroes: '[Aristotle] adds the word 'perhaps' (*isôs*) because the proof of such statements does not belong to this science [i.e. first philosophy], nor is the discussion of it proper to it, but to psychology' (fr. 14F=*Tafsīr* 1487–8; tr. Genequand). Freudenthal (1884, 42) rather misleadingly represents Ps.-Alexander as affirming the immortality of the soul and Alexander in Averroes as denying it (cf. note 131).

101 [678,9] Averroes (*Tafsīr* 1491–2) and Aquinas (*Commentary on Metaphysics* 2454) both understand Aristotle's point to be that the principle that effects have synonymous causes does not establish that Forms are necessary, because this principle is satisfied by individual causes in the case of both natural entities and artefacts.

102 [678,9] The art of healing is identified with the concept (or account) of health, which is identified with the form of health in the mind of the artist. Cf. 7.7, 1032b1–14; 7.9, 1034a9–25; 12.4, 1070b33; 12.9, 1075a1–3; *PA* 1.1, 640a31–2; and note 82.

# [Chapter 4]

103 [678,11] Several puzzles under this general heading are discussed in *Metaph.* 3.3–4, in particular the tenth puzzle: are the principles of perishable and imperishable things the same or different?

104 [678,14] According to Ps.-Alexander 'universally' is equivocal: it is equivalent to 'by analogy' at 1070a32, but contrasted with 'individually' at 1071a17 (cf. 684,8–9). According to Aquinas (*Commentary on Metaphysics* 2464), however, 'universally' is univocal, with the occurrence at 1070a32 looking forward to 1071a17.

105 [678,14] In an analogy A is related to B as C is related to D (see *Poet.* 21, 1457b16–19). Cf. *Metaph.* 5.6, 1016b31–1917a3 where things that are one in genus are also said to be one by analogy.

106 [678,23] Translates *kata ta suntetagmena*. *Suntattein* means literally 'to put items together in a certain order'. For example, although a statue and a door have different proximate principles, the principles can be placed in the same order: that of matter, form, and privation. Compare Plato *Laws* 10,903D where soul is said to be 'put together' (*suntetagmenê*) with different bodies in different lifetimes.

107 [678,35] Ps.-Alexander takes Aristotle's puzzle to be about whether the elements and principles are the same for all ten categories (as suggested at 1070a34–5,b1–2

and 1071a30). Judson (143), in contrast, takes the puzzle to be directed at Platonists such as Xenocrates who distinguish only beings *per se* and relatives (as suggested by 1070B3–4).

108 [679,9] An accident (*sumbebêkos*) is defined in *Metaph.* 5.30 as a characteristic which belongs to a subject at a particular place and time but does not do so necessarily or essentially (see also note 56). A relative (*pros ti*) is something that is said to be just what it is in relation to something else which is its correlative: e.g. the double is a relative because it is a double *of* a half (*Cat.* 7). It is assumed here that a relative (e.g. shorter than Simmias) is an accident of a substance (e.g. Socrates). Ps.-Alexander again understands Aristotle to be claiming that the same conclusions concerning relatives hold for all the non-substantial categories.

109 [679,12] Alexander in Averroes (fr. 17F=*Tafsīr* 1510–11) has a different interpretation: this is a new dialectical argument to the effect that if all the categories have a common element which is distinct from all the categories, this element must in turn have an element distinct from itself, and so on *ad infinitum*. The argument is dialectical because it tacitly assumes that every actual existent must be composed of elements.

110 [679,20] *Stoikheion* means 'letter' as well as 'element'.

111 [679,22] The lemma has *oude dê tôn noêtôn stoikheiôn* (as in Aristotle manuscripts EJCM), which is assumed in Ps.-Alexander's discussion. Most modern editors, however, prefer *oude dê tôn noêtôn stoikheion estin* (as in Aristotle manuscript A[b]), translated 'Nor, then, is any of the intelligible things an element', supposing that the genitive plural *stoikheiôn* in the first reading was misleadingly attracted to *noêtôn*. However, *stoikheiôn* may in fact be the correct reading if Aristotle has in mind the Platonic view that the Forms are 'intelligible' (*noêta*) and 'elements' (*stoikheia*) of perceptible objects (cf. 1.6, 987b18–20; 1.9, 990a31–2; 13.10, 1087a5). In support of *stoikheiôn* see Crubellier 2000, 146–8; cf. Judson note on 1070b7.

112 [679,23] The thesis that one and being are elements or principles of all things is also associated with Plato and the Pythagoreans (cf. 3.1, 996a5–6; 3.3, 998b9–11; 5.3, 1014b6–9). The reference to one and being is, therefore, to the point here because they seem to pose an obvious counter-example to Aristotle's thesis that there is no element or principle prior to the categories (a challenge which Aristotle also seeks to fend off in 3.3, 998b15–20).

113 [679,32] Translates *en* ('in') which is not found in EJA[b] but is present in CM. Ps.-Alexander understands Aristotle to be criticizing the view that one or being is an element contained in a compound as a part of it within a whole.

114 [679,34] Ps.-Alexander takes 'them' (*autôn*) to refer to compounds with being and one as elements, while Judson takes 'them' to refer to the elements, being and

one (2019,147). In contrast, Bonitz regards the reference to intelligible elements as an interpolation with 'them' referring back to 'elements' in a more general sense (1070b5). It is noteworthy that Alexander in Averroes mentions two interpretations, the first resembling Bonitz's and the second Ps.-Alexander's (fr. 18F=*Tafsīr* 1513–15). See also Salis, n. 157.

115 [680,3] This is an alternative paraphrase of Aristotle's sentence *ouden ar' estai autôn out' ousia oute pros ti*. Here Ps.-Alexander treats *out' ousia oute pros ti* as the subject whereas earlier at 679, 34–4 he treated it as the predicate.

116 [680,23] Ps.-Alexander's interpretation recalls *An. Post.* 1.22, 83a4–23 where Aristotle distinguishes between 'The white thing is wood' and 'The wood is white'. The latter, he says, is a strict (*haplôs*) predication because the wood becomes white, whereas the former is merely an accidental (*kata sumbebêkos*) predication because white is not the substratum of wood. However, at 1070b12 Aristotle implies further that the wood in itself (*kath' hauto*) primarily has the potentiality to be white.

117 [680,25] This may be what Aristotle means, but Ps.-Alexander does not comment on the omission of privation here. In contrast, Alexander in Averroes adds that 'cold is privation of heat, and cold, in cold bodies [e.g. earth and water], is that which produces their essence and essential properties in them' (fr. 19F=*Tafsīr* 1519; tr. Genequand).

118 [680,28] Judson calls Ps.-Alexander's proposal to move the clause 'a desperate remedy' (2019, 152). The words may be relevant here if they are intended to support the claim that compounds such as flesh or bone are substances distinct from their constituent elements ('those things').

119 [680,39] i.e. different proximate causes (i.e. matter, form, and privation) assigned to different effects in us. Things 'co-ordinated in us' is a gloss for Aristotle's 'immanent things' (*ta enhuparkhonta*). The commentary manuscripts have *katasuntetagmena*, a hapax legomenon, in place of which Hayduck conjectures *sunkatatetagmena* (which occurs at 685,20). I suggest *kata <ta> suntetagmena*, which is used earlier to describe proximate causes; cf. 678,23; 680,17; and note 106.

120 [681,3] Aristotle's claim that principle (*arkhê*) is more universal than element (*stoikheion*) is entailed by remarks in *Metaphysics* Book 5: that principles are immanent or external (5.1, 1013a19–20), that elements are principles (1013a20), and that elements are immanent (5.3, 1014b14–15). See Malink 2017 on Aristotle's distinction between elements and principles.

121 [681,6] Ps.-Alexander views 'the principle is divided into these' as a conditional clause supporting the following assertion that the efficient cause is a sort of principle, although the two clauses are independent in Aristotle's text. The phrase

recurs at 1070b29–30 (where it seems out of place) in some Aristotle manuscripts (EJ, though not in A$^b$, in Ps.-Alexander, or in Averroes' Arabic translation). Jaeger brackets the phrase in both places. See Salis, n. 170.

122 [681,6] This paraphrase differs from the Aristotle manuscripts, which disagree with each other: EJCM have *to d'hôs kinoun ê histan arkhê tis ousa* where the final feminine participle *ousa* does not agree with the neuter subject; while A$^b$, in place of *ousa*, has *kai ousia*, which does not seem apropos. Ps.-Alexander is closer to EJCM though he omits *ousa*, and his text agrees with the anonymous Latin translation ('quasi movens vero aut stans prinicipium est quoddam') and one of the Arabic translations quoted by Averroes (*Tafsīr* 1525). For discussion see Crubellier 2000, 153–5 and Judson note on 1070b23–5.

123 [681,14] This paraphrase agrees with the lemma reading *phusikois anthrôpois anthrôpos* (also in EMCV$^k$). According to Ps.-Alexander Aristotle intends to distinguish 'natural human beings' from Plato's Form of the Human Being Itself, which seems irrelevant to the context. It is widely suspected that *anthrôpois* (dative plural) may have been attracted to *phusikois*. Proposed solutions are to read *anthrôpôi* (dative singular) instead of *anthrôpois* (Zeller, 1919–1923, Ross, Jaeger, manuscript J$^b$) or simply to omit *anthrôpois* (manuscripts A$^b$J). Judson suggests a way the lemma reading might be retained, namely by taking *anthrôpois* with *anthrôpos* rather than with *phusikois*, permitting the translation: 'what brings about movement is, in natural things, a human being for human beings' (see his note on 1070b31).

124 [681,17] *Phys.* 2.7, 198a26.

125 [681,21] See note 102.

126 [681,22] This implies that there are *individual* forms which function as proximate causes of individual products. Cf. 678,22–8 where Socrates is said to have a distinct matter, form, and privation along with a distinct efficient cause (namely, his father Sophroniscus). There is a long-standing controversy over whether Aristotle is in fact committed to individual forms. See Sharples 2003, 146–8 for discussion of individual forms in Ps.-Alexander's interpretation.

127 [681,23] The four causes here are matter, from, privation, and moving cause, not the more familiar four – material, formal, efficient, and final – listed in *Physics* 2.3 and *Metaphysics* 5.2. The latter are not listed as such in *Metaphysics* 12.

128 [681,25] This is Aristotle's own first allusion in *Metaphysics* 12 to the first cause, which he describes as 'moving all things'. Alexander in Averroes (fr. 20F=*Tafsīr* 1529–31) suggests that Aristotle adds this in order to indicate that there is a principle distinct from movable things which does not have to be synonymous with them because it is a final cause.

## [Chapter 5]

129 [681,33] 'These things' translates *tauta*, which would usually be rendered 'the latter' since it is contrasted with *ekeina*, 'the former'. But *tauta* clearly does not refer to non-substances here. Alternatively, *tauta* could have the same referent as *ekeina*, namely substances. Ps.-Alexander, however, understands Aristotle to be claiming that it is the *principles* of substances that are the causes of all things, which seems to fit better with Aristotle's examples of soul, body, etc. In keeping with this interpretation, *tauta* of the manuscripts is emended to *t'auta* ('the same things') by Christ, followed by Ross, Jaeger, *et al.* (cf. Judson note on 1071a1).

130 [681,35] Ps.-Alexander repeats Aristotle's unusual phrase *tôn ousiôn aneu*. This argument assumes the ontological priority of substance; cf. note 23.

131 [682,2] Alexander in Averroes (unlike Ps.-Alexander) suggests that Aristotle uses 'perhaps' (*isôs*) because some people think the soul is separate, and he mentions interpretations involving separable souls or celestial souls (fr. 21F=*Tafsīr* 1534–5). Ps.-Alexander's reference to the souls of non-rational animals suggests that he does not see immortal souls or celestial souls at issue here (cf. 678,5).

132 [682,4] The words *ê orexis kai sôma* ('or body and desire') are not in our Aristotle manuscripts. Either Ps.-Alexander found them in another source or else (more likely) he added them for completeness.

133 [683,10] *Phys.* 1.8, 191b33.

134 [682,22] This citation departs from Aristotle manuscripts EJA$^b$ but agrees with CM in reading *allote* ('sometimes') instead of *alla te* ('both different'), and it departs from all the Aristotle manuscripts in omitting *en* before *eniois*. The former may have crept into the text anticipating *hote men . . . hote de* in the next line. The latter may simply be an oversight.

135 [682,30] Jaeger's apparatus mentions the first part of Ps.-Alexander's example: '*oinos* est *dunamei oxos* velut *sarx* est *dunamei anthrôpos*'. The second part of Ps.-Alexander's example is bizarre, unless he was privy to an alchemical process for transmuting vinegar into wine. In any case our Aristotle manuscripts do not mention vinegar, so another, more plausible interpretation of the example is simply that the same liquid is sometimes wine in potentiality and at another wine in actuality (cf. Averroes *Tafsīr* 1537).

136 [682,35] Ps.-Alexander (followed by some scholars) aligns privation here with potentiality, whereas most scholars align it with actuality. However, Aristotle's text (1071a8–10) is confusing because it combines two different triads (form, privation, matter; and form, matter, compound) together with unclear syntax, thus allowing for different interpretations. In any case, it is arguable that Aristotle

137 [683,2] By 'separable in thought' (*khôriston têi epinoia*) Ps.-Alexander evidently means 'separable in definition'. Hence, he takes the reference to be to form in so far as it is understood (i.e. defined) independently of matter. Alternatively, many scholars understand the reference to be a special class of forms, but there is not agreement on what class this might be. The phrase 'the enmattered forms' (*ta enüla eidê*) here seems to mean merely 'forms which exist in matter'. The phrase 'enmattered' was commonly used by the commentators, but it is debatable whether it is found in Aristotle himself. A widely discussed possible occurrence is at *DA* 1.1, 403a25 in manuscripts UX.

does not clearly commit himself one way or the other on the status of privation. For different interpretations see Code 2000, 168; Rapp 2016, 108; and Judson,161–2.

138 [683,5] Aristotle describes this example elliptically, mentioning only darkness as a privation. Ps.-Alexander fills out the example: light is the form, transparent air the matter, and day the compound of matter and form (cf. 12.4, 1070b21 discussed at 680,34–7). On the definition of light as the actualization of the transparent in so far as it is transparent see *DA* 2.7, 418b7–13.

139 [683,9] Translates *sterêsis de to skotos*. Hayduck treats this as a citation, but it is more likely a paraphrase of *sterêsis de hoion skotos* (1071a9–10; see lemma 1071a3 for the context).

140 [683,10] In the lemma Bonitz and Hayduck insert *diapherei*, which is missing from the commentary manuscripts (although 'differunt' occurs in Sepúlveda's translation). The omission may be a copyist's error because *diapherei* occurs in the citation at 683,23.

141 [683,22] Ps.-Alexander tacitly assumes that the sun's matter and form are temporally prior to Socrates'.

142 [683,27] Although this sounds like a mere tautology, Ps.-Alexander probably means that Aristotle's statement amounts to the claim that in another way things which have neither the same matter nor the same form differ in actuality and potentiality (on different interpretations see Salis 2005, 151–6). As Ross (364) points out, however, there may be more to the passage than this. For Aristotle's first 'which' clause uses *mê* for 'not' while the second uses *ou*, indicating that they are not on a par. That is, the first provides the basis for the second, e.g. it is because things have different matters that they have different forms.

143 [683,29] The inclined orbit of the sun is the cause of the seasons and hence of growth and decay; cf. *Phys.* 2.2, 194b13; *GC* 2.10, 336a31-b15; *Metaph.* 12.6, 1072a10–18; 12.8, 1272a15–16; 692,23–30.

144 [684,3] Translating *anastrepsanti*, instead of which Bontiz conjectures *antistrepsanti*, 'conversely'.

145 [684,12] The words 'in actuality and another thing that is in potentiality' are missing from the citation but are alluded to in the paraphrase. Ps.-Alexander understands the referent to be the proximate efficient cause understood as an individual hylomorphic compound.

146 [684,16] Here again Ps.-Alexander seems to imply that universals exist only in the soul (see note 28). Cf. also Alexander in Averroes fr. 22F=*Tafsīr* 1544.

147 [684,18] i.e. universal; translating *holês* as emended by Bonitz (who notes that Sepúlveda translates 'universalis'). Hayduck reads *holôs* (with L), though he also conjectures *haplôs* (which occurs in Aristotle's text but not in attributive position). Manuscript A has *hulês* which looks like a copyist error or misguided correction.

148 [684,21] Translates *eidê tôn ousiôn* (A, while L has *ta eidê tôn ousiôn*). The introduction of 'forms' seems rather abrupt here, and the Aristotle manuscripts disagree over whether *eidê* in fact occurs. Most of them have *eidê*, though they divide (like the commentary manuscripts) over whether to omit an initial *ta*: $E^1A^b$ reading *epeita eidê ta tôn ta ousiôn* and $CMV^k$ reading *epeita ta eidê ta tôn ousiôn*. In contrast, manuscript $J^1$ reads *êdê* instead of *eidê*. (An indication of the copyists' uncertainty over the correct reading is that E was corrected to *êdê* and J to *eidê*!) Modern editors in general eschew *eidê*: Jaeger accepts *êdê*, so the passage would be translated 'already the [causes] of substances [are causes and elements of things not in the same genus]'; and Ross (with Rolfes 1928 also followed by Fazzo and Alexandru) emends to *ei dê*, translated 'if then the [causes] of substances [are the principles of everything]'. Judson (with Christ) however retains *ta eidê*, translating: 'and then the forms of substances'. A possible back reference is to 1070b25-6 if *eidê* or *ta eidê* is read; to 1070b17 if *êdê* is read; and to 1070b31-1071a2; or 1070b17 if *ei dê* is read. See Judson's note on 1071a24 for further discussion of this difficult passage.

149 [684,23] E.g. Sophroniscus and Socrates are the same in species but different in number (cf. 681,19).

150 [684,27] According to Ps.-Alexander all three causes – material, formal, efficient – are distinguished as 'your' and 'my'. This passage (along with 1071a14-20) is often appealed to as evidence that Aristotle had a conception of *individual* form. Ps.-Alexander reinforces this impression by adding that the matter and form of different substances are themselves different in number (cf. also 709,1-25). Judson (139-41, 170-2) defends the individual form interpretation against Konstan and Ramelli 2006 and others.

151 [685,4] Omitting *ê* before *tôi analogon* with Bonitz based on A (Hayduck retains *ê* following L). Cf. Jaeger and Judson on 1071a33.

152 [685,4] Sepúlveda adds 'et id quod movet' ('and the moving cause'), probably attending to Aristotle's text instead of the commentary manuscript. Ps.-Alexander

no doubt postpones mention of the moving cause until 685,11 ff. because he views it as contrasted with the other three.

153 [685,10] e.g. when the sun melts snow together with its coldness, the sun causes the additional destruction of the coldness.

154 [685,13] Ps.-Alexander understands a reference back to 1070a18–19; cf. 684,8–19. See Judson, 173 for a different interpretation.

155 [685,14] See above 678,27 f.; 683,13.28; 684,12 ff. The term *entelekheia* (actualization), however, occurs only twice in Book 12: here and at 1074a36. It plays an important role in Aristotle's other works, however, especially DA 2.1.

156 [685,19] Aristotle elsewhere compares the species to a compound of matter (the genus) and form (the differentiae); see 5.6, 1016a28; 5.28, 1024b9; 7.12, 1038a6; 10.8, 1058a22.

157 [685,20] Translates *hetera*, omitted in the commentary manuscripts; cf. 1071a36.

158 [685,23] Rather than merely paraphrasing Alexander in Averroes explains that the perceptible objects mentioned here include everlasting as well as perishable substances (fr. 24F=*Tafsīr* 1557–8).

# [Chapter 6]

159 [685,28] See 12.7, 1072b25–30, where Aristotle himself first describes the prime mover as a god. The translation 'god' is in lower case because Aristotle does not treat *theos* as a proper name. (Greek writers commonly use 'the god' to refer to different deities depending on the context.) Also, the pronoun 'it' is used to refer to the god even though *ho theos* is masculine, because there is no indication that Aristotle regards the god as male. According to Ps.-Alexander Aristotle recognizes a plurality of gods among which the prime mover is the first (cf. 12.8, 1074b8–10 and 721,31–3).

160 [685,30] Cf. note 23.

161 [685,30] The remainder of this introductory section (685,30–687,29) is reproduced by Ps.-Alexander with many minor alterations from the genuine Alexander's *Quaestiones* 1.1 (ed. Bruns). The following notes report changes made by Ps.-Alexander which affect the meaning. Other trivial variations are noted in Hayduck's apparatus. The translation is indebted to Sharples 1992 but frequently modified for the sake of consistency.

162 [685,31] *Quaest.* begins simply, 'If all substances are perishable, all things will be perishable' (2,20).

163 [685,34] Instead of 'And it is clear ... imperishable', *Quest.* 2,22–3 has 'But not all things are perishable, because it is impossible for movement to be imperishable; for it is everlasting.' For Aristotle's proof see *Phys.* 8.1, 251a8–252a5.

164 [685,36] The verb *poiein* is translated 'affect' when it is opposed to *paskhein* (be affected). The alternative rendering 'act' is reserved for *energein* in this translation.

165 [686,3] Instead of 'Since, therefore, ... everlasting', *Quaest.* 3,1 has 'Now, movement is in that which is moved, so that the everlasting [movement], too, is in that which is moved everlastingly'.

166 [686,9] Instead of 'So the body ... everlasting', *Quaest.* 3,7 has 'the everlasting body which undergoes everlasting movement' (Bruns) or 'the body which undergoes everlasting movement is everlasting' (with B²).

167 [686,13] Instead of 'And what ... then this', *Quaest.* 3,10–11 has 'And what undergoes the first of all movements is also animate'. This is the peculiar interpretation of Alexander of Aphrodisias, taken over by Ps.-Alexander (cf. also fr. 25F=*Tafsīr* 1567). Although Aristotle does not say that the celestial spheres are animate in *Metaphysics* 12, he implies it at *Cael.* 2.2, 285a29–30; 2.12, 292a20–1,b1–2. See also 706,331–707,6 for Ps.-Alexander's explanation of why Aristotle does not mention souls in *Metaphysics* 12.

168 [686,17] Instead of 'for this reason' (*dia touto*), *Quaest.* 3,15 has 'this being so' (*touto on*).

169 [686,19] The term *ephesis* is rare in Aristotle (cf. *EN* 3.5, 1114b6) but more common in the commentators. It recurs at 694,2–3.

170 [686,21] Instead of 'And if it is moved ... it yearns', *Quaest.* 3,18 begins with a genitive clause translated, 'And in the case of that which is moved in accordance with impulse and yearning, there must be something for which this [body] yearns'.

171 [686,24] This remark of Alexander is important for Ps.-Alexander's own interpretation (cf. note 200). The term *energeia* can imply either 'actuality' or 'activity', a difference in connotation significant for Ps.-Alexander's account.

172 [686,26] The words 'but no potentiality ... Hence' are absent from *Quaest.* 3,22. The reference here is to *De Caelo* 1.12, 281a28-b25.

173 [686,28] The sentence 'So ... potentiality' is absent from *Quaest.* 3,23.

174 [686,30] The words 'and this [will go on] without limit' (*kai touto eis apeiron*) are absent from *Quaest.* 2,24.

175 [686,32] The words 'So' (*ara*) and 'cause' (*aitia*) are absent at *Quaest.* 3,26. However, Bruns adds *aitia* following Ps.-Alexander in order to make sense of the corresponding passage in *Quaestiones*.

176 [686,33] Instead of 'the body capable of circular motion' (*to kuklophorêtikon sôma*) *Quaest.* 4,2 has 'the divine body' (*to theion sôma*).

177 [686,34] Instead of 'affinity' or 'attraction' (*oikeiôseôs*) *Quaest.* 4,3 has 'being assimilated' (*homoiôseôs*). Unlike the genuine Alexander, Ps.-Alexander perhaps holds that a finite being cannot become similar to an infinite being; cf. 695,37–9 and see Salis 2005, 177, 402.

178 [686,36] Analysis is a method of distinguishing the factors involved in a case of causation; cf. *EN* 3.3, 1112b23. In ch. 7, Ps.-Alexander says that Aristotle uses the method of analysis to establish that there is an unmoved mover (693,13).

179 [687,1] 'That thing' (*ekeinou*) evidently refers to the first principle. Hayduck reads *ekeinou* following *Quaest.* 4,7, instead of *ekeinôn* ('these things') found in the commentary manuscripts (and 'illorum' in Sepúlveda).

180 [687,5] Plato, *Tim.* 52B.

181 [687,6] Translates *energeia tis*; alternatively, 'a sort of actuality'. Instead *Quaest.* 4,11 has 'something in actuality (dative)' (*energeiai ti*). Ps.-Alexander is more inclined than Alexander of Aphrodisias to describe the first mover as an actuality.

182 [687,6] The phrase 'and by itself' (*kai kath' hauto*) is absent from *Quaest.* 4,12.

183 [687,7] The word 'exists' (*esti*) is absent from *Quaest.* 4,12.

184 [687,11] Instead of 'contemplates' (*theôrêi*), *Quaest.* 4,16 has 'is active' (*energêi*). However, Bruns reads *theôrêi* with Ps.-Alexander in order to make better sense of the passage in *Quaestiones*.

185 [687,13] Instead of 'I mean ... most of all' *Quaest.* 4,17 has simply 'This is intelligible most of all.'

186 [687,16] 'Well' translates *eu*, which is bracketed by Hayduck. It is absent from *Quaest.* 4,20 and is not translated by Sepúlveda.

187 [687,18] 'So' (*ara*) is absent from *Quaest.* 4,22.

188 [687,22] 'So' (*ara*) is absent from *Quaest.* 4,26.

189 [1071b22] Translates *energeiai* (dative) as in EJ, while $A^b$ has *energeia* (nominative) as in Ross and Jaeger. Ps.-Alexander does not cite or comment this sentence.

190 [687,34] 'In effect' (*dunamei*) suggests that the argument at 1071b5–11 is enthymematic; cf. note 192.

191 [687,35] Translates *aidion* added by Hayduck with Bonitz (based on 'sempiternum' in Sepúlveda).

192 [687,38] Ps.-Alexander understands this to be implied by Aristotle's argument, since it lays the basis for arguing that this substance must be kept in everlasting motion by something else.

193 [688,2] *Phys.* 8.1, 251a18–28. Aristotle's argument is, in brief, that if a movement occurs, there must be a thing capable of being moved and something capable of moving it, both of which must have come to be as a result of a prior movement,

and so forth. Here and in the following lines Ps.-Alexander is contented with highly abbreviated allusions to the more elaborate arguments of the *Physics*. Freudenthal (1884, 19, 187) points out that the corresponding passage (685,33–686,16) taken from *Quaestiones* mentions a different line of argument involving the ensouled nature of the heavenly bodies rather than the eternity of time.

194 [688,2] More expansively in Sepúlveda: 'he thinks that the reason should not be left unspoken' ('rationem non putat silentio esse praetermittendam').

195 [688,4] Cf. *Phys.* 4.11, 219a34-b3: 'When [we perceive] a before and an after, then we say that there is time; for time is this, a number of movement in respect of before and after.'

196 [688,9] Cf. 686,5–7. On the continuity of movement see *Phys.* 5.4, 228a20-b1.

197 [688,11] Paraphrase of 1071b10: time 'is either the same as or some affection of movement'; cf. *Phys.* 8.1, 251b27–8: 'time [is] some affection of movement'. Cf. *Phys.* 4.11, 219a1–2,b2–3. Sharples (2003, 201–2) seems to have overlooked this comment of Ps.-Alexander.

198 [688,14] *Phys.* 7.1.

199 [688,15] This is tantamount to saying it is a moving cause and an efficient cause; cf. note 98.

200 [688,17] Translates *amoirousa dunameôs*. Similar phrases recur throughout this chapter, the first time in the text borrowed from Alexander (cf. 686,24). As is evident in the next sentence, however, being an actuality, for Ps.-Alexander, entails 'acting' (*energein*); cf. Salis 2005,182–3. This passage, incidentally, suggests that the mover is an immaterial form.

201 [688,20] Ps.-Alexander understands the claim that 'there will not be movement' literally, and interprets Aristotle's argument along the lines of *Cael.* 1.12, 283a27–8: 'that which is perishable at some time perishes, and if it is generable, it [at some time] has come to be'. That is, Ps.-Alexander supposes that, for Aristotle, if movement is merely possible (i.e. not necessary) then there will actually fail to be movement at some time. As Hintikka (1973, 95–9) points out, this is a special case of the so-called 'principle of plenitude'. Ross interprets Aristotle's claim differently: 'there need not be (always) movement'. This seems, however, too weak for Aristotle, because it leaves it open that there is always movement as a merely contingent fact. In the conditional at 1071b12–13, Ross, Jaeger, and Alexandru agree with Ps.-Alexander in reading *esti* ('is') in the protasis and *estai* ('will be') in the apodosis, although most manuscripts (e.g. EA[b]) have *esti* in both clauses, except for J which has *estai* in both.

202 [688,27] 'Over' and 'under' are of course relative to our viewpoint. As a celestial sphere revolves around the stationary earth, at any given time only half of it is 'over' us while the other half is 'under' us.

203 [688,30] Though Aristotle does not mention numbers here, see *Metaph.* 7.2, 1028b20.
204 [688,32] For similar objections that the Forms could not be efficient causes see *GC* 2.9, 335b7-24 and *Metaph.* 1.9, 991a8-b9.
205 [688,34] 'It' (*autê*) refers to the substance other than the Forms; alternatively, 'this' (*hautê*, as emended by Bonitz based on 'haec' in Sepúlveda).
206 [688,37] A reference to certain Neoplatonists according to Freudenthal (1884, 22); see also 719,19-22.
207 [689,3] i.e. its substantial form or essence. See note 91.
208 [689,5] Alexander in Averroes (fr. 25F=*Tafsīr* 1567) adds that the eternal mover must be the object of love by the noblest body (i.e. the celestial sphere). Ps.-Alexander makes no mention of this additional requirement, nor is there any trace of it here in the Aristotle manuscripts, though it obviously anticipates 1072b3.
209 [689,10] Although Aristotle makes reference to the fixed or 'non-wandering' stars (*aplanê astra*), the commentators also applied the shorthand label 'the non-wandering sphere' (*hê aplanês sphaira*, or often simply *hê aplanês*) to the sphere containing the fixed stars. This will be translated here by the more perspicuous 'the sphere of the fixed stars' (implied at 1073b25). The fixed stars are contrasted with the seven planets or 'wanderers' (*planêtês*) which change position relative to each other and to the fixed stars over time. See notes 33 and 338.
210 [689,15] In ch. 8 Aristotle will argue that fifty-five spheres are required to explain the movements of the seven planets. Ps.-Alexander understands the planetary spheres to constitute a unified system.
211 [689,19] Ross takes this as evidence that Ps.-Alexander's source has *energeia* (sing.) at 1071b22 with $A^b$, 'which is the preferable reading', rather than *energeiai* (pl.) with E. Ps.-Alexander may however be referring further back to *energeia* at 1071b20. See Fazzo 2016 who favours reading *energeiai* here and elsewhere in Book 12.
212 [689,23] Or 'another principle is prior (prius) to the first principle' as in Sepúlveda.
213 [689,27] Averroes (*Tafsīr* 1569) offers the same analogy with similar wording. Genequand (139 n. 129) conjectures that the genuine Alexander was the source.
214 [689,31] Ps.-Alexander seems to understand Aristotle to be arguing that if X has the (mere) potential to exist then at some time X will not exist (cf. note 201). Ross construes the claim less literally as 'nothing that is need be'.
215 [689,38] *Cael.* 1.12.
216 [690,3] This is the first reference to Aristotle by name in the commentary on Book 12; cf. note 4. For the second solution to the puzzle see 691,16-27.

217 [690,8] According to Aristotle the *theologoi* ('theologians' or 'mythologists') beginning with Hesiod (fl. 700 BCE) were 'ancients who lived before the present generation and first gave accounts of the gods' in mythical language ( *Metaph.* 1.3, 983b28-9; 14.4, 1091a33-b8) whereas the *phusikoi* ('natural theorists' or 'physicists') beginning with Thales (620-540 BCE?) were those who explained natural phenomena in terms of their material constituents (cf. *DA* 1.1, 403a29-b1).

218 [690,11] Hesiod, *Theodicy* 116-17 and *Works and Days* 17. Hesiod is described as a theologian at 3.4, 1000a9.

219 [690,14] This doctrine of Anaxagoras was mentioned at 12.2, 1069b20-1; cf. 673,4-22. In contrast Alexander in Averroes denies that Aristotle is referring to Anaxagoras here, though Averroes points out that this is based on a misunderstanding (fr. 26F=*Tafsīr* 1571).

220 [690,18] Translates *to auto aition*. Ps.-Alexander may be reading a corrupt text, for all the Aristotle manuscripts have *to auto adunaton*, 'the same impossibility', and Ps.-Alexander, is at pains to explain what 'the same cause' could mean here. Bonitz emends Ps.-Alexander's text *to auto adunaton* (based on 'impossibile' in Sepúlveda). However, all the commentary manuscripts have *to auto aition*, and *aition* occurs again at line 19 (where Bonitz conjectures that *legomenon*, 'what he is saying', should be read instead).

221 [690,28] cf. 1071b30. This interpretation presupposes Aristotle's hylomorphic theory of reproduction set forth in *GA*, e.g. 1.19, 724b12-21. In the case of animals the male factor is active and the female factor passive. The female 'menstrual fluid' (*katamênia*, paraphrasing Aristotle's *epimênia*) is the matter or potentiality from which the fetus develops, and the male 'seminal fluid' (*gonê*) is the source of its form. In the case of plants there is no sexual differentiation according to Aristotle, so that the 'seed' (*sperma*) as a whole, combining male and female functions, plays the active role, and earth the passive role of matter.

222 [690,32] Paraphrase of *Tim.* 30A: 'He took over all that was visible, which was not at rest but undergoing discordant and disorderly movement.' Cf. 52D-53B.

223 [690,33] Cf. *Cael.* 3.2, 300b8-10: 'Leucippus and Democritus say the [atoms] always undergo movement in the void or unlimited.'

224 [690,36] This is how Ps.-Alexander construes a compressed and possibly corrupt clause in the Aristotle manuscripts: *alla dia ti kai tina ou legousin oude hôdi oude tên aitian* (1071b33-4). Modern editors offer various repairs along similar lines. The criticism of Plato may anticipate the problem of pre-cosmic disorderly motion; see note 228.

225 [690,38] A sphere is called 'planetary' (*planômenos*) if it contributes to the motion of a planet. Ps.-Alexander is referring to the observed retrograde motion of planets.

226 [691,4] Cf. 694,3–4: 'yearning (*ephexis*) is in the rational part' of the soul.
227 [691,7] Ps.-Alexander interprets Aristotle's phrase *biai de ê hupo nou ê allou hôdi* as 'but by force, *either* by intellect *or* by something else, in another way'. He then understands being moved by intellect and by imagination as two ways of being moved 'by force', which is inconsistent with the contrast between voluntary and forced action in *EN* 3.1. The alternative, more generally accepted, translation is 'but *either* by force *or* by thought *or* by something else in another way'.
228 [691,16] On this interpretation Plato is accused of inconsistent claims: the soul came to be with the cosmos (*Tim.* 34A-C), there was movement before the cosmos was created (*Tim.* 30A; cf. 690,32), and the soul is the cause of all movement (*Tim.* 46D-E; cf. *Phdr.* 245C-246A; *Laws* 10,894C-899B).
229 [691,21] Earlier in this chapter (1071b21–6) Aristotle has mentioned potentialities which are not yet actualized. The two senses in which potentiality may be said to be prior to actuality are illustrated with biological kinds at 9.8, 1049b17–27. In the individual case it is true that potentiality is prior to actuality (e.g. the acorn is prior in time to the oak tree that grows from it); but in the universal case it is false (e.g. acorns are posterior in time to the oak trees by which they were produced).
230 [691,22] Instead of 'For Socrates ... Nevertheless' another translation is 'For if Socrates, who was also musical in potentiality before, became also such in actuality, nevertheless ...' (based on Bonitz with manuscript M).
231 [691,27] *DA* 3.7, 431a2–7; cf. 3.5,430a20–1. See also *Metaph.* 9.8, 1049b24–6; *Cael.* 1.12, 283a20–4.
232 [691,33] Translates *tên energeian*. Assuming that this reflects what Ps.-Alexander saw, Ross, Jaeger, and Alexandru read *energeia* at 1072a5 as in Aristotle manuscripts MC. Fazzo, however, reads *energeiai* (dative) with EJA[b] (followed by Judson).
233 [692,1] According to Empedocles the cosmos underwent a perpetual cycle in which the four roots or elements alternately merged together and came apart in a process taking thousands of years. 'These never stop altering continuously, now everything coming together by Love, now each being carried apart by the enmity of Hate' (DK 31B17). Cf. *Phys.* 8.1, 250b26–251a5; *Cael.* 1.10, 279b14–17.
234 [692,4] Ps.-Alexander understands 'cycle' (*periodos*) in this passage as referring narrowly to the cycles in Empedocles' cosmology (see previous note), so that the proposed 'or in some other way' would refer to Aristotle's own theory of eternal celestial motions. In contrast, Alexander in Averroes (fr. 27F=*Tafsīr* 1578–9) understands *periodos* here as referring to the eternally recurring cycle of the seasons which Aristotle himself acknowledges and explains in *GC* 2.10, 336a31-b15. On the latter interpretation Ps.-Alexander's reconstruction would be unnecessary and indeed inappropriate.

235 [692,7] Ps.-Alexander's interpretation relies on two observable facts about the sun: it appears to rise, pass overhead, and sink every day; and it comes closer and then moves away over the course of a year. These two facts have, according to Aristotle, two separate causes. The first is due to the diurnal revolution of the solar sphere around the stationary earth, a motion which is ultimately caused by the motion of the outermost sphere of the so-called fixed stars. The second fact is due to the oblique orbit of the solar sphere. This is the cause of the seasons. Because the solar sphere revolves at a slight angle to the equator, the earth's northern hemisphere is tilted closer to the sun for half the year so that the sun appears closer, the days are longer, and temperatures are warmer; and it is tilted away from the sun for the other half so that the sun appears further away, days are shorter, and temperatures are cooler. At the same time the southern hemisphere experiences the opposite of these effects.

236 [692,14] Translates *paro*, 'rather than'; Bonitz emends to *kai ou*, 'and not', based on Sepúlveda's 'non'.

237 [692,16] Translates *ekeino autôi te aition kakeinôi*, in the commentary manuscripts (although Sepúlveda translates 'ipsi'). However, some Aristotle manuscripts including EJ have *hautôi* instead of *autôi*, which would imply that the outermost sphere moves *itself* as well as the other sphere. Ps.-Alexander understands the clause to say that the outer sphere moves both the solar sphere and Saturn's sphere. Although earlier editors read *hautôi*, following Ross most later editors have read *autôi* with Ps.-Alexander and Themistius (17,27).

238 [692,19] In this simplified model Saturn's sphere receives diurnal motion from the outermost sphere and transmits it in turn to the solar sphere (there is a far more detailed scheme in ch. 8). Thus, Saturn's sphere is, as it were, a mere cog in the cosmic machinery.

239 [692,25] During the course of the year the sun appears to pass through the zodiac (a belt of twelve constellations of stars in the outermost sphere) which is at an inclined angle of nine degrees to the equator. In antiquity the sun was in Scorpio in the autumn from 24 October until 21 November and in Capricorn in winter from 22 December 22 until 19 January. It now passes through these constellations later in the year due to the precession of the zodiac.

240 [692,30] Aristotle presents an explanation of the cycle of the seasons along these lines in *GC* 2.10, 336a31-b15 and *Meteor.* 1.9, 346a20-347a8. Cf. note 143.

241 [692,34] Another translation is 'the way we have described', as in Bonitz (reading *legomena* instead of *ginomena*) following manuscript A and 'nos ... disseramus' in Sepúlveda.

## [Chapter 7]

242 [692,36] Although editors customarily begin ch. 7 at 1072a19, Ps.-Alexander takes 1072a19–26 to conclude the argument of ch. 6.

243 [692,37] Ps.-Alexander takes the clause 'and if they are not … from not-being' to be parenthetical; cf. lemma 1072a4. The three theories of how the world came to be have been mentioned before: from Night (1071b27; 690,9–13), from a primordial mixture (1069b21–7; 1071b28; 673,4–22; 690,13–14), and from not-being (1069b18–20; 672,37–673,4).

244 [693,13] On the method of analysis see note 178.

245 [693,16] On the contrast between observable fact (*ergon*) and argument or theory (*logos*) see *EN* 9.8, 1168a35; 10.9, 1179a21.

246 [693,17] 'That which it moves' translates *ho kinei*, on the assumption that *ho* is in apposition with *to planômenon pan sôma*, 'the entire planetary body' (on which see following note). This assumes a comma following *kinei* (the comma is in Hayduck's text but missing in Bonitz's). However, *ho kinei* is ambiguous, since *ho* can refer to the subject of *kinei* rather than the object, i.e. 'that which moves it' rather than 'that which it moves'. Ps.-Alexander thus takes *ho* to refer to the object moved by the outer sphere. Ross, on the contrary, takes it to refer to the mover of the outer sphere on the grounds that 'from the existence of a *kinoumenon* [thing moved] there cannot be inferred the existence of something which it moves, but only the existence of something that moves it' (endorsed by Sharples 2003, 201). However, Ps.-Alexander clearly supposes that the claim as he understands it has been established earlier because the sphere of the fixed stars moves the planetary spheres (1072a10–15; cf. 692,7–25).

247 [693,18] Translates *to planômenon pan sôma*, namely, the system of planetary spheres and the planets which they carry.

248 [693,19] Or 'something which' (cf. 'aliquid' in Sepúlveda).

249 [693,22] Translates *energeia* as in the Aristotle manuscripts at 1072a25.

250 [693,24] Ps.-Alexander omits *ti* before *ho* but includes it in line 27.

251 [693,25] This crucial sentence is the subject of considerable debate. Regarding the text itself Ps.-Alexander's reading is close to that of Aristotle manuscripts E¹CM: *epei de kinoumenon kai kinoun kai meson toinun esti ti ho ou kinoumenon kinei* (cf. previous note). Slight variations are the inclusion of *to* before *kinoumenon* (JE²A^b) and the omission of the second *kai* (A^b ² V^k). But the main problem is that if (as proposed by Ps.-Alexander) a comma is inserted after *meson*, the apodosis begins with *toinun*, which according Denniston 'is never, in classical Greek (though occasionally in later writers), placed at the opening of a sentence' (1950, 568). Accordingly, Jaeger inserts an ellipse before *toinun*

indicating some kind of corruption. Others emend *toinun esti* to *esti toinun* or to *kinoun esti*, though there is no support for either of these in the manuscripts. Various proposed solutions are summarized in Judson note on 1072a24–5.

252 [693,26] Ross objects that this cannot be understood. However, Ps.-Alexander takes this as supported by his construal of *ho kinei* at 1072a22–4; see note 246.

253 [693,30] On Ps.-Alexander's interpretation the argument turns on the general principle that if the intermediate and either of two extremes exist, the other extreme must also exist. (See Introduction, 13–14 for fuller discussion.) Similar interpretations are offered by Themistius (*in Metaph.* 16,20 ff.) and Alexander in Averroes (fr. 28F=*Tafsīr* 1588–9). However, the text presents difficulties (mentioned in note 251), and other interpretations of this crucial argument have been proposed: see Alexandru, 113–15; Elders 1972, 162–4; Salis 2005, 203–6; Fazzo, 275–80; Judson, 221–2.

254 [693,32] *Orekton* is translated 'object of desire' and *noêton* as 'intelligible object'. The *-ton* ending can indicate either a possible object or an actual object.

255 [693,35] The causality of the prime mover of the cosmos is analogous to that of ordinary objects of desire. Aristotle distinguishes three factors in animal movement: 'that which is unmoved (namely, the good, which is to be done), that which both brings about movement and is moved (namely, the faculty of desire), . . . and that which is moved (namely, the animal)' in *DA* 3.10, 433b14–18. Moreover, in animals the object of desire brings about movement by being an object of awareness: 'that which brings about movement, namely, the faculty of desire as such, is one in form. But first of all it is the object of desire, for without being moved this brings about movement by being thought or imagined' (*DA* 433b10–12; cf. *MA* 6, 700b23–9).

256 [693,38] The examples are, presumably, a particular loaf of bread and evils as a general kind.

257 [694,1] Translates *kalon*, which implies here that the object is supremely good and the aim of rational desire and worthy of choice. Aristotle elsewhere distinguishes the 'noble' (*kalos*) from the (merely) 'good' (*agathos*) in two ways. First, the good is 'always involved in action' whereas the noble is 'also present in immovable things' (*Metaph.* 13.3, 1078a31–2). Second, 'all goods have ends which are worthy of choice for their own sake. Of these, the noble are those which, existing for themselves, are all worthy of praise' (*EE* 7.15, 1248b17–20).

258 [694,4] Aristotle distinguishes three types of 'desire' (*orexis*): 'appetite' (*epithumia*), 'spirit' or 'emotion' (*thumos*), and 'wish' (*boulêsis*, in the sense of rational desire) (*DA* 2.3, 414b2; *MA* 6, 700b22). Appetite (along with spirit, which usually, as here, is not mentioned) is viewed as a non-rational desire, whereas

wish is closely linked to the rational faculty (*logistikon*). Here, Ps.-Alexander also treats *ephesis* ('yearning') as a rational desire, but its precise relation to *boulêsis* is not explained (cf. note 169). Similarly, *epheton* refers to the 'object of yearning'.

259 [694,5] Cf. *EN* 3.4, 1113a23–4: 'ought we to say that the good is without qualification and truly the object of wish, or that the apparent [good] is [the object of wish] for each person?' Cf. also *DA* 3.10, 433a27–8.

260 [694,6] Hayduck incorporates emendations by Bonitz based on Sepúlveda's translation ('potius quam ediverso'). The readings in the commentary manuscripts, as in Aristotle manuscript E$^1$, seem to be garbled, e.g. with *kalon* instead of *mallon*.

261 [694,8] In this context 'principle' (*arkhê*) may be understood as 'starting point' or 'source' of movement. Cf. *DA* 3.10, 433a19–20 where the object of desire is the *arkhê* of practical thought.

262 [694,11] Aristotle's verb *noein* and related terms are notoriously difficult to render into English, since strictly consistent translation can deviate from ordinary English usage and result in awkward, confusing, and misleading verbiage. Granting that there is much room for disagreement, the terms are translated here as follows: *noein* is rendered 'think' following most translators (some prefer 'understand'). Although the verb *noein* is transitive with a direct object, it is translated 'think of' when it has an object. Thus, *noein heauto* is translated 'think of itself' rather than 'think itself' (a common translation which, though literal, is misleading in English). In a similar vein *noêsis* is translated as 'act of thinking' understood as a mental act, and *noêma* as 'thought' in the sense of the content of thinking (cf. note 430). *Nous* presents the greatest difficulty. Although it often has roughly the sense of 'mind', 'thought', 'reason', 'insight', Aristotle sometimes (e.g. in *DA* 3.4–8) uses it more technically for a psychic faculty analogous to perception. In the latter sense Ps.-Alexander applies it systematically to a faculty with distinctive powers, dispositions, and activities, a usage which parallels 'intellectus' in the medieval Latin commentators. (This probably explains Sepúlveda's shift from the ordinary 'mens' to the scholastic 'intellectus' at 694,29.) Accordingly 'intellect' will be used in the present translation in order to convey this more technical understanding of *nous*. On the term *noêtos* ('intelligible') see note 443.

263 [694,18] Aristotle describes the Pythagorean use of two co-ordinated columns or series (*sustoikhiai*), positive and negative, as follows: 'they say that there are ten [opposing] principles, which they say are arranged in [two] columns: limit and unlimited, odd and even, one and plurality, right and left, male and female, resting and moving, straight and curved, light and darkness, good and bad, square and oblong' (1.5, 986a22–6). Note that substance does not appear in this

list, although it is at the head of Aristotle's own version of the positive column. He also describes the principles in the negative column as 'privative, for none of them is either a this or a such or any of the remaining categories' (*Phys.* 3.2, 201b24–6; cf. *Metaph.* 11.9, 1066a15–17; cf. *GC* 1.3, 319a15). Further, as Ps.-Alexander suggests here, the positive column is 'intelligible in itself' in the sense that the items in it are intelligible in their own right. For example, one must know what it is to be straight before one can know what it is to be curved. It is noteworthy that Alexander in Averroes lays out four different interpretations of the opposing columns (fr. 29F=*Tafsīr* 1601–2): (1) the good versus the negation of the good; (2) form versus privation; (3) form without privation versus form involving privation; and (4) form (of which substantial form is first) versus matter. Ps.-Alexander's interpretation seems to combine features of (1) and (4).

264 [694,19] Compare Aristotle's phrase, 'the column of the noble' (14.6, 1093b12–13). On his concept of the noble see note 257.
265 [694,27] Reading *dê* as conjectured by Salis ('igitur' in Sepúlveda). The passage 694,27–39 is reproduced from the real Alexander's *Mantissa* 2, 108,3–15.
266 [694,32] Sepúlveda does not translate the words following 'beforehand'.
267 [694,32] For further explanation of the actual intellect (*ho kat' energeian nous*) see note 300.
268 [694,40] See *DA* 3.4, 430a3–5.
269 [695,1] Hayduck adopts Bonitz's emendation of *ex hautou* (based on 'a se' in Sepúlveda; *ex autou* in the manuscripts).
270 [695,3] Sepúlveda translates 'actu semper' ('always actual'), which would imply that it is not a human intellect.
271 [1072b6] Reading *de* with the Aristotle manuscripts. See note 286.
272 [695,12] In ch. 8. Aristotle has already intimated this at 6,1071b20–1; cf. 689,8–16. Laks (2000, 225 n. 50) defends Ps.-Alexander's interpretation against Ross' contention that Aristotle is concerned merely with terminological precision.
273 [695,16] The one is a measure in the sense that we measure the quantity of something by counting the units in it, e.g. we measure a person's height as a number of cubit lengths (cf. 10.1, 1053a33-b6).
274 [695,17] The Aristotle manuscripts have 'that which is because of itself an object of choice' (*to di' hauto haireton*). It is possible that the whole phrase was in Ps.-Alexander's copy, because *di' hauto haireton* occurs in his paraphrase at 695,20.
275 [695,22] For the relationship between the 'actual intellect' (*ho energeiai nous*) and the 'dispositional intellect' (*ho kath' hexin nous*) see note 300.
276 [695,24] 'The final cause' translates *to hou heneka*, more literally, 'the that-for-the-sake-of-which'. The same translation serves for *to telikon aition*. This is Aristotle's first explicit mention of teleology, though he hints at it at 1070a11–12.

277 [695,26] This cryptic reference by Aristotle has occasioned much speculation. In his lost work *On the Good* Aristotle reported on Plato's unwritten lectures (Philoponus *in DA* 75,34–76,1). The contraries are all aligned with either the One or the many according to the genuine Alexander (*in Metaph.* 250,17–20), who adds that the definitive treatment is in Aristotle's *Selection of the Contraries* (also lost) although they are also discussed in *On the Good* Book 2. Aristotle himself (*Phys.* 2.2, 194a36) mentions that he distinguished two senses of 'final cause' (*to hou heneka*) in his lost work *On Philosophy*. The distinction (also found in *Cael.* 2.12, 292b4–7; *DA* 2.4, 415b2–3,21–2; *EE* 8.3, 1249b15) is between the aim or benefit and the beneficiary of some action or process.

278 [695,27] Ps.-Alexander's citation *esti gar tini to hou heneka* (1072b2) agrees with most Aristotle manuscripts and with most Arabic and Latin translations. However, A[b] has *tini* followed by *tinos*, and most editors read *tini <kai> tinos* in agreement with Alexander in Averroes (fr. 29F=Tafsir 1601–2) and as suggested by Ps.-Alexander's interpretation (cf. Freudenthal 1884, 47 and Judson note on 1072b2).

279 [695,35] Because the clause 'since (*gar*) the final cause is for someone' does not spell out the distinction between two senses of 'final cause', Ps.-Alexander understands *gar* as having the unusual adversative force of *de*. The main point, as he understands it, is that when a thing aims at an end or benefit for a beneficiary, it is the latter which is in the strict sense the final cause and it does not undergo change. Later, however, Ps.-Alexander speaks of the beneficiary also as a final cause, though presumably in a secondary sense (see 708,38–9 and Introduction, 18–20).

280 [695,39] Translates *akatalêpton*, which can mean 'unattainable' as well as 'incomprehensible'.

281 [696,2] This implies that the celestial bodies are in motion because they yearn for the unmoved mover. Since 'yearning is in the rational part' (694,3–4), this implies further that these bodies possess rational awareness, although Ps.-Alexander does not explicitly say this here. There is a long-standing disagreement among commentators (ancient and modern) over whether the argument of *Metaphysics* 12 assumes that that the celestial bodies are animate and sentient (for an overview see Wolfson 1973).

282 [696,3] Here and often elsewhere 'the heaven' (*ho ouranos*) refers to the outermost sphere of the fixed stars. Ps.-Alexander does not quote in full the crucial sentence (1072b3–4) in Aristotle's text, but he offers a clue here as to what he might have read. The following appears in our principal Aristotle manuscripts: *kinei dê hôs erômenon, kinoumenôi de t'alla kinei*. Though commentators generally concur that the first clause means that the unmoved mover moves the celestial bodies by being loved, there is widespread disagreement over the second clause. Many agree with Ross that *kinoumenôi* is 'hardly possible Greek' and

suggest emendations. It is also disputed whether *t'alla* is the subject or object of *kinei*, and if it is the object, then what the subject might be. If, however, *kinoumenôi* is retained with Jaeger, the clause might mean: '*by what is moved* (i.e. the outer sphere) it (i.e. the unmoved mover) moves the others (i.e. the inner spheres)' (cf. Laks 2000, 220 and Judson note on 1072b4). The manuscript A$^b$ contains *kinoumenon* (as a correction by a later hand), which Ross conjectures might have been read by Ps.-Alexander: 'while *what is moved* (i.e. the outer sphere) moves the others (i.e. the inner spheres)'. Ross instead emends to *kinoumena*: '*by being moved* the others (i.e. the celestial spheres) move (*sc.* still other things)' (as in Reeve's translation). Barnes' translation silently omits *kinoumenôi*: 'and it [i.e. the unmoved mover] moves the others'.

283 [696,4] The verb *existanai* ('disestablish') is opposed to *histanai* ('establish'). *Existanai* here implies changing or altering a thing utterly so that it is no longer the same thing and thus in effect ceases to exist.

284 [696,7] Omitting *kinoumenos*, bracketed by Hayduck following Bonitz. The word is not translated by Sepúlveda.

285 [696,8] The commentary manuscripts have *energeia* in agreement with the Aristotle manuscripts, although Jaeger emends to *energeiai* (dative). Here and in the following lines *energeia* could also be translated 'activity', since it is closely tied to the verb *energein*, 'to act'.

286 [696,9]. The particle *de* ('however') in the apodosis is unusual but not impossible. On proposed reconstructions of this difficult passage of Aristotle see Laks 2000, 228-30 and Judson note on 1072b5. Based on his own text Ps.-Alexander offers a plausible paraphrase: although the outer sphere possesses a circular motion which is as such an actuality, it can nevertheless be otherwise in the sense of undergoing rotation.

287 [696,13] Translates *kineitai* in the broad sense.

288 [696,14] Bonitz adds *aei* ('always') with manuscript M, which is missing from the other manuscripts and not translated by Sepúlveda.

289 [696,15] The commentary manuscripts have *energeiai* (dative) in agreement with most Aristotle manuscripts. Alexandru however reads *energeia* (reporting that this reading is found in E and some other independent manuscripts, a fact that was misreported by earlier editors). The latter would seem to be more consistent with Ps.-Alexander's own reading of *energeia* at 693,22 and 696,8 (see Golitsis 2016b, 497). The word order is altered, perhaps for emphasis, in Ps.-Alexander's quotation.

290 [696,19] See 1072b8-9; cf. *Phys.* 8.9, 265a13-b16.

291 [696,22] The commentary manuscripts have *anankê*, whereas the Aristotle manuscripts have *anankêi*, which is closer to *ex anankês* in the paraphrase at 696,26-7.

292 [696,22] 'First principle' or 'principle' translates *arkhê* which in this context implies 'starting point [*sc.* of movement]'.

293 [696,30] Although Aristotle has just said that the prime mover cannot exist in a different state from the one it is in (1072b7–8), which is the third sense of necessity listed by Aristotle, Ps.-Alexander takes the second sense to be pertinent, because he is trying to explain the connection between existing of necessity and existing nobly.

294 [696,31] 'All' (*pasa*) is not in the Aristotle manuscripts.

295 [696,36] cf. *EN* 10.8, 1178b21–3: 'the activity of the god, which surpassing in blessedness, must be contemplative; and of human activities, therefore, that which is most akin to this must be happiest.'

296 [696,37] The term *diagôgê*, 'way of carrying on' (cf. *diagein*, 'to carry on') implies a leisurely and intrinsically pleasurable activity, e.g. doing philosophy or enjoying music, that is carried on for its own sake and not in order to satisfy needs or produce further results (cf. *Metaph.* 1.1, 981b17–19; 1.2, 982b19–24; *EN* 10.7, 1177a26–7; *Pol.* 8.5, 1339b15–19).

297 [697,4] 'Activity' translates *energeia* in contexts where acts such as perceiving and thinking take place (see 697,10). 'Activity' highlights the contrast with disposition (*hexis*), whereas the alternate 'actuality' emphasizes the opposition to potentiality (*dunamis*). In many instances either translation is appropriate because the two senses are so intimately interrelated. On the close connection of *energeia* with pleasure see *EN* 7.13, 1153b9–11.

298 [697,6] Sepúlveda adds 'semper' ('always'). Norman (1969, 72–3) quotes this passage (696,32–697,6, with the pagination of Bonitz 671,8–18) as evidence that Ps.-Alexander views divine self-thinking of the divine intellect as the same in kind as human abstract thinking. Later, however, Ps.-Alexander speaks of the divine intellect as thinking *only* of itself (699,1–10).

299 [697,7] Translates *tautên*. Bonitz conjectures that Ps.-Alexander wrote *tautêi* or else *ekhei* dropped out. The point is that first (i.e. divine) intellect consists in pure actuality or activity; cf. 698,6.20. See Introduction, 20–1.

300 [697,17] On this interpretation Aristotle is comparing the thinking of the prime mover with that of human beings. The commentary spells this comparison out systematically in terms of analogy between 'our' (i.e. human) intellect and the 'first' (i.e. divine) intellect. Three different levels or stages of the human intellect are distinguished: the 'actual' (*kat' energeian*), 'dispositional' (*kath' hexin*), and 'potential' (*dunamei*). The actual intellect is the mind when it is fully engaged in the activity of contemplating an intelligible object (see especially 697,38). The dispositional intellect is the mind when it is capable of engaging in such activity, for example, because it has already formed the concepts necessary to contemplate

such objects. The potential intellect is the mind when it is merely capable of forming concepts by separating the common form of individuals from the matter. Thus the dispositional intellect is 'intermediate' between the actual and dispositional intellects. It is the actual intellect which most directly parallels the divine intellect, because by means of actually contemplating intelligible objects (which include, most notably, the divine intellect) it thinks of itself. This paragraph for the most part (697,19–39) reproduces the real Alexander's *DA* 85,11–86,6. See Tuominen 2010, Herzog 2016, and Judson, 230–2 for similar interpretations.

301 [697,18] Bonitz brackets *kai dunamis*, 'and a potentiality'. However, it is in all the manuscripts and translated by Sepúlveda. Its inclusion implies that the dispositional intellect is only a partially actualized intellect.

302 [697,25] Salis obelizes *touto gar en autêi*, which is not translated by Sepúlveda. Ps.-Alexander's sentence is a garbled substitute for the real Alexander's 'For the difference between human beings comes from the matter' (85,16–17). Cf. Freudenthal 1884, 27 n. 2.

303 [697,39] This paragraph is reproduced by Ps.-Alexander with a few alterations from the genuine Alexander's *DA* 86,14–87,1.

304 [698,2] Instead of 'just as ... object' Alexander's *DA* 86,15–16 has 'as has been proven in the case of perception'.

305 [698,3] Sepúlveda adds 'qui is esse intelligitur' ('which it is thought to be').

306 [698,8] Hayduck emends to *kath' hauto* ('per se' in Sepúlveda). The manuscripts have *kath' hauton* (masc.), i.e. 'in virtue of the intellect', as in Alexander *DA* 86,21. Bonitz reads *hath' hautên*, i.e. 'in virtue of the disposition'.

307 [698,12] Instead of 'fit under' (*upharmozein*) Alexander's *DA* 86,26 has 'accord with' (*epharmozein*).

308 [698,14] This is a brief summary of Aristotle's argument in *DA* 3.4–8.

309 [698,15] Instead of *autos* (masc.) Alexander's *DA* 86,29 has *auto* (neut.).

310 [698,18] Hayduck emends to *kath' hauto* ('per se' in Sepúlveda). The manuscripts have *kath' hauton* (masc.), i.e. 'in virtue of the intellect'.

311 [698,20] The 'first intellect' (*ho prôtos nous*) is the divine intellect, which is the first cause of cosmic motion. Ps.-Alexander again borrows from the real Alexander, *DA* 89,21–2; cf. Sharples 2003, 211 n. 119.

312 [698,22] Translates *hê kath' hauto malista noêsis*, more loosely, 'thinking in its truest form'.

313 [698,26] Aristotle uses the metaphor of 'making contact' or 'touching' (*thinganein*) for the act of thinking of a simple intelligible object or essence. In the case of a complex object one's judgement (e.g. whether the wood is white) may be true or false, but in the case of a simple object or essence one's thought

either makes contact with the object or else fails to do so (e.g. one either grasps the essence of wood or white, or else one is ignorant of it); cf. 9.10, 1051b17–32 with 599, 1–600, 36.

314 [698,32] Translates *ekeino mallon toutou*, more literally, 'that rather than this' or 'the former rather than the latter'. Here the lemma agrees with the Aristotle manuscripts rather than Ps.-Alexander's own paraphrase (which incidentally agrees with Philoponus and Themistius) at 698,32: *ekeinou mallon touto*, 'this rather than that' (cf. also 37–8: *touto mallon ekeinou*, which is a more common construction). Ross, Jaeger, and Alexandru emend the Aristotle text in agreement with Ps.-Alexander's paraphrase, whereas Laks, Fazzo, and Judson adhere to the manuscript reading.

315 [698,34] Aristotle argues in *Nicomachean Ethics* 10.7 that contemplation is the highest form of human happiness and in 10.8, further, that 'the activity of the god, which is superior in blessedness, will be contemplative' (1178b21–2).

316 [698,38] Reading here *ekeinou mallon touto*, Ps.-Alexander takes the point to be that the latter (i.e. genuine thinking of itself) is the divine state belonging to the former (i.e. the divine intellect) more so than to the human intellect. Reading the same phrase Ross understands that the latter (i.e. actual contemplation) rather than the former (i.e. the capacity to contemplate) is the divine state (cf. Herzberg 2016, 173). If, however, *ekeino mallon toutou* is read with the lemma and Aristotle manuscripts (cf. note 314) it might mean: the former (thinking of itself) is more divine than partaking of an intelligible object (Laks (2000, 235 n. 72). See also Judson note on 1072b23 and Salis 2005, 229 n. 334; 2007, n. 396.

317 [699,4] If 'always' (*aei*) is included, as here, the point is that the first intellect is always an object of thinking by itself because it is always actually thinking. The word *aei* ('always') is found in only one commentary manuscript (M) and it is not translated by Sepúlveda. Nor is it to be found in the corresponding passage in the manuscripts of the real Alexander's *Mantissa* (699,1–11 of Ps.-Alexander's commentary is virtually identical with *Mantissa* 109,25–110,3). Bonitz reads *aei*, while Hayduck omits it without explanation. Bruns also adds *aei* in his edition of the *Mantissa* 109,27 (following Freudenthal 1884, 26) based on the parallel with commentary manuscript M.

318 [699,8] Translates *heauton ara monon noêsei*. The divine intellect is aware of itself and nothing else (cf. 699,1–2). This anticipates the argument of ch. 9.

319 [699,10] Following Hayduck's placement of a comma after *monos*. Bonitz and Sepúlveda place the comma before *monos* so that the translation is: 'in so far as it is simple, it alone (*monos*) will think of itself alone'. There is apparent tension with Ps.-Alexander's interpretation that the subordinate intellects are also simple (cf.

695,9–16), since this implies that the subordinate intellects too think only of themselves. Perhaps he supposes that they think of the first intellect by the way or *per accidens*.

320 [699,11] This explains Aristotle's unsupported claim that the divine intellect is superior to the human (cf. Herzberg 2016, 178). The commentary manuscripts vary. The translation follows Hayduck's text based on L with an emendation. Bonitz's text, reconstructed from A and M, is translated, 'And in so far as it is simple (A), only it among the intelligible things will think of itself alone (M)'.

321 [699,17] Ps.-Alexander reads *ekeino* (neut.) as in EJ, whereas $A^b$ has *ekeinos* (masc.). Nevertheless Ps.-Alexander understands the first intellect (*nous*, masc.) as the referent, whereas Ross takes it to be *ho theos*. See Judson note on 1072b27.

322 [699,18] Translates *kath' hautên* (i.e. in virtue of the activity) with M. A has *kath' hauton* (i.e. in virtue of the intellect).

323 [699,24] On the meaning of 'duration' (*aiôn*) see *Cael.* 1.9, 279a23–8: 'For the end that encompasses the lifetime of each individual that is not outside of nature has been called the duration (*aiôn*) of each. For the same reason also, the end of the entire heaven, and the one that encompasses all of time and its unlimitedness is a duration (*aiôn*) – having received its name from its always (*aei*) existing – that is immortal and divine.'

324 [699,31] The Pythagoreans and Speusippus understand 'principles' (*arkhai*) as 'starting points' or 'origins'. There may be a fuller statement of Speusippus' view at 14.4, 1091b15–1092a5. See also 717,37–718,5 and note 489.

325 [699,37] Aristotle offers a similar objection at 14.5, 1092a9–17; cf. 14.4, 1091a33–6.

326 [699,38] Though Hayduck treats this as a citation, it is more likely a paraphrase.

327 [700,1] *Phys.* 8.10, 267b17–22. Ps.-Alexander refers to *Physics* Book 8, probably because he does not find arguments in *Metaphysics* Book 12 for the claims made in this concluding paragraph. Against this Ross contends that these claims are supported by what has gone before, but the external passages referenced by Ps.-Alexander contain clearer and fuller proofs. It is also possible that 1073a5–13 is a later addition.

328 [700,4] *Phys.* 8.10, 266a12–24, 267b17–26.

329 [700,6] *Phys.* 8.10, 266a24-b6; cf. *Cael.* 1.7, 275b21–3.

330 [700,7] See *Phys.* 3.5; *Cael.* 1.5.

331 [700,8] Translates *apathes kai analloiôton*. Aristotle applies the same terms to whatever exists outside of the cosmos in *Cael.* 1.9, 279a20–1.

332 [700,10] Cf. 1072b8–9 with 696,19–20. For the proof see *Phys.* 8.7, 260a26–261a26.

## [Chapter 8]

333 [700,14] The proof is to be found not earlier in *Metaphysics* 12 but in the *Physics*, where Aristotle argues that the first cause of eternal continuous motion must be unmoved accidentally as well as in its own right (8.6, 258b13–16, 259b20–8). For the distinction see *Phys.* 8.4, 254b7–12: things impart or undergo movement accidentally (*kata sumbebêkos*) if they [merely] belong to or contain as a part things that impart or undergo movement, while things do so in themselves or in their own right (*kath' hauto*) if they do so not by [merely] belonging to or containing as a part the things that impart or undergo movement. In this chapter Ps.-Alexander will argue that there are other movers which cannot be moved in either way; cf. note 345. See also Sharples 2002, 8 n. 34 and Salis 2005, 248.

334 [700,16] Translates *de*, which is not in our Aristotle manuscripts. Ps.-Alexander understands 'but (*de*) we must not overlook' to go with the following clause referring to the claims made by Aristotle's predecessors. In our Aristotle manuscripts the *de* is missing, so that 'we should not overlook' more naturally goes with the preceding indirect question of how many first principles there are. The lemma however agrees with the Aristotle manuscripts.

335 [700,20] Ps.-Alexander, following Aristotle, uses two terms, *arithmos* and *plêthos*, often, it seems, interchangeably. Elsewhere Aristotle says that a *plêthos* is a quantity comprising discrete parts, and a number is an amount that can be measured by the units of which it is composed; hence, an *arithmos* is a definite (*hôrismenon*) or numerable (*arithmêton plêthos*) amount (cf. 1073b13; 5.13, 1020a7–13; 10.6, 1057a2–4). *Arithmos* is standardly translated 'number' but there is unfortunately no convenient English counterpart for *plêthos* in this sense. Because the argument of this chapter does not seem to hinge on the distinction, this translation follows others in rendering both words as 'number', except when they are used together as in this sentence or when *plêthos* evidently has another sense such as 'multitude'
(cf. 709,34; 710,19).

336 [700,24] It is uncertain whom exactly Aristotle (and Ps.-Alexander for that matter) has in mind; cf. notes 36 and 38.

337 [700,25] Aristotle criticizes Plato's doctrine that number goes only up to ten at *Metaph.* 13.8, 1084a12-b2 (discussed by Ps.-Alexander at 770,11–772,28); see also *Phys.* 3.6, 206b27–33.

338 [700,36] There are two sorts of stars: a few are called 'wandering' (*planêtês*) because they are observed to change position relative to other stars (cf. note 209), and a large mass of stars called fixed or non-wandering (*aplanês*) because they

maintain the same position relative to each other. According to the theory of homocentric spheres the observed movement of these stars can be explained in terms of the motions of celestial spheres (cf. note 357). The theory of the spheres is described further in the Introduction, 15–20.

339 [700,36] Translates *gegonasin*, not literally because the spheres are eternal (cf. 708,31–3). The claim that the spheres exist on account of the stars is explained in 708,3–17.

340 [701,4] Ps.-Alexander's interpretation of this chapter hinges on this claim, which he takes to be implied by Aristotle's argument; cf. notes 333, 345, and 399, and Introduction, 16.

341 [701,7] Ps.-Alexander may mean that an animal's soul sometimes forces its body to move in an unnatural way; cf. note 227.

342 [701,8] *Cael.* 2.12, 292a18-b25.

343 [701,9] Translates *prodiôristhô* as emended by Hayduck with Brandis (cf. Sepúlveda 'hactenus'). The commentary manuscripts have *prosdiôristhô*, 'let these things have been determined besides'.

344 [701,10] Translates *dedeigmenôn rhêteon*. The Aristotle manuscripts have instead *diôrismenôn lekteon*.

345 [701,17] Cf. *Phys.* 8.6, 259b16–20: the soul is moved accidentally because when it makes the body change its place it also moves itself coincidentally since it is in the body. Unlike souls the immovable movers cannot be moved even accidentally. See also 706,31–709,11.

346 [701,19] *Phys.* 8.6, 259a16–20.

347 [701,22] The outermost sphere is called 'the universe' (*to pan*) because it encompasses all perceptible substances; cf. *Cael.* 1.9, 279a11–17.

348 [701,24] Translates *to kuklôi sôma* which is short for *to kuklôi sôma pheromenon*; cf. 1073a31–2 and *Cael.* 1.3, 270a33 with 269b29–30.

349 [701,25] The reference is uncertain. Perhaps Ps.-Alexander means that a body can be everlasting *only* if it is in circular motion. In *De Caelo* Aristotle argues that the heaven is in everlasting motion because 'it possesses the circular body which by nature is always moved in a circle' (2.3, 286a1–9). In the *Physics* he argues that circular motion is the only movement that can be everlasting (8.9, 265a13–27).

350 [701,26] Translates *kai kath' hautên akinêtou*, whereas the Aristotle manuscripts have only *kath' hautên*. The extra words may be added to indicate that *kath' hautên* modifies *akinêtou ousias* rather than *phoran*.

351 [701,27] Translates *kath' hauto*, which is in fact the reading of Aristotle manuscripts J and A[b], instead of *kath' hautên* read by Ps.-Alexander (also in Aristotle manuscripts ECV[k]).

352 [701,36] Hence, there is a one-to-one correlation between individual motions and individual movers.

353 [702,8] Translates *sphairôn*. The Aristotle manuscripts have *phorôn*. Ps.-Alexander assumes that the number of spheres equals the number of motions; cf. 702,22.

354 [702,8] Translates *philosophiai* (dat.) in commentary manuscript A (cf. 782,14 and 16) and Aristotle manuscripts MC. Commentary manuscript L and the Aristotle manuscripts EJA$^b$ (and the sources for the Arabic and Latin translations) have *philosophias* (gen.), which implies that mathematics is a part of philosophy. *Philosophias* may be an error due to attraction to *oikeiotatês*.

355 [702,17] Aristotle elsewhere remarks that, unlike other mathematical objects, those of astronomy are perceived to involve movement (cf. 1.8,989b32–3). At 704,25 Ps.-Alexander illustrates how he understands this: the astronomer thinks of the planet as if it were a geometrical point in motion along a circular line traced by the central point of the planet.

356 [702,22] See note 353.

357 [702,24] According to Simplicius, 'As Eudemus [fl. 325 BCE] recorded in the second book of his astronomical history (and Sosigenes [the Peripatetic, 2nd cent. AD] took this over from Eudemus), Eudoxus of Cnidus [408?-355? BCE] is said to be the first of the Hellenes to have made use of such hypotheses [concerning concentric spheres], Plato (as Sosigenes says) having created this problem for those who concerned themselves with these things: on what hypotheses of uniform and ordered motions could the phenomena concerning the motions of the planets be preserved? ... Callippus of Cyzicus [*c*. 370-*c*. 310 BCE], who studied with Polemarchus [of Cyzicus], the associate of Eudoxus, went to Athens after him and lived with Aristotle [*c*. 330 BCE] and together with him corrected and filled out the discoveries of Eudoxus' (*in Cael*. 488,18–24; 493,4–8; tr. Mueller).

358 [702,35] Mueller provides an annotated translation of Aristotle's text 1073b17–1074a15 along with Ps.-Alexander's exegesis as follows at 702,38–706,15 (in Mueller 2005, Appendix 1, 123–8), which was very helpful in preparing the present translation and notes for this passage.

359 [702,36] The lemma omits *hekaterou* found in the Aristotle manuscripts.

360 [1074a6] See note 387.

361 [703,2] It is uncertain which commentary on *De Caelo* Ps.-Alexander intends here. He borrows liberally (without attribution and often almost verbatim) from Simplicius' commentary, which often quotes Sosigenes (who relied on Eudemus), perhaps via the latter's pupil, Alexander of Aphrodisias, to whom Simplicius also refers repeatedly (cf. Moraux 1984, 347–51; 2001,224–5). Assuming that the

subject of 'we have also interpreted' is the authorial 'we', it might be charitably conjectured that Ps.-Alexander supposes that Simplicius was copying the commentary of the real Alexander, whose commentary he is trying to reconstruct from whatever source he can lay his hands on. In any case Simplicius' commentary is (in addition to *Metaph.* 12.8) our primary source for Eudoxus' theory of homocentric spheres. Modern scholarship is heavily influenced by the reconstruction of Schiaparelli 1875 (e.g. Dreyer 1906, ch. 4 and Heath 1913, chs 16–17) although some details of his interpretation have been questioned recently (references in Beere 2003, 4–5).

362 [703,4] This replicates Simplicius' lemma at 491,12–14. The entire passage from *Cael.* 2.12, 293a4–11 is translated as follows: 'And further for the following reason the other motions involve a single body: the motions before the last, which involves a single star, move many bodies; for the last sphere which undergoes motion is embedded [in the other spheres], and each sphere is in fact a body. Therefore, the work of the last will be common [to the others]; for each has its own proper natural motion, while this motion is, as it were, added. But the potentiality of any limited body is related to a limited [body].' The 'last' sphere contains the moon, 'the star that is stationed the lowest'; cf. 705,24–5.

363 [703,9] Ps.-Alexander's discussion is almost entirely confined to the sun and the moon, each of which has three spheres according to Eudoxus.

364 [703,11] i.e. the outermost sphere containing the fixed stars. Its motion is replicated by the first or outermost sphere associated with each planet, which thus keeps the planet's diurnal motion synchronous with that of the fixed stars. Figure 1 (adapted from Evans 1998, 76) depicts the sphere of the fixed stars, which rotates westward around the axis with poles A (north) and B (south) with its equator midway between the poles. Obliquely inclined to the equator is the ecliptic, the circle running through the middle of the zodiac, close to which the sun is carried by its own second sphere over the course of a year, turning at the northern tropic at the summer solstice and the southern tropic at the winter solstice.

365 [703,13] The three solar spheres correspond to those of the moon, depicted in Figure 2 (adapted from Evans 1998, 307): the first explains the sun's diurnal motion from east to west, the second its annual movement along the zodiac, and the third its supposed deviation from the ecliptic, as explained below.

366 703,16] See Simplicius, *in Cael.* 493,11–13: 'the sun is moved from east to west in the sphere of the fixed stars' (tr. Mueller). On the plural subject cf. note 361.

367 [703,22] i.e. not star-bearing. Cf. Simplicius, *in Cael.* 491,17–28 and 493,17–20. These passages are Theophrastus texts 165A–C in Fortenbaugh *et al.* 1992.

368 [703,23] Ps.-Alexander passes over Aristotle's remark that 'the second [sphere] is in the [circle] along the middle of the zodiac', which plays the following role

according to Simplicius: 'to turn from west to east around an axis which is at right angles to the plane through the middle of the signs of the zodiac' (494,5–6; tr. Mueller).

369 [703,25] According to Simplicius, the moon's second sphere 'was hypothesized to turn in the same direction as the second, but around a different axis which should be conceived as perpendicular to the plane of a certain great, oblique circle which the sun is thought to describe with its own central point when it is carried by the smallest sphere in which it is fastened'. He later remarks that this sphere explains 'why it is observed that it is not further north and south in the same points of the zodiac but that these points in the signs of the zodiac always shift toward preceding signs'; that is, the moon's greatest deviations in latitude take place through the zodiac in a progressively westward direction (*in Cael.* 494,6–9; 495,10–13; tr. Mueller).

370 [703,26] The verb *pheresthai* up to this point has been translated 'to be in (or undergo) motion', as applied in particular to the spheres, e.g. 696,12. The verb *pherein*, however, commonly means 'to carry' and Ps.-Alexander, following Aristotle, subsequently uses it in this sense, because spheres carry planets. The second sense implies the first; for when a planet is carried by its spheres it is in motion. While Aristotle says that the spheres carry (*pherein*) the stars, he says that the separate substances move (*kinein*) the spheres, and Ps.-Alexander follows this distinction (see Bodnár 2016, 265).

371 [703,27] The term *sêmeia* ('signs') refers to constellations and *tropika* is related to *tropê*, i.e. the turning of the sun at the solstices. (The term *tropê* is translated 'turning' because it is applied to the moon as well as the sun.) According to Simplicius, '[the sun] turns to the sides of the middle of the signs of the zodiac (this was determined by the fact that it does not always rise at the same place in the summer and winter solstices)' (*in Cael.* 493,14–17; tr. Mueller). Eudoxus evidently postulated that the third sphere carrying the sun varies slightly from the ecliptic. Later ancient astronomers, however, determined that although it is true that the moon's path is at an incline (of about five degrees) to the ecliptic, the sun's path is not (see Heath 1913, 198–9).

372 [703,33] From Cancer and Capricorn at the summer and winter solstice respectively.

373 [703,34] The first lunar sphere rotates from east to west with the same motion as the fixed stars. The second sphere follows the zodiac rotating slowly westward along the ecliptic taking about 18.6 years to complete a single rotation. The third sphere rotates eastward once a month. Note that the equator of the second sphere (the ecliptic) is aligned obliquely to that of the first, and the equator of the third (carrying the moon) is aligned obliquely to the second, which is closely followed

by the sun according to Eudoxus. Hence the claim that the moon's circle is more obliquely aligned to the middle of the zodiac. Although Eudoxus' claim that the sun veers slightly from the ecliptic is mistaken (cf. note 371), he is correct that the moon's path is obliquely aligned with the ecliptic.

374 [703,34] As in Sepúlveda's translation. The commentary manuscripts have AGBMCD, as Mueller points out, 'if that order is used in the diagram the moon would never be south of the sun's path in the zodiac' (2005, 127 n. 11; see also Salis 2005, 262, 267–9). Sepúlveda evidently spotted and fixed the error, unless he was relying on a manuscript with the correct reading. Figures 3A and 3B illustrate the example from different points of view. In Figure 3A (from Sepúlveda) the horizontal line represents the horizonal circle (viewed from the edge). DEB represents the equatorial circle, AEC the sun's circle, and GEM the moon's circle. The line DG (representing the greatest distance between moon rises) is greater than DA (representing the greatest between sunrises). In Figure 3B (from Mueller 2005, 124) the circle represents the horizon (viewed from the celestial pole). DEB represents a section of the equatorial circle, AEC a section of the sun's circle, and GEM a section of the moon's circle. Once again, the arc DG (representing the greatest distance between moon rises) is greater than the arc DA (representing the greatest distance between sunrises).

375 [704,10] The commentary manuscripts have *taxin* ('order') instead of *thesin* ('position') as in the Aristotle manuscripts. The words in parenthesis (*toutesti tôn apostêmatôn*) also occur in Simplicius (*in Cael.* 497,10) as part of what is obviously a gloss: *toutesti tôn apostêmatôn taxin*. Simplicius' phrase is missing from Aristotle manuscript E but has made it into other manuscripts. It is obelized by most modern editors.

376 [704,11] Sepúlveda includes 'ut secundas'.

377 [704,13] Although Ps.-Alexander shows little interest in Callippus' revisions, Simplicius reports that 'Eudemus recounts briefly for the sake of which phenomena [Callippus] thought that these spheres had to be added. He says that [Callippus] says that since the time between the solstices and the equinoxes differ as much as Euctemon and Meton [who made these observations in 432 BCE] thought, the three spheres for each [of sun and moon] were not sufficient to preserve the phenomena, obviously because of the non-uniformity of their motions. And Eudemus also recounts briefly and clearly for what reason [Callippus] added one sphere in the case of each of the planets Mars, Venus, Mercury' (*in Cael.* 497,17–24; tr. Mueller).

378 [704,21] i.e. in Simplicius' commentary. In contrast to the carrying spheres which impart planetary motion, the counteracting spheres ensure that extra motion is not transmitted to the next planet inward (cf. 708,9–10). As Sosigenes explains, 'It is

necessary for these spheres (which <Aristotle> calls counteracting) to be attached to the hypotheses for two reasons: so that there will be the proper position for both the sphere of the fixed stars for each planet and for the spheres under it; and so that the proper speed will be present in all of the spheres. For it was necessary both that a sphere move in the same way as the sphere of the fixed stars or as some other sphere around the same axis at it and that it rotate in an equal time, but neither <property> could possibly belong to it without the addition of the spheres mentioned by Aristotle' (ap. Simplicius, *in Cael.* 498,4–10; tr. Mueller). As Sosigenes further explains, an inner sphere counteracts an outer sphere by moving at the same speed about the same axis but in the opposite direction (cf. 504,7–15).

379 [704,23] The following example appears to be modelled after an illustration of Sosigenes (recounted by Simplicius, *in Cael.* 499,16–500,14) involving three homocentric spheres: the outermost AB contains DE, which in turn contains FG. Ps.-Alexander's example differs, however, in important details from Sosigenes' and is at times hard to follow (cf. Salis 2005, 262, 267–9 and 2007, n. 458). Figures 4A and 4B (from Mueller 2005, 125) may depict the sorts of diagrams Ps.-Alexander has in mind.

380 [704,27] The straight line represents the horizon.

381 [704,32] 'If the speeds [of two homocentric spheres] are equal, [Sosigenes] will prove that the compound motion is double; ... for if the greater causes the smaller to move a quarter circle and the smaller moves at the same speed, then the smaller itself also moves a quarter circle, and a quarter circle will have been moved through twice, so that the motion compounded of both is double the motion of the one' (Simplicius, *in Cael.* 500,24–501,1; tr. Mueller).

382 [704,28] Ps.-Alexander evidently envisages a case in which outer sphere AB moves in the opposite direction to both ED and GF. The reversal of letters suggests that ED and GF rotate in the same direction as each other but in a direction opposite to AB, which supposedly has a direct counteracting effect on ED and an indirect counteracting effect on GF.

383 [704,38] And hence DE is moved towards E.

384 [704,38] This seems mistaken. Even if AB impedes DE, it does not follow that DE will in turn impede FG but only that DE will be prevented from adding extra motion to FG. FG will still have a motion of its own.

385 [705,5] 'DE' is inadvertently omitted from Mueller's translation. Here Ps.-Alexander evidently considers a second case in which AB moves in the opposite direction to DE (on which it has a counteracting effect) but in the same direction as FG. This seems to be a more in line with Aristotle's intention: in order for AB and FG to rotate synchronously, AB must move in an opposite direction to either DE or FG but not to both (cf. Simplicius, *in Cael.* 500,5–14).

386 [705,11] Mueller (2005, 128 n. 19) aptly remarks, 'it is tempting to emend the text here and in the following line', reading 'the sphere in which the stars are embedded' (*endedentai hoi asteres*) in place of 'the sphere in which the star is embedded' (*endedetai ho astêr*), taking the reference to be to the sphere of the fixed stars. The point would be that the counteracting spheres of Saturn are supposed to ensure that Jupiter circles the earth daily along with the fixed stars.

387 [705,13] Translates *hôste*, rather than *epei oun* ('since then') as in the Aristotle manuscripts ('cum igitur' in Sepúlveda).

388 [705,21] This disagrees with the Aristotle manuscripts, which say that Callippus 'assigned the same number [of spheres] to Jupiter and Saturn as Eudoxus, but he held that two spheres must be assigned in addition to the sun and moon, ... and one [in addition] to each of the remaining planets' (1073b34–8). This is a temporary lapse because Ps.-Alexander later mentions 'the two spheres of the sun and the two spheres of the moon, which Callippus has added' (706,1).

389 [705,24] Translates *to katô*. The Aristotle manuscripts have *katôtatô tetagmenon* (which is placed lowest in order); cf. *katôtatô* at 705,25.

390 [705,36] Ps.-Alexander's reckoning closely follows Simplicius, *in Cael.* 502,27–503,9 disregarding his miscount mentioned in note 388.

391 [705,41] This paragraph closely follows Simplicius, *in Cael.* 503,10–504,1. At 503,33–4 Simplicius reports that Alexander of Aphrodisias and Porphyry expressed confusion in their commentaries on the *Metaphysics*. It is uncertain why Aristotle suggests that Callippus' extra spheres for the moon and sun might not be necessary.

392 [706,5] For Callippus' reasons for adding the spheres see note 377.

393 [706,8] Ps.-Alexander's 706,8–15 is substantially the same as Simplicius, *in Cael.* 503,35–504,1. However, the words in brackets are in Simplicius' text but omitted in Ps.-Alexander's, resulting in an awkward sentence (cf. Sharples 2003, 205 n. 90). This suggests that Ps.-Alexander copied Simplicius rather than the reverse.

394 [706,14] Deleting *phêsi legein*.

395 [706,15] The scribal error would consist in writing *hepta* ('seven') instead of *ennea* ('nine'). This final clause alludes to a flaw in Aristotle's theory detected by Sosigenes (cf. Simplicius, *in Cael.* 502,20–7; 503,19–27): The purpose of the counteracting spheres is to ensure that the first (outermost) sphere of each planet has the same motion as the sphere of the fixed stars. But in Aristotle's scheme it turns out that the first (outermost) and last (innermost) spheres for each planet both have the same motion as the sphere of the fixed stars. For example, the motion of the seventh sphere (Saturn's innermost sphere) is the same as that of the eighth (Jupiter's outermost sphere) so that the latter is redundant. This recurs for all six planets beneath Saturn. (Recent discussions of this problem include Yavetz 1998, Mendell

2001, Beere 2003, Bodnár 2005, Judson, 213–8.) If Aristotle realized this himself, he would have seen that only forty-nine are required (in which case there would be no need for 'numerological' interpretations as in Sedley 2000, 331 n. 7). But, as Sosigenes suggests, this would not explain why Aristotle says 'forty-seven' at 1074a13. The following table compares the number of spheres assigned to each planet by Callippus, Aristotle, and Sosigenes (with counteracting spheres indicated in italics).

Number of Spheres Required for Each Planet's Motion

|  | Eudoxus | Callippus | Aristotle | Sosigenes |
|---|---|---|---|---|
| Saturn | 4 | 4 | 4+*3* | 4+*3* |
| Jupiter | 4 | 4 | 4+*3* | 4+*3*−*1* |
| Mars | 4 | 4+1 | 4+1+*4* | 4+1+*4*−*1* |
| Sun | 3 | 3+2 | 3+2+*4* | 3+2+*4*−*1* |
| Venus | 4 | 4+1 | 4+1+*4* | 4+1+*4*−*1* |
| Mercury | 4 | 4+1 | 4+1+*4* | 4+1+*4*−*1* |
| Moon | 3 | 3+2 | 3+2 | 3+2−*1* |
| Total spheres | 26 | 33 | 55 | 49 |

396 [706,16] Translates *sphairôn* in the commentary and Aristotle manuscripts. Simplicius and Themistius read *phorôn*.

397 [706,16] The words *kai aisthêtas* ('and perceptible'), also missing from the citation at 706,24, are found in the Aristotle manuscripts (along with most Arabic and Latin translations as well as Themistius and Simplicius, *in Cael.* 506,5), but are obelized by modern editors on the grounds that the immovable movers are imperceptible.

398 [706,30] In their mastery of astronomy.

399 [706,32] Ps.-Alexander assumes that the spheres have souls (although Aristotle nowhere says this explicitly) in basic agreement with Simplicius: 'We should think about [the heavenly bodies] as having soul, a rational soul, so that they also share in action and a life of action (cf. *Cael.* 2.12, 292a20–1). However, we also speak of doing and making in the case of irrational souls and bodies without soul, but we predicate action uniquely in the case of rational souls. If we do conceive them in this way what occurs in the case of the motion of the heavenly bodies will not be thought at all paradoxical' (*in Cael.* 482,10–15; tr. Mueller) On Ps.-Alexander's interpretation Aristotle makes no reference to ensouled spheres because he wants to emphasize the more fundamental causal role of the immovable movers. On the difference between celestial souls and immovable movers cf. notes 340 and 345.

400 [707,1] This distinction follows Simplicius (*in Cael.* 381,2-18) who criticizes the real Alexander for confounding nature and the soul; cf. Merlan 1935 and Sharples 2003,199-200.

401 [707,2] Ps.-Alexander envisages a hierarchy of immovable movers dependent on the prime mover (cf. 701,39-702,1; 709,28; 721,33). This seems to be required in order to reconcile the conclusion of ch. 8 that there are fifty-five unmoved movers with the thesis of ch. 7 that there is one principle on which depend the heavens and nature (1072b13-14). This is also suggested by Aristotle's comparison of the prime mover to a 'general' (*stratêgos*) and 'commander' (*koiranos*). This political theme is also emphasized by Themistius, Aquinas, and Suárez, who compare the celestial rule to kingship.

402 [707,8] Cf. Simplicius, *in Cael.* 380,5-7: 'Alexander says that not the soul of the heavens but the first mover is the cause of its being moved *ad infinitum*' (tr. Mueller). Ps.-Alexander's 706,34-707,11 is also substantially the same as Simplicius, *in Cael.* 382,10-16.

403 Cf. 706,38-707,1.

404 [707,34] Translates *telos* as in Hayduck with commentary manuscript AL ('finem' in Sepúlveda) and corrected Aristotle manuscripts. *Telous* is in commentary manuscript M and the uncorrected Aristotle manuscripts. The latter may be a mistaken reading supposing that *telous* agrees with *tou aristou* (the best end). See Judson note on 1074a20.

405 [708,11] i.e. fifty-five, understanding *tosautai* as suggested by Bonitz based on Sepúlveda 'hoc numero habentur'.

406 [708,20] The word *aitian* is omitted by Bonitz and Brandis following manuscript M.

407 [708,23] Translates *ei*, which Jaeger reads instead of *eite* in the Aristotle manuscripts.

408 [708,25] i.e. movement as a genus including alteration and growth and diminution as well as locomotion.

409 [708,32] The argument is clearer in the Greek, because *pherein* can mean 'carry' as well as 'impart motion'. When Aristotle says 'everything imparting motion is naturally for the sake of the object in motion' (1074a25-6) this could also be translated 'everything carrying something is naturally for the sake of the object carried by it'. The thing 'carrying' (*to pheron*) is a sphere and not the separately existing mover (called *to kinoun*); cf. note 370.

410 [708,37] After 'heaven' manuscript L adds 'and the divine stars are in motion through the heaven, so that every motion is an end', which looks like a confused gloss.

411 [708,39] Presumably a star is an end or final cause in a secondary sense, i.e. as beneficiary; cf. note 279 and Introduction, 18-20.

412 [709,1] Ps.-Alexander generally understands *ho ouranos* as referring to the entire perceptible universe; cf. *Cael.* 1.9, 278b9–21.

413 [709,5] Cf. 497,38–40 on 7.8, 1034a7–8: 'Callias and Socrates are the same in species but different in matter'. Note that *eidos* ('species') could also be translated 'form' in this context.

414 [709,7] This assumes that each effect has its own unique cause; cf. 701,36.

415 [709,14] Omitting *touto ekhei* which is evidently repeated by error from the previous sentence; cf. Sharples 2003, 197 n. 46.

416 [709,16] Translates *energeia*. Bonitz reads *energeiai* ('in actuality') with manuscript A (Sepúlveda 'actu').

417 [709,17] Ps.-Alexander does not mention an objection raised by the real Alexander: 'for what reason will the first mover, though it is one, not be able to move more than one body in circular motion, if after all it brings about movement by being the object of yearning and love, for nothing prevents more than one thing from yearning for it' (ap. Simplicius, *in Cael.* 270,5–12; tr. Mueller).

418 [709,19] Translates *ho Sôkratous*. Ps.-Alexander evidently interprets this difficult passage as follows: If many things are human beings, then in so far as they are human they will have a different account (*sc.* from things that are horses). Similarly, Socrates in so far as he is Socrates will have a different account (*sc.* from Plato). Each individual human being will be an enmattered compound individual with a distinct account of its form. Hence, if there are many prime movers, each will be an enmattered compound individual with a distinct account of its form. But this is impossible (since the first causes are immaterial). So there can only be one first cause. This interpretation fits well with the view that Aristotle subscribes to individual forms; cf. note 150. Sharples (2003, 197) offers a different interpretation: he takes 'the account of Socrates' to refer to an account shared by many individuals, but it is hard to square this with Ps.-Alexander's reference to 'the account of Socrates *in so far as he is Socrates*'.

419 [709,30] Translates *ainottomenoi* (acc.) modifying *hêmeis* ('we'). Bonitz however conjectures *ainottomenôn* modifying *tôn arkhaiôn kai pampalaiôn*, 'those who were ancient and very early'.

420 [709,35] A *medimnos* was an Attic corn measure equalling approximately twelve gallons.

421 [709,39] Translates *proêktai*. The Aristotle manuscripts have *prosêktai*, 'has been added'.

422 [710,9] Translates *eplasanto*. Manuscript L has *aneplasanto*, 'refabricated'.

423 [710,25] Herodotus (2.3,5; 2.76,3) relates a similar anecdote: he heard tell from the Arabs that the Egyptians venerated the ibises because they prevented swarming winged serpents from entering Egypt. He also mentions that in Egypt

anyone who killed an ibis, whether intentionally or not, was sentenced to death. The god Thoth was often depicted with the head of an ibis.

424 [710,30] Elsewhere Aristotle suggests that the same ideas are preserved or else rediscovered through endlessly recurring cycles: *Cael.* 1.3, 270b19–20; *Meteor.* 1.3, 339b27–9; *Pol.* 7.10, 1329b25–30.

# [Chapter 9]

425 [710,36] The missing lemma in the commentary is presumably an oversight.
426 [710,36] Although Hayduck treats *polutimêton* as part of the citation, it belongs more likely to the paraphrase along with *kai prôton*. Ps.-Alexander sees a reference here to the prime mover, whom he previously called *ho polutimêtos nous* (707,21). The phrase also occurs in the commentary to Book 7 (463,34) but not in the commentary on Books 1–5 by the real Alexander.
427 [710,37] Translates *phaneron* which is stronger than Aristotle's *dokei* (it seems).
428 [710,40] cf. *EN* 10.8, 1178b19–20: 'Surely [the gods] are not sleeping like Endymion.'
429 [711,11] The term 'dominant' (*kurios*) implies that an intellect would be subservient to anything that determines or controls whether, and what, it is thinking.
430 [711,12] Translates *noêsis*, which implies that the intellect is actively engaged in thinking; cf. 697,8–11. Ps.-Alexander's citation, however, omits *alla dunamis* ('but a potentiality'), present in the Aristotle manuscripts, either because it was missing from his source or because he regarded it as irrelevant to the present argument. The addition of *alla dunamis*, however, would suggest that if the intellect were a *potentiality* then something else *outside* of it would have control over whether it was actualized or not (see Salis 2005, 299–300). In any case, Ps.-Alexander understands Aristotle's point to be that the dominant causal factor (*to kurion*) cannot be a *part* of the intellect.
431 [711,19] Translates *holos* as emended by Hayduck (cf. 'totus' in Sepúlveda). If *holôs* is retained with the manuscripts (as in Bonitz), the translation is 'it is not as a whole but only with a part that it thinks'.
432 [711,24] Translates *allote de allo*, which is more likely a paraphrase than a citation.
433 [711,37] Translates *heautou* with manuscripts AL. Bonitz emends to *autou* ('its') following Sepúlveda. Ps.-Alexander views movement here as merely a change for the worse. Other commentators (e.g. Brunschwig 2000, 285) see a reference to the unmoved mover, although there is no mention of this in ch. 9.

434 [712,3] Translates *dunamis*, which could also be translated 'power', 'capacity', or 'faculty' in the present context (cf. 'facultas' in Sepúlveda). 'Potentiality' is used here in order to convey the contrast with actuality (cf. 712,15).

435 [712,8] Translates *autôi* as emended by Bonitz and Hayduck (cf. 'illi' in Sepúlveda), instead of *autou* ('of it') in the manuscripts.

436 [712,13] Likewise, there is no need to worry that the stars will eventually stop rotating because they find it toilsome; see 9.8, 1050b22–8; cf. 592,25–40.

437 [712,18] Cf. *DA* 3.4, 429a13–18.

438 [712,23] *Eti* would indicate that at 1074b31 Aristotle starts a new argument rather than supporting what immediately precedes it.

439 [712,29] Ps.-Alexander does not comment on the implication that Aristotle's divine intellect would not be omniscient (cf. Salis 2005, 306–7; 2007, n. 531).

440 [712,34] That is, if the act of thinking (*noêsis*) *were* a potentiality, it would not be the best thing.

441 [712,35] Translates *esti*. Bonitz conjectures *estai*, 'will be', following Sepúlveda 'erit'.

442 [712,35] Translates *hê noêsis noêseôs*. Ps.-Alexander understands the genitive *noêseôs* as indicating the object of thinking, as do most commentators, rather than the subject which thinks.

443 [712,36] On this interpretation the divine intellect consists of a completely actualized state of self-consciousness (see 1072b19–21; cf. 697,21–8 and 698,14–16). Throughout this discussion Ps.-Alexander uses *to nooumenon* (passive participle, translated 'the object of thinking') for what is *actually* thought of as distinguished from *to noêton* (verbal adjective, translated 'the intelligible object'), which is or *can* be thought of. As remarked by Brunschwig (2000, 302 n. 24) Aristotle himself uses only *noêton* in ch. 7 and exclusively *nooumenon* in ch. 9.

444 [713,11] Translates a second *allo* missing in the Aristotle manuscripts. This may be a paraphrase. See 712,4–5 for a similar turn of phrase.

445 [713,20] See notes 82 and 102.

446 [713,30] Translates *to eidos to aneu hulês*. Although Aristotle's word order might suggest that 'without matter' modifies 'productive knowledge', Ps.-Alexander takes it with 'the form' understood as substantial form or essence. For a similar interpretation see Brunschwig 2000, 295–6 and Judson, 318.

447 [713,32] Or 'productive sciences' (*epistêmê* is translated 'science' or 'knowledge', depending on context). Elders (1972, 263–4) criticizes Ps.-Alexander's interpretation on the grounds that 'productive sciences without matter' would more naturally be understood to refer to mathematical disciplines. But as Ps.-Alexander remarks, the latter are classified by Aristotle as theoretical sciences, and 'without matter' more likely refers here to the way the productive sciences treat their objects.

448 [713,33] That is, Aristotle explicates the account (*logos*) as the object (*pragma*), which is in turn identified with the act of thinking (*noêsis*).
449 [713,37] The reasoning is in general as follows: thinking of X has the essence of X as its object, the essence of X is identical with X, and thinking is the same as its object; therefore, thinking of X is the same as X. The example of the eclipse recalls *An. Post.* 2.2, 90a15; cf. 668,20–4. On Ps.-Alexander's interpretation see Judson 2019, 319.
450 [713,41] See *DA* 3.4, 430a3–5; 3.5, 430a19–20; 3.7, 431a1–2, b16–17.
451 [714,1] These words together with those cited at 713,37–9 form a continuous passage: *to oukh heterou oun ontos tou nooumenou kai tou nou, hosa mê hulên ekhei, tauton estai, kai hê noêsis tôi nooumenôi mia*. Different rather substantial portions of this cited material are missing from the original texts of two important Aristotle manuscripts: *tou nooumenou kai tou nou, hosa mê hulên ekhei, to auto estai, kai hê noêsis* from J; and *kai tou nou, hosa mê hulên ekhei, to auto estai, kai hê noêsis tôi nooumenôi mia* from E. In both manuscripts, however, the missing material is added by later hands in the margins, although J (like $A^b$) has *tou nooumenou* before *mia* instead of *tôi nooumenôi*. Modern editors use the version in Ps.-Alexander and the redacted E. See Brunschwig 2000, 294–5 and Fazzo, 330–1 for discussion. On Ps.-Alexander's interpretation see also note 443.
452 [714,3] Translates *zêtêsai* in the commentary manuscripts; the Aristotle manuscripts have *aporia*. This appears as a lemma in Sepúlveda and Hayduck, while Bonitz treats it as a citation, though it may be merely a paraphrase.
453 [1075a7] Cf. note 456.
454 [714,14] See *Metaph.* 12.7, 1073a6–7; cf. 700,1–2.
455 [714,17] Translates *tôn sunthetôn* (genitive), which Ps.-Alexander understands as denoting the *possessors* of intellect (i.e. hylomorphic entities) rather than the *objects* thought of by the intellect (i.e. composite objects). A problem for the former interpretation is that 'composite' (*suntheton*) refers to the object of thinking just before, at 1075a5. Nonetheless, Ross and Judson (324–6) agree with Ps.-Alexander, while Bonitz, Brunschwig (2000, 299–300), and others favour the latter interpretation.
456 [714,17] Translates *oun*, which according to Alexandru is also present in all the available representatives of the *beta* family of manuscripts and in E as corrected by a later hand. Alexandru adds that 'the particle is written in abbreviated form and was not recognized even by later editors such as Christ, Ross and Jaeger'. The latter editors' texts are lacking *oun*, which did not appear in $A^b$ or in the first draft of E. Ross and Jaeger insert a dash, understanding the *hôsper* clause as parenthetical. Reading *oun* Ps.-Alexander understands the sentence as concluding the discussion of the puzzle. Further, he paraphrases the sentence as

having a *hôsper* ... *houtô* ('just as ... so ...') structure, which requires omitting *de* at 1075a10 or understanding it as non-connective (cf. Denniston 1950, 181).

457 [714,18] Translates *ê*. The Aristotle manuscripts have *ê gar* ('or at least').

458 [714,23] Translates *ton hapanta aiôna*, understood here as of unlimited duration, i.e. forever; cf. note 323.

459 [714,25] *DA* 3.6. See note 300.

460 [714,28] This is Ps.-Alexander's interpretation of Aristotle's clause 'which is something else' (*on allo ti*).

461 [714,31] By 'a certain whole' (*holon ti*) Ross understands instead 'a certain whole period, i.e. in a well-organised life of activity'.

462 [714,33] Sharples (2003, 210–11) remarks that 'one may doubt that the real Alexander would have called 'divine intellect the *form* of human intellect'. However, Ps.-Alexander does not make this bald claim, because he adds the qualification: *whenever* the intellect is capable of grasping the divine intellect. Although Sharples calls attention to similar uses of 'supervene' (*epigignesthai*) in the genuine Alexander's *DA* 25,2–3 and 26,21–2, the present discussion also recalls repeated claims that form supervenes in an individual instant, in Ps.-Alexander's own commentary on *Metaph.* 7 and 8: cf. 455,12; 486,17; 495,23; 496,22; 559,20; 561,24.

## [Chapter 10]

463 [714,37] Ps.-Alexander understands the cosmos to comprise the entire perceptible universe including the sublunary realm (cf. 715,15; also 687,30; 690,3; 709,1).

464 [715,4] The word *kosmos* implies order, in virtue of which the cosmos is described in terms of praise: good, best, excellent, and noble.

465 [715,12] More periphrastically, the army is good and excellent (*eu*) if it has a good and excellent general.

466 [715,22] Translates *megista*. Bonitz reads *malista*, 'most' (with A), the *lectio difficilior*.

467 [715,31] This paragraph translates a single complex sentence with several parenthetical asides, which has been broken up for the sake of clarity.

468 [715,33] Jaeger suggests that these words may be misplaced in the Aristotle manuscripts and it might be better to move them from 1075a16 to a19, so that they precede the example of the household, as in Ps.-Alexander's commentary.

469 [715,34] Ps.-Alexander extends Aristotle's analogy of the cosmos to the household to include the 'city-state' (*polis*) or 'commonwealth' (*politeia*), which

helps set the stage for the political analogy which concludes Book 12 (cf. *politeuesthai* at 1076a3). The term *politeia* can also be translated 'constitution' or 'regime', and Aristotle identifies the *politeia* with the *politeuma* ('government') at *Pol.* 3.7, 1279a25–7; 3.6, 1278b11.

470 [715,34] The 'free persons' (*eleutheroi*) in the household are the paterfamilias and his wife and legitimate children, and the other members are 'slaves' (*douloi*) (*Pol.* 1.3). In the political analogy Ps.-Alexander implies that free persons are citizens 'partaking in the laws' rather than mere non-slaves. The translation of *exesti* as 'are at liberty' (following Ross) highlights the paradoxical juxtaposition with *eleutheroi*. Sharples (2003, 206) misleadingly remarks that Ps.-Alexander understands 'Aristotle's point to be that free men have *more* choices'. His point is rather that the choices of free men are limited to actions that benefit the polis to a greater extent than are those allowed to slaves. See Keyt 2018.

471 [715,41] Translates *ho ti etuche*. The manuscripts disagree over whether this phrase also occurs earlier at 1075a20 in connection with free persons, where it looks like a replacement for *hotioun* which occurs in EMC. JA[b], have *ho ti etuche* and it is added in E by a later hand (cf. Fazzo, 301). Ross and Jaeger report Ps.-Alexander's citation in support of reading *ho ti etuche* at 1075a20, but in fact he reports the phrase only for 1075a22. See also Golitsis 2016b, 497.

472 [716,4] Translates *tote*. This aside may suggest the commentary was written long after Aristotle's time, for example in the Byzantine era (Salis 2005, 335). Or it may indicate that the commentator was unfamiliar with Epictetus' origins (R. Sorabji in Sharples 2003, 207 n. 93).

473 [716,11] Translates *toiautê gar hakastou arkhê autôn hê phusis esti* (on the text cf. Judson note on 1075a22–3). Commentators disagree over whether 'nature' (*phusis*) here refers to the overarching nature of the entire universe (e.g. Sedley 2000) or to the nature immanent in each individual in it (e.g. Judson, 348–9). On Ps.-Alexander's interpretation the claim involves 'nature' in both senses. The term *arkhê* is translated 'principle' throughout this chapter (as generally throughout Book 12) in order to trace the thread of argument, but in some contexts its meaning is close to 'source' or 'rule' (cf. note 533). See *Metaph.* 5.1 and 5.4 on the terms *arkhê* and *phusis* respectively.

474 [716,17] Ps.-Alexander assumes that Aristotle is here talking about the reciprocal transformation of the elements in the sublunary realm. He may have in mind the explanation in *Generation and Corruption* of how the ongoing process of coming-to-be and perishing contributes to the common good of the universe: 'Since in all cases, we say, nature always desires what is better, and being is better than not-being ... but this is not possible in all cases because they are too far away from the principle, in the remaining fashion the god fulfilled the whole, by making

coming-to-be uninterrupted; for in this way being would be most connected, because coming-to-be always comes to be the closest to the [eternal] substance' (2.10, 336b27–34). In *Generation and Corruption*, however, Aristotle also says, 'Coming-to-be and perishing are not due to aggregation and dispersal [of pre-existing materials], but they occur when a thing comes to be from one thing to another as a whole' (1.3, 317a20–2). Therefore, according to Ps.-Alexander, the latter is what Aristotle really means to say at 1075a23–4; cf. also note 476.

475 [716,26] An unknown teacher is also mentioned at 610,34–5 and, interestingly, also by Michael of Ephesus, *in PN* 142,5.

476 [716,33] See *Phys.* 8.9, 265b22–3: 'Anaxagoras says that Intellect, which first brought about movement, disperses (*diakrinein*)'. According to Ps.-Alexander, the aorist passive *diakrithênai* ('have been dispersed') indicates that the present universe was established (*sustênai*) after things of the same kind came to be separated from other things after they were dispersed by the Intellect from the primordial mixture. Ps.-Alexander's point may be that cosmic order requires the 'dispersal', i.e. the permanent separation, of the cosmic spheres.

477 [716,34] Against this interpretation Elders (1972, 274) objects, 'The clause obviously is to be connected with the immediately preceding words.' However, Ps.-Alexander takes the immediately preceding clause to be parenthetical (as punctuated in the lemma).

478 [717,2] The lemma is abridged in the commentary: '"The impossible and absurd consequences for those who say otherwise" until "ought not be overlooked"'. The word 'until' (*heôs tou*), occurring only in M, looks like an editorial addition.

479 [717,9] Sc. from which it came to be, since it is everlasting. Cf. 716,29–30.

480 [717,15] See *Phys.* 1.7, 190b33: 'it is impossible for the contraries to be affected by each other' and in reference to Empedocles 1.6, 189a24–6: 'Love does not bring Hate together to produce something from it, nor does Hate do so from Love, but rather both act on a third thing.'

481 [717,20] Aristotle suggests that Plato conflated the substratum with the contraries at *Phys.* 1.9, 192a11–15, when he says that an unnamed theorist identified an underlying nature (the Dyad, i.e. the great and small), but failed to distinguish it from the contrary from which change proceeds. Aristotle adds that the underlying factor is viewed as *kakopoion* ('bad-making'). Cf. *Metaph.* 14.4, 1091b31–2: it follows for Plato that 'the contrary element, whether it is plurality or the unequal, that is the great and small, is the Bad Itself'.

482 [717,21] This seems to refer to the distinction made at 14.1, 1087b4–6: 'Some thinkers make one of the contraries matter, some of them making the unequal matter for the one, i.e. the equal, ... and others making plurality the matter for the one'. In the commentary on this passage, however, the former view is

attributed to Plato and his followers, and the latter to Pythagoras and his followers (796,10–797,17). The latter view is also attributed to Speusippus in the commentary at 828,12–14 on 14.4, 1091b32–5.

483 [717,29] Translates *kai mallon* (omitted in L).

484 [717,32] Cf. *Phys.* 1.7, 190b33–5: 'The problem is solved by the fact that the substratum is different [from the form and privation]; for it is not a contrary'.

485 [717,33] Translates *kai gar hê hulê hê mia*, which Ps.-Alexander evidently found in an alternative manuscript. This is close to Aristotle manuscripts EJA$^b$: *hê gar hulê hê mia oudeni enantion* ('the one matter is contrary to nothing'). The intended referent of 'the one matter' is unclear from the context. This difficulty is skirted by changing *hê mia* to *hêmin* with Aristotle manuscripts MCV$^k$ ('matter for us is contrary to nothing'). See Judson note on 1075a34. Though Ps.-Alexander may have read *hêmin* at 1075a34 (as in Jaeger's apparatus), he in fact cites it only in conjunction with *luetai* at 1075a31(cf. 717,30). In any event, Ps.-Alexander himself understands *hê hulê hê mia* ('the one matter') to be equivalent to *hê hulê hê prôtê*, the first or prime matter which has no qualities.

486 [717,35] i.e. water and air. Cf. *GC* 2.3, 330a30-b7: On the elemental level there are two pairs of contraries: hot-cold and moist-dry. The four 'apparently simple elements' are characterized by one from each pair. 'Fire is hot and dry, air is hot and moist, water cold and moist, earth cold and dry'. 330b33–331a1: 'fire and earth are extremes and purest, while water and air are intermediate and more mixed'. Cf. 679,15.

487 [717,37] At 1.6, 988a14 Aristotle says that Plato 'assigned the cause of excellence (*to eu*) and of evil to the elements', i.e. to the One and the Dyad (great and small) respectively; cf. Alexander, *in Metaph.* 60,13–16.

488 [718,2] The Aristotle manuscripts have 'the good and the bad are not principles'. The words 'and the bad' (*kai to kakon*) may have been missing from Ps.-Alexander's source manuscript, or he may have mistaken *kalon* for *kakon* (cf. Salis 2005, 344).

489 [718,5] At 14.4, 1091b31–2 Aristotle says, 'the contrary element, either plurality or the unequal or great and small [i.e. the Dyad] will be the Bad Itself'. The commentary on this passage indicates that Speusippus refused to apply the good to the one because 'if the one is good then the not-one, which is the material [i.e. the plurality or Dyad], is bad' (823,12–14).

490 [718,5] Viz. the Platonists who were just mentioned.

491 [718,10] In this sentence 'capable of producing' and 'efficient' both translate *poiêtikos*. At 1.4, 985a21–31 Aristotle says that Empedocles viewed Love and Hate as countervailing moving causes.

492 [718,13] i.e. depending on which description of Love is relevant.

493 [718,16] Cf. 1.4, 985a4–7: 'If one follows and understands according to Empedocles' thought and not what he inarticulately says, he will find that that Love is the cause of good things and Hate of bad things'.
494 [718,17] If A and B are contraries and C and D are contraries, then if C is true of A, then D is true of B. Cf. Alexander of Aphrodesias in Top. 126, 16–17.
495 [718,21] Ross objects that this interpretation does not explain how the perishability of Hate is due to its *badness*. However, Ps.-Alexander's interpretation depends on the claim that if Hate is identified with badness it is a *contrary* and consequently perishable.
496 [718,22] At 1075b8 Aristotle infers that Anaxagoras treated the good as a moving principle *because* he regarded Intellect as a moving principle. In Book 1 he says Anaxagoras treated Intellect as the source of motion in 1.3, 984b8–22 and 1.4, 985a18–21 but he does not mention the good in those passages. It is unclear whether Ps.-Alexander recognizes this distinction.
497 [718,24] Unless, that is, Anaxagoras speaks of the Intellect as a final cause as well as efficient cause.
498 [718,25] See note 102.
499 [718,28] Translates *kineitai*. Bonitz suggests *kinei* following 'movere' in Sepúlveda, in which case the clause would be translated: 'everything which brings about movement *moves* that which is moved for the sake of it [i.e. Intellect]'.
500 [718,30] The translation 'he' is intentionally ambiguous. The manuscripts have *legôn* (nominative, as read by Bonitz) which would refer to Aristotle, whereas Hayduck emends to *legonta* (accusative) referring to Anaxagoras. The former would be more apt if the goodness of Intellect was inferred by Aristotle rather than explicitly asserted by Anaxagoras. At 1.6, 988a14–17 Aristotle says that Anaxagoras like Empedocles 'sought' to assign the good and bad to the elements, though he may only mean that this assignment is implied by their remarks (cf. notes 493 and 496).
501 [718,33] The commentary manuscripts have *rhathumêsêi* (literally, 'to shirk'), which is the basis for Ps.-Alexander's interpretation. Aristotle manuscript E originally had *rhuthmisêi* ('fine-tune') but a later hand added *rhathumêsêi*, which is also in CM.
502 [719,7] At 690,9–13 Hesiod was quoted in connection with the view that everything came to be from Chaos and Night; cf. note 243. Aristotle may be referring more generally to thinkers before Parmenides.
503 [719,10] See note 474.
504 [719,13] The commentary manuscripts differ slightly from the Aristotle manuscripts, but the point remains essentially the same: both those who posit the

contraries and those who posit the Forms must accept an additional 'more dominant' principle, namely, the efficient cause (cf. 4,1070b22–5 with 680,38–681,3).

505 [719,14] Translates *ex autou kai eis auton*: i.e. the first intellect is both efficient cause and final cause of the universe.

506 [719,16] Freudenthal (1884, 22) sees a reference here to Neoplatonists. Cf. 688,37–9 on emanations from the Forms.

507 [719,22] It is uncertain what 'theologians' Ps.-Alexander has in mind. There may be a reference to Plato's *Republic* 5, 477A: 'knowledge (*gnôsis*) is concerned with being and ignorance (*agnôsis*) with not-being'.

508 [719,23] 'To wisdom' (*sophiai*) in the Aristotle manuscripts.

509 [719,32] This sentence seems garbled because the first clause of the protasis appears to contradict the apodosis. Perhaps in view of this Sepúlveda substitutes for the first clause: 'which will obtain for the same reason in the first principle, if we posit a contrary to it' (quae ratio eadem in principio primo valebit, si quidquam ipsi contrarium faciamus). However, the argument is a *reductio ad absurdum* (as was pointed out to me by David Keyt), so the sentence needs no repair.

510 [719,35] On matter as potentiality see 11.2, 1060a20–1.

511 [719,37] This is a paraphrase of Aristotle's difficult phrase *hê de enantia agnoia eis to enantion*. If ignorance is the contrary of knowledge, the object of ignorance will be the contrary of the object of knowledge.

512 [720,1] Translating *eti ei mê*, found in commentary manuscripts AL and Aristotle manuscripts CM and followed by Jaeger. EJA[b] have *eite mê* (followed by Ross).

513 [720,8] *Cael.* 1.3, 270a12-b25.

514 [720,10] Ps.-Alexander omits 'and the natural theorists' (*kai tois phusikois*). But his point is that without the immovable mover there will be an infinite regress of movers; cf. 686,28–30.

515 [720,11] The name 'Heracles' can also refer to the planet Mars (cf. Ps.-Aristotle, *de Mundo* 2, 392a25). Since, however, Ps.-Alexander mentions only the theologians (omitting the reference to 'the natural theorists' at 1075b27), it is assumed in the translation that he is referring to a succession of deities which are related as father and son, rather than a sequence of planets, though the latter might be suggested by 'heavenly objects' (1075b26; cf. 720,8).

516 [720,12] Reading *hetera* (fem.) with L; A has *heteros* (masc.), which would refer to another god. Here the *arkhê* is the proximate mover.

517 [720,14] It is not obvious what the objection would be against the Platonists unless it is some version of the 'third man' argument.

518 [720,16] See 1.9, 991b9–21; 13.5; 14.2 and 14.6.

519 [720,19] Cf. 1.9, 991b4–5 on Plato's *Phaedo* 100D: 'and yet, although the Forms exist, nonetheless the things that participate [in them] will not come to be ...'.
520 [720,20] See *Cat.* 6, 4b22–31: Unlike lines which are 'continuous' (*sunechês*), numbers are 'discrete' (*diorismenos*) because their parts do not have a common boundary at which they are in contact together. 'For example, if five is a part of ten, the two fives are not in contact together at any common boundary but are discrete.'
521 [720,22] Ps.-Alexander mentions no support for the claim that a number cannot be an efficient cause. Aristotle's reasons may, however, be along the same lines as his criticisms of the doctrine that the soul is a self-moving number in *DA* 1.4, 408b32–409a30.
522 [720,27] That is, actualities are posterior in time to the corresponding potentialities in the case of individual subjects, e.g. Socrates is potentially musical before he becomes actually musical. Cf. notes 229 and 231.
523 [720,29] i.e. (presumably) there are always things that exist.
524 [720,32] Ps.-Alexander understands the reference to be to 1072a3–4. Elders 1972, 293, suggests 1071b19–20, which is also possible. The thesis is illustrated and qualified at 9.8, 1049b17–29.
525 [720,36] This problem is elaborated in 13.9, 1085b4–12; cf. 780,12–5.
526 [720,36] Here begins a long sentence (720,36–721,8) that is broken up in the translation.
527 [721,6] Cf. *DA* 2.1, 412b6–8: 'there is no need to enquire whether the soul and the body are one, just as there is no need to ask why the wax and its shape are one, nor more generally whether the matter and that to which the matter belongs are one'.
528 [721,11] Reading *gegone* with L; A has *etelesan* (Bonitz conjectures *apetelesan*), in which case it would mean: 'they completed one thing out of them'.
529 [721,11] This doctrine is attributed to Speusippus in 7.2, 1028b20–4 on which the commentator states: 'Speusippus, the pupil of Plato, said that the intelligible substances are more than three [as Plato had said], namely the first is the One-Itself, another is the principle of number, another is the principle of magnitude, and another the principle of the soul; and thus he extended the kinds of goodness into a multitude' (462,34–463,1).
530 [721,14] Translates *pentados*. The number five embodies justice because it divides equally the perfect number ten (cf. 741,5–6). Sepúlveda translates 'ex numero septem' ('out of the number seven'); cf. 720,35.
531 [721,15] Cf. 14.3, 1090b13–20 where Aristotle compares Speusippus' 'episodic' ontology to a 'bad tragedy', on which Ps.-Alexander drolly comments: 'Many mediocre tragedians interject masks, actors, and dialogue which in a like manner

possess neither continuity nor appropriateness to what went before or after. For example, if after the tragedian has brought Ajax in the interim after he has committed suicide, he has then brought in Hecuba singing a dirge for Troy, what connection would this have with what precedes or follows, as when Menelaus makes his entrance and does not permit Teucrus to bury the body of Ajax? What, then, occurs in a dreadful tragedy would also occur in nature if anything is composed of numbers and planes' (816,9–16).

532 [721,23] Translates *gar* of dissent; cf. Denniston 1950, 74–5.
533 [721,30] This assumes a close connection between *arkhê* as political rule and *arkhê* as metaphysical principle; see also note 473.
534 [721,31] Aristotle quotes Homer's *Iliad* 2.204. Some editors add *estô* as in Homer's text, but it is not appropriate at 1076a4, it is omitted by most Aristotle manuscripts, and there is no suggestion of it in the commentary manuscripts.

# APPENDIX I

# Freudenthal's Comparison of the Two Alexanders

The following overview by Jacob Freudenthal (1884) is translated here with updated information.

Key to references:

F = frr. in J. Freudenthal, *Die durch Averroes erhaltenen Fragmente Alexanders zur Metaphysik des Aristoteles* (Berlin: Königliche Akademie der Wissenschaften, 1884).

Hayduck = *Alexandri Aphrodisensis in Aristotelis metaphysica commentaria*, ed. M. HBayduck (Berlin: Georg Reimer, 1888).

Bonitz = *Alexandri Aphrodisensis Commentarius in libros metaphysicos Aristotelis*, ed. H. Bonitz (Berlin: George Reimer, 1847).

*Tafsīr* = Ibn Rushd [Averroes], *Tafsīr mā baʿd aṭ-Ṭabīʿa*, ed. M. Bouyges (Beirut: Dār al-Mashriq 1938).

## Comparison of Alexander in Averroes with Ps.-Alexander

| Alexander in Averroes | Ps.-Alexander on *Metaphysics* 12 |
|---|---|
| fr. 1F (*Tafsīr* 1393–5) On the connection of the individual books of the *Metaphysics* and the ordering of the twelve books. | Hayduck 668,2–12; Bonitz 641,4–14 Entirely different. |
| fr. 2F (*Tafsīr* 1406) On the object of the *Metaphysics* and the beginning of the twelfth book. | Hayduck 668,14–18; Bonitz 641,15–19 Entirely different. |
| fr. 3F (*Tafsīr* 1408–9) Commentary on 1069a19f. | Hayduck 669,2–24; Bonitz 642,1–19 Entirely different. |
| fr. 4aF (*Tafsīr* 1420) On the meaning of 1069a32: *hês anankê ta stoikheia labein*. | Hayduck 670,31–4; Bonitz 643,29–30 Same conclusion but different commentary and terminology. |

| | |
|---|---|
| fr. 4bF (*Tafsīr* 1420–1)<br>On different versions of 1069a30–3. | Hayduck 670,24–34; cf. 671,7–21; Bonitz 643,23–31<br>Based on the reading which is explicitly rejected by Alexander in Averroes. |
| fr. 5F (*Tafsīr* 1427)<br>On the opinions of earlier philosophers regarding immovable substance. | Hayduck 671,1–7; Bonitz 644,1–8<br>Mentioning only Plato and Pythagoreans, while Alexander in Averroes rightly mentions Plato's students too. |
| fr. 6F (*Tafsīr* 1429)<br>On the objects of physics and metaphysics. | Hayduck 671,7–17; Bonitz 644,8–16<br>Corresponding only in so far as here, as in Alexander in Averroes, Aristotle's text is paraphrased. |
| fr. 7F (*Tafsīr* 1430–3)<br>On the principles of perceptible substance. | Hayduck 671,23–672,21; Bonitz 644,21–645,21<br>Offering only some similarity, as far as the text of Aristotle and its sketchy paraphrase are considered. However, none of the exegeses of Alexander in Averroes are found here. |
| frr. 8aF (*Tafsīr* 1439) & 8bF (*Tafsīr* 1442)<br>On the earlier enquiries into the concepts of possibility, actuality and matter. | Hayduck 672,24–673,4; Bonitz 645,22–646,7<br>Entirely different. |
| fr. 9F (*Tafsīr* 1445–6)<br>On the words attributed by Aristotle to Democritus: *ên homou panta*. | Hayduck 673,19–22; Bonitz 646,21–3<br>In stark contradiction with Alexander in Averroes. |
| frr. 10aF (*Tafsīr* 1457–9), 10bF (1460–2) & 10cF (1462–5)<br>On products of nature and art, especially concerning generation from synonyms. | Hayduck 675,18–676,4; Bonitz 648,18–649,8<br>Containing nothing of all the wide-ranging discussions of Alexander in Averroes. |
| fr. 11F (*Tafsīr* 1467–72)<br>Several interpretations of 1070a9–10: *hê men hulê ktl.* | Hayduck 676,5–29; Bonitz 649,9–31<br>Containing none of the commentary offered by Alexander in Averroes. |
| fr. 12F (*Tafsīr* 1481–2)<br>Commentary on 1070a18: *dio dê ou kakôs ktl.* | Hayduck 677,12–14; Bonitz 650,18–20<br>Containing no trace of the different readings and commentary of Alexander in Averroes. |
| fr. 13aF (*Tafsīr* 1483) & 13bF (1484–5)<br>Commentary on 1070a18: *alla toutôn ktl.* | Hayduck 677,14–24; Bonitz 650,20–9<br>Entirely different. |
| fr. 14F (*Tafsīr* 1487–8)<br>On the immortality of the soul. | Hayduck 677,37–678,5; Bonitz 651,6–12<br>Completely contradicting the discussion of Alexander in Averroes. |

fr. 15F (*Tafsīr* 1497)
On the reliability of Aristotelian doctrine.

No parallel for this.

fr. 16F (*Tafsīr* 1506–9)
On the identity or difference of the principles of beings.

Hayduck 678,11–31; Bonitz 651,16–652,2
Agreeing in meaning on subordinate points.

fr. 17F (*Tafsīr* 1509–11)
Objections of Alexander.

Hayduck 678,31–679,21; Bonitz 652,2–27
Showing no trace of agreement.

fr. 18F (*Tafsīr* 1513–16)
One and being are not principles of the categories.

Hayduck 679,23–680,33; Bonitz 652,28–654,5
Agreeing with only one of several explanations by Alexander in Averroes.

fr. 19F (*Tafsīr* 1519)
On negations as essential determinations of a thing.

Hayduck 680,33–681,13; Bonitz 654,5–23
Showing no trace of agreement.

fr. 20F (*Tafsīr* 1529–31)
Commentary on 1070b34f.

Hayduck 681,24–5; Bonitz 654,32–3
Showing no trace of agreement.

fr. 21F (*Tafsīr* 1534–5)
Commentary on 1071a2f.

Hayduck 681,28–682,14; Bonitz 655,1–14
Completely different.

fr. 22F (*Tafsīr* 1544–5)
On the universal and individual.

Hayduck 684,8–27; Bonitz 657,16–658,2
Completely different.

fr. 23F (*Tafsīr* 1554–5)
Commentary on 1071a36f.

Hayduck 685,14–20; Bonitz 658,21–7
Completely different.

fr. 24F (*Tafsīr* 1557–8)
Commentary on 1071b11f.

Hayduck 685,22–5; Bonitz 658,27–30
Completely different.

fr. 25F (*Tafsīr* 1567)
On a necessary condition of eternal motion not mentioned by Aristotle.

Hayduck 687,25–688,27; Bonitz 661,3–662,8
Showing no trace of agreement; cf. however Hayduck 686,12–13; Bonitz 659,21–2; i.e. Alexander, *Questions* 1.1.

fr. 26F (*Tafsīr* 1571)
On 1071b27.

Hayduck 690,14–17; Bonitz 663,31–664,3
Agreeing in part (since Aristotle himself provides the explanation with 1072a5f).

fr. 27F (*Tafsīr* 1578–80)
On the causes of regularity and of changes of appearances.

Hayduck 692,5–12; Bonitz 665,29–666,4
Differing on essential points.

fr. 28F (*Tafsīr* 1588–9)
On the proof of the existence of the unmoved mover.

Hayduck 693,13–30; Bonitz 667,10–25
Completely different.

fr. 29F (*Tafsīr* 1601–2)
On 1072a30f.

Hayduck 694,17–20; Bonitz 668,16–17
With only one (and the most obvious) of the four explanations of Alexander in Averroes.

| | |
|---|---|
| fr. 30F (*Tafsīr* 1605) On the essential and inessential perfection of being. | Hayduck 695,26-39; Bonitz 669,26-670,9 Showing no trace of agreement. |
| fr. 31F (*Tafsīr* 1619) On the blessedness of god. | Hayduck 697,23-698,3; Bonitz 672,2-19 Showing no trace of agreement. |
| fr. 32F (*Tafsīr* 1623) On thinking of itself which Aristotle attributes to the intellect. | Hayduck 697,16-698,31; Bonitz 671,26-673,11 Showing no trace of agreement. |
| frr. 33 & 34F (*Tafsīr* 1660-77) On Aristotle's theory of the spheres. | Hayduck 702,55-706,21; Bonitz 677,25-681,21 Showing no trace of agreement. |

Two more fragments, 35 (on whether the stars have souls) and 36 (on providence), are drawn from Averroes' (spurious) *Epitome on Metaphysics*. Freudenthal (112 n. 2) notes that it is uncertain whether they are taken from Alexander of Aphrodisias' commentary on the *Metaphysics*.

APPENDIX II

# Comparison of Ps.-Alexander's Readings with the Aristotle Manuscripts

Noteworthy agreements and disagreements between Ps.-Alexander's lemmata (L) or citations (C) (or on occasion paraphrases (P)) and the two principal families of Aristotle's *Metaphysics* 12 are registered in the following three lists of passages. The *alpha* family is represented by EJ and the *beta* family by A$^b$CM until 1073a1 (cf. 699,30), after which A$^b$ switches allegiance to *alpha*. (Deviations of manuscripts from their families are noted in parentheses and frequently indicate cross-contamination.) Manuscript V$^k$ offers selections from *Metaphysics* 12 and generally agrees with *beta*. Apparently trivial variations (e.g. involving spelling, word order, elision, incidental omissions, and minor slips) are disregarded. Readings are based on the critical apparatus in Alexandru. See Introduction §5 for further information concerning manuscripts.

### Ps.-Alexander's agreements with the *alpha* family against the *beta* family

| Hayduck | Bekker | Ps.-Alexander | *alpha* (EJ) | *beta* (A$^b$CM) |
|---|---|---|---|---|
| 669,25C | 1069a22 | tauta | tauta | t'álla (E$^2$) |
| 672,11C | 1069b11 | omitted | omitted (CM) | hê$^1$ |
| 677,19C | 1070a10 | omitted | omitted | estin (E$^2$) |
| 678,10L | 1070a31 | ta de | ta d' | ésti de ta |
| 678,10L | 1070a31 | éstin hôs | éstin hôs | omitted (J$^1$) |
| 678,15L | 1070a33 | pantôn (pantas A) | pantôn (CM) | panta |
| 679,22L | 1070b7 | stoikheiôn | stoikheiôn (CM) | stoikheion estin |
| 681,14L.19P | 1070b31 | anthrôpois anthrôpos | anthrôpois anthrôpos | anthrôpos (J) |
| 682,37C | 1071a8 | energeíai | energeíai | energeia (JV$^k$) |
| 684,6L | 1071a17 | de | de (CM) | omitted |
| 684,12C | 1071a19 | todi | todi (CM) | tôi eidei |

| Hayduck | Bekker | Ps.-Alexander | *alpha* (EJ) | *beta* (A$^b$CM) |
|---|---|---|---|---|
| 684,16P | 1971a20 | *ta* | *ta* (CM) | omitted |
| 684,28L | 1071a29 | *dê* | *dê* | *de* (J) |
| 685,22P | 1071b1 | *arkhai* | *arkhai* | *hai arkhai* |
| 685,24P | 1071b2 | *pôs*$^2$ | *pôs*$^2$ (CM) | omitted |
| 688,28C | 1071b14 | *ouden* | *ouden* | *outhen* |
| 688,35C | 1071b17 | *energêsei ... estai* | *energêsei ... estai* (CM) | *energêsê ... esti* |
| 691,36C | 1072a8 | *khronon* | *khronon* (CM) | *khronou* |
| 691,24C | 1072a24 | omitted | omitted (E$^1$CMV$^k$) | *to* (E$^2$JA$^b$) |
| 693,24C | 1072a24 | *kai*$^2$ | *kai*$^2$ (A$^{b1}$CM) | omitted (A$^{b2}$V$^k$) |
| 694,5P | 1072a29 | *kalon* | *kalon* (E$^1$) | *mallon* (E$^2$) |
| 694,7C | 1072a30 | *gar* | *gar* (E$^1$CMV$^k$) | *de* (E$^2$) |
| 694,16C | 1072a30 | *kineitai* | *kineitai* (CM) | omitted |
| 695,9C | 1072a33 | omitted | omitted (CM) | *to*$^1$ |
| 695,27C | 1072b3 | omitted | omitted (CMV$^k$) | *tinos* (A$^b$) |
| 696,8C | 1072b6 | *tautêi* | *tautêi* (CM) | *tautên* |
| 696,8C | 1072b5 | *hê prôtê* | *hê prôtê* (V$^k$Cmg.) | *prôtê* (E$^2$) |
| 699,17C | 1072b27 | *ekeino* | *ekeino* (CMV$^k$) | *ekeinos* |
| 704,21C | 1074a3 | *apokathistasas* | *apokathistasas* (CM) | *apokathistôsas* (A$^b$J) |

Postscript: In two instances Ps.-Alexander agrees with J against all the other manuscripts at 669,31C (1069a22), reading *ê* rather *hê*, and at 688,19P (1071b13), reading *estai* rather than *esti*. On the other hand, he agrees with all other manuscripts against J at 677,27.32C (1070a21), reading *hôs progegenêmena* rather than *hôsper gegenêmena*. Also, he agrees with ECM against A$^b$ and J at 714,1C (1075a5), reading *tôi nooumenôi* rather than *tou nooumenou*, and he agrees with the other manuscripts against J and E$^2$ at 688,17C (1071b12), reading *esti* rather than *estai*.

## Ps.-Alexander's agreements with the *beta* family against the *alpha* family

| Hayduck | Bekker | PsAlexander | alpha (EJ) | beta (A$^b$CM) |
|---|---|---|---|---|
| 669,32C.P | 1069a23 | to ouk (L, ouk A) | ouk (CM) | to ouk |
| 670,20C | 1069a29 | hekasta | hekaston (CM) | hekasta |
| 671,21C | 1069a31 | omitted | aidios hê de (A$^b$C$^1$) | omitted (C$^2$MV$^k$) |
| 672,9C | 1069b9 | to | omitted (E$^1$CM) | to |
| 677,15C | 1070a19 | álla | allà (CMA$^{b1}$) | álla (A$^{b2}$) |
| 678,9P | 1070a30 | omitted | ho (CM) | omitted |
| 678,10L | 1070a31 | állai | álla (CM) | állai |
| 679,32C | 1070b8 | en | omitted (A$^b$) | en |
| 681,6P | 1070b25 | histôn | histan (C) | histôn |
| 681,8P | 1070b26 | aitia | aitiai | aitia |
| 681,12P | 1070b29f | omitted | kai ... arkhê | omitted |
| 682,21C | 1071a5 | allote | álla te (A$^b$) | allote |
| 684,20C | 1071a24 | ta eidê (eidê A) | êdê (J$^1$E$^2$) | ta eidê (V$^k$) eidê (A$^b$E$^1$?J$^2$) |
| 689,19P | 1071b22 | energeia | energeíai | energeia |
| 690,13C | 1071b28 | ên homou | homou (J$^1$CM) | ên homou (J$^2$) |
| 691,19C | 1072a3 | proteran | proteron (A$^b$) | proteran |
| 691,29L.20P | 1072a5 | energeia$^2$ | energeíai (A$^b$) | energeia$^2$ |
| 692,16C | 1072a15 | autôi | hautôi (C) | autôi |
| 696,15C | 1072b8 | energeíai | energeia (C) | energeíai (J) |
| 701,26C | 1073a34 | kath' hautên | kath' hautên (CV$^k$) | kath' hauto (J) |
| 702,8C | 1073b4 | philosophíai | philosophias | philosophíai |
| 711,11C | 1074b19 | omitted | ho estin | omitted (V$^k$) |
| 712,38L | 1074b36 | heautês | autês (A$^b$) hautês (J) | heautês (V$^k$) |
| 713,39C | 1075a4 | t'auton | to auto | t'auton (V$^k$) |
| 714,17C | 1075a7 | oun | omitted (E$^1$A$^b$) | oun (V$^k$E$^2$) |
| 717,33P | 1075a34 | hêmin hê mia (alt.) | hê mia (A$^b$) | hêmin (V$^k$) |
| 717,38C | 1075a35 | panta | hapanta | panta (V$^k$) |
| 718,33C | 1075b12 | rhathumêsêi | rhuthmisêi | rhathumêsêi (CME$^2$) rhathumêsi (V$^k$) |
| 720,1L | 1075b24 | eti ei | eite | eti ei (V$^k$) |

## Ps.-Alexander's disagreements with both the *alpha* and *beta* families

| Hayduck | Bekker | PsAlexander | *alpha* (EJ) | *beta* (A^bCM) |
|---|---|---|---|---|
| 669,9C | 1069a20 | ei kai | kai ei | kai ei |
| 669,24f.C | 1069a22 | haplôs hôs eipein | hôs eipein haplôs | hôs haplôs eipein |
| 671,26C | 1069a22 | hoion | allà | allà |
| 669,27C | 1069a22 | omitted | kai | kai |
| 671,19C | 1069a32 | *kai* after *hês* | omitted | omitted |
| 671,19C | 1069a32 | omitted | hê d' aïdios | hê d' aïdios |
| 671,19C | 1069a31 | hên...homologousin after *aisthêtê* | hên...homologousin after *phthartê* | hên...homologousin after *phthartê* |
| 673,20C | 1069b23 | homou | hêmin | hêmin homou (E²M) |
| 674,7C | 1069b28 | esti to (*ti esti* 8P) | ti esti | ti esti |
| 676,30P | 1070a11f | kai hexis tis eis hên | eis hên kai hexis tis | eis hên kai hexis tis |
| 677,20C | 1070a19 | álla | allà | allà (álla A^b2) |
| 677,27C | 1070a21 | omitted | aitia | aitia |
| 679,22L | 1070b7 | on kai to hen | hen ê to on (CM) | on ê to hen |
| 682,21C | 1071a6 | omitted | en | en |
| 684,11C | 1071a18 | de | dê | dê |
| 685,18f.C | 1071a37 | oute ... oute | mête ... mête | mête ... mête |
| 688,29C | 1071b14 | oud' an | oud' ean | ean (oude an CM) |
| 689,34C | 1071b25 | ouden | outhen | outhen |
| 690,18C | 1071b28 | aition (sic?) | adunaton | adunaton |
| 691,18C | 1072a3 | oun | dê | dê |
| 692,8C | 1072a13 | men | omitted | omitted |
| 692,31C | 1072a17 | houtô | houtôs | houtôs (houtô C) |
| 693,17C | 1072a23 | omitted | ti | ti (omitted V^k) |
| 693,40C | 1072a27 | men | men gar (C) | gar men men (M) |
| 696,8C | 1072b5 | hôste ei phora | hôsth' hê phora (V^kC²) | hôst' ei hê phora (E²) |
| 696,22C | 1072b10 | anankê | anankêi | anankêi |
| 699,38P | 1073a4 | kekhôrismenê kai allê | akinêtos kai kekhôrismenê | akinêtos kai kekhôrismenê |
| 700,16C | 1073a15 | de | omitted | omitted |
| 701,10C | 1073a23 | dedeigmenôn rhêteon | diôrismenôn lekteon | diôrismenôn lekteon |
| 702,8C | 1073b4 | sphairôn | phorôn | phorôn |
| 702,36LC | 1073b17 | omitted | hekaterou | hekaterou |

| | | | | |
|---|---|---|---|---|
| 704,9fC | 1073b32–4 | tên autên etitheto taxin toutetsti tôn apostêmatôn | tên men thesin tôn sphairôn tên autên etitheto Eudoxôi | tên men thesin tôn sphairôn tên autên etitheto Eudoxôi tout' estin tôn apostêmatôn tên taxin (A[b]) |
| 705,13C | 1074a6 | hôste | epei oun | epei oun |
| 705,18C | 1073b36 | omitted | eti | eti |
| 705,23C | 1074a8 | katô (katôtatô tetagmenon 39P) | katôtatô tetagmenon | katôtatô tetagmenon |
| 706,17L.24C | 1074a16 | omitted | kai tas aisthêtas | kai tas aisthêtas (CV[k]) kai ouk aisthêtas (V[k]) |
| 707,34C | 1074a20 | telos (AL) telous (M) | telous (E[1]J) telos (E[2]) | telous |
| 708,22P | 1074a22 | ei | eite | eite |
| 709,19C | 1074a35 | ho de Sôkratês | Sôkratês | Sôkratês |
| 709,39C | 1074b4 | proêktai | prosêktai | prosêktai |
| 710,38C | 1074b16 | ekhon | ekhôn | ekhôn |
| 710,40P | 1074b17 | mê noei | mêden noei mêd' ennoei (A[b]J) | mêden noei |
| 713,11C | 1074b37 | állo[2] | omitted | omitted |
| 713,15C | 1074b38 | ou | oude | oude (ou V[k]) |
| 713,15C | 1074b38 | t'auton | t'auto | t'auto |
| 714,3L | 1075a5 | zêtêsai | aporia | aporia |
| 713,15C | 1074b38 | ou | oude | oude (CM) ou (V[k]) |
| 714,18C | 1075a8 | omitted | ge | ge |
| 717,33C | 1075a34 | kai gar hê | hê gar | hê gar |
| 718,2C | 1075a37 | omitted | kai to kakon | kai to kakon |
| 718,13P | 1075b5 | kai hôs hulêi | hôs hulê kai | hôs hulê kai |
| 720,14P | 1075b27 | ê hoi arithmoi | ê arithmoi | ê arithmoi (arithmoi V[k]) |

# Bibliography

Alexandru, S. (1999), 'A new manuscript of Pseudo-Philoponus' commentary on Aristotle's *Metaphysics* containing a hitherto unknown ascription of the work', *Phronesis* 44, 347–52.

Alexandru, S. (2003), 'Reflections regarding Milan manuscripts of the commentary on Aristotle's *Metaphysics* ascribed to George Pachymeres', *Revue d'histoire des textes* 31, 117–27.

Alexandru, S. (2014), *Aristotle's Metaphysics Lambda: Annotated critical edition based upon a systematic investigation of Greek, Latin, Arabic, and Hebrew Sources*, Leiden: Brill.

Aquinas, St. Thomas (1995), *Commentary on Aristotle's Metaphysics*, tr. John P. Rowan, South Bend, IN: Dumb Ox Books.

Armstrong, A. H. (1960), 'The background of the doctrine "that the intelligibles are not outside the intellect"', in *Les sources de Plotin*, Entretiens Hardt 5, Genevaz: Fondation Hardt, 391–425.

Arnim, H. von (1931), 'Die Entwicklung der aristotelischen Gotteslehre', *Sitzungsberichte der Akademie der Wissenschaften in Wien, philosophisch-historische Klasse*, 212:5, 3–80; repr. in Hager, 1–74.

Baghdassarian, F. (2017), 'L'intellection divine en *Métaphysique Lambda* 7 and 9: les indices d'un approfondissement d'Aristote par lui même', in Baghdassarian and Gyomarc'h, 33–58.

Baghdassarian, F. and G. Gyomarc'h (2017) (eds), *Réceptions de la théologie Aristotélicienne d'Aristote à Michel d'Éphèse*, Louvain-la-Neuve: Peeters.

Baltzly, D. (2015), 'Two Aristotelian puzzles about planets and their Neoplatonic reception', *Apeiron* 48, 483–501.

Barker, E. F. (1957), *Social and political thought in Byzantium from Justinian I to the last Palaeologus: Passages from Byzantine writer and documents*, Oxford: Oxford University Press.

Barnes, J. (1984) (ed.), *The complete works of Aristotle: The revised Oxford translation*, 2 vols., Princeton: Princeton University Press.

Barnes, J. (1997), 'Roman Aristotle', in J. Barnes and M. Griffin (eds), *Philosophia togata II: essays on philosophy and Roman society*, Oxford: Oxford University Press, 1–69.

Beere, J. B. (2003), 'Counting the unmoved movers: Astronomy and explanation in Aristotle's *Metaphysics* XII.8', *Archiv für Geschichte der Philosophie* 85, 1–20.

Berti, E. (1997), 'Da chi è amato il motore immobile? Su Aristotele *Metaph*. XII 6–70', *Methexis* 10, 59–82.

Berti, E. (2000), 'Unmoved mover(s) as efficient cause(s) in *Metaphysics Lambda* 6', in Frede and Charles, 181–206.

Berti, E. (2000b), 'Il movimento del cielo in Alessandro di Afrodisia', in A. Brancacci (ed.), *La filosofia in età imperiale, Atti del colloquio Roma, 17–19 giugno 1999*, Naples: Bibliopolis, 227–43.

Berti, E. (2004), *Aristotel: dalla dialettica alla filosofia prima con saggi integrativi*, Milan: Bompiano.

Berti, E. (2016), 'The program of *Metaphysics Lambda* (chapter 1)', in Horn, 67–86.

Bertolacci, A. (2005), 'On the Arabic translations of Aristotle's *Metaphysics*', *Arabic Sciences and Philosophy* 15, 241–75.

Blyth, D. (2015), 'Heavenly soul in Aristotle', *Apeiron* 48, 427–65.

Bodéüs, R. (2000), *Aristotle and the theology of the living immortals*, Albany: SUNY.

Bodnár, I. (1997), 'Alexander of Aphrodisias on celestial motions', *Phronesis* 42, 190–205.

Bodnár, I. (2005), 'Aristotle's rewinding spheres: Three options and their difficulties', *Apeiron* 38, 257–75.

Bodnár, I. (2016), 'Cases of celestial teleology in *Metaphysics Lambda*', in Horn, 247–67.

Bonitz, H. (1847) (ed.), *Alexandri Aphrodisensis Commentarius in libros Metaphysicos Aristotelis*, Berlin: Georg Reimer.

Bordt, M. (2006), *Aristoteles 'Metaphysik XII'*, Darmstadt: Wissenschaftliche Buchgesellschaft.

Bordt, M. (2011), 'Why Aristotle's God is not the unmoved mover', *Oxford Studies in Ancient Philosophy* 40, 91–109.

Bouyges, M. (1938) (ed.), *Averroes, Tafsīr Mā Baʻd aṭ-Ṭabīʻa*, Beirut: Dār al-Mashriq.

Bradshaw, D. (2001), 'A new look at the first mover', *Journal of the History of Philosophy* 39, 1–22.

Broadie, S. (1993), 'Que fait le premier moteur d'Aristote? (Sur la théologie du livre Lambda de la "Métaphysique")', *Revue philosophique de la France et de l'Étranger* 183, 375–411.

Brown, L. (1994), 'The verb "to be" in Greek philosophy: Some remarks', in S. Everson (ed.), *Companions to ancient thought 3: Language*, Cambridge: Cambridge University Press, 212–36.

Browning, R. (1962), 'An unpublished funeral oration on Anna Comnena', *Proceedings of the Cambridge Philological Society* 188, 1–12; repr. in Sorabji 1990a, 393–406.

Bruns, I. (1887) (ed.), *Alexandri Aphrodisiensis De Anima liber cum Mantissa, consilio et auctoritate Academiae Literarum Regiae Borussicae*, Berlin: Georg Reimer.

Brunschwig, J. (2000), 'Metaphysics Lambda 9: A short-lived thought experiment?', in Frede and Charles, 275–306.

Burnyeat, M. (2008), '*Kinêsis* vs. *energeia*: A much-read passage in (but not of) Aristotle's *Metaphysics*', *Oxford Studies in Ancient Philosophy* 34, 219–92.

Buckler, G. (1929), *Anna Comnena*, Oxford: Clarendon Press.

Cassin, B. and M. Narcy (1989), *La decision du sens: le livre Gamma de la Métaphysique de Aristote: introduction, texte, traduction et commentaire*, Paris: Vrin.

Charles, D. (2000), 'Metaphysics Lambda 2: Matter and change', in Frede and Charles, 81–110.

Charles, D. (2018), 'Physics I.7' in D. Quarantotto (ed.), *Aristotle's Physics: A systematic exploration*, Cambridge: Cambridge University Press, 178–205.

Christ, W. (1895), *Aristotelis Metaphysica*, Leipzig: Teubner.

Code, A. (2000), 'Some remarks on *Metaphysics Lambda 5*', in Frede and Charles, 161–79.

Comnena, A. (1969), *The Alexiad*, tr. E. R. A. Sewter, Harmondsworth: Penguin.

Crubellier, M. (2000), '*Metaphysics Lambda 4*', in Frede and Charles, 137–60.

Crubellier, M. (2016), 'What the form has to be and what it needs not be (*Metaphysics Lambda 3*)', in Horn, 119–37.

Curnis, M. (2016), 'La *Politica* di Aristotele tra Michele Efesio e Demetrio Petrizzopulo', *Erytheia. Revista de estudios bizantinos y neogriegos* 37, 247–99.

De Filippo, J. G. (1994), 'Aristotle's identification of the prime mover as God', *Classical Quarterly* 44, 393–409.

De Filippo, J. G. (1995), 'The "thinking of thinking" in *Metaphysics Lambda 9*', *Journal of the History of Philosophy* 33, 91–8.

De Koninck, T. (1994), 'Aristotle on God as thought thinking itself', *Review of Metaphysics* 47, 471–515.

De Koninck, T. (1991), '"La pensée de la pensée" chez Aristote', in T. De Koninck and G. Planty-Bonjour (eds), *La question de dieu chez Aristote et Hegel*, Paris: Presses universitaires de France, 69–51.

Denniston, J. D. (1950), *The Greek particles*, 2nd edn, Oxford: Oxford University Press, 1950; orig. 1934.

Di Giovanni, M. and O. Primavesi (2016), 'Who wrote Alexander's commentary on *Metaphysics Lambda*? New light on the Syro-Arabic tradition', in Horn, 11–66.

Dillon, J. and D. O'Meara (2006), (tr.), *Syrianus on Aristotle's Metaphysics 13–14*, London: Duckworth.

Donini, P. L. (1968), 'Il "De anima" di Alessandro di Afrodisia e Michele Efesio', *Revista Filologia e di Istruzione Classica* 96, 316–23.

Dooley, W. (1989) (tr.), *Alexander of Aphrodisias on Aristotle* Metaphysics *1*, London: Duckworth.

Dooley, W. (1993a) (tr.), *Alexander of Aphrodisias on Aristotle* Metaphysics *4*, London: Duckworth.

Dooley, W. (1993b) (tr.), *Alexander of Aphrodisias on Aristotle* Metaphysics *5*, London: Duckworth.

Dooley, W. and A. Madigan (1992) (tr.), *Alexander of Aphrodisias on Aristotle* Metaphysics *2–3*, London: Duckworth.

Dreyer, J. L. E. (1906), *History of the planetary systems from Thales to Kepler*, Cambridge: Cambridge University Press; 2nd edn as *A history of astronomy from Thales to Kepler*, ed. W. H. Stahl, New York: Dover, 1953.

Easterling, H. J. (1961), 'Homocentric spheres in *de caelo*', *Phronesis* 6, 158–63.

Easterling, H. J. (1976), 'The unmoved mover in early Aristotle', *Phronesis* 21, 252–65.

Ebbesen, S. (1981), *Commentators and commentaries on Aristotle's* Sophistici Elenchi*: A study of post-Aristotelian ancient and modern writings on fallacies* 3 vols, Leiden: Brill, vol. 2, 153–99.

Ebbesen, S. (1990), 'Philoponus, "Alexander" and the origins of medieval logic', in Sorabji 1990a, 481–99.

Elders, L. (1972), *Aristotle's theology. A commentary on Book Lambda of the* Metaphysics, Assen: Van Gorcum.

Evans, J. (1998), *The history and practice of ancient astronomy*, New York and Oxford: Oxford University Press.

Fazzo, S. (2002), 'Lambda 7, 1072b2–3', *Elenchos* 23, 357–76.

Fazzo, S. (2010), 'Lo stemma codicum dei libri *Kappa* e *Lambda* della *Metafisica*: una revisione necessaria', *Aevum* 84 (2), 339–59.

Fazzo, S. (2012) (ed., tr.), *Il libro Lambda della* Metafisica *di Aristotele*, Naples: Bibliopolis.

Fazzo, S. (2013), 'Heavenly matter in Aristotle: *Metaphysics Lambda 2*', *Phronesis* 58, 160–75.

Fazzo, S. (2014), *Commento al libro Lambda della* Metafisica *di Aristotele*, Naples: Bibliopolis.

Fazzo, S. (2016), 'Unmoved mover as pure act or unmoved mover in act? The mystery of a subscript iota', in Horn, 181–205.

Fazzo, S. (2016), 'Aristotle's *Metaphysics* – current research to reconcile two branches of the tradition', *Archiv für Geschichte der Philosophie* 98, 433–57.

Fine, G. (1984), 'Separation', *Oxford Studies in Ancient Philosophy* 2, 31–87; repr. in G. Fine, *Plato on knowledge and the Forms: Selected essays*, Oxford: Clarendon Press, 2003, 252–300.

Fortenbaugh, W. W. et al. (1992) (ed., tr.), *Theophrastus of Eresus: Sources for his life, writings, thought, and influence*, Leiden: Brill.
Frede, M. (2000), 'Introduction', in Frede and Charles, 1–52.
Frede, M. (2000), '*Metaphysics Lambda* 1', in Frede and Charles, 53–80.
Frede, M. and D. Charles (2000) (eds), *Aristotle's* Metaphysics Lambda*: Symposium Aristotelicum*, Oxford: Oxford University Press.
Freudenthal, J. (1884), *Die durch Averroes erhaltenen Fragmente Alexanders zur Metaphysik des Aristoteles. Mit Beiträgen zur Erläuterung des arabischen Textes durch S. Fränkel*. Berlin: Königliche Akademie der Wissenschaften.
Genequand, C. (1986) (tr.), *Ibn Rushd's Metaphysics: A translation with introduction of Ibn Rushd's Commentary on Aristotle's* Metaphysics, *Book Lâm*, Leiden: Brill.
Genequand, C. (2001), *Alexander of Aphrodisias 'On the Cosmos'*, Leiden: Brill.
George, R. (1989), 'An argument for divine omniscience in Aristotle', *Apeiron* 22, 61–74.
Giacon, Carlo (1969), *La causalità del motore immobile*, Padua: Antenore.
Gill, M. L. (1994), 'Aristotle on self-motion', in Gill and Lennox, 15–34.
Gill, M. L. and J. G. Lennox (1994) (eds), *Self-Motion from Aristotle to Newton*, Princeton: Princeton University Press.
Golitsis, P. (2008), 'Georges Pachymère come didaschale: Essai pour use reconstitution de sa carrière et de son enseignement philosophique', *Jahrbuch der Österreicheischen Byzantinistik* 58, 53–68.
Golitsis, P. (2014), 'La Recensio Altera du commentaire d'Alexandre d'Aphrodise à la *Métaphysique* d'Aristote et le témeoignage des manuscrits byzantins Laurentianus Plut. 87,12 et Ambosianus F 113 Sup.', in J. S. Codoñer and I. P. Martín (eds), *Textual transmission in Byzantium*, Belgium: Turnhout, 201–32.
Golitsis, P. (2015), 'Collation but not contamination: On some textual problems of Aristotle's *Metaphysics Kappa* 1065a25sqq', *Revue d'Histoire des Textes* 10, 1–23.
Golitsis, P. (2016a), 'Editing Aristotle's *Metaphysics*: A response to Siliva Fazzo's critical appraisal of Oliver Primavesi's edition of *Metaphysics Alpha*', *Archiv für Geschichte der Philosophie* 98, 458–73.
Golitsis, P. (2016b), 'The manuscript tradition of Alexander of Aphrodisias' commentary on Aristotle's *Metaphysics*: Towards a new critical edition', *Revue d'Histoire des Textes* 11, 55–94.
Golitsis, P. (2016c), 'Who were the real authors of the *Metaphysics* commentary ascribed to Alexander and Ps.-Alexander?', in Sorabji 2016a, 565–88.
Golitsis, P. (2016d), Review of Alexandru 2014, *Journal of the History of Philosophy* 54, 497–8.
Golitsis, P. (2017), 'La réception de la théologie d'Aristote chez Michel d'Ephèse et quelques autres néoplatoniciens', in Baghdassarian and Guyomarc'h, 239–51.

Gottschalk, H. B. (1990), 'The earliest Aristotelian commentators', in Sorabji 1990a, 55–81.
Graham, D. (1999) (tr.), *Aristotle Physics Book VIII: Translated with a commentary*, Oxford: Clarendon Press.
Guthrie, W. K. C. (1933/34), 'The development of Aristotle's theology', *Classical Quarterly* 27, 162–71 and 28, 90–8.
Guthrie, W. K. C. (1939) (tr.), *Aristotle 'On the Heavens'*, Cambridge, MA: Harvard University Press.
Guthrie, W. K. C. (1978), *A History of Greek philosophy*, vol. V: *The later Plato and the Academy*, Cambridge: Cambridge University Press.
Guthrie, W. K. C. (1981), *A History of Greek philosophy*, vol. VI: *Aristotle: an encounter*, Cambridge: Cambridge University Press.
Hadot, I. (1987), 'Recherches sur les fragments du commentaire de Simplicius sur la *Métaphysique* d'Aristote', in I. Hadot (ed.), *Simplicius, sa vie, son oeuvre, sa survie*, Berlin and New York: Walter de Gruyter, 225–45.
Hager, F.-P. (1969) (ed.), *Metaphysik und Theologie des Aristoteles*, Darmstadt: Wissenschaftliche Buchgesellschaft.
Hankinson, R. J. (2002) (tr.), *Simplicius on Aristotle's On the Heavens 1.1–4*, Ithaca: Cornell University Press; London: Duckworth.
Hankinson, R. J. (2004) (tr.), *Simplicius on Aristotle's On the Heavens 1.5–9*, Ithaca: Cornell University Press; London: Duckworth.
Hankinson, R. J. (2006) (tr.), *Simplicius on Aristotle's On the Heavens 1.10–12*, Ithaca: Cornell University Press; London: Duckworth.
Harlfinger, D. (1975), 'Edizione critica del testo del "*De ideis*" di Aristotele', in W. Leszl (ed.), *Il 'De Ideis' di Aristotele e la teoria platonica delle idee*, Florence: Olschki, 15–54.
Harlfinger, D. (1979), 'Zur Überlieferungsgeschichte der *Metaphysik*', in P. Aubenque (ed.), *Études sur la Métaphysique d'Aristote*, Paris: Vrin, 7–33.
Hatzimichali, M. (2013), 'The text of Plato and Aristotle in the first century BC', in M. Schofield (ed.), *Aristotle, Plato and Pythagoreanism in the first century BC: New directions for philosophy*, Cambridge: Cambridge University Press, 1–27.
Hayduck, M. (1888) (ed.), *Alexandri Aphrodisiensis in Aristotelis metaphysica commentaria (CAG 1)*, Berlin: Georg Reimer.
Hayduck, M. (1901) (ed.), *Michaelis Ephesi in librum quintum ethicorum nicomacheorum commentaria (CAG 22.3)*, Berlin: Georg Reimer.
Hayduck, M. (1904) (ed.), *Michaelis Ephesi in libros de partibus animalium, de motu animalium, de incessu animalium (CAG 22.2)*, Berlin: Georg Reimer.
Heath, T. (1913), *Aristarchus of Samos: The ancient Copernicus*, Oxford: Clarendon Press.

Heiberg, J. L. (1894) (ed.), *Simplicii in Aristotelis De Caelo Commentaria* (*CAG* 7), Berlin: Georg Reimer.

Herzberg, S. (2016), 'God as pure thinking: An interpretation of *Metaphysics* Lambda 7', in Horn, 157–80.

Heylbut, G. (1892) (ed.), *Eustrati (et Michaelis et Anonymo) in ethica nicomacheoreum commentaria* (*CAG* 20), Berlin: Georg Reimer.

Hintikka, J. (1973), *Time and necessity: A theory of modality*, Oxford: Clarendon Press.

Horn, C. (2002), 'In welchem Sinn enthält *Metaphysik Lambda* eine Theologie?' *Jahrbuch für Religionsphilosophie* 1, 28–49.

Horn, C. (2016) (ed.), *Aristotle's* Metaphysics *Lambda – new essays*, Boston/Berlin: De Gruyter.

Horn, C. (2016b), 'The unity of the world-order according to *Metaphysics Lambda* 10', in Horn, 269–93.

Jackson, H. (1904), 'On some passages in Aristotle's *Metaphysics Lambda*', *Journal of Philology* 29, 138–44.

Jaeger, W. (1917), 'Emendationen zur Aristotelischen *Metaphysik*', *Hermes* 52, 481–519.

Jaeger, W. (1948), *Aristotle: Fundamentals of the history of his development*, tr. R. Robinson, 2nd edn, Oxford: Oxford Clarendon Press; rev. tr. of *Aristoteles: Grundlegung einer Geschichte seiner Entwicklung*, Berlin: Weidmann, 1923.

Jaeger, W. (1957) (ed.), *Aristotelis Metaphysica*, Oxford Classical Texts, Oxford: Clarendon Press.

Judson, L. (1994), 'Heavenly motion and the unmoved mover', in Gill and Lennox, 135–53.

Judson, L. (2000), 'Formlessness and the priority of form: *Metaphysics Zeta* 7–9 and *Lambda* 3', in Frede and Charles, 81–110.

Judson, L. (2018), 'First philosophy in *Metaphysics Lambda*', *Oxford Studies in Ancient Philosophy* 54, 227–77.

Judson, L. (2019) (tr.), *Aristotle* Metaphysics *Lambda, translated with an introduction and commentary,* Oxford: Clarendon Press.

Kahn, C. H. (1966), 'Sensation and consciousness in Aristotle's psychology', *Archiv für Geschichter der Philosophie* 21, 235–76; repr. in J. Barnes, M. Schofield, and R. Sorabji (eds), *Articles on Aristotle*, vol. 4: *Psychology and Aesthetics*, London: Duckworth: 1979, 1–31.

Kahn, C. H. (1973), *The verb 'to be' in ancient Greek*, Dordrecht: Reidel; repr. Indianapolis: Hackett, 2003.

Kahn, C. H. (1985), 'The place of the prime mover in Aristotle's teleology', in A. Gotthelf (ed.), *Aristotle on nature and living things*, Pittsburgh: University of Pittsburgh Press, 183–205.

Kahn, C. H. (1992), 'Aristotle on thinking', in M. C. Nussbaum and A. O. Rorty (eds), *Essays on Aristotle's De Anima*, Oxford: Clarendon Press, 359–80.

Katayama, E. G. (1999), *Aristotle on artifacts: A metaphysical puzzle*, Albany: State University of New York Press.

Katz, E. (2017), 'Ontological separation in Aristotle's *Metaphysics*', *Phronesis* 62, 26–68.

Keyt, D. (2018), 'Aristotelian freedom' in D. Schmidtz and C. Pavel (eds), *The Oxford handbook of the philosophy of freedom*, Oxford: Oxford University Press.

Konstan, D. (2001) (tr.), *Aspasius, Michael of Ephesus, Anonymous on Aristotle's Nicomachean Ethics 8–9*, London: Duckworth.

Konstan, D. and I. Ramelli (2006), 'Aristotle and individual forms: The grammar of the possessive pronouns at *Metaphysics* Lambda 5, 1071a27–9', *Classical Quarterly* 56, 105–12.

Konstan, D. (2008) (tr.), *Aspasius on Aristotle's Nicomachean Ethics 1–4, 7–8*, London: Bloomsbury.

Kosman, A. (1994), 'Aristotle's prime mover', in Gill and Lennox, 155–71.

Kosman, A. (2000), '*Metaphysics Lambda* 9: Divine thought', in Frede and Charles, 307–26.

Kotwick, M. (2016), *Alexander of Aphrodisias and the text of Aristotle's Metaphysics*, Berkeley: California Classical Studies.

Krämer, H. J. (1969), 'Grundfragen der AristotelischenTheologie', *Theologie und Philosophie* 44, 363–382; 481–505.

Kroll, W. (1902) (ed.), *Syriani in metaphysica commentaria (CAG 6.1)*, Berlin: Georg Reimer.

Kukkonen, T. (2014), 'On Aristotle's world', *Oxford Studies in Ancient Philosophy* 46, 311–52.

Laks, A. (2000), '*Metaphysics Lambda* 7', in Frede and Charles, 207–43.

Landauer, S. (1903) (ed.), *Themistii in Aristotelis Metaphysicorum librum Lambda paraphrasis (CAG 55)*, Berlin: Georg Reimer.

Lang, H. (1993), 'The structure and subject of *Metaphysics Lambda*', *Phronesis* 38, 257–80.

Lefebvre, D. (2012), 'La question de l'unité d'une science des substances', in M. Bocelli (ed.), *Physique et métaphysique chez Aristote*, Paris: Vrin, 113–32.

Lemerle, P. (1971), *Le première humanisme byzantin*, Paris: Presses Universitaires de France.

Liatsi, M. (2016), 'Aristotle's silence about the prime mover's *noêsis*', in Horn, 229–45.

Lloyd, G. E. R. (2000), '*Metaphysics Lambda* 8', in Frede and Charles, 245–73.

Luna, C. (2001), *Trois études sur la tradition des commentaires anciens à la Métaphysique d'Aristote*, Leiden: Brill.

Makin, S. (2006) (tr.), *Aristotle* Metaphysics *Book Theta, translated with an introduction and commentary*, Oxford: Clarendon Press.

Malink, M. (2000), 'Aristotle on principles as elements', *Oxford Studies in Ancient Philosophy* 53, 163–213.

Marrou, H. I. (1963), 'Synesius of Cyrene and Alexandrian Neoplatonism', in A. Momigliano (ed.), *The conflict between paganism and Christianity in the fourth century*, Oxford: Clarendon Press, 126–50.

Martin, T. H. (1879), 'Questions connexes sur deux Sosigène, l'un astronome et l'autre péripatéticien, et sur deux pèripatéticiens Alexandre, l'un d'Egée et l'autre d'Aphrodisias', *Annales de la Faculté es Letrres de Bordeaux* 1, 174–87.

Matthen, M. (2001), 'The holistic presuppositions of Aristotle's cosmology', *Oxford Studies in Ancient Philosophy* 20: 171–99.

Matthen, M. and R. J. Hankinson (1993), 'Aristotle's universe: its form and matter', *Synthese* 96, 417–35; repr. in L. P. Gerson (ed.), *Aristotle: critical assessments*, vol. 2: *Physics, cosmology and biology*, London and New York: Routledge, 1999, 209–26.

Mendell, H. (1998), 'Reflections on Eudoxus, Callippus and their curves: Hippopedes and callippopedes', *Centaurus* 40, 177–275.

Mendell, H. (2001), 'The trouble with Eudoxus', in P. Suppes, J. Moravcsik, and H. Mendell (eds), *Ancient and medieval traditions in the exact sciences: Essays in memory of Wilbur Knorr*, Stanford: CSLI, 59–138.

Menn, S. (1992) 'Aristotle and Plato on God as *nous* and the good', *Review of Metaphysics* 45, 543–75.

Menn, S. (2012), 'Aristotle's theology', in C. S. Shields (ed.), *The Oxford handbook of Aristotle*, Oxford: Oxford University Press, 422–64.

Mercken, H. P. F. (1990), 'The Greek commentators on Aristotle's Ethics', in Sorabji 1990a, 407–44.

Merlan, P. (1963), *Monopsychism, mysticism, and metaconsciousness*, The Hague: Nijhoff.

Meyrav, Y. (2019), *Themistius' Paraphrases of Aristotle's Metaphysics 12: A critical Hebrew-Arabic edition of the surviving textual evidence, with an introduction, preliminary studies, and a commentary*, Leiden: Brill.

Meyrav, Y. (2020), *Themistius On Aristotle's* Metaphysics *12*, London: Bloomsbury.

Miller, F. D. (2012), 'Aristotle on the separability of mind', in C. S. Shields (ed.), *The Oxford handbook of Aristotle*, Oxford: Oxford University Press, 306–39.

Miller, F. D. (2013), 'Aristotle's divine cause', in E. Feser (ed.), *Aristotle on Method and Metaphysics*, London and New York: Palgrave Macmillan, 277–98.

Miller, F. D. (2018) (tr.), *Aristotle* On the soul *and other psychological works*, Oxford: Oxford University Press.

Minio-Paluello, L. (1952), 'Jacobus Veneticus Grecus', *Traditio* 8, 265–304.

Minio-Paluello, L. (1960), 'La tradition aristotélicienne dans l'histoire des idées', *Association Budé: Congrès de Lyon 8–13 Septembre 1958*, Paris, 166–85.

Moraux, P. (1965) (ed., tr.), *Aristote 'Du Ciel'*, Paris: Les Belles Lettres.

Moraux, P. (1976), *Aristoteles Graecus: Die Griechischen Manuskripten des Aristoteles*, vol. 1: *Alexandrien – London*, Berlin: Walter de Gruyter, 1976.

Moraux, P. (1984), *Der Aristotelismus bei den Griechen*, vol. 2, Berlin: Walter de Gruyter.

Moraux, P. (2001), *Der Aristotelismus bei den Griechen*, vol. 3, Berlin: Walter de Gruyter.

Mueller, I. (2004) (tr.), *Simplicius on Aristotle's* On the Heavens *2.1–9*, Ithaca: Cornell University Press; London: Duckworth.

Mueller, I. (2005) (tr.), *Simplicius on Aristotle's* On the Heavens *2.10–14*, Ithaca: Cornell University Press; London: Duckworth.

Mueller, I. (2009) (tr.), *Simplicius on Aristotle's* On the Heavens *3.1–7*, Ithaca: Cornell University Press; London: Duckworth.

Mueller, I. (2009b) (tr.), *Simplicius on Aristotle's* On the Heavens *3.7–4.6*, Ithaca: Cornell University Press; London: Duckworth.

Mueller, I. (2011) (tr.), *Simplicius on Aristotle's* On the Heavens *1.2–3*, Ithaca: Cornell University Press; London: Duckworth.

Mueller, I. (2011b) (tr.), *Simplicius on Aristotle's* On the Heavens *1.3–4*, Ithaca: Cornell University Press; London: Duckworth.

Mugnier, R. (1930), *La théorie du premier moteur et l'évolution de la pensée aristotélicienne*, Paris: Vrin.

Natali, C. (1997), 'Causa mortice e causa finale nel Libro Lambda della Metafisica di Aristotele,' *Methexis* 10, 105–23.

Natali, C. (2004), 'On *Generation and Corruption* I.6', in F. De Haas and J. Mansfeld (eds), *Aristotle's Generation and Corruption I*, Oxford: Clarendon Press, 195–217.

Norman, R. (1969), 'Aristotle's philosopher-god', *Phronesis* 14, 63–74; repr. in J. Barnes, M. Schofield, and R. Sorabji (eds), *Articles on Aristotle*, vol. 4: *Psychology and Aesthetics*, London: Duckworth, 1979, 93–102.

Oehler, K. (1955), 'Der Beweis für den unbewegten Beweger bei Aristoteles', *Philologus* 99, 70–92; repr. in Oehler, *Antike Philosophie und byzantinisches Mittelalter*, Munich: Beck, 1969, 162–83.

Oehler, K. (1964), 'Aristotle in Byzantium', *Greek, Roman, and Byzantine Studies* 5, 133–46.

Oehler, K. (1984), *Der Unbewegte Beweger des Aristoteles*, Frankfurt a. M.: Klostermann.

O'Meara, D. and J. Dillon (2008) (tr.), *Syrianus on Aristotle's* Metaphysics *3–4*, London: Duckworth.

Owens, J. (1979), 'The relation of God to the world in the *Metaphysics*', in P. Aubenque (ed.), *Études sur la métaphysique d'Aristote*, Paris: Vrin, 207–28.

Patzig, G. (1960–61), 'Theologie und Ontologie in der *Metaphysik* des Aristoteles', *Kant-Studien* 52, 185–205.

Peters, F. E. (1968), *Aristoteles Arabus: The oriental translations and commentaries of the Aristotelian corpus*, Leiden: Brill.

Praechter, K. (1906), 'Michaelis Ephesii' [Review of *CAG* 22.2], *Göttingische Gelehrte Anzeigen* 168, 861–907.

Praechter, K. (1909), 'Die griechischen Aristoteleskommentare', *Byzantinische Zeitschrift* 18, 516–38.

Praechter, K. (1990), 'Review of the *Commentaria in Aristotelem Graeca*', tr. V. Caston, in Sorabji 1990a, 31–54; a translation of Praechter 1909.

Preus, Anthony (1981) (tr.), *Aristotle and Michael of Ephesus* On the Movement *and* Progression of Animals, Hildesheim: Olms.

Primavesi, O. (2012) (ed.), 'Aristotle *Metaphysics Alpha*: A new critical edition with introduction', in C. Steel (ed.), *Aristotle's Metaphysics Alpha*, Oxford: Oxford University Press, 385–516.

Rapp, C. (2016), 'The principles of sensible substance in *Metaphysics Lambda* 2–5', in Horn, 87–117.

Rashed, M. (2007), *Essentialisme: Alexandre d'Aphrodise entre logique, physique et cosmologie*. Berlin: Walter de Gruyter.

Reeve, C. D. C. (2016) (tr.), *Aristotle Metaphysics*, Indianapolis, IN: Hackett.

Reeve, C. D. C. (2018) (tr.), *Aristotle Physics*, Indianapolis, IN: Hackett.

Reeve, M. D. (2011), *Manuscripts and methods: Essays on editing and transmission*, Rome: Edizioni di storia e letteratura.

Rolfes, E. (1928) (tr.), *Aristoteles' Metaphysik*, 2 vols, Leipzig: F. Meiner.

Rose, V. (1854), *De Aristotelis librorum ordine et autoritate commentio*, Berlin: Georg Reimer.

Ross, A. (2016), 'The causality of the prime mover in *Metaphysics Lambda*', in Horn, 207–27.

Ross, W. D. (1923), *Aristotle*, London: Methuen; 6th edn, London: Routledge, 1995.

Ross, W. D. (1924) (ed.), *Aristotle Metaphysics: A revised text with introduction and commentary*, 2 vols, Oxford: Clarendon Press.

Ross, W. D. (1936) (ed.), *Aristotle's Physics: A revised text with introduction and commentary*, Oxford: Clarendon Press.

Ryan, E. (1973), 'Pure form in Aristotle', *Phronesis* 18, 209–24.

Salis, R. (2005), *Il commento di pseudo-Alessandro al libro* Lambda *della* Metafisica *di Aristotele*, Rubbettino: Soveria Manneli.

Salis, R. (2007) (tr.), 'Commento al libro *Lambda* (dodicesimo)', in G. Movia, (ed.), *Alessandro di Afrodisia e Pseudo Alessandro Commentario Alla 'Metafisica' di Aristotele*. Milan: Bompiani, 1870–2042.

Salis, R. (2009), 'La causalidad del motor immóvil seguin Pseudo Alejandro', *Estudios de Filosofia* 40, 201–9.

Sandbach, F. H. (1954), 'A transposition in Aristotle, *Metaphysics* Lambda c. 9, 1074b', *Mnemosyne* 7, 39–43.

Schiaparelli, G. V. (1875), 'Le sfere omocentriche di Eudosso, di Callippo e di Aristotele', *Publicazioni del R. Osservatorio di Brera in Milano*, no. ix; repr. in Schiaparelli, *Scritti sulla storia della astronomia antica*, Bologna: Nicola Zanichelli, 1925–27, vol. 2, 3–112; tr. by W. Horn as 'Die homocentrischen Sphären des Eudoxus, des Kallippus und des Aristoteles', *Abhandlungen zur Geschichte der Mathematik* 1 (1877), 101–98.

Sedley, D. (2000), '*Metaphysics Lambda* 10', in Frede and Charles, 327–50.

Sepúlveda, J. G. (1527) (tr.), *Alexandri Aphrodisiei commentaria in duodecim Aristotelos libros de prima philosophia*, Rome: Silber; 2nd edn, Paris: Simon Colinaeus, 1536.

Sharples, R. W. (1983a) (tr.), *Alexander of Aphrodisias On Fate*, London: Duckworth.

Sharples, R. W. (1983b), 'The unmoved mover and the motion of the heavens in Alexander of Aphrodisias', *Apeiron* 17, 62–6.

Sharples, R. W. (1987), 'Alexander of Aphrodisias', *Aufstieg und Niedergang der römischen Welt*, 2.36.2, 1176–1243.

Sharples, R. W. (1990), 'The school of Alexander?', in Sorabji 1990a, 89–118.

Sharples, R. W. (1992) (tr.), *Alexander of Aphrodisias 'Quaestiones' 1.1–2.15*, Ithaca: Cornell University Press; London: Duckworth.

Sharples, R. W. (1994) (tr.), *Alexander of Aphrodisias 'Quaestiones' 2.16–3.15*, Ithaca: Cornell University Press; London: Duckworth.

Sharples, R. W. (2002), 'Aristotelian theology after Aristotle', in D. Frede and A. Laks (eds), *Traditions of theology: Studies in Hellenistic theology, its background and aftermath*, Leiden: Brill, 1–40.

Sharples, R. W. (2003), 'Pseudo-Alexander on Aristotle, *Metaphysics Lambda*', in G. Movia (ed.), *Alessandro di Afrodisia e la 'Metafisica' di Aristotele*, Milan: Vita e pensiero, 187–219.

Sharples, R. W. (2004) (tr.), *Alexandria of Aphrodisias 'Supplement to On the Soul'*, Ithaca: Cornell University Press; London: Duckworth.

Shields, C. (2016) (tr.), *Aristotle De Anima: Translated with an introduction and commentary*, Clarendon Aristotle, Oxford: Clarendon Press.

Sondregger, E. (2006), *Aristoteles' Metaphysik Lambda: Ein spekulativer Entwurf*, Bern: Peter Lang.

Sorabji, R. (1990a) (ed.), *Aristotle transformed: The ancient commentators and their influence*, London: Duckworth; 2nd edn, London: Bloomsbury, 2016.

Sorabji, R. (1990b), 'Infinite power impressed: The transformation of Aristotle's physics and theology', in Sorabji 1990a, 181–98.

Sorabji, R. (2004), *The philosophy of the commentators*, 3 vols, London: Duckworth.

Sorabji, R. (2016a) (ed.), *Aristotle re-interpreted: New findings on seven hundred years of the ancient commentators*, London: Bloomsbury.

Sorabji, R. (2016b), 'Universals transformed in the commentators on Aristotle', in Sorabji 2016a, 291–312.

Tarán, L. (1981), Review of Moraux 1976 in *Gnomon* 50:6, 721–50

Tarán, L. (1987), 'Syrianus and Pseudo-Alexander's commentary on *Metaphysics* E-N', in J. Wiesner (ed.), *Aristoteles: Werk und Wirkung*, vol. 2, Berlin and New York: Walter de Gruyter, 215–32.

Thillet, P. (1958), 'Remarques et notes critiques sur les traductions arabes du livre Lambda de la *Métaphysique d'Aristote*', *Actes du Congrès de Lyon*, 114–24.

Trizio, M. (2014), 'Eleventh-to-twelfth century Byzantium', in S. Gersh (ed.), *Interpreting Proclus from antiquity to Renaissance*, Cambridge: Cambridge University Press, 186–225.

Tweedale, M. (1984), 'Alexander of Aphrodisias' view on universals', *Phronesis* 29, 297–303.

Verrycken, K. (2015), 'Philoponus' Neoplatonic interpretation of Aristotle's psychology', *Apeiron* 48, 502–20.

Vitelli, G. H. (1897) (ed.), *Ionnis Philoponi (Michaelis Ephesi) in Aristotelis libros de generatione commentaria (CAG 14.3)*, Berlin: Gerog Reimer.

Vlastos, G. (1963), 'A note on the unmoved mover', *Philosophical Quarterly* 13, 246–7; repr. in G. Vlastos, *Studies in Greek philosophy*, vol. 2, Princeton: Princeton University Press, 283–4.

Vries-van de Velden, E. de (1987), *Théodore Métochite, une réévaluation*, Amsterdam: Gieben.

Wallies, M. (1898) (ed.), *Alexandri (quod fertur Michael Ephesius), in Aristotelis sophisticos elenchos (CAG 2.3)*, Berlin: Georg Reimer.

Walzer, R. (1958), 'On the Arabic versions of Books *Alpha, alpha*, and *Lambda* [I, II, XII] of Aristotle's *Metaphysics*', *Harvard Studies in Classical Philology* 63, 217–31.

Wedin, M. V. (1988), *Mind and imagination in Aristotle*, New Haven: Yale University Press.

Wendland, P. (1901) (ed.), *Alexandri Aphrodisiensi in librum de sensu commentaria (CAG 3.1)*, Berlin: Georg Reimer.

Wendland, P. (1903) (ed.), *Michaelis Ephesi in parva naturalia commentaria (CAG 22.1)*, Berlin: Georg Reimer.

Wilberding, J, J. Trompeter, and A. Rigolio (2018) (tr.), *Michael of Ephesus on Aristotle's* Nicomachean Ethics *10 with Themisitus* On Virtue, London: Bloomsbury.

Westerink, L. G. (1962) (ed.), *Anonymous Prolegomena to the Platonic Philosophy*, Amsterdam: North-Holland Publishing Company.

Wolfson, H. A. (1973), 'The problem of the souls of the spheres from the Byzantine commentaries on Aristotle through the Arabs and St. Thomas to Kepler', in Wolfson, *Studies in the history of philosophy and religion*, Cambridge, MA: Harvard University Press, 22–59.

Woods, M. (1991), 'Universals and particulars in Aristotle's *Metaphysics*', *Oxford Studies in Ancient Philosophy*, supp. vol.: 'Aristotle and the later tradition', 41–56.

Yavetz, I. (1998), 'On the homocentric spheres of Eudoxus', *Archive for History of Exact Sciences* 52, 221–78.

Zahlfleisch, J. (1900), 'Einige Gesichtspunkte für die Auffassung und Beurtheilung der Aristotelischen Metaphysik', *Archiv für Geschichte der Philosophie* 13, 85–9.

Zeller, G. (1919–1923), *Die Philosophie der Griechen in ihrer geschichtlichen Entwicklung*, Leipzig: O. R. Reisland.

Zingano, M. (2016), 'Individuals, form, movement: from *Lambda* to *Zeta-Eta*', in Horn, 139–55.

# English–Greek Index

absurd: *atopos*
absurdly: *atopôs*
accident, accidental: *sumbebêkos*
accidental, be: *sumbainein*
accidentally: *kata sumbebêkos*
account: *logos*
accurately: *akribôs*
act (v.): *energein, prattein*
act of thinking: *noêsis*
action: *praxis*
activity: *energeia*
actualization: *entelekheia*
actuality: *energeia*
advantage: *sumpheron*
affect (v.): *poiein*
affected, be: *paskhein*
affection: *pathos*
affinity: *oikeiôsis*
after: *husteros*
air: *aêr*
align obliquely: *loxoun*
allow: *ephienai*
allude: *ainittesthai*
alter: *alloioun*
alteration: *alloiôsis*
always: *aei*
amount: *plêthos*
analogous: *analogos*
analogous, be: *analogein*
analysis: *analusis*
ancient: *arkhaios*
animal: *zôion*
animate: *empsukhos*
answer (v.): *apokrinesthai*
appear: *phainesthai*
appearance: *phantasia*
appetite: *epithumia*
appetitive: *epithumêtikos*
appropriate (adj.): *oikeios*
Aquarius (astron.): *hudrokhoos*
arc: *periphereia*
argument: *epikheirêma*
arithmetic: *arithmêtikê*
army: *strateuma*
art: *tekhnê*

artefact: *tekhnêtês*
ask: *erôtan*
assertion: *apophasis*
assumption: *axiôma*
astronomy: *astrologia, astronomia*
atemporally: *akhronôs*
atom: *atomos*
attribute: *pathos*

bad: *kakos*
bastard reasoning: *nothos logismos*
be: *einai*
beast: *thêrion*
become, come to be: *gignesthai*
beholding: *periôpê*
being (n.): *ontotês, to einai*
being, that which is: *to on*
belief (religious): *doxa*
benefaction: *agathodosia*
best: *aristos*
better: *ameinos, kreittos*
birthday: *genethlios hêmera*
black: *melas*
blackness: *melania*
blessed: *makarios*
body: *sôma*
bone: *ostoun*
bottom: *edaphos*
box: *kibiôton*
breadth: *platos*
brick: *plinthos*
bright: *lampros*
bring forth: *paragein*
bronze: *khalkos*
building art: *tektonikê*
bushel: *medimnos*

capable of imparting movement: *kinêtikos*
capable of circular motion: *kuklophorêtikos*
capable of thinking: *noêtikos*
capacious: *khorêtikos*
Capricorn (astron.): *aigokerôs*
carry: *pherein*
carry on: *diagein*

category: *katêgoria*
cause: *aitia, aition*
centre: *kentron*
chance, randomness: *tukhê*
change (n.): *metabolê*
change (v.): *metaballein, kinein*
changeable: *metablêtos*
Chaos (myth.): *Khaos*
chiefly: *kuriôs*
chop wood: *xulotomein*
circle: *kuklos*
circular: *enkuklios*
circular motion: *kuklophoria, periphora*
claim: *axiôma*
cognize: *dianoeisthai*
cold: *psukhros*
coldness: *psukhrotês, to psukhron*
colour: *khrôma*
column: *sustoikhia*
coming-to-be: *genesis*
common: *koinos*
common, have in: *koinônein*
commonality: *koinônia*
commonwealth: *politeia*
complaint: *enklêma*
complete (v.): *teleioun*
complete (adj.): *teleios*
completion: *teleiotês*
composed of elements: *stoikheiotos*
compound (adj.): *sunthêtos*
compound whole: *to sunolon*
comprehension: *perilêpsis*
confirmation: *pistis*
confusion: *tarakhê*
congenital: *autophuês*
constellation: *sêmeion*
constellation of the zodiac: *zôidion*
contact (n.): *haphê*
contact (v.): *haptesthai*
contemplate: *theorein*
contemplation: *theôria*
continuous: *sunekhês*
contradict: *antilegein*
contrariety: *enantiôsis, enantiotês*
contrary: *enantios*
contribute: *sumballesthai, sunteinein*
contribute together: *suntelein*
cook: *magireuein*
co-ordinate: *suntattein*
corporeally: *sômatikôs*
cosmos: *kosmos*
counteract: *anelittein*
criticize: *aitiasthai*
Cronus (myth.): *Kronos*

cube: *kubos*
culmination: *apartismos*
cycle: *periodos*

darkness: *skotos*
day: *hêmera*
definition: *horos*
demonstration: *apodeixis*
demonstrative: *apodeiktikos*
depend on: *exartêsthai*
desirable: *orektos*
desire (n.): *orexis*
desire (v.): *oregesthai*
destroy: *anairein*
destroy in addition: *sunanairein*
detailed: *eskeumennôs*
determinate: *hôrismenos*
devoid of, be: *apallattein*
devoutly: *theophilôs*
different: *allos, heteros*
differentia: *diaphora*
dignified: *semnos*
dilemma: *diairesis*
diminution: *phthisis*
discordantly: *plêmmelôs*
disestablish: *existasthai*
disorder: *ataxia*
disorderly: *ataktôs*
disperse: *diakrinein*
distance: *apostêma*
distinction: *diairesis*
divide: *diorizein*
divine: *theios*
divisible into parts: *meristos*
dominant: *kurios*
door: *thura*
drinking party: *sumposion*
duration: *aiôn*
Dyad (Platonic): *duas*

each: *hekastos*
ear of corn: *astakhus*
earth (astron.), earth (element): *gê*
Earth (myth.): *Gaia*
east: *anatolê*
eclipse (v.): *ekleipein*
eclipse: *ekleipsis*
efficient cause: *poiêtikon aition*
effigy: *indalma*
elaboration: *paramuthia*
element: *stoikheion*
elliptical: *ellipês*
elliptically: *ellipôs*
emanate: *aporrhein*

emanation: *aporrhoia*
embed: *endein*
end: *telos*
enmattered: *enülos*
enmattered form: *enülon eidos*
enquire: *zêtein*
enquiry: *zêtêsis*
envisage: *phantazein, phantazesthai*
envision: *oneirôttein*
episodic: *epeisodiôdês*
equal: *isos*
equally fast: *isotakhôs*
equinoctial: *isêmerinos*
equinox: *isêmeria*
essence (or being): *to einai*
essence: *to ti ên einai*
establish: *sunhistanai*
establishment: *sustasis*
eternal: *aïdios*
everlasting: *aïdios*
everlastingly: *aïdiôs*
evident: *phaneros*
evil: *phaulos*
exacting: *akribês*
exactly: *akribôs*
example: *hupodeigma, paradeigma*
excellence: *to eu*
exist: *einai*
existence: *to einai*
explanation: *aitia, aition*
express in a roundabout way: *periphrazein*
external: *ektos*

fabricate: *plattein*
fact: *ergon*
failure: *apotukhia*
false: *pseudês*
father: *patêr*
feel regret: *metameleshai*
festival: *panêguris*
final cause: *telikon aition, to hou heneka*
fire: *pur*
firm: *bebaios*
first: *prôtos*
fixed star: *aplanês astêr*
flesh: *sarx*
flood: *kataklusmos*
for the sake of: *heneka*
force (v.): *biazesthai*
force: *bia*
forebear: *progonos*
forefathers, of: *patrios*
foreign: *allotrios*
foreign, be: *allotrioun*

Form (Platonic): *eidos*
form: *eidos*
formal cause: *eidikon aition*
formidable: *iskhus*
formless matter: *aneideos (eskhatê) hulê*
fornicate: *porneuein*
fount: *pêgê*
free: *eleutheros*
friendly, be: *philein*
fulfilment: *sumplêrôsis*

generable: *genêtos*
general: *genikos, stratêgos*
generate: *gennan*
generated: *apogennêma*
generative: *genêtikos*
genus: *genos*
geometry: *geômetria*
god: *theos*
godless: *atheos*
good: *agathos*
good, make: *agathunein*
good life: *euzôïa*
goodness: *agathotês*
govern: *politeuein*
grasp (n.): *katalêpsis*
grasp (v.): *ephaptesthai, katalambanei*
grow together: *sumphuesthai*
growth: *auxêsis*
growth together: *sumphusis*

haphazard, be: *tunchanein*
happiness: *eudaimonia*
hate: *neikos*
head: *kephalê*
heal: *iatreuein*
healer: *iatros*
healing art: *iatrikê*
health: *hugieia*
healthy: *hugieinos*
healthy, be: *hugiainein*
heap: *sôros*
heaped up: *sôrêdon*
heat: *thermotês, to thermon*
heaven: *ouranos*
heavenly: *ouranios*
hemisphere: *hêmisphairion*
Heracles (myth.): *Heraklês*
honourable: *timios*
honourable, highly: *polutimêtos*
hope: *elpis*
horizon: *horizôn*
horse: *hippos*
horse form: *hippeion eidos*

hot: *thermos*
house, household: *oikia*
housebuilder: *oikodomos*
housebuilding art: *oikodomikê*
human: *anthrôpeios, anthrôpinos*
human being: *anthrôpos*
human-being-itself: *autoanthrôpos*
human form: *anthrôpoeidês*
humour: *khumos*

ibis: *ibis*
Idea (Platonic): *idea*
ignorance: *agnoia*
illuminate: *phôtizein*
imagination: *phantasia*
imagine: *phantazesthai*
immaterial: *aülos*
immovable: *akinêtos*
impart motion: *pherein*
impart movement: *kinein*
impede: *empodizein*
impediment: *empodôn*
imperishable: *aphthartos*
impious: *asebês*
impossible: *adunatos*
impulse: *hormê*
in itself, by itself, in its own right: *kath' hauto*
in passing: *parergos*
inanimate: *apsukhos*
incomplete: *atelês*
incorporeal: *asômatos*
indescribable: *anêrmêneutos*
indeterminate: *aoristos*
indicate: *emphainein*
indication: *sêmeion*
indicative: *deiktikos*
individual: *atomos, kath' hekaston*
individual (n.): *to kath' hekaston*
individual (adj.): *hekastos*
indivisible: *adiairetos, atomos*
induction: *epagôgê*
infallible: *aptaistos*
ingenerable: *agenêtos*
inseparable: *akhôristos*
intangible: *alêptos*
intellect: *nous*
intelligible: *noêtos*
intermediary: *mesos*
intermediate: *metaxu*
intermittent, be: *dialimpanein*
interpret: *exêgeisthai*
interpretation: *exêgêsis*
interval: *paratasis*

intimate (v.): *ainittesthai*
investigation: *theôria*

judgement: *hupolêpsis*
Jupiter (astron.): *Zeus*
justice: *dikaiosunê*

keen intelligence: *ankhinoia*
killer (fem.): *phoneutria*
knowable: *epistêtos*
knower: *epistêmôn*
knowing: *gnôsis*
knowledge: *epistêmê*

law: *nomos*
learning: *mathêsis*
liberty, be at: *exeinai*
life: *zôê*
light: *phôs*
limit: *perainein*
liquid: *hugrotês*
live: *zên*
live well: *eu zên*
locomotion: *phora*
logically: *logikôs*
love (n.): *philia*
love (v.): *eran, philein*
lunar: *selêniakos*

magnitude: *megethos*
Mars (astron.): *Arês, Heraklês*
mass: *khuma*
material: *hulikos*
material cause: *hulikon aition*
mathematical: *mathêmatikê*
mathematical object: *mathêmatikon, mathêmatos*
mathematician: *mathêmatikos*
matter: *hulê*
measure: *metron*
memory: *mnêmê*
menstrual fluid: *katamênion*
Mercury (astron.): *Hermês*
mistake: *hamartêma*
mixture: *migma*
moist exhalation: *hugra anathumiôsis*
moon: *selênê*
mortal: *thnêtos*
mother: *mêtêr*
motion: *phora*
movable: *kinêtos*
move (trans.): *kinein*
move together with: *sunkinein*
moved object: *to kinoumenon*

movement: *kinêsis*
mover: *to kinoun*
moving cause: *kinêtikon aition*
multitude: *plêthos*
myth: *muthos*
mythically: *muthikôs*

natural: *phusikos*
natural theorist: *phusikos*
nature: *phusis*
necessary: *anankaion*
necessary, necessity: *anankê*
negation: *apophasis*
negligent, be: *rhathumein*
night: *nux*
noble: *kalos*
non-rational: *alogos*
north: *boreion*
not know: *agnoein*
not standing still: *astatos*
not-being, nothingness: *to mê einai*
not-being, that which is not: *to mê on*
notion: *ennoia*
not-one: *mê hen*
number: *arithmos, plêthos*

object: *pragma*
object of appetite: *epithumêtos*
object of choice: *hairetos*
object of desire: *orektos*
object of opinion: *doxastos*
object of thinking: *nooumenon*
object of wish: *boulêtos*
object of wonder: *thaumastos*
object of yearning: *ephetos*
objection: *enstasis*
oblique alignment: *loxôsis*
oblique: *loxos*
obliquely aligned: *loxôs*
observation: *paratêrêsis, parorhama*
odd: *perittos*
olive tree: *elaia*
old, very: *pampalaios*
omit: *elleipein*
one: *heis*
opined, be: *dokein*
opinion: *doxa*
oppose: *antikeisthai*
opposition: *antithesis*
order (n.): *taxis*
order (v.): *tattein*
orderliness: *eukosmia*
orderly: *eutaktos, tetagmenôs*
other: *allos, heteros*

otherness: *heterotês*
overfull: *huperplêrês*
overlook: *epilanthanesthai*

part: *meros*
partake: *metekhein*
partial: *merikos*
participation: *metalêpsis, methexis*
particular: *merikos*
partless: *amerês*
partlessly: *amerôs*
paternal, of forefathers: *patrios*
perceptible: *aisthêtos*
perception: *aisthêsis*
perceptual basis: *aisthêtikê hupobathra*
perhaps: *isôs*
perish: *phtheiresthai*
perishable: *phthartikos, phthartos,* en *phthorai*
perishing: *phthora*
permissible: *themis*
persuasion (sect.): *hairesis*
philosophically: *philosophôs*
philosophize: *philosophein*
philosophy: *philosophia*
picture: *eikôn*
Pisces (astron.): *ikhthues*
place: *topos*
plane: *epipedon*
planet, planetary star: *planêtês astêr*
planetary: *planômenos*
plant: *phuton*
pleasant: *hêdus*
pleasure: *hêdonê*
point: *sêmeion*
pole: *polos*
polis (city-state): *polis*
ponder: *enthumeisthai*
position: *thesis*
possible (adj.): *dunatos*
possible, be: *dunasthai*
posterior: *husteros*
potential, potentiality: *dunamis*
potential, have: *dunasthai*
predicate (v.): *katêgorein*
present, now: *nun*
present in, be: *enhuparkhein*
principle (origin, source): *arkhē*
prior: *proteros*
privation: *sterêsis*
probably: *isôs*
produce, make: *poiein*
producing: *poion*
productive: *poiêtikos*

progression: *anodos*
proof: *deixis*
prove: *deiknunai*
providential: *pronooumenos*
proximate: *prosekhês*
puzzle (n.): *aporia*
puzzle (v.): *aporein*
pyramid: *puramidês*

quality: *poiotês*
quantity: *poson*

random: *tukhos*
rational: *logistikos*
rational (part): *logikos*
reality: *huparxis, hupostasis*
reason: *logos*
reasonable: *eulogos*
reasonably: *eulogôs*
receive in succession: *diadekhesthai*
receptive: *dektikos*
reduction of the contraries: *anagôgê tôn enantiôn*
reject: *anairein*
relative: *pros ti*
remember: *mimnêskein*
rest (n.): *êremia*
rest (v.): *êremein*
ridiculous: *katagelastos*
rigour: *spoudê*
rise: *anatellein*
rise before: *proanatellein*
rise together: *sunanatellein*
roundness: *strongulotês*
rule of many: *poluarkhia*
ruler: *arkhos*

same: *autos*
same in species: *homoeidês*
Saturn (astron.): *Kronos*
Saturn, of (astron.): *Kroniakê*
saviour (fem.): *sôteira*
saying: *gnômê*
Scorpio (astron.): *skorpion*
sculptor: *andriantopoios*
see: *horan*
seed: *sperma*
seem: *dokein*
semen: *gonê*
separable: *khôristos*
separate (adj.): *khôristos*
separate (v.): *khôrizein*
separately: *khôris*
separation: *khôrismos*

set: *dunein*
set before: *produnein*
set together: *sundunein*
shadow: *skia*
shameful: *aiskhros*
shape: *skhêma*
sick: *nosôdês*
sicken: *nosein*
sickness: *nosos*
signify: *sêmainein*
simple: *haplous*
simple things (i.e. elements): *ta hapla*
simply: *haplôs*
sinew: *neuron*
slave: *andrapodon, doulos*
sleep (v.): *katheudein*
snake: *ophis*
solar: *hêliakos*
solar (sphere): *hêliakos*
soldier (v.): *strateuesthai*
solstitial: *tropikos*
solution: *lusis*
soul: *psukhê*
sovereign: *koiranos*
sovereignty of many: *polukoiraniê*
species: *eidos*
speech: *logos*
sphere: *sphaira*
Sphere (Empedocles): *sphairos*
sphere of the fixed stars: *aplanês sphaira*
spontaneous: *automatos*
stand, make a: *histasthai*
star: *astêr*
starless: *anastros*
state: *hexis*
statue: *andrias*
steer: *kubernein*
stone: *lithos*
straight: *euthus*
subject: *hupokeimenon*
submit in evidence: *tekmairesthai*
subsequently: *akolouthôs*
subsist, be present: *huparkhein*
subsistence: *huparxis*
substance: *ousia*
substantial, be: *ousiousthai*
substantial form: *ousiôdes eidos*
substantiation: *parastasis*
substratum: *hupokeimenon*
succession: *diadokhê*
successively: *ephexês*
summer (solstice): *therinos*
sun: *hêlios*
supervene: *epigignesthai*

sweetening: *glukansis*
swimming: *plôtos*
syllable: *sullabê*
synonymous: *sunônumos*

teacher: *kathêgemôn*
temporal: *khronikos*
ten: *dekas*
terminate: *apoperatoun*
text: *lexis*
theologian: *theologos*
theoretical: *theôrêtikos*
theoretical knowledge: *theôria*
thing: *pragma*
think: *noein*
thinker: *nooun*
this-something: *tode ti*
thought: *epinoia, noêma*
thrice-blessed: *trismkaristos*
time: *khronos*
together (Anaxagoras): *homou*
toilsome: *epiponos*
touch (v.): *thinganein*
transition: *metabasis*
transitional: *metabastikos*
transparency: *diaphanês*
treatise: *pragmateia*
triangle: *trigônos*
true: *alêthês*
truth: *alêtheia*
turn into a beast: *apotherioun*
turning (i.e. solstice): *tropê*

ultimate: *eskhatos*
unaffectable: *apathês*
unalterable: *analloiôtos*
unceasing: *apaustos*
unclarity: *asapheia*
undergo motion: *pherein*
undergo opposite motion: *antipheresthai*
underlie: *hupokeisthai*
unequal: *anisos*
unforced: *abiastos*
ungenerated: *agennêtos*
ungraspable: *akatalêptos*
unification: *henôsis*
unify: *henoun*
unintelligently: *anoêtôs*
unity: *hê henas*
universal (n.): *to katholou*
universal (adj.): *katholikos*

universe: *to pan*
unlimited potential: *apeirodunamos*
unlimited, without limit: *apeiros*
unmixed: *amigês*

vain: *matên*
valuable: *timios*
value (v.): *agapein*
Venus (astron.): *Aphroditê*
vinegar: *oxos*
vine plant: *ampelos*
vision: *opsis*
void: *kenon*

waking: *egrêgorsis*
walk: *badizein*
walking: *badisis*
water: *hudôr*
wax: *kêros*
way of carrying on: *diagogê*
way of life: *bios*
welcome (v.): *aspazesthai*
well: *eu*
west: *dusis, dusmê*
white: *leukos*
whiteness: *leukotês*
whitening: *leukansis*
whole (n.): *holotês*
whole (adj.): *holos*
whole (i.e. the universe): *to holon*
will: *boulêma*
wine: *oinos*
winged: *ptênos*
wisdom: *sophia*
wise: *sophos*
withdrawal: *ekstasis*
without a share: *amoiros*
without a share, be: *amoirein*
without magnitude: *amegethos*
without qualification: *haplôs*
without quality: *apoios*
witness (v.): *marturesthai*
wonderful: *thaumasios*
wood: *xulon*
worse: *kheiros*
worth: *axiôma*

yearn: *ephiesthai*
yearning: *ephesis*

zodiacal: *zôidiakos*

# Greek–English Index

References are to the page and line numbers of the Greek text (indicated in the margins of the translation).

*abiastos*, unforced, 706,37
*adiairetos*, indivisible, 714,11
*adunatos*, impossible, 717,1.3
*aei*, always, 679,8; 686,24; 687,8f; 688,31; 690,30; 691,34ff; 692,22ff; 693,8ff; 695,39; 696,37ff; 698,4ff; 699,12; 718,10
*aêr*, air, 672,37; 676,26; 680,35f
*agapein*, value, 697,13
*agathodosia*, benefaction, 707,19
*agathos*, good, 694,21; 695,34ff; 711,25.38; 714,36ff; 717,19.21.37ff; 718,2.7; 721,31
*agathotês*, goodness, 695,37
*agathunein*, make good, 707,14.36; 709,36
*agenêtos*, ingenerable, 673,30; 687,29ff; 720,9
*agennêtos*, ungenerated, 676,6; 719,9
*agnoein*, not know, 715,17
*agnoia*, ignorance, 719,37
*aïdios*, everlasting, 670,30.32.38; 685,29ff; 686,2ff; 687,32ff; 688,1ff; 689,12ff; 693,14ff; 696,14; 699,19–25.28.38; 700,3; 701,1.17.29ff; 706,21; 709,9ff; eternal, 709,25
*aïdiôs*, everlastingly, 688,7; 709,3.7
*aigokerôs*, Capricorn, 692,24
*Aiguptios*, Egyptian, 710,18ff
*ainittesthai*, allude, 670,17; 690,11.14; intimate, 683,23; 717,20
*aiôn*, duration, 699,23f; 714,23
*aiskhros*, shameful, 712,30
*aisthêsis*, perception, 694,35f; 697,8; 698,2; 713,1.7
*aisthêtikê hupobathra*, perceptual basis, 697,32
*aisthêtos*, perceptible, 669,4.18f; 670,26; 671,15ff; 673,27f; 676,5; 677,16; 694,35; 697,29; 698,2; 699,38; 706,23; 713,7; 715,1; 716,25; 720,1
*aitia*, *aition*, cause, 668,11.20–22; 674,30; 678,10ff; 680,10ff; 681,29ff; 684,8ff.26; 690,18ff; 691,12; explanation, 685,9; *eidikon aition*, formal cause, 677,34.37; 681,22; 718,7; 720,23; *hulikon aition*, material cause, 718,11; *kinêtikon aition*, moving cause, 700,33ff; 701,35f; 702,25; 707,16; 708,20; 720,23.25; *poiêtikon aition*, efficient cause, 674,23; 677,29.33; 681,17ff; 706,32; 718,7.9f; *telikon aition*, final cause, 708,19f.23; 718,7; *to prôton aition*, the first cause, 681,24; 685,27; 694,14; 695,18f.36; 696,1.27f; 697,2f.7; 701,1; 709,2.8.20; 712,27.30; 714,22; 719,28.30
*aitiasthai*, criticize, 690,7.14; 691,9; 699,28; 700,31
*akatalêptos*, ungraspable, 695,39
*akhôristos*, inseparable, 681,30; 685,31
*akhronôs*, atemporally, 677,8; 714,24
*akinêtos*, immovable, 668,3; 670,38; 686,28ff; 687,32ff; 688,16.37; 693,30; 695,11ff.24; 696,16; 700,14; 701,2.4.15; 706,17ff
*akolouthôs*, subsequently, 670,11; 720,5
*akribês*, exacting, 702,31; *akribôs*, with exactness, 672,24; accurately, 718,33
*alêptos*, intangible, 690,12
*alêtheia*, truth, 690,4; *kat' alêtheian*, in truth, 676,28f
*alêthês*, true, 674,5; 676,24
*alloiôsis*, alteration, 672,13
*alloioun*, undergo alteration, 677,8
*allos* (cf. *heteros*), different, other, 674,16; 677,15; 678,10ff; 681,1ff
*allotrios*, foreign, 690,3; 721,17
*allotrioun*, be foreign, 690,3; 721,16
*alogos*, non-rational, 678,5; 682,4; 691,6; 694,3; 715,40
*amegethos*, without magnitude, 720,20
*ameinos*, better, 686,12.14
*amerês*, partless, 700,2; 706,22; 709,35; 714,11.14f.22; *amerôs*, partlessly, 714,24

*amigês*, unmixed, 699,7
*amoirein*, have no share in, 688,17.19.28; 689,7.19; 719,35
*amoiros*, without a share, 686,24.27; 687,20; 689,4
*ampelos*, vine plant, 674,16.27
*anagôgê tôn enantiôn*, reduction of the contraries, 695,25f
*anairein*, destroy, 685,9ff; reject, 720,29
*analloiôtos*, unalterable, 700,9
*analogein*, be analogous, 682,37
*analogos*, analogous, 697,34; *tôi analogon, kat' analogian*, by analogy, 678,14; 682,7.18ff; 680,37; 684,33ff; 685,2.6; 695,20
*analusis*, analysis, 686,36; 687,1; 693,13
*anankaion*, necessary, 670,19; 694,25; 696,14f.23–30; 706,30
*anankê*, necessity, necessary, 670,31; 692,5.7; 696,21–7
*anatellein*, rise, 692,20f; 703,28.37; 704,2; 705,2f
*anatolê*, east, 690,38; 703,15.33
*andrapodon*, slave, 715,39
*andriantopoios*, sculptor, 678,28; 683,10
*andrias*, statue, 678,18ff; 680,13; 684,9f
*anelittein*, counteract, 704,15; opp. *pherein*, 708,9–10; cf. *sphaira*
*anërmêneutos*, indescribable, 696,36
*anison, to*, the unequal (Plato), 717,18.21f; 720,26
*agnoein*, keen intelligence, 690,3
*anodos*, progression, 675,9
*anoêtôs*, unintelligently, 670,27
*anthrôpoeidês*, in human form, 710,12.16
*anthrôpeios*, human, 674,15; 683,35; 710,4.17
*anthrôpos*, human being, 671,36; 674,14f; 675,30.32; 676,1f; 682,3f.28; 683,12ff; 684,21; 689,26f; 691,3; 695,15; 697,22ff; 699,36; 709,10ff; 710,6; 711,2f.37f; 712,9ff
*antikeisthai*, oppose, 671,29ff; 672,1ff; 683,35; 698,11
*antilegein*, contradict, 720,3
*antipheresthai*, undergo opposite motion, 704,35f
*antithesis*, opposition, 698,12
*aoristos*, indeterminate, 687,18
*apallasthai*, be devoid of, 688,23
*apartismos*, culmination, 715,18
*apathês*, unaffectable, 700,8; 708,16.18
*apaustos*, unceasing, 693,14

*apeirodunamos*, having unlimited potentiality, 700,3f.8
*apeiros*, unlimited, without limit, 674,24; 675,9.13; 686,25.30; 690,33; 691,36; 695,37; 700,4.25–30; 707,7f.10; 720,10
*Aphroditê*, Venus (planet), 705,30
*aphthartos*, imperishable, 670,33; 671,9.27; 673,28f; 685,34; 687,30ff; 715,26; 718,18.21.40ff; 719,2.4; 720,9
*aplanês*, fixed (star), 703,10f; cf. *sphaira*
*apodeiktikos*, demonstrative, 696,26; *apodeiktikê spoudê*, demonstrative rigour, 700,30f
*apodeixis*, demonstration, 686,36; 691,30; 693,15; 702,6.12
*apogennêma*, generated from, 669,22
*apoios*, without quality, 717,34
*apokrinesthai*, answer, 684,31
*apoperatoun*, terminate, 700,25
*apophasis*, negation, 671,30.33.35; assertion, 700,17
*aporein*, pose a puzzle, 673,33; 674,4; 678,33; 689,20; 693,2
*aporia*, puzzle, 668,11; 673,24; 689,20; 690,2; 691,17; 693,2; 710,37; 713,9f.17; 714,2
*aporrhein*, emanate, 719,20
*aporrhoia*, emanation, 688,38; 719,19
*apostêma*, distance, 704,10
*apotherioun*, turn into a beast, 710,7f
*apotukhia*, failure, 675,27; 676,3
*apsukhos*, inanimate, 686,14
*aptaistos*, infallible, 713,12
*Arês*, Mars (planet), 704,17; 705,30
*aristos*, best, 686,11.13; 695,20f; 696,34; 699,12.21–31; 700,2; 707, 20ff.34; 710,38ff; 714,36ff; 718,3ff
*arithmêtikê*, arithmetic, 702,16.18f; 713,33
*arithmos*, number, 700,20ff; *hoi arithmoi*, the numbers (Pythagoreans or Plato), 688,30; 720,12ff; *arithmôi* (opp. *eidei*), in number, 681,19; 684,23; 688,23.30; 709,4ff
*arkhaios*, ancient, 709,31
*arkhê*, principle (origin, source), 668,3ff; 670,13; 673,24ff; 675,29f; 678,10ff; 681,28ff; 694,7ff; 696,22–31; 716,10f.14; 721,31; distinguished from *stoikheion*, 681,1ff; *hê prôtê arkhê*, the first principle, 686,36; 687,25; 688,23.30; 689,23f; 693,13ff; 699,28; 700,13; 701,10f; 709,8; 719,32ff
*arkhos*, ruler, 721,26
*asapheia*, unclarity, 677,31

*asebês*, impious, 711,30; 712,31
*asômatos*, incorporeal, 686,30; 694,40; 700,1.8.12; 703,2; 720,6f
*aspazesthai*, welcome, 697,14
*astakhus*, ear of corn, 674,26f
*astatos*, not standing still, 701,24
*astêr*, star, 670,31.36; 692,18; 700,36ff; 704,24.26; 705,11ff; 708,38
*astrologia*, *astronomia*, astronomy, 702,13
*ataktôs*, disorderly, 676,19; 690,32; 691,11
*ataxia*, disorder, 681,12; 721,26ff
*atelês*, incomplete, 672,17.21; 699,33
*atheos*, godless, 670,27
*atomos*, indivisible, 677,24; 688,39; 709,15; individual (instant), 714,15.23.30-4; atom (atomists), 690,33
*atopos*, absurd, 690,18f.28; 711,6.28; 712,28; 715,5.30; 717,1.3
*atopôs*, absurdly, 718,8
*aülos*, immaterial, 689,12; 694,40; 695,2; 699,7; 709,15; 713,39; 719,34
*autoanthrôpos*, human-being-itself, 681,18
*automatos*, spontaneous, 675,26; 676,2
*autophuês*, congenital, 706,37
*autos, t'auton*, same, 678,10ff; 682,7ff
*auxêsis*, growth, 672,12
*axiôma*, worth, 695,22; claim, 712,24

*badisis*, walking, 708,29
*badizein*, to walk, 712,10f
*bebaios*, firm, 719,24
*bia*, force, 691,2.6; 696,24
*biazesthai*, to force, 691,4; 701,7
*bios*, way of life, 710,4
*boreion, to*, the north, 704,1
*boulêma*, will, 721,32
*boulêtos*, object of wish, 693,40

*de*, but, 695,27f
*deiknunai*, prove, 668,11 et passim
*deiktikos*, indicative, 708,17.23f
*dekas*, ten, 700,24-8
*dektikos*, receptive, 690,13; 698,28
*deixis*, proof, 686,36; 712,24
*diadekhesthai*, receive in succession, 686,5
*diadokhê*, succession, 686,9
*diagein*, carry on, 710,38
*diagogê*, way of carrying on, 687,26; 696,32.37; 697,6; 711,37; 714,26.29

*diairesis*, distinction, 695,25; dilemma, 678,37; 710,39
*diakrinein*, disperse, 716,14ff.31f
*dialimpanein*, be intermittent, 699,23
*dianoeisthai*, cognize, 711,28.30
*diaphanês*, transparency, 683,6-8
*diaphora*, differentia, 697,24.26
*dikaiosunê*, justice, 721,14
*diorizein*, divide, 720,20
*dokein*, seem, 689,25.31-3; 694,5f; be opined, 670,25; 717,3
*doulos*, slave, 716,4
*doxa*, opinion, 670,18.21; 713,7; 719,8; (religious) belief, 709,32; 710,31f
*doxastos*, object of opinion, 713,8
*duas*, the Dyad (Plato), 720,13
*dunamis* (opp. *energeia*), potential, potentiality, 682,8ff; 689,3ff.19ff; 691,17ff; 692,40; 700,4f; 712,3ff; 720,27ff; *dunamei, kata dunamin*, potentially, in potentiality, 672,22ff; 674,10ff; 686,24ff; 687,16; 688,17ff; 697,18; 712,19; 719,34f; cf. *nous*
*dunasthai*, have the potential, 672,19ff; 688,20.32; 689,25ff
*dunein*, set, 692,20; 705,3
*dusis*, west, 703,15
*dusmê*, west, 690,38

*edaphos*, bottom, 676,13
*egrêgorsis*, waking, 697,8
*eidos*, form, 668, 6; 672,18; 673,5.29; 674,19.30ff; 675,22.24; 676,7.31ff; 677,35ff; 678,3.9.15ff; 680,12ff; 682,6ff.33ff; 684,20ff.33ff; 687,3ff.18; 688,16.31; 690,6ff; 694,38; 695,4; 697,18.20ff; 698,1ff; 706,32ff; 709,5ff; 713,19ff; 714,31f; 715,27ff; 717,25ff; 720,37ff; Form (Plato), 671,3; 676,36; 688.36; 717,19.21; 720,12ff; *eidei* (opp. *arithmôi*), in species, 681,19; *enülon eidos*, enmattered form, 683,2; 694,27; *ousiôdes eidos*, substantial form, 672,10
*eikôn*, picture, 693,35
*einai*, be, exist, 669,10.24.30.39; 670,6; 677,27.32; 689,29ff; *ontotês*, being, 669,29; *to einai*, being, existence, or essence, 669,30.35; 670,1.6; 681,29ff; 694,27.29; *to on*, being, that which is, 669,24; 672,22.26-32; 679,24; 689,29ff; 720,28; *to on* (in Plato), Being, 679,22ff; *to mê einai*, not-being, nothingness, 678,2; 686,26; *to mê on*,

not-being, that which is not, 670,16; 672, 28ff; 673,1ff; 674,4ff; 679,29f; 680,2; 692,38; 719,6-9
*ekleipein*, be eclipsed, 668,21ff; 713,34
*ekleipsis*, eclipse, 668,21ff; 713,35-7
*ekstasis*, withdrawal, 711,36
*ektos*, external, 681,1
*elaia*, olive tree, 674,15.27
*eleutheros*, free, 715,34
*elleipein*, be omitted, 692,2
*ellipês*, elliptical, 683,24
*ellipôs*, elliptically, 674,8; 712,20
*elpis*, hope, 697,11.13
*emphainein*, indicate, 673,20; 718,11
*empodizein*, impede, 704,38
*empodôn*, as an impediment, 685,38
*empsukhos*, animate, ensouled, 678,3; 682,2; 686,13ff
*enantios*, contrary, 685,15ff; 695,25; 717,7ff
*enantiôsis*, contrariety, 672,15ff; 717,36
*enantiotês*, contrariety, 717,12
*endein*, embed, 704,26; 705,11
*energeia* (opp. *dunamis*), actuality, 682,8ff; 686,22ff; 687,4.17; 688,16.19; 689,19.22; 691,27; 692,39; 696,8ff; 709,15f.25; 712,18f; 719,34; 720,27ff; activity, 697,4ff; 699,17f; 706,38; *energeiai, kat' energeian*, 672,26ff; 674,10ff; 694,22f; cf. *nous*
*energein*, to act, 688,18.20.35f.38; 689,1ff.25ff; 691,18ff; 692,4ff; 693,22; 697,10; 720,27f
*enhuparkhein*, be present in, 688,22
*enklêma*, complaint, 718,32
*enkuklios*, circular, 708,37f
*ennoia*, notion, 697,30; 702,24; 709,31
*enstasis*, objection, 695,10; 707,33; 713,2
*entelekheia*, actualization, 685,11.13f.17
*enthumeisthai*, ponder, 700,17
*enülos*, enmattered, 683,2; 694,27; 709,12
*epagôgê*, induction, 679,20; 680,18; 689,22
*epeisodiôdês*, episodic, 721,25
*ephaptesthai*, grasp, 714,21
*ephienai*, allow, 715,34
*ephesis*, yearning, 686,20f.34; 694,2
*ephetos*, object of yearning, 694,2f; 695,2; 701,8f.12.22; 707,34-7; 708,23f
*ephexês*, in succession, 669,6.10.23
*ephiesthai*, yearn, 686,21; 691,4; 695,38f; 707,20.35ff
*epigignesthai*, supervene, 714,33f; 721,4.7

*epikheirêma*, argument, 679,11; 704,14; 712,21
*epilanthanesthai*, overlook, 706,8
*epinoia*, thought, 670, 16; 676,2; 683,1f
*epipedon*, plane, 721,12
*epiponos*, toilsome, 711,6ff
*epistêmê*, knowledge, 696,24.33; 697,35-7; science, 671,10ff; 710,19.31; 713,1ff; 719,24ff; *akra epistêmê*, highest knowledge, 696,33; *poiêtikê* versus *theôrêtikê epistêmê*, productive versus theoretical knowledge, 713,31; *prôtê epistêmê*, first science, 668,14ff
*epistêmôn*, knower, 697,35ff
*epistêtos*, knowable, 713,1ff; 719,25f
*epithumêtikos*, appetitive, 694,3
*epithumêtos*, object of appetite, 693,40f
*epithumia*, appetite, 694,2
*eran*, to love, 695,39; 696,2; 707,21
*êremein*, be at rest, 697,39; 701,24
*êremia*, rest, 671,11
*ergon*, fact, 693,16
*erôtan*, ask, 674,7; 685,7.12
*eskeumennôs*, in detail, 700,22f
*eskhatos*, ulitmate, 675,3ff
*eu, to*, excellence, 696,24.30; 713,14.26; 714,26; 715,10ff
*eu zên*, live well, 711,23
*eudaimonia*, happiness, 695,30
*eukosmia*, orderliness, 709,36f
*eulogos*, reasonable, 706,23.28ff; 707,3
*eulogôs*, reasonably, 698,14
*eutaktos*, orderly, 686,8
*euthus*, straight, 695,23; 705,2
*euzôïa*, good life, 696,34
*exartêsthai*, depend on, 707,17; 709,28; 721,33
*exêgeisthai*, interpret, 713,7
*exêgêsis*, interpretation, 703,2
*exeinai*, be at liberty, 715,34f.39; 716,3
*existanai*, disestablish, 696,3.5.13

*Gaia*, Earth (goddess, Hesiod), 690,10
*gê*, the earth, 688,26f; 692,10ff; 718,39; earth (element), 670,21; 676,26; 679,15ff.27ff; 690,27; 717,35; 721,18f
*genesis*, coming-to-be, 672,10f; 673,33; 674,6.8.12; 676,32ff; 692,27.30; 693,1.7f; 719,10; 720,8; *en genesei*, subject to generation, 715,26ff; 716,13ff; 719,3
*genethlios hêmera*, birthday, 710,11
*genêtikos*, capable of making [things] come to be, 692,6f.

*genêtos*, generable, 687,31ff; 691,24
*genikos*, general, 679,3
*gennan*, generate, 718,38; 719,7
*genos*, genus, 670,13; 679,3; 684,22; 685,19; race, 710,14
*geômetria*, geometry, 702,16.18; 713,32
*gignesthai*, become, come to be, 672,29; 673,1–30; 674,31ff; 675,19ff; 678,16ff; 695,28f; 717,7ff
*glukansis*, sweetening, 708,30
*gnômê*, saying, 700,17
*gnôsis*, knowing, 714,34
*gonê*, semen, 690,27

*hairesis*, persuasion, 671,6
*hairetos*, object of choice, 695,17.20
*hamartêma*, mistake, 676,3
*haphê*, contact, 676,24; 677,6.21; 714,26.34
*haplous*, simple, 672,10; 674,22; 679,33f; 687,8ff; 694,22; 699,5ff; 701,21.35–7; 706,21; distinguished from *heis*, 695,9–16; *ta hapla*, the simple things, i.e. material elements, 674,22; 679,33f
*haplôs*, without qualification, 669,24
*haptesthai*, be in contact, 676,11
*hêdonê*, pleasure, 696,35; 697,5
*hêdus*, pleasant, 697,9; 699,12
*heis*, one, 669,10.22; 686,6; 701,35–7; 706,21; 709,1ff; distinguished from *haplos*, 695,9–15; *to hen*, the One (Anaxagoras), 673,7; 679,24; the One (Plato), 679,22ff; 717,22f.38; 720,13; *hê henas*, unity, 689,15; *mê hen*, not-one, 679,30; 680,2
*hekastos*, each, 682,15; *to kath' hekaston*, the individual, 676,34ff
*hêliakos*, solar, 692,29; cf. *sphaira*
*hêlios*, sun, 673,31; 683,12ff.28ff; 692,7ff; 693,3; 703,13.18.25ff
*hêmera*, day, 680,36; 683,7; 692,27ff; 693,1.7
*hêmisphairion*, hemisphere, 688,26
*heneka*, for the sake of, 695,29.31–5; *hou heneka, to*, final cause (the that-for-the sake-of-which), 695,24.27–35
*henôsis*, unification, 676,17.25
*henoun*, unify, 676,21f; 720,34.36
*Heraklês*, Mars (planet), 720,11
*Hermês*, Mercury (planet), 705,30
*heteros*, other, different (cf. *allos*), 672,32; 673,23ff; 678,24ff; 679,14ff; 680,5ff.32ff; 682,7ff
*heterotês*, otherness, 672,32

*hexis*, state, 669,37; 676,31; 677,23.36
*hippeion eidos*, form of a horse, 678,19
*hippos*, horse, 672,37; 675,26; 684,21; 695,15; 709,14
*histasthai*, make a stand, 695,36
*holos*, whole (adj.), 669,3; 709,34; 711,1ff; 714,4ff.22ff; *to holon*, the whole (i.e. the universe), 714,27.35; 715,19; 716,7.10.22f.34
*holotês*, whole (n.), 669,14.20; 687,29; 695,37; 716,39
*homoeidês*, same in species, 684,22
*homou*, together (Anaxagoras), 673,8.13ff; 690,13; 692,38; 693,10
*horan*, see, 701,21.25; 712,5.29f
*hôrismenos*, determinate, 686,8; 687,17
*horizôn*, horizon, 703,34
*hormê*, impulse, 686,18ff
*horos*, definition, 668,23
*hudôr*, water, 670,21; 672,36; 674,24; 675,14; 676,26; 718,38
*hudrokhoos*, Aquarius, 673,31
*hugiainein*, be healthy, 682,23
*hugieia*, health, 675,23f; 677,11f.36; 678,9; 681,10.19–21; 713,4f.20; 718,25f
*hugieinos*, healthy, 713,6
*hugra anathumiôsis*, moist exhalation, 675,13
*hugrotês*, liquid, 682,29
*hulê*, matter, 668,5; 672,6.19.30; 673,6.12ff; 674,19ff; 675,7; 676,5ff; 678,15ff; 680,12ff.20ff; 682,6ff.33.35; 683,14ff; 684,14.23ff.32ff; 685,19ff; 687,4.15.18; 690,6ff; 691,11; 694,27.38; 695,2ff; 697,20.24; 709,25; 716,21; 717,16ff; 719,17ff; 721,1ff; *aneideos* (*eskhatê*) *hulê*, formless matter, 674,22.34; 675,3.5.14; 715,31; *aneu hulês*, without matter, 677,11; 713,29f; *khôris tês hulês*, separately from the matter, 697,21ff; 698,15ff; *mê ekhôn hulên*, not possessing matter, 714,10; *para tês hulês*, apart from the matter, 709,13f; *prosekhês hulê*, proximate matter, 674,21.23; 677,26; 717,30.35; *hê protê hulê*, the first (i.e. prime) matter, 674,34; 717,34; *teleutaia hulê*, last matter, 677,22f.25
*hulikos*, material, 697,23; 718,11
*huparkhein*, subsist, be present, 677,32f; 679,32; 681,30ff; 721,6
*huparxis*, reality, subsistence, 679,37; 684,16; 688,6; 721,3.8.10
*huperplêrês*, overfull, 707,18

*hupodeigma*, example, 669,12; 674,12; 716,9.35
*hupokeimenon, to*, subject, 668,16f; substratum, 670.36; 675,9ff; 677,20ff; 680,23; 682,32.35; 715,25ff; 717,16ff
*hupokeisthai*, underlie, 670,35–6; 672,3; 715,24ff; 717,10ff
*hupolêpsis*, judgement, 691,31; 710,34
*hupostasis*, reality, 677,1
*husteros*, posterior, 683,17; 686,37; after, 687,4–7

*iatreuein*, heal, 715,35
*iatrikê*, art of healing, 678,8; 681,20; 713,4.6.19; 718,25
*iatros*, healer, 675,24
*ibis*, ibis, 710,21–5
*idea*, Idea (Plato), 671,3.5.7; 676,36ff; 678,6; 688,29.40; 720,6.14.20ff
*ikhthues*, Pisces, 673,32
*indalma*, effigy, 697,9
*isêmeria*, equinox, 703,38
*isêmerinos*, equinoctial (circle), 703,34
*iskhus*, formidable, 706,27.29
*isos*, equal, 717,19.22
*isôs*, perhaps, probably, 678,5; 680,19
*isotakhôs*, equally fast, 704,29–31

*kakos*, bad, 693,38; 711,40; 717,17.20.30ff; 720,26
*kalos*, noble, 687,14ff; 694,1.19; 695,17.22; 696,22.27; 699,29; 715,8; 718,5
*katagelastos*, ridiculous, 708,29
*kataklusmos*, flood, 710,29
*katalambanei*, to grasp, 695,35f; 713,12
*katalêpsis*, grasp, 713,12
*katamênion*, menstrual fluid, 674,15; 690,26f; 699,31–5
*katêgorein*, to predicate, 670,33
*katêgoria*, category, 668,15.26; 669,2.10; 672,7; 678,34ff
*kathêgemôn*, teacher, 716,26
*katheudein*, to sleep, 710,40
*kath' hauto*, by itself, in its own right, 669,34; 671,2; 672,30; 680,21ff; 681,31ff; 684,17; 687,6; 693,36; 695,18ff; 697,15ff; 698,18; 713,40; *kath' hauto – kata sumbebêkos*, 672,33; 698,8; 700,13f; 701,2–4.11f.15; 713,5
*kath' hekaston, to; hekastos*, individual, 670,20; 682,15; 684,14ff
*katholikos*, universal in character, 681,2.4

*katholou, to*, universal, 670,8.12–13.16–17.22; 678,13ff; 680,16; 682,13ff; 684,9ff.32ff; 695,7; 697,19.22.30
*kenon* (atomists), void, 690,32
*kentron*, centre, 703,25.30ff
*kephalê*, head, 676,10ff; 677,16.22
*kêros*, wax, 721,6–7
*khalkos*, bronze, 674,31ff; 675,8.13; 677,35; 678,18ff
*Khaos* (Hesiod), Chaos, 690,9.11f; 691,37
*kheiros*, worse, 711,35ff; 712,20.24.28
*khorêtikos*, capacious, 690,12
*khôris*, separately, 670,2; 685,31
*khôrismos*, separation, 678,1
*khôristos*, separable, 669,39; 681,30ff; 683,1ff; separate, 670,38; 671,2
*khôrizein*, to separate, 669,5; 683,2.6; 686,35; 694,28f.38; 695,2ff; 697,20; 698,30; 699,38; 721.10
*khrôma*, colour, 671,31; 712,4; 715,26; 716,19
*khronikos*, temporal, 677,2; 714,8f
*khronos*, time, 677,30; 683,19; 687,38; 688,2ff; 690,33; 691,37; 696,37; 704,34; 714,7ff
*khuma*, mass, 691,25; 703,21
*khumos*, humour, 675,4
*kibiôton*, box, 678,20; 690,26
*kinein*, move, impart movement, 686,4ff.23ff; 688,1f; 691,8f; 693,31ff; 700,8f; 701,14ff; change, 696,13; *to kinoun*, mover, 681,1ff.14; 693,19–30; 701,15ff; 718,22.27; 719,21; 721,5; *to kinoumenon*, that which is moved, 686,2ff.16ff; 693,19ff; 701,14ff; 718,28
*kinêsis*, movement, 669,27; 671,10f; 672,7; 681,35; 685,33ff; 687,37ff; 690,30ff; 691,1ff; 693,4ff; 694,8ff; 700,21ff; 711,36; 720,18; *hê kuklôi kinêsis*, circular movement, 693,14f; 696,19; 695,22ff
*kinêtikos*, capable of bringing about movement, 686,22; 687,3.11f; 688,15.17f; 689,9.14.16; 701,36; 707,13; cf. *aition; to prôton kinêtikon*, the first mover (i.e. moving cause), 707,12.14
*kinêtos*, movable, 686,31
*koinônein*, have in common, 671,15; 715,27ff; 716,21ff.36ff; 721,19
*koinônia*, commonality, 715,24
*koinos*, common, 670,22; 671,16; 697,22f; 715,24
*koiranos*, sovereign, 721,31

*kosmos*, cosmos, 687,30; 691,10.38; 692,3; 709,1ff.34; 714,37; 715,4.11.17
*kreittos*, better, 711,35ff
*Kroniakê* (*sc. sphaira*), of Saturn, 689,11; 692,11ff
*Kronos*, Saturn (planet), 692,7.19ff; 700,35; 703,18.22; 705,16ff; 720,11; Cronus (god), 710,2
*kubernein*, to steer, 709,36
*kubos*, cube, 721,22
*kuklophoria*, circular motion, 686,10
*kuklophorêtikos*, capable of circular motion, 686,14f.33; 696,1f; 716,29-31; 717,9
*kuklos*, circle, 703,23.30ff; 704,23ff; *kuklôi*, circular, in a circle, 683,28ff; 686,11f; 687,3; 690,35; 695,22; 696,12ff; 701,24; 703,34; 706,34; cf. *kinêsis*
*kurios*, dominant, 711,7f.9.11; 719,13.15.17
*kuriôs*, chiefly, 668,22; 670,6.15; 678,35; 680,37; 682,7; 687,3.21; 691,27; 692,41; 693,38ff; 703,24ff

*lampros*, bright, 715,28f
*leukansis*, whitening, 708,30
*leukos*, white, 671,31ff; 672,34-6; 680,22ff; 719,32
*leukotês*, whiteness, 717,14
*lexis*, text, 671,18
*lithos*, stone, 691,1ff
*logikos*, rational, 711,6
*logikôs*, in a logical way, 670,14
*logistikos*, rational, 694,3f
*logos*, account, 675,24; 678,8; 683,15; 709,17f.21; 713,33; reason, 693,15; speech, 696,35
*loxos*, oblique (orbit), 683,28ff
*loxôs*, obliquely aligned, 683,28ff; 692,6f.28
*loxôsis*, oblique alignment, 692,24.39; 703,30f; 704,3f
*loxoun*, align obliquely, 703,23ff; 704,5
*lusis*, solution, 668,10; 678,11; 689,35; 690,2; 713,25

*magireuein*, cook, 716,6
*makarios*, blessed, 696,35f; 721,33
*marturesthai*, call as a witness, 691,32
*matên*, in vain, 708,6.12f; 710,12
*mathêmatikê epistêmê*, mathematical science, 702,8f.15
*mathêmatikon, mathêmatos*, mathematical object, 671,2.4ff; 702,21
*mathêmatikos*, mathematician, 702,23

*mathêsis*, learning, 696,24
*medimnos*, bushel, 709,35
*megethos*, magnitude, 702,18; 707,23; 716,24f; 720,21
*melania*, blackness, 717,14f
*melas*, black, 719,32
*merikos*, particular, 681,4; 684,12ff; partial, 695,7.38
*meristos*, divisible into parts, 714,14.21
*meros*, part, 669,3.5.15-16.20; 694,3; 711,2ff; 714,4ff
*mesos*, intermediary, 693,20.24f
*metaballein*, change, 672,20ff; 673,5.12.29; 711,33f; 714,4
*metabasis*, transition, 697,28
*metabastikos*, transitional, 706,38
*metablêtos*, changeable, 671,22.28
*metabolê*, change, 671,26ff; 672,1.9.11; 677,3
*metalêpsis*, participation, 698,24f
*metameleshai*, feel regret, 711,39f
*metaxu*, intermediate, 671,29; 672,1; 679,15; 697,36; 717,35
*metekhein*, partake, 669,29; 717,38
*mêtêr*, mother, 699,34
*methexis*, participation, 719,16; 721,32
*metron*, measure, 695,14
*migma*, mixture, 673,17.19; 691,33
*mimnêskein*, remember, 697,12
*mnêmê*, memory, 697,11.13
*muthikôs*, mythically, 709,33f; 710,2.9.26
*muthos*, myth, 709,32f.38f; 710,2.4.9.26

*neikos*, Hate (Empedocles), 690,16; 691,34; 718,16ff
*neuron*, sinew, 676,9; 677,26; 683,14,16
*noein*, think, 686,33; 694,10ff.30ff; 698,1ff; 699,1ff; 705,5.8; 711,1f.23ff; *noein heauto*, think of itself, 697,4.6; 698,4ff.35ff; 711,1f.23ff; *to nooun*, that which thinks, 699,4; 712,36ff; *to nooumenon*, the object of thinking, 694,38; 699,3; 712,36ff
*noêma*, thought, 697,30.39
*noêsis*, act of thinking, 694,8ff; 697,8; 698,17ff; 711,11ff; 712,1ff
*noêtikos*, capable of thinking, 699,11
*noêtos*, intelligible, 670,26.37; 671,12.15; 679,23f; 687,2ff.22; 693,31ff; 695,8.18; 696,33f; 698,8ff; 699,2ff; 713,12ff; 720,4.6; *to prôton noêton*, the first intelligible object, 694,7
*nomos*, law, 710,3.23; 716,4

*nosein*, be sick, 682,24f
*nosôdês*, sick, 713,6
*nosos*, sickness, 681,10; 682,24
*nothos logismos*, bastard reasoning (Plato), 687,5
*nous*, intellect, 678,4; 682,3; 687,10; 691,3; 694,9ff; 695,8; 696,33; 697,1; *ho anthrôpinos (hêmeteros) nous*, the human (or our) intellect, 696,33 697,1.10; 712,13.15; 714,16ff; *ho dunamei nous*, the potential intellect, 697,18f; 698,26; *ho energeiai nous*, the actual intellect, 694,32; 695,21; 697,16ff; 698,1ff.35ff; 712,15; 714,25; *ho kath' hexin nous*, the dispositional intellect, 695,21; 697,17ff; *ho polutimêtos nous*, the highly honoured intellect, 710,36; 719,13f.28f; *ho prôtos nous*, the first intellect, 698,20.23.36ff; 699,1ff.16f.19–21; 707,2.5f.21; 710,36f; 711,20; 712,12; 713,13; 714,12.23ff; 715,7.14f; 721,33; *ho theios nous*, the divine intellect, 710,37; 711,32; 714,32; *ho nous*, the Intellect (Anaxagoras), 673,8; 674,23; 690,17; 691,34; 718,22ff
*nun, to*, the present, 677,8ff; 714,6.15.23.30.32
*nux*, night, 680,37; 692,27ff; 693,1.6.7; Night (Hesiod), 690.11f; 691,37; 692,37; 693,10

*oikeios*, appropriate, 671,30ff
*oikeiôsis*, affinity, 686,34
*oikia*, house, household, 675,22; 677,11f.31; 681,11.21; 713,19.22; 715,33; 716,37ff
*oikodomikê*, art of housebuilding, 681,21; 713,18ff
*oikodomos*, housebuilder, 675,23; 677,30f; 681,12
*oinos*, wine, 682,27.30
*oneirôttein*, envision, 673,9
*ontotês*, being, 669,29
*ophis*, snake, 710,19.21
*oregesthai*, desire, 694,5f
*orektos*, object of desire, 687,2.22; 693,31ff; 701,9; *to prôton orekton*, the first desirable object, 694,7
*orexis*, desire, 682,3f; 686,34
*ostoun*, bone, 676,9; 677,26; 680,27; 683,14ff
*ouranios*, heavenly, 719,3; 720,8
*ouranos*, heaven, 691,12–14; 696,4.10.31; 707,11f.22; 708,37; 709,1; 718,38; 721,14; *ho prôtos ouranos*, the first heaven, 693,16f; 707,22
*ousia*, substance as individual, 669,13ff; 670,8ff.25ff; 671,23ff; 672,9.11f.17; 675,19ff.31ff; 676,5f; 677,24; 681,28ff; 684.20; 685,27ff; 687,6.18ff; 689,8; 694,19ff; 696,12; 699,37; 701,33–5; 706,15ff; 720,4; substance as category, 668,13ff; 678,33ff; 680,3ff.24ff; 687,33; substance as substantial form or essence, 672,17; 676,30; 680,25; 687,11f; 689,3.7; 696,12; 698,7; 698,28; 711,4ff; 713,30; *hê prôtê ousia*, the first substance, 668,17; 685,27; 695,11; 710,27
*ousiousthai*, have substance, 712,2.8ff
*oxos*, vinegar, 682,30

*pampalaios*, very old, 709,26.31; 710,32
*pan, to*, universe, 669,3; 673,8; 674,23; 701,21; 715,13.15
*panêguris*, festival, 710,5.9
*paradeigma*, example, 682,28
*paragein*, bring forth, 709,3.37
*paramuthia*, elaboration, 688,2
*parastasis*, substantiation, 690,3
*paratasis*, interval, 677,2; 714,9
*paratêrêsis*, observation, 706,20
*parorhama*, oversight, 706,14
*parergos*, in passing, 674,4; 720,3
*paskhein* (opp. *poiein*), be affected, 685,36–9; 687,16
*patêr*, father, 681,3; 694,34.36
*pathos*, affection or attribute, 669,30; 672,14; 681,35
*patrios*, of forefathers, 700,34
*pêgê*, fount, 691,12.16
*perainein*, limit, 700,5.26.30; 703,3f
*perilêpsis*, comprehension, 697,19f
*periodos*, cycle, 691,38; 692,2f
*periôpê*, beholding, 711,35
*periphereia*, arc, 704,1.3
*periphora*, circular motion, 708,32
*periphrazein*, express in a roundabout way, 702,3
*perittos*, odd, 694,20
*phainesthai*, appear, 676,8ff; 694,1
*phaneros*, evident, 669,31; 675,25; 676,35; 685,3; 686,36
*phantasia*, appearance, 677,9; imagination, 677,12; 691,6; *kata phantasian*, in appearance, 676,20ff

*phantazein, phantazesthai*, envisage, 669,23; 673,10.18; 677,6ff; imagine, 676,20
*phaulos*, evil, 711,26ff; 712,31
*pherein*, carry, 703,26ff; 704,15ff; 705,24ff; 706,4; 708,9.36; opp. *anelittein*, 708,9–10
*pheresthai*, be carried or be in motion, 691,5; 692,23ff; 695,10; 696,12.14; 704,5ff
*philein*, love, 697,12; be friendly, 702,29
*philia*, Love (Empedocles), 690,16; 691,34; 718,8ff
*philosophein*, practise philosophy, 716,4
*philosophia*, philosophy, 671,13; 702,14; 719,23
*philosophôs*, in a philosophical manner, 706,31; 715,16
*phoneutria*, killer (fem.), 710,21
*phora*, locomotion, motion, 672,13; 673,31; 691,6; 692,16; 701,23ff; 702,20; 708,25ff; *hê prôtê phora*, the first motion, 696,8.10
*phôs*, light, 680,35ff; 683,5ff; 694,19
*phôtizein*, illuminate, 683,7
*phthartikos, phthartos*, perishable, 670,30.33; 671,8ff.27; 673,28f; 676,6; 685,30.32; 687,31ff; 691,24; 718,40f; 719,1.4
*phtheiresthai*, perish, 672,4; 686,27; 688,25; 695,7; 718,19
*phthisis*, diminution, 672,12
*phthora*, perishing, 672,11; 677,3ff; 688,7; 692,27.30; 693,1.8; *en phthorai*, subject to perishing, 716,13
*phusikos*, natural, 672,9ff; 675,25; 681,15–17; 687,28; *hê phusikê*, natural science, 671,10ff; *ho phusikos*, natural theorist, 690,10ff
*phusis*, nature, 669,22; 670,28; 675,20.33ff; 676,18.30.38; 677,13ff.23; 687,1.26; 688,31.33; 691,1.8; 692,5; 696,5.13.31; 706,36ff; 708,13; 709,34; 714,35f; 715,32; 716,10ff
*phuton*, plant, 670,30.35; 690,28; 715,20
*pistis*, confirmation, 689,21; 691,31; 711,37.39
*planêtês astêr*, planetary star, 700,35f; planetary sphere, cf. *sphaira*
*planômenos*, planetary (lit. wandering), 693,18.20; cf. *sphaira*
*platos*, breadth, 703,30f.39; 704,2ff
*plattein*, fabricate, 710,9
*plêmmelôs*, discordantly, 690,32

*plêthos*, amount, 700,18ff; multitude, 709,34; 710,19; 721,26; syn. *arithmos*, 700,32ff.
*plinthos*, brick, 681,12
*plôtos*, swimming, 715,20
*poiein*, produce, make, 675,29; (opp. *paskhein*), affect, 685,36–9; 687,14f.19
*poiêtikos*, productive, 674,23; 677,29.33; 678,26ff; 680,12ff; 681,1ff; 683,28ff; 684,33ff; 688,15.18; 720,25; cf. *aition, epistêmê*
*poion*, quality, 669,7–8.19; 678,34ff; *poiotês*, quality, 669,27
*polis*, city-state, 710,7; 715,36ff
*politeia*, commonwealth, 715,34; 716,5.9.35
*politeuein*, govern, 721,25ff
*poluarkhia*, rule of many, 721,26–8
*polukoiraniê*, sovereignty of many, 721,31
*polos*, pole, 704,6
*polutimêtos*, highly honourable, 699,16; cf. *nous*
*porneuein*, fornicate, 711,30
*poson*, quantity, 669,7.9.19; 672,13; 678,34ff; 687,33
*pragma*, thing, object, 670,15; 674,18; 713,28.34; 720,32f
*pragmateia*, treatise, 668,4; 674,36; 675,16; 690,4; 717,3f
*prattein*, do, act, 695,29–32; 715,36ff
*praxis*, action, 695,32
*proanatellein*, rise before, 705,10
*produnein*, set before, 705,4
*progonos*, forebear, 693,16
*pronooumenos*, providential, 710,20
*pros ti*, relative, 678,34ff; 679,35; 680,3ff.30ff; 698,11.13
*prosekhês*, proximate, 678,22.31.35; 682,1f; 685,12–13; 695,2; 715,30; cf. *hulê*
*proteros*, prior, 683,17ff; 688,3–7; 689,24ff; 691,17ff; 720,31ff
*prôtos*, first, 668,4.14ff; 684,11ff; cf. *aition, arkhê, epistêmê, hulê, kinêtikos, noêtos, nous, orekton, ouranos, ousia, phora, to ti ên einai*
*pseudês*, false, 674,5
*psukhê*, soul, 675,23f; 682,2; 686,17f; 691,11–16; 701,16f; 711,3ff; *alogos psukhê*, non-rational soul, 678,5; *logikê psukhê*, rational soul, 678,4; *hai tôn sphairôn sphairai*, souls of the spheres, 706,32; 707,1ff
*psukhron, to*, the cold, 672,4.7; 680,20ff

*psukhrotês*, coldness, 672,4
*ptênos*, winged, 715,20
*pur*, fire, 670,21; 676,26; 677,16ff; 679,15ff.27ff; 691,2; 717,35; 721,13.16f
*puramidês*, pyramid, 721,13
*Puthagoreios*, Pythagorean, 694,19

*rhathumein*, be negligent, 718,33.40
*Rhea*, Rhea (goddess), 710,2.10

*sarx*, flesh, 675,5; 676,9; 677,16.21.26; 680,26; 682,28; 683,14ff
*selênê*, moon, 703,6.29ff
*sêmainein*, signify, 690,18; 695,14.16
*sêmeion*, indication, 676,1; constellation, 703,27; point, 703,38f; 704,24, 705,2.12f
*semnos*, with dignity, 711,1.15f
*skhêma*, shape, 678,18.20; 715,25.27; 716,24.26
*skia*, shadow, 697,9
*skorpion*, Scorpio, 692,24
*skotos*, darkness, 680,36; 683,9; 690,11
*sôma*, body, 670,22.34; 675,23; 681,10; 682,3f; 686,9ff.30ff; 696,2; 700,5f; 701,8; 720,36; *ho pempton sôma*, the fifth body, 670,37; 683,21; 715,26ff; 718,3; 719,3
*sômatikôs*, corporeally, 709,34f
*sophia*, wisdom, 668,16.26f; 670,9; 719,27
*sophos*, wise, 710,5.21
*sôros*, heap, 676,12; *sôrêdon*, heaped up, 676,20
*sôteira*, saviour, 710,23
*sperma*, seed, 674,15; 690,28; 699,30–7
*sphaira*, sphere, 670,30.35; 700,36f; 709,28; 677,35; *hê aplanês (prôtês) sphaira*, the sphere of the fixed stars, 689,10.13.14; 690,37; 692,12ff.40; 693,3.10.13f; 701,4f.22; 703,11ff; *hai planômenai sphairai*, the planetary spheres, 689,10f; 690,38; 693,18.20; 701,25ff; 707,12f; 721,32; *hê hêliakê sphaira*, the solar sphere, 692,29.30.32; 693,3.7; *hê selêniakê sphaira*, the lunar sphere, 703,6.29ff; *anastrai sphairai*, starless spheres, 703,22; *anelittousa sphaira*, counteracting sphere, 704,15ff; 705,6ff.25ff; 708,10
*sphairos*, Sphere (Empedocles), 673,17; 718,9.11
*sterêsis*, privation, 668,5; 669,35; 671,37; 672,18.20.31; 673,6; 675,1; 678,15ff;
680,12ff.35ff; 682,6ff.33.35; 683,32ff; 684,25; 685,4ff; 717,26.32
*stoikheion*, element, 670,31ff; 671,26; 673,24–5; 678,33ff; 679,1ff.20ff; 680,10ff; 716,18f; distinguished from *arkhê*, 681,1ff
*stoikheiotos*, composed of elements, 679,2
*stratêgos*, general, 715,11–13
*strateuma*, army, 715,9.12
*strateuesthai*, be a soldier, 715,36; 716,4
*strongulotês*, roundness, 675,8–11.35; 721,6f
*sullabê*, syllable, 679,19f; 684,15f.19
*sumbainein*, be accidental to, 672,35–6; *sumbebêkos*, accident, accidental, 669,4; 679,9; 681,28ff; 685,8; *kata sumbebêkos*, accidentally, 672,35; 673,1 (cf. *kath' hauto*)
*sumballesthai*, contribute, 721,18ff
*sumpheron, to*, advantage, 710,4.9.13
*sumphusis*, growth together, 676,18.25; 677,21; *sumphuesthai*, grow together, 676,11
*sumplêrôsis*, fulfilment, 715,18f.23.32; 716,23
*sumposion*, drinking party, 710,5
*sunanairein*, destroy in addition, 685,10
*sunanatellein*, rise together, 705,13
*sundunein*, set together, 705,13
*sunekhês*, continuous, 685,5.6.32; 686,32; 688,9f; 699,23f; 701,18; 712,7ff; 720,20
*sunhistanai*, establish, 716,32; establish (i.e. demonstrate) 670,4; 685,28; 687,1.26; 700,34; 720,4
*sunkinein*, move together with, 693,5
*sunolon*, compound whole, 669,16
*sunônumos*, synonymous, 675,17ff
*suntattein*, co-ordinate, 678,23; 680,17.39; 685,20; 715,16ff
*sunteinein*, contribute, 708,4.8.11; 716,5ff
*suntelein*, contribute together, 708,10.32; 715,17ff; 716,1.12.25
*sunthêton, to*, compound, 679,34; 687,10; 709,21; 713,22; 714,6ff; 716,18ff
*sustasis*, establishment, 715,37.41; 716,1ff
*sustoikhia*, column, 694,17; 695,18

*tarakhê*, confusion, 705,11
*tattein*, put in order, 704,22; 705,7.39; 715,4ff
*taxis*, order, 676,17.22; 704,9; 715,3ff; 720,2.7
*tekhnê*, art, 675,20.28ff; 678,8; 710,29f
*tekhnêtês*, artefact, 677,1; 678,8

*tekmairesthai*, submit in evidence, 683,8f
*tektonikê*, art of building, 690,26
*teleios*, complete, 672,17.21; 699,34
*teleioun*, to complete, 707,13; 712,18f
*telos*, end, 707,34; 708,24.36.38
*teleiotês*, completion, 697,18
*tetagmenôs*, in an ordered way, 673,34; 721,28
*thaumasios*, wonderful, 699,15f
*thaumastos*, object of wonder, 697,15; 699,13.15f
*theios*, divine, 670,26; 671,12; 698,34.37; 699,13; 708,37; 709,29.34.36; 701,37; 711,30f.32f; 712,32f; 713,8; 715,26; cf. *nous*
*themis*, permissible, 714,15
*theologos*, theologian, 690,7ff; 719,22; 720,10
*theophilôs*, devoutly, 715,16
*theorein*, contemplate, study, 671,13.17; 687,11
*theôrêtikê opsis*, theoretical vision, 697,29f
*theôrêtikos*, theoretical, 713,32; cf. *epistêmê*
*theôria*, investigation, 668,13.18; theoretical knowledge, 702,17; contemplation, 698,34; 699,12; 711,16; 714,27
*theos*, god, 685,27; 699,12ff; 706,33; 707,5; 708,13; 709,28ff; 710,1; 721,31f
*thêrion*, beast, 715,39
*therinos*, summer (solstice), 703,38
*thermon, to*, the hot, 672,5; 680,20ff
*thermotês*, heat, 672,4.14
*thesis*, position, 704,21.39

*thinganein*, touch, 698,26
*thnêtos*, mortal, 678,5
*thura*, door, 678,19ff
*timios*, honourable, 698,37; 711,5.32f; 719,24; valuable, 712,17.19
*to ti ên einai to prôton*, essence, the first, 709,23f
*tode ti*, this-something, 676,8.16.30; 677,23
*topos*, place, 672,13; 688,11; 696,12
*trigônos*, triangle, 694,19; 721,12.22
*trismakaristos*, thrice-blessed (experience), 714,19
*tropê*, turning (i.e. solstice), 703,27.33.38; 704,1
*tropikos*, solstitial, 703,26f
*tunchanein*, be at random, 715,41
*tukhê*, chance, 675,26; 676,2
*tukhos*, random, 671,29; 674,13-14.28; 711,26.31

*xulon*, wood, 678,19ff; 690,25
*xulotomein*, chop wood, 716,6

*zên*, live, 697,2.5
*zêtein*, enquire, 668,8 *et passim*
*zêtêsis*, enquiry, 670,15
*Zeus*, Jupiter (planet), 689,11; 700,35; 703,18.22; 705,16ff; 720,11; Zeus (god), 710,2.10
*zôê*, life, 696,35ff; 699,16ff.23ff.31; *hê aristê zôê*, the best life, 697,7
*zôidion*, constellations of the zodiac, 703,21ff; 704,7ff
*zôidiakos*, zodiacal, 692,24
*zôion*, animal, 670,30.34; 676,17; 680,14; 681,9f.14-16; 689,26; 690,27; 691,7; 699,20ff; 700,1; 701,6.18; 709,9.25

# Index of Passages from Other Works

References are to ancient and medieval authors and commentators excluding Aristotle's *Metaphysics* 12 and Ps.-Alexander's commentary on Book 12. Page references in **bold** are to the introduction, and other references in regular type are to the end notes keyed to the page and line numbers of the Greek text.

Alexander of Aphrodisias
  *De Anima (DA)*
    25,2–3: 714,33
    26,21–2: 714,33
    79,16–18: 670,16
    85,11–86,6: **27**; 697,17
    86,14–87,1: **27**; 697,39
    89,21–2: 698,20
    90,4–7: 670,16
  *De Fato*
    1, 164,3–5,13 ff.: **28 n. 5**
  *in Aristotelis Metaphysica commentaria*
    (*in Metaph.*)
    60,13–16: 717,37
    250,17–20: 695,26
  *Mantissa*
    108,3–15: 694,27
    109,25–110,3: **27**; 699,4
  *Quaestiones (Quaest.)*
    1.1, 2,20–4,26: 685,30–687,29
    1.24, 38,25 ff.: 672,36
    2.28, 78,18–20: 670,16
  *Fragments in Averroes's Tafsīr*
    fr. 1F=Tafsīr 1394: 668,17
    fr. 2F=Tafsīr 1406: 668,17
    fr. 3F=Tafsīr 1408: 669,7
    fr. 4bF=Tafsīr 1421: 671,21
    fr. 5F=Tafsīr 1427: 671,3
    fr. 6F=Tafsīr 1428: 671,17
    fr. 9F=Tafsīr 1445–6: 673,22
    fr. 10a-cF=Tafsīr 1457–65: 675,34
    fr. 11F=Tafsīr 1467–72: 676,8
    fr.12F=Tafsīr 1481–2: 677,13
    fr. 14F=Tafsīr 1487–8: 678,5
    fr. 17F=Tafsīr 1510–11: 679,12
    fr. 18F=Tafsīr 1513–15: 679,34
    fr. 19F=Tafsīr 1519: 680,25
    fr. 20F=Tafsīr 1529–31: 681,25
    fr. 21F=Tafsīr 1534–5: 682,2
    fr. 22F=Tafsīr 1544: 684,16
    fr. 24F=Tafsīr 1557–8: 685,23
    fr. 25F=Tafsīr 1567: 686,13; 689,5
    fr. 26F=Tafsīr 1571: 690,14
    fr. 27F=Tafsīr 1578–9: 692,4
    fr. 28F=Tafsīr 1588–9: 693,30
    fr. 29F= Tafsīr 1601–2: 694,18; 695,27
Anaxagoras
  fr. 1: 673,9
Aquinas, Thomas
  *Sententia libri metaphysicae*
    2439: 674,24
    2454: 678,9
    2464: 678,14
Aristotle
  *Categories (Cat.)*
    1, 1a6–8: 675,19
    4, 1b25–2a4: 669,2
    5, 2b3–6: 670,3
    5, 2b17–21: 670,13
    5, 2b37–3a1, 2b22: 670,13
    6, 4b22–31: 720,20
    7: 679,9
    10: 671,30
  *De Interpretatione (Int.)*
    7, 17a39-b1: 670,13
  *Posterior Analytics (An. Post.)*
    1.22, 83a4–23: 680,23
    2.2, 90a15: 668,23
  *Topics (Top.)*
    1.9, 103b22–3: 669,2
    2.8: 671,30
    8.12, 162b27: 670,14
  *Physics (Phys.)*
    1.5, 188a31-b3: 671,31
    1.5, 188a32–3: 674,15
    1.6, 189a24–6: 717,15
    1.7: 672,6
    1.7, 190b33–5: 717,15; 717,32
    1.7, 191a8–12: 668,6
    1.8, 191a36: 671,13
    1.8, 191b13–15: 672,33
    1.8, 191b33: 683,10

1.9, 192a25–34: 674,35
2.2, 194a36: **31 n. 55**; 695,26
2.2, 194b13: 683,29
2.2, 194b14: 671,13
2.3: 677,28; 681,23
2.5–6: 675,27
2.7, 198a26: 681,17
2.7, 198a27–8: 671,17
3.2, 201b24–6: 694,18
3.4, 203a20: 673,22
3.5: 700,7
3.6, 206b27–33: 700,25
4.10, 218b19: 671,31
4.11, 219a1–2, b2–3: 688,11
4.11, 219a34–b3: 688,4
5.1–3: 671,31
5.3, 227a23–7: 676,11
5.4, 228a20–b1: 688,9
7.1: 688,14
8.1, 250b26–251a5: 692,1
8.1, 251a8–252a5: 685,34
8.1, 251a18–28: 688,2
8.1, 251b27–8 688,11
8.4, 254b7–12: 700,14
8.5, 256b14–20: **14**
8.6, 258b10–16: 701,4
8.6, 258b13–16: 700,14
8.6, 259a16–20: 701,19
8.6, 259b20–8: 700,14
8.6, 259b20–31: 701,4
8.7, 260a26–261a26: 700,10
8.7, 261a27: 671,31
8.9, 265a13–27: 701,25
8.9, 265a13–b16: 696,19
8.9, 265b22–3: 716,33
8.10, 266a12–24: 700,4
8.10, 266a24–b6: 700,6
8.10, 267b17–22: 700,1
8.10, 267b17–26: 700,4
*De Caelo* (*Cael.*)
1.3, 269b29–30: 701,24
1.3, 270a33: 701,24
1.3, 270b1: 670,31
1.3, 270b19–24: 670,31
1.3, 270b19–20: 710,30
1.5: 700,7
1.7, 275b21–3: 700,6
1.9, 278b9–21: 709,1
1.9, 279a11–17: 701,22
1.9, 279a20–1: 700,8
1.9, 279a23–8: 699,24
1.10, 279b14–17: 692,1
1.11, 280b22–9: 677,6
1.12: 689,38

1.12, 281a28–b25: 686,26
1.12, 283a20–4: 691,29
1.12, 283a27–8: 688,20
2.1, 283b26–9: 670,31
2.2, 285a29–30: 686,13
2.3, 286a1–9: 701,25
2.3, 286a10–11: 670,31
2.4, 287b14–21: 670,31
2.6, 288a34–b1: 670,31
2.12, 292a18–b25: 701,8
2.12, 292a20–1, b1–2: 686,13; 706,32
2.12, 292b4–7: 695,26
2.12, 293a4–11: 703,4
3.1, 298b19–20: 671,17
3.2, 300b8–10: 690,33
3.4, 303a16: 673,22
*Generation and Corruption* (*GC*)
1.2, 315a26: 672,12
1.2, 316a11: 670,14
1.3, 317a20–2: 716,17
1.3, 318a5–6: 671,17
1.3, 319a15: 694,18
1.7, 324b13: **24**
1.7, 324b17–18: 676,31
2.3, 330a30–b7: 717,35
2.3, 330b33–331a1: 717,35
2.10, 336a31–b15: 692,4.30
2.10, 336a31ff: 683,29
2.10, 336b27–34: 716,17
*Meteorology* (*Meteor.*)
1.3, 339b27–9: 710,30
1.9, 346a20–347a8: 692,30
4.6–10: 674,21
4.12, 390a15: 675,5
*De Mundo* (spurious)
2, 392a25: 720,11
*De Anima* (*DA*)
1.1, 403a2: 670,14
1.1, 403a25: 683,2
1.1, 403a29–b1: 690,8
1.2, 404a3: 673,22
1.2, 405b2: 670,27
1.4, 408b18–30: 678,4
1.4, 408b32–409a30: 720,22
2.1, 412a6–9: 676,7
2.1, 412a8–9: 676,31
2.1, 412b6–8: 721,6
2.1, 413a3–7: 678,4
2.1: 685,14
2.3, 414b2: 694,4
2.4, 415b2–3,21–2: 50 n. 55; 695,26
2.5, 417b3–4: 670,16
2.5, 417b16: 676,31
2.7, 418b7–13: 683,5

## Index of Passages from Other Works

3.4–8: 694,11; 698,14
3.4, 429a13–18: 712,18
3.4, 430a3–5: 694,40; 713,41
3.5, 430a12: **24**
3.5, 430a19–20: 713,41
3.5, 430a20–1: 691,29
3.7, 430b27–31: **25**
3.7, 431a1–2: 713,41
3.7, 431a2–7: 691,29
3.7, 431b16–17: 713,41
3.10, 433a19–20: 694,8
3.10, 433a27–8: 694,5
3.10, 433b10–12: 693,35
3.10, 433b14–18: 693,35
*Parts of Animals (PA)*
  1.1, 640a31–2: 678,9
  1.1, 641a32-b10: 678,4
*Movement of Animals (MA)*
  6, 700b22: 694,4
  6, 700b23–9: 693,35
*Generation of Animals (GA)*
  1.19, 724b12–21: 690,28
  1.21, 729b13: **24**
  2.3, 736b15–29: 678,4
*Metaphysics (Metaph.)*
  1.1, 981b17–19: 696,37
  1.1, 981b28–9: 668,16
  1.2, 982b19–24: 696,37
  1.3: 670,20
  1.3, 983b28–9: 690,8
  1.3, 984a3: 670,27
  1.3, 984a8–11: 673,17
  1.3, 984b8–22: 718,22
  1.4, 985a4–7: 718,16
  1.4, 985a18–21: 718,22
  1.4, 985a21–9: 673,17
  1.4, 985a21–31: 718,10
  1.5, 986a22–6: 694,18
  1.5, 987a19: 671,3
  1.6, 987b14–18: 670,38
  1.6, 987b18–20: 679,22
  1.6, 987b31–3: 670,14
  1.6, 988a14: 717,37
  1.6, 988a14–17: 718,30
  1.8, 989a20–6: 673,17
  1.8, 989a33-b21: 673,9
  1.8, 989b32–3: 702,17
  1.9, 990a31–2: 679,22
  1.9, 991a8-b9: 688,32
  1.9, 991b4–5: 720,19
  1.9, 991b5–7: 677,13
  1.9, 991b9–21: 720,16
  2.1, 993b25: 675,19
  2.2, 994a3–5: 675,16

  3.1, 996a5–6: 679,23
  3.3–4: 678,11
  3.3, 998b9–11: 679,23
  3.3, 998b15–20: 679,23
  3.4, 999b18–20: 676,38
  3.4, 1000a5–1001a3: 673,24
  3.4, 1000a5–1001a13: 668,9
  3.4, 1000a9: 690,11
  4.3, 1005b3: 670,14
  5.1, 1013a19–20: 681,3
  5.2: 681,23
  5.3: 677,28
  5.3, 1014b14–15: 681,3
  5.4, 1014b22–6: 676,11
  5.6, 1016a28: 685,19
  5.6, 1016b12: 669,3
  5.6, 1016b31–1917a3: 678,14
  5.7: 672,33
  5.8, 1017b24–6: 676,31
  5.13, 1020a7–13: 700,20
  5.28, 1024b9: 685,19
  5.30: 679,9
  6.1, 1026a5–6: 678,4
  6.1, 1026a12: 671,11
  6.1, 1026a19: 671,13
  6.1, 1026a23–32: 671,13
  7.1, 1028a31-b2: 670,3
  7.2, 1028b19–20: 670,38
  7.2, 1028b20: 688,30
  7.2, 1028b20–4: 721,11
  7.2, 1028b21–4: 671,3
  7.3, 1029a2–7: 676,7
  7.4, 1029b13: 670,14
  7.7, 1032b1–14: 678,9
  7.8, 1033a24-b19: 674,35
  7.8, 1033a24-b5: 675,5
  7.8, 1033b5–8: 674,36
  7.8, 1034a7–8: 709,5
  7.9, 1034a9–25: 678,9
  7.10, 1035b30: 675,5; 677,26
  7.12, 1038a6: 685,19
  7.13: 670,16
  7.13, 1038b5: 676,31
  7.13, 1038b11: 670,23
  7.14, 1309a24–34: 670,13
  7.17, 1041a28: 670,14
  8.1, 1042a14–16: 670,13
  8.1, 1042a26–31: 676,7
  8.1, 1042a29: 676,31
  8.1, 1042b5–6: 673,31
  8.2, 1043a26–8: 676,7
  8.3, 1043b14–16: 677,6
  8.3, 1043b16–17: 674,36
  8.3, 1043b18–21: 678,4

8.3, 1043b19–21: 676,38
8.4, 1044b6–8: 673,31
8.5, 1044b31–4: 676,31
8.6, 1045b18: 677,26
9.8, 1049b17–27: 691,21
9.8, 1049b24–6: 691,29
9.8, 1050b21–2: 673,31
9.8, 1050b22–8: 712,13
9.10, 1051a34-b2: 674,6
9.10, 1051b17–32: 698,26
10.1, 1052a22: 669,3
10.1, 1053a33-b6
10.1, 1053b4–6: 669,8
10.3–4: 671,30
10.6, 1057a2–4: 700,20
10.7: 671,30
10.8, 1058a22: 685,19
11.1, 1059b16–18: 671,11
11.2, 1060a20–1: 719,35
11.4, 1061b17–19: 671,13
11.4, 1061b19: 671,13
11.7, 1064a15: 671,11
11.7, 1064b3: 671,13
11.9, 1066a15–17: 694,18
11.11, 1067b25–30: 674,6
13.1, 1076a17–22: 670,38
13.1, 1076a20–1: 671,3
13.3, 1078a31–2: 694,1
13.5: 720,16
13.5, 1079b8–9: 670,13
13.5, 1080a5–6: 677,13
13.9, 1085b4–12: 720,36
13.10, 1087a5: 679,22
14.1, 1087b4–6: 717,21
14.2: 720,16
14.2, 1089a26–31: 674,6
14.3, 1090b13–20: 671,3; 721,15
14.4, 1091a33–6: 699,37
14.4, 1091a33-b8: 690,8
14.4, 1091b15–1092a5: 699,31
14.4, 1091b31–2: 717,20; 718,2
14.4, 1091b32–5: 717,21
14.5, 1092a9–17: 699,37
14.6: 720,16
14.6, 1093b12–13: 694,19
Nicomachean Ethics (EN)
1.13, 1102a26–1103a3: 678,4
3.3, 1112b23: 686,36
3.4, 1113a23–4: 694,5
3.5, 1114b6: 686,19
6.6, 1141b2–3: 668,16
7.13, 1153b9–11: 697,4
9.8, 1168a35: 693,16
10.7: 698,34
10.7, 1177a26–7: 696,37

10.8, 1178b19–20: 710,40
10.8, 1178b21–3: 696,36; 698,34
10.9, 1179a21: 693,16
Eudemian Ethics (EE)
1.8, 1217b21: 670,14
2.1, 1219b26–1220a2: 99
7.15, 1248b17–20: 694,1
8.3, 1249b15: 695,26
Politics (Pol.)
1.3: 715,34
3.6, 1278b11: 715,34
3.7, 1279a25–7: 715,34
3.13, 1284b25–34: **23**
3.16, 1288a15–29: **23**
7.10, 1329b25–30: 710,30
8.5, 1339b15–19: 696,37
Poetics (Poet.)
21, 1457b16–19: 678,14
Averroes
Tafsīr mā baʿd aṭ-Ṭabīʿa (Tafsīr)
1491–2: 678,9
1525: 681,6
1537: 682,30
1569: 689,27

Empedocles
fr. 17: 692,1
frr. 22, 25, 36: 673,17

Herodotus
Histories
2.3,5; 2.76,3: 710,25
Hesiod
Theodicy
116–17: 690,11
Works and Days
17: 690,11
Homer
Iliad
2.204: **2,23**; 721,31

Michael of Ephesus
in librum quintum ethicorum
Nicomacheorum commentarium
(in EN)
50,6–9: **9**
142,5: 716,26
570,21: **6**
in parva naturalia commentaria (in PA)
149,8–16: **5**

Philoponus
in Aristotelis de anima libros
commentaria (in DA)
75,34–76,1: 695,26

Plato
  *Laws*
    10,894C-899B: 691,16
    10,903D: 678,23
  *Parmenides (Parm.)*
    130C-D: 677,20
  *Phaedo*
    100D: 720,19
  *Phaedrus*
    245C-246A: 691,16
  *Republic (Rep.)*
    5,477A: 719,22
    6,510B-511D: 670,38
  *Timaeus (Tim.)*
    30A: 690,32
    30A: 691,16
    34A-C: 691,16
    46D-E: 691,16
    52D-53B: 690,32
    52B: 687,5
Plotinus
  *Enneads*
    5.2.1: **24**
Porphyry
  *Life of Plotinus*
    14: **4**
Ps.-Alexander
  *in Aristotelis Metaphysica commentaria
    (in Metaph.)*
    455,12: 714,33
    462,29-31: 670,27
    462,34-463,1: 721,11
    486,17: 714,33
    494,26-496,6: 674,35
    495,23: 714,33
    496,22: 714,33
    497,38-40: 709,5
    559,20: 714,33
    561,24: 714,33
    567,24: **8**
    592,25-40: 712,13
    611,27-612,7: 669,8
    630,31-2: **8**
    641,11-12: **8**
    723,37-724,7: 671,3
    741,36-7: **8**
    745,29-32: **5**
    745,31-2: 671,3
    766,6-8: 671,3
    770,11-772,28: 700,25
    780,12-5: 720,36
    782,14.16: 702,8
    782,31-2: 671,3
    794,13: **6, 24**
    796,10-797,17: 717,21
    797,12-17: **29 n. 22**
    815,26-816,19: 721,15
    823,12-14: 718,2
    828,12-14: 717,21

Simplicius
  *in Aristotelis de caelo commentaria
    (in Cael.)*
    270,5-12: 709,17
    380,5-7: 707,8
    381,2-18: 707,1
    382,10-16: 707,8
    482,10-15: 706,32
    488,18-24: 702,24
    491,12-14: 703,4
    491,17-28: 703,22
    493,11-13: 703,16
    493,14-17: 703,27
    493,15-17: 703,34
    493,17-20: 703,22
    493,4-8: 702,24
    494,5-6: 703,23
    494,6-9; 495,10-13: 703,25
    497,17-24: 704,13
    498,4-10: 704,21
    499,16-500,14: 704,23
    500,24-501,1: 704,32
    500,5-14: 705,5
    502,20-7: 706,15
    502,27-503,9: 705,36
    503,10-504,1: 705,41
    503,19-27: 706,15
    503,35-504,1: 706,8
    504,7-15: 704,21
    506,5: 706,16
  *in Aristotelis physicorum libros
    quattuor priores commentaria
    (in Phys.)*
    238,8-14: 672,36
  *in Aristotelis physicorum libros
    quattuor posteriores
    commentaria (in Phys.)*
    1226,10-1227,33: **14**
    1360,24-1363,24: **24**
Syrianus
  *in metaphysica commentaria (in
    Metaph.)*
    166,26-8: **29 n. 22**

Themistius
  *in Aristotelis metaphysicorum librum
    12 paraphrasis (in Metaph.)*
    2,6: 670,16
    6,32: 676,38
    16,20 ff.: 693,30

# Subject Index

This index lists philosophical topics, ancient philosophers and astronomers, and Greek commentators. Page references in **bold** are to the introduction. Page and line references in regular type are to the Greek text of the commentary (the suffix '-n' indicates additional information in the accompanying note).

accidental – in itself, *kata sumbebêkos – kath' hauto* 672,33n; 672,33; 673,1; 680,23n; 698,8; 700,13f; 701,2–4.11f.15; 713,5
accidents, *ta sumbebêkota*, distinguished from substances 669,4; 679,9n; 681,28ff; 685,8
 be accidental to, *sumbainein* 672,35–6
account, *logos*, as form 675,24; 678,8
 as definition 683,15; 709,17f.21; 713,33
 *see also* definition
Achilles, as example 682,26; 684,15
action, *praxis*, for the sake of an end 695,32
 to act, *prattein*, for the sake of an end 695,29–32; 715,36ff
activity, *energeia*, of prime mover 697,4n; 699,17f
 of heavenly spheres 706,38
 to act, *energein* **12**; 688,18 *passim*; 697,10; 720,27f
 *see also* actuality
actuality, *energeia*, opposed to potentiality **2, 12, 14**; 682,8ff; 688,16.19; 689,19.22; 712,18f
 and the heaven 686,22ff; 696,8ff
 as prime mover 709,15f.25; 719,34
 prior to potentiality 691,21n; 692,39; 720,27n
 *see also* activity
actualization, *entelekheia*, as efficient cause 685,11 *passim*
actually – potentially, *energeiai – dunamei* 672,26ff; 674,10ff; 694,22f
affection, attribute, *pathos*, of substance 669,30
 change of, i.e. alteration 685,36–9
 *see also* quality

affecting – being affected, *poiein – paskhein* 685,36–9; 687,16
air, *aêr*, a primary element 672,37; 676,26; 680,35f
Alcibiades, as example 682,26
Alexander of Aphrodisias, commentator **3–4, 15, 23**; 670,16n; 685,30n; 699,4n; 709,17n
 as cited by Averroes **3–4**; 668,17n *passim*
 as copied by Ps.-Alexander **7–10**
 *see also* Alexander of Aphrodisias in Index of Passages from Other Works
alteration, *alloiôsis*, change of quality 672,13; 677,8
Ammonius, commentator **23**
analogy, *analogia, analogos*, principles (causes, elements) same by analogy 678,14n; 680,37; 682,7 *passim*; 695,20
 form analogous to actuality 682,37
 intellect analogous to knower 697,34
analysis, *analusis*, method of proof 686,36; 693,13
Anaxagoras, said all things were together 673,7.9n; 674,17; 690,17
 on the good as cause 717,30ff
 on the Intellect **23**; 691,32; 716,32; 718,22 *passim*
animal, living being, *zôion*, as perishable substance 670,30.34
 as example 676,17; 680,14; 681,9f.14–16; 690,27
 as genus prior to human species 689,26
 immovable mover 699,20 *passim*; 709,9.25
 moved by soul 701,6.18
 rational – non-rational 678,4n; 691,7

animate things, *ta empsukha*, substances possessing soul 678,3; 682,2
  better than inanimate, *ta apsukha* 686,13ff
  *see also* soul
Anna Comnena, patroness of commentators **6–7**
appearance, imagination, *phantasia*, as mental occurrence 677,9.12; 691,6
  'by appearing' (*tôi phainesthai*) understood as 'in appearance' (*kata phantasian*) 676,8 *passim*
  appearing noble, 694,1
appetite, *epithumia*, non-rational desire 694,2f
  object of appetite, *epithumêtos* 693,40f
Aquarius, *hudrokhoos*, a constellation 673,31
Ariston, father of Plato, as example 678,8
Aristotle, mentioned by name 691,30; 692,1; 701,9–10; 703,1; 704,20; 705,38; 706,12–13; 710,25; 717,29; 719,2
  keen intelligence of 690,3
arithmetic, *arithmêtikê*, a mathematical science 702,16ff; 713,33
army, *strateuma*, analogous to cosmos 715,9.12
art, *tekhnê*, as cause 675,20 *passim*; 678,8
  and form 675,22–4; 678,9; 713,19ff
  repeatedly perishing and being rediscovered 710,29f
artefact, *tekhnêtês*, caused by form in soul 677,1; 678,8
astronomy, *astrologia, astronomia*, science concerned with stars 702,13
atom, *atomos*, Leucippus 690,33

bad, *kakos*, contrary to good 693,38; 711,40; 720,26
  Plato on the Bad 717,17
becoming, *genesis, to gignesthai see* coming-to-be
being, existence, reality, *to einai, ontontês*, belongs to substances in the strict sense and to non-substances on account of substance 669,10ff.31n; 681,29ff
  does not come to be from not-being except accidentally 672,28ff;
  in actuality prior to being in potentiality 686,26; 689,29ff; 720,28
  not an element 679,24ff

Plato on Being-Itself 679,22ff
  that which is, *to on*, is twofold potential and actual 672,22.26–32; 718,9
  *see also* not-being
belief, opinion, *doxa*, distinguished from perception and knowledge 713,7f
  religious belief 709,32; 710,31f
  'On Opinion' (Parmenides) 670,21
black, *melas*, an extreme of colour 717,14f; 719,32
body, *sôma*, opposed to soul 675,23; 681,10; 682,3f; 701,8; 720,36
  common, i.e. universal element 670,23n
  heavenly 670,34; 686,9ff.30ff; 696,2; 700,5f
  movable 686,30ff;
  planetary 693,17n.18n
  the fifth 670,37n; 683,21; 715,26ff; 718,3; 719,3
bone, *ostoun*, part of proximate matter of an animal 676,9; 677,26; 680,27; 683,14ff
bronze, *khalkos*, example of matter 675,8; 677,35; 678,18ff

Callias, as example 672,37; 676,34–5; 677,24; 709,5
Callippus, astronomer **15**; 702,24n.34; 703,1; 704,11 *passim*; 705,15.21n.41n; 706,1 *passim*
Capricorn, *aigokerôs*, a constellation 692,24
carry, *pherein see* motion
carrying on, way of, *diagogê*, way of life of the prime mover 687,26; 696,32.37n; 697,6; 710,38; 711,37; 714,26.29
category, *katêgoria*, ten kinds of being 668,15,26; 669,2n.10; 672,7; 678,34ff
cause, *aitia, aition*, first causes and principles **22–3**; 668,11 *passim*; 674,30; 678,10ff; 680,10ff; 681,29ff; 684,8ff.26
  efficient, *poiêtikon*, in general **18, 24**; 677,29ff; 681,17ff; 706,32; Anaxagoras 674,23; Pythagoreans 720,23
  final, *telikon*, in general **2, 18–19, 23**; 708,19f.23; 718,7; that for the sake of which, *hou heneka* 695,24 *passim*

## Subject Index

formal, *eidikon*, in general 677,34.37; 681,22; Platonists 718,7ff; Pythagoreans 720,23
material, *hulikon*, theologians 690,18ff; Empedocles 718,11
moving, *kinêtikon*, in general **2, 11, 18**; 701,35f; of the stars 702,25; 707,16; 708,20 Plato 691,12; 700,33ff; Pythagoreans 720,23ff
the first cause, i.e. prime mover 681,25n; 685,27; 694,14; 695,18f.36; 696,1.27f; 697,2f.7; 701,1; 709,2.8.20; 712,27.30; 714,22; 719,28.30

chance, randomness, *tukhê*, deviation from nature or art 675,27n; 676,2
change not from random opposites 671,29; 674,13–14.28

change, *metabolê*, of quantity, quality, place, and substance 672,1 *passim*
and matter 673,5 *passim*
first intellect not changeable 711,33f; 714,4
forms of artefacts not result of change 677,3
from opposites or intermediates 671,26ff

Chaos, *Khaos*, Hesiod 690,9–12
Christianity **4, 7, 10, 21, 23, 25**
cold, *to psukhron, psukhrotês*, privation of heat 672,4.7; 680,20ff
colour, *khrôma*, a genus of quality 671,31; 716,19
object of sight, 712,4
of heavenly bodies, 715,26
columns, *sustoikhiai*, rankings of opposites (Pythagoreans) 694,18n; 695,18
coming-to-be, generation, *genesis, to gignesthai*, change in substance 672,10f
caused by matter, form, and privation 678,16ff
directed towards form 676,32ff; 693,1.7f
everlasting **13**; 691,30ff; 719,10; 720,8
for the sake of something 695,28f
from what is in actuality and from what is not in potentiality 672,29 *passim*
not of matter or form 674,31ff
of effects from synonymous causes 675,19ff
whether all things come to be 717,7ff

coming-to-be – perishing, *gignesthaii – phtheiresthai* 692,27.30; 716,13ff; 719,3
common, *to koinon*, as universal 670,22; 671,15f; 697,22f
commonality, *koinônia*, of the cosmos 715,24ff; 716,21ff; 721,19
commonwealth, *politeia*, analogous to the cosmos 715,34 *passim*
compound, *to sunthêton*, a unity consisting of elements 679,34; 716,18ff
material substances 687,10; 709,21; 713,22; 714,6ff
compound whole (*sunolon*) of substance and non-substance 669,16
constellations of the zodiac, *sêmeia zôidia* 692,25n; 703,21ff.27n; 704,7ff
contact, touching, *haphê*, of bodies 676,11.24; 677,6.21
thinking as touching or being in contact (*haptesthai, thinganein*) **24**; 698,26n; 714,26.34
contemplation, *theôria*, as investigation 668,20; 671ff; 702,17
divine contemplation 698,34; 699,12; 711,16; 714,27
thinking of simple objects 687,11; 697,29f
contraries, contrariety, *ta enantia, enantiôsis, enantiotês*, all change is into a contrariety 672,15ff
and elements and intermediates 717,36
form and privation 685,15ff
other philosophers make everything from contraries 717,7–15
the reduction of 695,25
cosmos, *kosmos*, everlasting **1, 11, 23**; 687,30
Empedocles 715,4.11.17
orderly and good 714,37ff; 715,4n
Plato 691,10
steered by the gods 709,34–7
unique 709,1–17
*see also* heaven, universe
counteracting sphere, *anelittousa sphaira see* sphere counteracting
Cronus, *Kronos*, a god 710,2; 720,11
cycle, *periodos*, cosmic cycle (Empedocles) 691,38ff; 692,4n

darkness, *skotos*, privation of light 680,36; 683,9
Hesiod 690,11

day, *hêmera*, compound of air and light 680,36; 683,7
cause of 692,27ff; 693,1.7
definition, *horos*, same as cause 668,23; cf. 713,33
see also account
Democritus, said all things were together in potentiality 673,19–22
demonstration, *apodeixis*, deduction or proof 691,30; 693,15; 702,6.12
and necessary truth 696,26
no demonstration of first principle 686,36
Platonists as lacking demonstrative rigour 700,30f
desire, *orexis*, faculty of the soul 682,3f; an object is desired because it seems good 694,5f
of heavenly body 686,34; 701,9
prime mover as the first object of desire (*orekton*) **18**; 687,2.22; 693,31ff; 694,7
see also appetite, yearning
difference, otherness, *to allon, heterotês*, the causes of all things are in a way the same and in a way different 674,16; 678,10 *passim*; 682,7ff
difference of Forms from particulars (Plato) 677,15
efficient cause as different from elements 681,1ff
elements as different from compounds 680,5ff.32ff
not-being as due to otherness 672,32
superlunary and sublunary bodies have different matter 673,23ff
differentia, *diaphora*, as form 697,24.26
disorder, *ataxia*, a certain privation of form 676,19; 681,12
Plato 690,32; 691,11;
social disorder due to the rule by many 721,26ff
divine, *to theion*, substance 670,26; 671,12; 709,29.36; 712,32f
body 708,37; 715,26
intellect 710,37 *passim*; 713,8
multitude 709,34
state of the human intellect 698,34.37; 699,13
duration, timespan, *aiôn* 699,24n; 714,23
Dyad, *duas*, Plato 720,13

earth, *gê*, a primary element 676,26; 679,15ff.27ff; 690,27; 717,35; 721,18f; Parmenides 670,21
central terrestrial sphere **1, 11, 13**; 688,26f; 692,10 *passim*; 718,39
east – west, *anatolê – dusmê* 690,38; 703,15.33
eclipse, *ekleipsis*, cause and definition 668,23n; 713,37n
Egyptians, *Aiguptioi*, concerning the gods 710,18–25
elements, *ta stoikheia*, of perceptible substances 670,31ff; 671,26
and principles 673,24–5; 678,33ff
distinguished from principles 681,1ff
matter, form, and privation as elements 681,7–8
not identical with compounds 679,20ff; 716,18f
the simple things (*ta hapla*), material elements 674,22n; 679,33f
whether the elements of all things are the same 673,24; 678,35n; 680,10 *passim*
emanation, *aporrhoia*, from Forms (Platonists) 688,38; 719,19–20
Empedocles, said everything came from the mixture 673,16
cosmic cycle 692,1–3
Love and Hate **23**; 673,17n; 690,15; 691,34; 718,8 *passim*
end, *telos*, as the best and an object of yearning 707,34; 708,24.36
of heavenly bodies 707,13; 708,38
what completes, *to teleioun*, as more valuable than what is completed 712,18f
equal – unequal, *to ison – to anison*, Plato 717,18–22
essence, *to ti ên einai*, the first essence 709,23f
see also being, substance
Euctemon, astronomer 704,13n
Eudemus, astronomer 702,24n
Eudoxus, astronomer **15**; 702, 24n *passim*; 704,27n.34n; 705–18–19; 706,18–19
Eustatius, commentator 7
everlastingness, eternity, *to aïdion*, of spheres and stars 670,30.32.38
of heavenly motion 700,3; 701,17; 706,21
of prime mover 685,29ff; 686,2ff; 687,32ff; 699,19–25.28.38; 701,1; 709,9ff

## Subject Index

of the first heaven 693,14ff; 696,14
subordinate immovable movers
  689,12ff; 701,29ff
excellence, the 'well-', *to eu*, implies
  necessity 696,24.30
  of the cosmos **2, 21**; 715,10 *passim*
  of the first intellect divine thought
  713,14.26

father – mother, *patêr – mêtêr*, principles
  not elements 681,3; 694,34–6;
  699,34
fire, *pur*, a primary element 676,26;
  677,16ff; 679,15ff.27ff; 691,2;
  717,35
  Heraclitus 670,21
  Pythagoreans 721,13.16f
first, *to proton see* cause; essence; heaven;
  intellect; intelligible object; matter;
  motion; mover; object of desire;
  principle; science; substance
flesh, *sarx*, as matter 676,9; 677,16.21.26;
  680,26; 682,28; 683,14ff
  as form 675,5
force *bia*, opposed to nature 691,2.6
  and necessity 696,24
  animal body forced by soul 701,7
  unforced (*abiastos*) as natural
  706,37
form, *eidos*, in general **18**; 668,6; 674,30;
  678,15ff; 680,12ff; 682,6ff; 684,44ff;
  709,5ff; 717,25ff
  and art 675,22–4; 678,9; 713,19ff
  and change 673,5.29; 675,22.24;
  677,35ff
  and knowledge 687,3ff; 694,38; 695,4;
  697,18ff; 698,1ff; 714,31f
  and matter 690,6ff; 720,37ff;
  enmattered form, *enülon eidos*
  683,2n; 694,27
  and prime mover 688,16.31; 706,32ff;
  715,27ff
  and substance 672,18; 676,7.31ff;
  687,3.18
  cause of difference of things **17**;
  674,19ff; 681,22n; 684,20ff.27n
  substantial form, *ousiôdes eidos* 672,10
Forms, the, *ta eidê*, Platonic [In discussing
  Plato's doctrine, ps.-Alexander uses
  *idea* and *eidos* as equivalent terms.
  The principal texts are reported
  below under 'Ideas'.]
free, *eleutheros*, opposed to slave **21**;
  715,3n

Gaia, a goddess (Hesiod) 690,10
general, *stratêgos*, analogous to prime
  mover 715,11–13
generation *see* coming-to-be
genus, *genos*, as universal 670,13
  and species 684,22
  as category 679,3
  as matter 685,19
  as race 710,14
geometry, *geômetria*, a mathematical
  science 702,16.18; 713,32
god, the, *ho theos*, the prime mover and
  first intellect **1–2, 5, 21–5**; 685,28n;
  699,12ff
  and nature 708,13
  divine multitude 709,34
  the gods, subordinate immovable
  movers **16, 23**;706,33; 707,5;
  709,28ff; 710,1; 721,31f
good, the, *to agathon*, object of desire
  695,34ff
  and the prime mover 695,37;
  707,14.19.34–6; 711,25.38; 717,36
  *passim*; 721,31
  the column of the good 694,21
  the Good-Itself (Plato) 717,19.21.37ff
growth, *auxêsis*, change in quantity
  672,12
  joint growth, *sumphusis*, of organs
  676,18.25; 677,21

healing art, medicine, *iatrikê*, example of
  an art 675,24; 678,8; 681,20;
  713,4–6.19; 718,25
health, *hugieia*, good condition of the
  body 675,23f; 677,36; 681,10; 682,23
  form of health identical with healing
  art 677,11; 678,9; 681,19–21;
  713,4f.20; 718,25f
heat, *to thermon, thermotês*, quality
  opposed to cold 672,4–5.14;
  680,20ff
heaven, *ouranos*, outermost heavenly
  sphere **1, 11, 17**; 696,4 *passim*
  the first 693,16f; 707,22
  the universe outside of the earth
  708,37; 709,1; 718,38; 719,3;
  720,8
  Plato 691,12–14
  Pythagoreans 721,14
Heracles, a god 720,11n
Heraclitus, on fire as principle 710,21
Hesiod, cosmogony 690,9; 719,6
  followers of 719,6

Hippo, called 'godless' 670,27
Homer **11, 22–3**; 721,31n
horse, *hippos*, example of a natural
  substance 672,37; 675,26; 678,19;
  684,21; 695,15; 709,14
house, *oikia*, example of an artefact 675,22;
  677,11f.31; 681,11.21; 713,19ff;
  716,37ff
  housebuilder 675,23; 677,30f; 681,12
  housebuilding 681,21; 713,18ff
  household 715,33
human being, *anthrôpos*, as species
  posterior to genus animal 689,26f
  as example of a natural substance
    671,36; 674,14f; 675,30–32;
    676,1f; 684,21; 695,15; 697,22ff;
    709,10ff
  causes of human generation 683,12
    *passim*; 699,36
  human soul opposed to divine intellect
    711,2 *passim*; 712,9ff
  proximate causes of 682,3f.28; 691,3
humour, *khumos*, Hippocratic 675,4n

ibis, sacred bird in Egypt 710,21–5
Ideas, the, *hai idea* [Under this term are
  included citations to the Platonic
  Forms, *ta eidê*]
  as causes **23**; 678,6; 688,29–40;
    717,19ff; 719,12ff; 720,6 *passim*
  as genera or universals 676,36
  distinct from numbers 671,3ff
imagination *see* appearance
immaterial things, *ta aüla*, the heavenly
  movers **11**; 689,12; 694,40; 695,2;
  699,7; 709,15.25; 713,39; 714,10;
  719,34
  forms in soul separate from matter
    677,11; 697,21ff; 698,15ff;
    713,29f
immovable objects, *ta akinêta*, the Ideas
  (Plato) 671,1; 688,37
immovable mover *see* mover
imperishable things, *ta aphtharta*, the
  heavenly bodies and their
  motions 670,33; 671,9.27; 673,28ff;
  685,34; 687,30ff; 715,26; 719,2–4;
  720,9
  Hate (Empedocles) 718,18–21.40
incorporeality, *to asômaton*, of the
  heavenly movers 686,30; 694,40;
  700,1.8.12; 703,2; 720,6f
induction, *epagôgê*, method of proof
  679,20; 680,18; 689,22

ingenerable things, *ta agenêta*, the
  heavenly bodies 673,30; 676,6;
  687,29ff; 718,9; 720,9
  *see also* ungenerated
intellect *nous*, of human beings **11**; 678,4;
  682,3; 696,33; 697,1.10; 712,13.15;
  714,16ff
  actual human 694,32; 695,21; 697,16ff;
    698,1ff.35ff; 712,15; 714,25
  dispositional human 695,21; 697,17ff
  divine **2, 5, 20–5**; 695,8; 698,20.23.36ff;
    699,1ff.16f.19–21; 707,2.5f.21;
    710,36f; 711,20.32; 712,12; 713,13;
    714,12.23ff.32; 715,7.14f;
    719,13f.28f; 721,33
  potential human 697,18f; 698,26
  the Intellect (Anaxagoras) 673,8;
    674,23; 690,17; 691,34; 718,22ff
intelligible object, *ta noêta*, in general
  693,31ff; 696,33f; 698,8ff;
  712,36n;713,12ff
  element 679,23f;
  first substance 694,7
  prime mover **1, 8, 20–1**; 670,26.37;
    687,2ff.22; 694,7 695,8.18; 699,2ff;
    720,4.6
  object of thinking *see* thinking
intermediary, *mesos*, between mover and
  moved **14**; 693,20.24f
intermediate *metaxu*, between opposites
  671,29; 672,1; 679,15; 717,35
  between actuality and potentiality
    697,36

Jupiter, *Zeus*, second outermost planet
  689,11; 700,35; 703,18.22; 705,16ff;
  720,11
justice, *dikaiosunê*, as a number
  (Pythagoreans) 721,14

knowledge, *epistêmê*, in general 696,24.33;
  697,35–7
  and perception 713,1ff
  human knowledge, *gnôsis*, of divine
    intellect 714,34
  *see also* science

law, *nomos*, function of 710,3.23; 716,4
Leucippus, on eternal movement
  690,29–33
life, *zôê*, of prime mover 697,2–5;
  699,16–31
  best human life 696,34ff; 697,7
  way of life, *bios*, of human beings 710,4

light, *phôs*, actuality of the transparent
    medium, i.e. air 680,35ff; 683,5ff
  Pythagoreans 694,19
living being *see* animal
logically, *logikôs*, in terms of definition
    670,14n
love, value, *philia, agapein, eran*, towards
    activities 697,12; 702,29
  Love – Hate (Empedocles) **23**; 690,16;
    691,34; 718,8ff
  prime mover as object of loving (*eran*)
    **2, 19**; 695,39–696,2; 707,2

manuscripts of Ps.-Alexander's
    commentary **25–6**
manuscripts of Aristotle's *Metaphysics* **27**
Mars, *Arês*, third outermost planet 704,17;
    705,30.33
mathematics, *mathêmatikê*, and astronomy
    702,8.15.21.23
  Plato 671,2.4ff
matter, *hulê*, as principle, underlying form
    and privation **17–18**; 668,5; 672,30;
    678,15ff; 682,6ff.33.35;
  and change and coming-to-be
    672,6.19; 673,6ff; 680,20ff; 716,21
  and form 687,4ff.15.18; 690,6ff;
    694,27.38; 695,2ff; 697,20–4;
    721,1ff
  as substance 676,5ff
  different things have different matter
    674,19ff; 680,12ff; 683,14ff; 684,14
    *passim*; 685,19ff
  local 673,31n
  Plato 687,5; 691,11; 717,16ff; 719,17ff
  prime 674,22n.34; 675,3.5n.14;
    677,22f.25; 715,31.34
  proximate 674, 21.23; 675,5n; 677,26n;
    717,30.35
menstrual fluid, *katamênion* 674,15n;
    690,28n; 699,31–5
Mercury, *Hermês*, second innermost
    planet 704.12; 705,30.33
Meton, astronomer 704,13n
Michael of Ephesus, commentator **3, 5–10**;
    668,1n
mind *see* intellect
mixture, *migma*, a condition of the
    cosmos, Empedocles 673,17.19;
    Anaxagoras 691,33
moon, *selênê*, innermost planet 703,6.29ff
mortal, *to thnêton*, characteristic of
    non-rational souls 678,5
mother *see* father – mother

motion, locomotion, *phora*; impart
    motion, carry, *pherein*; undergo
    motion, *pheresthai* defined as
    change of place 672,13; 703,26n
  circular 686.10.14f.33; 696,1f; 708,32;
    716,29–31; 717,9
  heavenly **11–12, 16, 19**; 673,31; 691,6;
    692,16,23ff; 695.10; 696,12.14;
    701,23ff; 702,20; 704,5ff; 708,25ff
  the first 696,8.10
  *see also* movement
movement, *kinêsis*; impart movement,
    *kinein*; be moved, *kineisthai*, in
    general 669,27; 671,10f; 672,7.13;
    681,35; 688,1f; 691,1ff
  Anaxagoras 718,28
  and efficient cause 681,1ff.14; 695,22ff
  and final cause 693,31ff; 694,8ff;
  and moving cause 686,16ff; 693,14ff;
    701,14ff;
  heavenly movement is circular
    695,22ff; 696,13ff
  heavenly movement is everlasting
    **11–12, 17, 19**; 685,33ff; 686,2ff;
    687,37ff
  Leucippus 690,29–33
  Plato 690,29–32; 700,21ff; 720,18
  Pythagoreans 720,18
  *see also* motion and mover
mover, *to kinoun, to kinêtikon*, cause of
    movement 686,22; 687,3.11f;
    689,9.14.16; 701,36
  immovable **2, 11, 13–19**; 668,23; 670,38;
    686,28 *passim*; 687,32ff; 688,15
    *passim*; 693,23–30; 695,11f.24;
    696,16; 700,8f.14; 701,1 *passim*;
    707,12–14; *see also* prime mover
  the mover missing from Plato's account
    719,21; 721,5
myth, *muthos*, traditional belief in the
    gods 709,32–710,16.25–35
  Egyptian 710,16–25

natural, *phusikos*, of a substance
    possessing a nature 672,9ff;
    675,25.33; 681,15–17; 687,28
  science, *hê phusikê* 671,10ff
  theorist *ho phusikos* 690,10ff
natural – unnatural movement 691,8
nature, *phusis*, essence 687,1.26; 692,5;
    696,5.13
  as formal cause 675,20; 676,18.30;
    688,31–3; 706,36ff; 708,13; 715,32;
    716,10ff

as perceptible universe **22**; 669,22; 670,28; 696,31; 709,34; 714,35f
does nothing in vain, *matên* 708,6.12f; 710,12
Plato 676.38; 677,13ff
necessity, *anankê, to anankaion*, belongs to everlasting motion and the first mover 696,14 *passim*
opposed to reasonableness 706,30
Neoplatonism **4–5, 9–10, 24–7**
night, *nux*, compound of air and darkness 680,37; 692,27ff; 693,1.6.7
Night (Hesiod) 690.11f; 691,37; 692,37; 693,10
not-being, nothingness, *to mê einai*, that which is not, *to mê on*, spoken of in three ways 674,6n *passim*
followers of Hesiod not-being as first principle 692,38; 719,6–9
universals as not-beings 670,16
whether forms (e.g. souls) when separated pass into nothingness 678,2
*see also* being
notion, *ennoia*, epistemic state inferior to knowledge 697,30; 702,24; 709,31
number, *arithmos*, number, distinguished from amount, *plêthos* 700,20n
same – different (or one – many) in number or in species 681,19; 684,23; 688,23.30; 709,4ff.13n
the number of heavenly spheres **15–20**; 700,13 *passim*
the numbers, *hoi arithmoi* (Pythagoreans and Platonists) 688,30; 720,12ff

obliqueness, *to loxon*, of a planetary orbit **13**; 683,28ff; 692,6 *passim*; 703,23 *passim*
one, *heis*, not an element 679,24ff
Anaxagoras 673,7; 679,24
cosmos as unitary and unique 669,10.22; 709,1ff
distinguished from *haplos* 695,9–15
one movement has one mover 701,35–7; 706,21
Plato 679,22ff; 717,22f.38
unity, *hê henas* 689,15
unification, *henôsis* 676,17.21ff; 720,34.36
opinion, *doxa see* belief
opposites, *ta antikeimena*, from which there is change 671,29 *passim*

order, *taxis*, of parts in a substance 676,17ff
of the heavens **1–2, 22**; 686,8; 704,9 *passim*; 709,36f; 715,3 *passim*; 721,28
otherness *see* difference

Parmenides, followers of 670,21; 719,7
participation, *metalêpsis*, partake, *metekhein*, in being 669,29
in intelligible object 698,24f
Plato 717,38
perception, *aisthêsis*, faculty of the soul 697,8
and its objects 694,35f; 698,2; 713,1.7
basis for intellectual thought 697,29–32
perceptible objects, *ta aisthêta*, bodies with magnitude and shape 716,25
as forms identical with perception 694,35; 698,2
Plato 677,16
substances 669,4.18f; 670.26; 671,15ff; 673,27f; 676,5; 706,23; 715,1
perishing *see* coming-to-be
philosophy, *philosophia*, distinguished from natural science 671,13; 702,14; 706,31; 715,16
first 671,13n
Pisces, *ikhthues*, a constellation 673,32
planet, planetary star, *planêtês astêr*, lit. wandering star **14–19, 23**; 693,18.20; 700,35f
*see also* sphere and star
plant, *phuton*, genus of living substance 670,30.35; 690,28; 715,20
Plato, son of Ariston **4, 7**; 678,8
lost writings 695,26n
as example 680,8; 682,26; 685,1; 709,5.10
on 'bastard reasoning' 687,5
on mathematical objects 670,38n; 671,3
on motion 690,29–31; 691,9–16.21n
on the contrary as substratum 717,19–21
on the Forms **12, 23**; 670,18; 677,12; 720.6.14ff
on the good and the bad 717,17.39ff; 719,20
pleasure, *hêdonê*, of contemplation 696,35; 697,5; 699,12
plenitude, principle of **12**; 688,20n

Plotinus, philosopher **24**
polis, *polis*, city-state 710,7
  analogous to cosmos **21-2**; 715,36ff
polytheism, opposed to Christianity **23**
Porphyry, philosopher **4**
potentiality, *dunamis*, relation to actuality **2, 12**; 682,8ff; 687,16; 689,3ff.19ff; 691,17ff; 692,40; 712,19
  and change 672,22ff; 674,10ff
  as matter 672,19ff
  Democritus 673,19-20
  is not always actual 688,20; 689,25ff
  none in prime mover 686,24; 688,17n *passim*; 719,34f
  posterior to actuality 691,21n; 692,39; 720,27n
  potential intellect 697,18; 712,3ff; 720,27f
  unlimited potentiality 700,4f
  *see also* actuality
prime mover, *to prôton kinêtikon*, first cause of heavenly motion **1-2, 11-12, 15-18, 20-5**; 707,12-14; 701,15ff
  as the Intellect in Anaxagoras 718,22.27
  *see also* mover, immovable
principle, *arkhê*, source or beginning **11, 22**; 668,3 *passim*
  and causes 678,10ff
  distinguished from element, *stoikheion* 681,1ff
  matter, form, and privation 675,1
  nature or art 675,29f; 716,10f.14
  of substance 681,28ff
  principles of all things in a way the same and in a way different 673,24; 680,10 *passim*
  the first principle 668,3ff; 686,36; 687,25; 688,23.30; 689,23f; 693,13ff; 696,22-31; 699,28; 700,13; 701,10f; 709,8; 719,32ff; 721,31ff
privation, *sterêsis*, contrary of state 668,9n; 669,35; 671,37; 672,18.20.31; 673,6; 675,1; 678,15ff; 680,12ff.35ff; 682,6ff.33.35; 683,32ff; 684,25; 685,4ff; 717,26.32
proximate – ultimate, *prosekhes – eskhaton* 675,5; *see also* matter proximate
Ps.-Alexander, commentator, identity of **3-7**
Ps.-Philoponus, commentator **5**

puzzle, *aporia*, whether all things have one principle and element 673,24
  book concerning puzzles, i.e. *Metaph*. 3 668,11
  from what kind of not-being there is coming-to-be 674,4
  whether potentiality is prior to actuality 689,20; 690,2; 691,17; 693,2
  whether the different categories have the same elements and principles 678,33
  whether the first intellect is best in virtue of thinking or in virtue of being thought 713,9f.17
  whether the first intellect thinks and, if so, whether it thinks of itself or of something else 710,37
  whether the object of thinking is simple or composite 714,2
Pythagoreans, on the numbers as principles 720,4-6.14-15
  on the relationship between mathematical objects and the Ideas 671,3n
  theory of columns 694,19-20
  deny that the good is a principle 699,29-30; 718,1-5
  make nature episodic 721,11-15
  posit many principles 721,25

quality, *to poion, poiotês*, a category of being 669,7-8.19; 678,34ff
  alteration as change of quality (or affection) 672,1 *passim*
  posterior to substance 669,2ff; 687,33
quantity, *to poson*, a category of being 669,7 *passim*; 678,34ff
  growth or diminution as change of quantity 672,13 *passim*
  posterior to substance 669,27ff; 687,33

rational part, *to logikon, to logistikon, ho logos*, a faculty of the soul 711,6; 694,3
reality, *huparxis*, existence or subsistence 679,37; 684,16; 688,6; 721,3.8.10
reality, *hupostasis*, as opposed to thought 677,1
reason, *logos*, distinguished from fact or observation, *ergon* 693,15
reasonable, *eulogos* 698,14; 706,23.28ff; 707,3

reduction, *anagoge*, of the contraries 695,25f
relative, *ta pros ti*, a category of being 678,34ff; 679,9n.35; 680,3ff.30ff; 698,11.13
rest, *êremia*, privation of movement 671,11; 697,39; 701,24
ruler, *arkhos*, one ruler opposed to many, *poluarkhia* **2**, **22**; 721,26–8
'let there be one sovereign', *koiranos* (Homer) **2**; 721,31

Saturn, *Kronos*, outermost planet **13**; 689,11; 692,7.11ff; 700,35; 703,18.22; 705,16ff; 720,11
science, *epistêmê*, study of first principles 684,14ff
    natural 671,11n
    productive versus theoretical 713,31
    perished and rediscovered 710,19.31
    *see also* knowledge
Scorpio, *skorpio*, a constellation 692,24
seed, semen, *sperma*, *gonê* 674,15n; 690,28n; 699,30–7
separation, separability, *khôrismos*, *khôris*, *khôrizein*, *khôristos*, of substance from non-substance 669,5; 669,39ff; 681,30ff
    of Ideas and mathematical objects from perceptible particulars (Plato) 670,38ff; 721.10
    of intelligible form (or universal) in thought from matter 683,1–6; 694,28–695,8; 697,20; 698,30
    of mover generally from thing moved 686,35
    of prime mover from perceptible objects 699,38
    of substantial form, e.g. of soul from body after death 678,1
shape, *skhêma*, a form of perceptible objects *skhêma*, shape 678,18.20; 715,25.27; 716,24.26
sickness, *nosos*, privation of health 681,10; 682,24f; 713,6
simple, *haplous*, of the intelligible object 687,8ff; 694,22
    of the divine intellect 699,5ff
    of the first heavenly movement 706,21
    of the prime mover 701,21.35–7
    stated simply (*haplôs*), without qualification 669,24 *passim*
    the simple distinguished from the one, *heis* 695,9–16; 701,35–7

simple things *see* elements
Simplicius, commentator **5**, **8**, **14–15**, **23**, **27**; 702,24n; 703,2n *passim*
    as copied by Ps. Alexander **8**, **27**
    *see also* Simplicius in Index of Passages from Other Works
slave, *andrapodon*, *doulos*, opposed to free **21–2**; 715,39; 716,4
Socrates, as example 672,31; 675,4.6; 676,9ff; 678,23ff; 679,14f; 680,8; 681,18; 682,22ff; 683,13ff; 690,7; 691,21.23; 695,30; 709,5ff; 720,33
solstice *see* turning
Sophroniscus, father of Socrates, as example 677,30; 678,7.28; 681,18; 683,13ff
Sosigenes, astronomer **3**, **15**; 702,24n; 704,21n.23n; 706,13
soul, *psukhê*, substantial form of living thing 682,2
    cause of movement 686,17f; 701,16f
    cosmic soul (Plato) 691,11–16
    rational – non-rational soul 678,4–5
    soul distinguished from intellect 711,3ff
    souls of the heavenly spheres 706,32; 707,1ff
    *see also* animate
sovereign, *koiranos*, analogous to prime mover 721,31
species, *eidos*, opposed to genus 689,26ff; 684,22
    same in species, *homoeidês* 684,22
    same (or different) in number – in species 681,19; 684,22f; 688,23.30; 709,4ff
Speusippus, the best is not a principle 699,29; 670,19n; 671,3n; 718,5n; 721,11n.15n
sphere, *sphaira*, cause of observed stellar motion **1**, **13**, **15–17**, **19**; 670,30.35; 677,35; 700,36f; 709,28
    counteracting (*anelittousa*) **15**; 704,15ff; 705,6ff.25ff; 706,15n; 708,10
    first, i.e. outermost sphere of the fixed stars **11–17**, **19**; 689,10.13.14; 690,37; 692,12ff.40; 693,3.10.13f; 701,4f.22; 703,11ff
    lunar 703,6.29ff
    planetary 689,10f; 690,38n; 693,18.20; 701,25ff; 707,12f; 721,32
    solar **13**; 692,29.30.32; 693,3.7
    starless (Theophrastus) 703,22

Subject Index 259

the Sphere, i.e. blended cosmos
(Empedocles) **23**; 673,17;
718,9.11
total number of planetary spheres
**15-17**; 700,13-20; 702,4 *passim*;
706,15n
spontaneity, *to automaton*, deviation from
nature or art 675,27n; 676,2
star, *astêr*, heavenly object formed of fifth
body **19**; 670,31.36; 708,38
fixed, *aplanês* **13**; 689,10n; 692,18;
700,36n; 703,10f
planetary, lit. wandering, *planêtês*,
*planômenos* 693,18.20; 700,36n;
704,24.26; 705,11ff
state, possession, *hexis* 669,37n; 671,30n
statue, *andrias* – sculptor, *andriantopoios*,
as example 678,18ff.28; 680,13;
683,10; 684,9f
substance, *ousia*, in general 668,13 *passim*;
675,19ff.31ff; 677,24; 678,33ff;
680,3ff.24ff; 681,28ff; 687,33
as substantial form or essence 672,9.17;
676,30; 680,25; 687,6ff; 689,3.7;
696,12; 698,7.28; 711,4ff; 713,30
first, i.e. prime mover **1-2, 8-12**;
668,17n; 685,27; 695,11; 699,37;
701,33-5; 710,27
Pythagoreans 694,19f
three kinds perceptible perishable,
perceptible imperishable, and
intelligible 670,25 *passim*; three
kinds matter, form, and compound
676,5ff
to have substance, *ousiousthai* 712,2.8ff
Substratum, *hupokeimenon*, and matter
670.36; 675,9ff; 677,20ff; 680,23;
682,32-5; 715,25ff; 717,16ff
subject matter of a science 668,16f
sun, *hêlios*, fourth innermost (or
outermost) planet **13**; 673,31
and solar sphere 692,29ff; 703,13
*passim*
efficient cause of coming-to-be and
perishing 683,12ff.28ff; 692,7-35
synonymous, *sunônumos*, sameness of
name of cause and effect 675,19n
*passim*
Syrianus, commentator **4-5, 8**

Themistius, commentator 670,16
theologian, *theologos*, explaining cosmos
in terms of gods 690,8n; 719,22;
720,10

Theophrastus, on 'starless' spheres 703,22
theoretical knowledge, investigation,
contemplation, *theôria*, as scientific
study 668,13.18; 671,13.17; 702,17
and divine intellect 698,34; 699,12;
711,16; 714,27
contemplation or 'theoretical vision' of
intelligible objects 687,11 697,29f
thing, object, *pragma*, being in the strict
sense 670,15
Anaxagoras 674,18; 720,32f
and matter 721,1
as object of thinking 713,28.34
thinking, *noein*, by the human intellect
694,11n.12ff; 698,1ff
by a divine intellect 686,33; 699,1ff
capable of thinking, *noêtikos* 699,11
that which thinks 699,4; 712,36ff
the object of thinking 694,38; 699,3;
712,36n
think of itself 697,4.6; 698,4ff.35ff;
699,1ff; 711,1f.23ff
thought, *noêma* 697,30.39
*see also* intelligible
thinking, act of, *noêsis* **20**; 694,8ff.11n;
697,8; 698,17ff; 711,12n; 712,1ff
this-something, *tode ti*, as individual
substance 676,8.16
as form 676.30; 677,23
time, *khronos*, as everlasting **12**; 687,38ff
a short time, or temporal interval
(*khronikê paratasis*) 677,2; 696,37;
714,7ff
priority in time of efficient cause
677,30; 683,19
touch *see* contact
transparency, *to diaphanês*, medium for
light 683,6-8
triangle, *trigônos*, Pythagoreans 694,19;
721,12.22
truth, *alêtheia, to alêthes alêtheia*, in
statement 676,24.28f; 690,4
as being 674,5
turning, *tropê*, of sun or moon at solstice
703,27n.33.38; 704,1

unaffectable, *apathês*, immovable movers
700,8; 708,16.18
ungenerated, *agennêtos*, heavenly
bodies 676,6
Eleatics on being 719,9
*see also* ingenerable
unity *see* one
universal, *to katholou*, as genus 670,16n

and causes 684,9ff.32ff
and principles 678,13ff; 680,16; 682,13ff
formed by intellect 670,16; 695,7; 697,19.22.30
Plato 670,8ff
universal – particular, *katholou – kath' hekaston* 670,13n; 681,2-4; 684,12ff; 695,7.38
universe, as everything, *to pan* **11, 21-2**; 669,3n; 673,8; 674,23; 701,21; 715,13.15
as the whole, *to holon* 709,34; 714,27.35; 715,19; 716,7.10.22f.34
see also cosmos, heaven
unlimited, the, *to apeiron*, and the first cause 695,37; 700,4; 707,7f.10
and time 690,33; 691,36;
regress 675,9.13; 686,25.30; 720,10
unmixed, *amigês*, first intellect 699,7

Venus, *Aphroditê*, third innermost planet 705,30
void, the, *to kenon*, Leucippus 690,32

waking, *egrêgorsis*, activity of soul 697,8
water, *hudôr*, a primary element 670,21; 672,36; 674,24; 675,14; 676,26; 718,38
west *see* east – west

white, *leukos*, an extreme of colour 671,31ff; 672,34-6
not a substratum 680,22ff; 717,14
potentially black 719,32
whole, *holos, holotês*, material compound (*sunolon*) of substance and characteristics 669,14-20; 716,39
whole, the *see* cosmos, heaven, universe
will, *boulêma*, of prime mover 721,32
wine – vinegar, *oinos – oxos* 682,30n
wisdom, *sophia*, knowledge of first principle 668,16n.26f; 670,9;
has no contrary 719,27
practical (*sophos*) 710,5.21
wonder, object of, *to thaumaston*, divine thinking 697,15; 699,13-16

Xenocrates, philosopher 670,19n; 671,3n

yearning, *ephesis*, rational desire 686,20ff; 691,4n; 694,2
immovable mover as object of yearning 686,21; 695,38f; 701,8fF; 707,20ff; 708,23f
intelligible object as object of yearning, *ephetos* 694,2f; 695,2

Zeus, a god 710,2.10f
zodiac *see* constellations of the zodiac